ALSO BY RONALD HINGLEY

Chekhov: A Biographical and Critical Study

The Undiscovered Dostoyevsky

Russian Writers and Society: 1825–1904

Nihilists

The Tsars: Russian Autocrats 1533–1917

A People in Turmoil: Revolutions in Russia

The Russian Secret Police

A Concise History of Russia

Joseph Stalin: Man and Legend

EDITOR AND TRANSLATOR OF:

The Oxford Chekhov:
Volumes 1–3 (*plays*); Volumes 4–9 (*stories*)

TRANSLATOR OF:

Alexander Solzhenitsyn:
One Day in the Life of Ivan Denisovich
(*with Max Hayward*)

A New Life of
Anton Chekhov

Chekhov at Melikhovo, April 1897.

RONALD HINGLEY

A New Life of
Anton Chekhov

ALFRED A. KNOPF

NEW YORK

1976

THIS IS A BORZOI BOOK
PUBLISHED BY ALFRED A. KNOPF, INC.

Copyright © 1976 by Ronald Hingley
All rights reserved under International and Pan-American Copy-right Conventions. Published in the United States by Alfred A. Knopf, Inc., New York, and simultaneously in Canada by Random House of Canada Limited, Toronto. Distributed by Random House, Inc., New York. Originally published in Great Britain by Oxford University Press, London.

ISBN: 0-394-49058-4
Library of Congress Catalog Card Number: 75-36818

MANUFACTURED IN THE UNITED STATES OF AMERICA
FIRST AMERICAN EDITION

CONTENTS

ILLUSTRATIONS

Sources

Novosti Press Agency: frontispiece, 3, 9, 11, 16, 21, 22, A, D; *Society for Cultural Relations with the USSR:* 1, 2, 5, 6, 7, 10, 12, 13, 14, 15, 20, B, C; *Radio Times Hulton Picture Library:* 4, 18, 19; *The Mander and Mitchenson Theatre Collection:* 8, 17.

PREFACE

The present work is entitled *A New Life of Anton Chekhov* to distinguish it from another book by myself, published in 1950: *Chekhov, a Biographical and Critical Study.**

That book was written when I was a very young man, and at a time when much of the abundant documentary material on Chekhov had not yet become available. For instance, I was not able to use the most important source of all: the eight volumes of Chekhov's letters (volumes 13–20, the last-issued items of the Moscow-published twenty-volume *Works* of 1944–51). Among other valuable contributions of post-1950 Russian literary scholarship two particularly useful items must also be mentioned: N. I. Gitovich's *Letopis zhizni i tvorchestva A. P. Chekhova* ["Chronicle of A. P. Chekhov's Life and Work"], which gives a day-by-day account, in over eight hundred pages, of almost all Chekhov's known activities; and *Literaturnoye nasledstvo: Chekhov* ["Literary Heritage: Chekhov", edited by V. V. Vinogradov and others], an important compilation containing many previously unpublished documents. There are also Olga Knipper's letters to Chekhov from 20 November 1902 onwards, as first published in full in V. Ya. Vilenkin's edition of 1972. And there are the extremely important unpublished letters to Chekhov from Lika Mizinov, Lydia Yavorsky and others, to which access has now become possible, though it remains restricted. To these must be added numerous other newly available Chekhov documents brought out in the last twenty-five years by the literary scholars of his native country. Not least among them is to be an entirely new, Moscow-published edition of Chekhov's complete works and letters—discussed in some detail below.

As for help from nearer home, a great debt is owed to Dr. Virginia Llewellyn Smith, whose study of women in Chekhov's life and work, *Anton Chekhov and the Lady with the Dog* (London, 1973), developed out of a D.Phil. thesis written under my supervision at the University of Oxford. This is the most illuminating book on Chekhov which I know. Its main topic, the love theme, is central to his biography and writings; but had previously been neglected or treated superficially, not least in my own

* For fuller references to this and other works mentioned in the Preface, see the Bibliography of Source Material, below.

earlier biography. Why did I then write so little about Chekhov's loves and marriage, on which the existing information—limited though it was— would have permitted a far more adequate treatment? Perhaps, in youth, I thought a man's experiences in this field unworthy of note unless they were triumphant, spectacular, eventful, heroic and romantic; or at least intriguingly unhappy and frustrated. Chekhov's were none of these things, yet become fascinating to the eye of discernment as focused on them by Dr. Llewellyn Smith. Seeing so clearly into this material in her way, she has taught me to see it in my way; which by no means contradicts hers, yet differs from it substantially. Having thus educated her former supervisor, she has also, since publishing her book, discussed drafts of the present study with me at length and on many occasions, providing valuable criticisms and suggestions, besides making available extensive transcripts of certain important archive material. For all this help I am more grateful than I can easily say.

Among further reasons for writing a second *Chekhov* was this: that I have now translated his entire dramatic *œuvre* and about two-thirds of his mature narrative fiction for *The Oxford Chekhov*, of which publication began in 1964, seven volumes having been completed. To render a major author as scrupulously as possible into one's own language, while also dealing with all the variants and providing histories of the texts—this is to get inside his skin to an extent which no research, however thorough, can make possible if confined to the biographical material alone.

Another consideration is that it is no disadvantage, when writing an author's life, to be some sort of author oneself. This is my fourteenth book, which means that I have had some experience in constructing these complex artefacts. My 1950 *Chekhov* was my first book, and I was not, when writing it, much excited to find my subject correcting proofs, cursing reviewers, haggling with publishers, lunching with editors, being driven to despair by misprints, meeting or failing to meet deadlines, and subjected in a literary context to those gusts of anger, boredom, cynicism and occasional delight which are part of the writer's life. Now, though a teacher by trade and an academic (not a professional) author, I yet have more insight than previously into a writer's practical concerns, and can therefore enter into Chekhov's professional doings more intimately. Moreover, my intervening publications happen to include a novel; and this work of fiction at least proves me capable of groping in the same area as that in which Chekhov soared. It also happens that several of my other books deal with Russian political, social and historical subjects about which I was, in 1950, lamentably ignorant. The background material to this new study is, accordingly, more authentic than the somewhat meagre corresponding passages in my earlier *Chekhov* could be.

Whereas my former book on Chekhov was billed as a critical as well as a biographical study, this one is biography pure and simple. The literary works do, however, figure no less prominently here than in the earlier book; for to write of Chekhov without discussing his art would be like writing about Stalin while leaving out his politics. The difference is this: that the concern is not, now, to assess or analyse Chekhov's writings for their own sake, but solely to bring out their significance in his evolution as man and author. And yet a far more comprehensive critical assessment of Chekhov's work does seem to emerge, purely as a by-product of this concentratedly biographical study, than is to be found in the many avowedly critical passages of my previous *Chekhov*.

The present study places Chekhov the author firmly, as a matter of conscious policy, in the context of his literary life. How Chekhov wrote what works for which publications is here set out in detail; and where plot summaries or sketches of individual fictional characters are necessary to chart his course as a writer, such summaries and sketches are provided. Nor do I apologize for blatantly dividing Chekhov's work into "periods", well aware though I am that he himself considered this procedure absurd. "You and I never suspected it, old son, but here I am in my Third Period", he once told his friend and personal physician Dr. Altshuller. Disregarding this, I split Chekhov into two main periods: Early (up to March 1888) and Mature (from March 1888 onwards), both periods being further subdivided into four phases, as is summarized in Appendix I, below.

Though literary criticism as such is avoided in this book, except as an inevitable by-product of biography, it does not follow that all judgements of value are excluded on principle. Far from it, for individual works are frequently invoked as good, bad or indifferent; even as superb or atrocious. These comments all represent considered opinion, but universal validity is not claimed for any of them. Like Chekhov himself I have no criterion for distinguishing good art from bad, or for saying why I prefer Shakespeare to Zlatovratsky.

The main source of the present study is, as indicated above, *Works, 1944–51*: the admirable, Moscow-published, twenty-volume *Complete Works and Letters of A. P. Chekhov* in Russian. As evidence on Chekhov's life this edition, and especially its last eight volumes (containing 4,200 letters), still remains more important than all the rest of the existing source material put together. Yet, even while saluting this publication, we must proclaim it as probably doomed to obsolescence within a decade, for it is to be progressively superseded by a new, revised, expanded and (on its form so far) still more admirable edition: the Moscow-published, thirty-volume *Complete Works and Letters*, to which brief reference was also made above. This has been announced for publication in 1974–82 by the Gorky

Institute of World Literature of the USSR Academy of Sciences. When completed it will contain all the works (in 18 volumes) and all the letters (in 12 volumes).

No volume of this *Works and Letters, 1974–82* was available to me while I was writing the present biography. However, the desirability of obtaining access to so ambitious a new edition was inevitably present in my mind. Would there be any significant fresh material? And if so when could I get hold of it? I naturally made strenuous efforts to secure copies at the earliest possible moment, all too conscious that Muscovite publishing and British bookselling conditions made it absurd even to attempt to discover just which volumes would surface when. Only a fool would have sought them in Moscow. I nevertheless did so; but it was on a North Carolina campus that I first sighted the only two volumes so far issued. The sighting occurred in the Wilson Library of the University of North Carolina at Chapel Hill on 16 April 1975, both volumes being datelined 1974. This happened three months after the manuscript of the present book had been delivered to the publishers. A few days later, after returning to England, I harpooned my own copies of these elusive tomes (volume 1 of the works and volume 1 of the letters) with the help of Holdan Books, Oxford; and am now able, after retrieving my own manuscript, to take account of one-fifteenth of the new Chekhov edition in giving the final revision to my biography.

My opinion, inevitably provisional under the circumstances, of this new edition of Chekhov is as follows. *Works and Letters, 1974–82* is in content a truly scholarly edition of a great author, though it is unfortunately less satisfactory in style, format and finish. It is on present showing worthy to supersede, in accordance with its editors' declared intentions, the far from negligible *Works, 1944–51*. However, though the 1974–82 edition is (so far) a magnificent monument to the skill and dedication of the numerous Chekhov scholars of the USSR involved in its preparation, the fresh evidence contained in the two volumes so far available, including that in the highly informative commentaries, is disappointing. It certainly will not lead to any major reappraisal of the subject. All the same, the new edition has enabled me to make certain minor last-minute corrections to my text.

In one important respect alone the scholarly standards of the new edition leave much to be desired: the continued maintenance, though in modified form, of the policy whereby certain material—accessible only to the editors and oracularly designated by them "unsuitable for publication"—has been censored out of Chekhov's letters. Thus opens yet another chapter in the long and complex saga of the mutilation of Chekhov's correspondence by its Russian editors. In the first comprehensive collection of his letters to be published—*Pisma, 1912–16,* edited by his sister—we find evidence of numerous cuts, these being indicated by repeated dots. Many of the deleted passages appear from their context to refer to Chekhov's amorous experiences, while elsewhere we infer that he used the Russian equivalent of "four-letter words" or expressed himself otherwise indecorously. On the whole these cuts have not been restored in subsequent editions. In *Works, 1944–51* they are even intensified: in one letter (to A. S. Suvorin of 10 November 1895) a reference of Chekhov's, included in his sister's edition, to his alleged "impotence" was struck out: no doubt as unbefitting the image of a Great Man. In a few such instances we may sometimes restore the cuts of 1944–51 from the Moscow 1912–16 six-volume edition; and also from the selection of letters in volumes 11 and 12 of the twelve-volume *Works* published in Moscow in 1960–4.

Using these techniques we can also restore certain references which might be judged derogatory to the Russians and to other peoples of what is now the USSR and of what is there termed the "socialist camp". I have found, among such excisions, disparaging comments on Moldavians, Buryats, Yakuts, the Slavs in general, and one in which Chekhov denounces the Russians' alleged addiction to vodka. A passage alluding to the Chinese as ideal domestic pets was also removed. So were passages in which peoples of the present-day "capitalist camp" are presented as possessing skills superior to those of peoples of the present-day "socialist camp": for instance, one in which Chekhov describes the Italian actress Eleonora Duse as head and shoulders above any Russian rival; and another in which he speaks of the British colonial administration of Hong Kong as immeasurably superior to that of Russia's far eastern empire.

Among the excisions made in *Works, 1944–51* the most frequent are of passages in which Chekhov alludes to Jews by the derogatory term жид (*zhid*) and its derivatives. This, since there is no other way of rendering it, I boldly translate "Yid": a distasteful word, not normally part of my active vocabulary. Even to apologize for this breach of taste may seem an impertinence, since any such apology must seem to imply that Chekhov needs defending against the charge of anti-Semitism. But certain brief factual points are worth making. Firstly, жид and its derivatives were somewhat less offensive in nineteenth-century Russia than they are in present-day Russia; or than "Yid" is in present-day England. Secondly, Chekhov normally confined these utterances to private remarks addressed to Gentiles; I should be astonished to find evidence that he ever abated his customary courtesy when addressing any of his many Jewish friends directly. Finally, there are certain episodes in his record, as discussed below, which speak for themselves. There is his stance over the Dreyfus Affair; there is the help which he once gave to a Jewish student who wished to enter Moscow University in defiance of the quota; there is his horror at the

Kishinyov pogrom of 1903. There is also his "engagement" to marry a Jewish girl in 1886, and his championship (if accurately reported) of his persecuted Jewish school friend Wolkenstein about ten years earlier.

That the editors of *Works, 1944–51* should have distorted the witness by censoring out жид and its derivatives was inevitable, since the excision of these terms from published correspondence (but not from belles-lettres) was then official policy in the USSR. Now, however, Chekhov's new editors seem to be admitting to the record material which the uninstructed might interpret as derogatory to Jews; six such passages, excised from the previous edition, have been restored.

Under the new dispensation Chekhov is also permitted to allude to such indecorous phenomena as masturbation, gonorrhoea, pederasty, buggery and his own "backside". But the Russian equivalents of "four-letter words" are still excised. Even here, though, one curious minor liberty has been permitted. What can in its context have been nothing other than the word жопа ["arsehole"] previously figured as follows:

[...]

Now, however, in keeping with the spirit of the times, this key word is printed, somewhat less delicately, as follows:

ж⟨ ... ⟩

But for other words of this type, such as those of the ебать ["fuck"] and хуй ["prick"] families, which Chekhov also seems to have used—albeit less freely than some American Presidents—the editorial fig-leaf remains securely in place, and they appear fully enclosed in their little chastity belts, as follows:

⟨ ... ⟩

As for the chauvinistic editing which involved the excision from *Works, 1944–51* of material disparaging to the present-day "socialist camp", and also of material praising the present-day "capitalist camp"—unfortunately the volumes of *Works and Letters, 1974–82* so far available provide no evidence on what that policy will eventually prove to be. Obviously Chekhov is now being less savagely bowdlerized in his own country than was the case in the Stalin era. However, the continued censoring of a great man's words, so long after the death of himself and his close relatives, is inexcusable. It leaves a disgraceful blot on the new thirty-volume Chekhov. My own unsubstantiated guess is that this castrating policy has been imposed by extraneous, non-literary authority on the devoted scholars responsible for the new edition. They may well have resisted the censoring bureaucrats as best they could.

Another, more disquieting, consideration also arises. Is it not conceivable that, in addition to cuts openly acknowledged in typographical form by the symbol ⟨. . .⟩, other—typographically unavowed—excisions may also have been made? Whole letters, or passages of letters, bearing on aspects of Chekhov's life deemed unsuitable for dissemination, could have been, and indeed may have been, simply suppressed without acknowledgement. Given the strict control maintained by Muscovite authority over its archive material, there are no means whereby unkremlinized scholars can prove or disprove this speculation. All one can say is that if in fact such underhand suppression has taken place, it runs very much contrary to the admirable scholarly spirit in which *Works and Letters, 1974–82* seems, on the evidence so far available, to have been prepared.

The only other edition of Chekhov important to the present study is the ten-volume "Collected Works" edited by Chekhov himself and published in St. Petersburg by A. F. Marks in 1899–1902. This edition was not, however, formally entitled a *Collected Works*; instead of that each individual volume bore its own title: *Stories, Tales and Stories, Plays* and so on. As will be seen below, the edition is particularly valuable as a guide to Chekhov's estimation of his own works. On the many other editions of Chekhov in Russian information will be found in the editorial preface to the first volume of the works in *Works and Letters, 1974–82.**

In the present study Russian names are transliterated or otherwise rendered along lines laid down in the Prefaces to volumes 1–9 of *The Oxford Chekhov*, edited and translated by myself and published by the Oxford University Press; see especially volume 3. That transliteration system is here modified in one small particular: ий is still rendered as "y", but only where it occurs as an adjectival-type ending (in practice as the last syllable in names); elsewhere it becomes "iy", as in "Novorossiysk".

* POSTSCRIPT. Further to the comments above on *Works and Letters, 1974–82*, another, third, volume of this edition came to hand at the last moment, just before the revised proofs of the present book went to press. This is volume 2 of the Letters, covering January 1887 to September 1888. A comparison of this latest text with corresponding material in *Works, 1944–51* shows that the policy of restoring some, but—alas—by no means all, of the previously censored material has been maintained. In particular thirteen previously censored references to Jews have been included in the new edition. So too has a previously censored disrespectful reference to certain peoples of the Caucasus contained in Chekhov's letter of 12 August 1888 to K. S. Barantsevich: "The natives are swine—not one poet, not one singer have those gentry produced."

Against these welcome restorations must be set the emergence of a sinister and barely credible policy, not followed in Letters, volume 1, of the same edition: that of imposing extra cuts—cuts not imposed even in the prudish *Works, 1944–51*. For instance, where (in a letter to N. A. Leykin of 4 June 1887) the earlier edition has the already mutilated "I'm bored and sad and have no one to [. . .]", the new edition supinely

Two-letter initials such as "Ye." in "Ye. P. Yegorov" occur where our transliteration code gives two letters in place of a single Cyrillic letter (in this case "e"). In the Reference Notes and Bibliography authors' (or their translators') spellings of their own names have been retained where these conflict with the above system; here too Russian lady authors of the appropriate grammatical category regain the endings -a or -aya which have been docked in the text. In rendering the names of hotels, parks, streets, ships and the like the practice of *The Oxford Chekhov* has also been followed: some are translated, others transliterated according to what seems appropriate in a given instance, and over-all consistency has not been sought—except of course that the same objects get the same name throughout.

As for the titles, in English, of Chekhov's works, all those occurring in *The Oxford Chekhov* are quoted as they appear in that edition, which contains all the drama in volumes 1–3 and all the stories of the mature period (1888–1904) in volumes 4–9. Since volumes 4 and 7 have not yet appeared, the titles of the stories which they will contain are given in the form which it is proposed to use when they are translated. For other titles those of Constance Garnett are used, despite their occasional quaintness, if a given work chances to appear in her extensive series of Chekhov translations. The titles of early works not appearing among Garnett's translations are either translated by myself or given in the form used by some other translator. With an author who has published between six and seven hundred variously-entitled items confusion is hard to avoid. This is why, in the interests of clarity, Chekhov's works are given their own separate index, with transliterated Russian titles and dates. The bracketed publication date of a given work is added in the body of the text, but only if that date falls outside the period under review in a particular chapter. Very occasionally, when confusion is especially apt to arise, a transliterated Russian title is also quoted in the text.

To assist readers to visualize the length of a given work—important in considering the shape and development of Chekhov's art—a rough unit of

---

offers the doubly castrated "I'm bored and sad ⟨. . .⟩". A similar supererogatory bowdlerization has also been imposed two pages later, in Chekhov's letter of 4–5 June 1887 to F. O. Shekhtel. In these two instances the 1974–82 edition accordingly shows itself yet more squeamish than its predecessor: an evil omen for the ten outstanding volumes of correspondence to be published by 1982.

Nothing is easier than to monitor these absurdities as volume suceeds volume, but one does so with sadness, since the inevitable effect is to cast an otherwise unmerited shadow on a fine piece of collective editing. I hope that it is not too late to appeal for a change of heart, and for the printing of Chekhov's correspondence in its entirety in subsequent volumes, together with addenda covering the material so far suppressed. [*Jan. 1976*] measurement was needed, and the word "page" was chosen. By this is meant, except where otherwise indicated, a typical page of a typical book: more specifically, a typical page in *Works, 1944–51*, consisting of 41 lines and containing up to 400 Russian words.

From the editors of Chekhov's correspondence in the 1944–51 *Works* I take over an ugly symbol already invoked above:

[. . .]

They use this to indicate the frequent points at which they omit words or passages of the original for censorship reasons. If, then, Chekhov is quoted here as writing "I am bored and have no one to [. . .]", this means that the symbol in question occurs at the corresponding point in *Works, 1944–51*; or that some similar notation has been used in some other edition of the letters to mark a cut.

All translations in this book are mine, except where the titles of early (pre-1888) works may be given in the rendering of Constance Garnett or others. Dates accord with the Julian Calendar used in Russia during Chekhov's lifetime, and lag behind the dates used in Western Europe: by twelve days in the nineteenth century, and by thirteen days in the twentieth century.

My warmest thanks and appreciation go to the following who have very kindly helped me, but must not of course be held responsible for any errors in the text: to Dr. Virginia Llewellyn Smith, as already acknowledged above; to Dr. Frank Ridehalgh, who read those parts of the text which have a medical bearing, and who, with a natural flair for nuances Chekhovian, advised on the interpretation and wording of certain passages; to Jeremy Newton, for generously vetting my drafts several times and for his expert advice; to Dennis O'Flaherty for specialized counsel on nineteenth-century Russian press and publishing matters; to Anne Abley and David Howells for assistance with bibliographical problems; to my son Martin for compiling some of the statistics; and above all to my wife for helping me even more than with any previous book. I am also greatly indebted for expert criticism of the interpretation contained in this biography to the distinguished participants in a conference which I was privileged to address in spring 1975 in the United States: the Chekhov Symposium held by the Department of Slavic Languages of the University of North Carolina at Chapel Hill; and most particularly (among many other specialists who were present) to Dr. Charanne Kurylo; to Professors Thomas Eekman, Karl D. Kramer and Thomas G. Winner; and not least to Professor Paul Debreczeny, who conceived and organized this most valuable meeting of Chekhovists from all over the world. And, finally, I

thank my friends at the Oxford University Press in London for skilled
editorial advice on the manuscript of this book; for more than twelve
years' expert help with *The Oxford Chekhov* and its numerous paperback
offshoots; for permission to quote from and otherwise use material from
those publications; for moral support and encouragement of a particularly
high order.

Poor Chekhov, alas, never had such luck with his publishers.

Frilford, Abingdon,   RONALD HINGLEY
1975

A New Life of
Anton Chekhov

CHAPTER ONE

Taganrog
1860–79

The Grocer's Son

Anton Pavlovich Chekhov, who introduced his own special brand of elusiveness into literature, was himself a most elusive man.

The mystery does not derive from any fundamental inconsistency of character, for if we study Chekhov patiently we shall eventually find him a model of harmony and integrity. Nor do difficulties in understanding Chekhov arise from lack of evidence. So many passing thoughts did he commit to paper in over four thousand private letters, and so lavish is the memoir material about him, that we are amply informed in great detail on his reactions to politics, medical practice, love, authorship, religion and countless lesser topics; and in many cases we also know exactly why he made this decision or adopted that course of action. The trouble is, rather, that his motives and opinions, though articulated with crystal clarity at any given moment, were apt to change radically from one moment to another: a characteristic shared, to an extent not always recognized, by lesser men.

Did Chekhov enjoy practising medicine, writing stories, dominating the Russian theatre, living in Moscow, visiting St. Petersburg? Or did he hate these things? Was he gregarious? Was he solitary? An optimist; or a pessimist? We shall learn not to leap in with a bald yes or no whenever such questions arise, as they frequently do. And we may in the end find ourselves not only compelled but even content to leave some of the mysteries unresolved, just as Chekhov himself leaves so many of his fictional and dramatic problems unresolved. That human personality is ultimately an enigma this enigmatic genius has demonstrated again and again in his works. Is there any reason why we should expect him to have contravened his own norm in his own life?

Perhaps he himself was that tantalizing phenomenon: a Chekhov character.

This most famous and puzzling of grocers' sons was born, the third of six children, on 16 or 17 January 1860 in the southern Russian port of Taganrog.[1] Here he spent the first nineteen years of his life, in the stifling atmosphere of a Russian provincial town.

A provincial born and bred, Chekhov was to include in his plays, stories and letters many a denunciation of the Russian provinces. Sharing the common view that provincial life was monotonous and culturally backward, he thought of all Russian towns as identical;[2] if you had seen one you had seen the lot. Only two of the Empire's cities escaped this stricture: the current capital, St. Petersburg; and the former capital, Moscow. These metropolises, each with its population of nearly a million, were twice as large as any rival Russian centre. Culturally, economically and administratively they dwarfed all potential competitors; among which Taganrog, with a mere fifty or sixty thousand souls, was not numbered.

Situated about six hundred miles south of Moscow on a cape in the Gulf of Taganrog, Chekhov's home town lurks at the far end of linked land-locked seas; its Gulf is an inlet of the Sea of Azov, itself an inlet of the Black Sea, that annexe to the Mediterranean. And yet this hemmed-in port had only recently lost its position to the fast-growing Odessa as the main channel for southern trade. During Chekhov's childhood Taganrog was in decline, partly because the harbour was silting up. And though the railway arrived in the 1870s, economic developments in general favoured near-by Rostov-on-Don at the expense of Chekhov's birthplace. But Taganrog was still an important outlet for grain exports in and beyond his boyhood. The port had a lively cosmopolitan atmosphere. Among its many foreign residents Turks were prominent; but less so than the Greeks, who held a near-monopoly over the grain trade. The local millionaires were Greek, and they owned the finest houses. But Taganrog was also a cultural centre for its Cossack and Ukrainian hinterland. There was a cathedral, a new public library, a theatre which was no stranger to touring Italian opera companies.

The harbour, the sea, the theatre, the library, a town park with band, the cliff-side Yelizaveta Park on the outskirts, two grammar schools, amusingly jabbering foreigners, a railway: with all these amenities Taganrog was not the dullest of Russian provincial backwaters. Other, more exotic, features included the occasional kidnapping in its very streets of young girls for Turkish harems. Judicially imposed public floggings, and also "civil executions"—ceremonies of degradation involving the breaking of a sword over the condemned man's head to accompanying drum rolls—were carried out in Mitrofaniyevsky Square. These barbarous rituals the little Chekhovs could observe from a window of their house in Monastyrsky Street: one in a succession of rented houses occupied during Anton's first fourteen years.[3] Otherwise, though, life could indeed grow tedious in a city of long, wide, straight, unpaved streets lined with squat, mainly one-storey houses with closed shutters. In wet weather pedestrians sank over the top of their jackboots in the churned mud of these thorough-fares while carriages lurched past in a flurry of slush; in hot weather there were choking clouds of dust; and at night the streets were still more uncomfortable and perilous owing to the absence of lighting. An eerie silence brooded over the place, broken, it might be, by the yelps of a demented dog careering frantically about as it tried to shake off the tin can tied to its tail by local hooligans as a preliminary to beating it to death.[4] Small wonder, in the light of this and similar anecdotes, that "Taganrogish behaviour" became, in the adult vocabulary of Anton and his brothers, a synonym for brutality, squalor and mindless vulgarity.

Chekhov himself often denounced his native town. In adolescence he lamented that there was "nothing, absolutely nothing, new" in so deadly a dump.[5] Revisiting it as a young man, he found all the houses squashed-looking; their roofs were unpainted, their shutters perennially closed. Along the sticky, drying, chunky mud of the so-called roads the cabs picked their way at walking pace. How dirty, empty, lazy, illiterate and boring Taganrog was, with its misspelt inn-signs, its deserted streets, its ugly, smug-looking dockers, its dandies in their long coats, its peeling stucco, its general air of idleness. True, Bolshoy Street had at last been paved, even acquiring a European air. But the general impression was "utterly Asiatic: such oriental squalor on all sides that I can't believe my eyes. Sixty thousand inhabitants do nothing but eat, drink, reproduce themselves. Of other interests they have none." All Chekhov could see were cakes, eggs, bottles of Santurin wine, babies at the breast: not one newspaper or book.[6]

Yet Chekhov—in this as in so many other matters difficult to pin down—was deeply attached to his native town. In the late 1890s we shall find him regretting that its climate did not permit him to return as a permanent resident. By then he had become Taganrog's tireless cultural benefactor, presenting many hundreds of books to its library; patronizing its regional museum; helping to acquire a huge statue of its founder, Peter the Great. He also drew on Taganrog, unavowedly, over the years as a background for stories set in unnamed provincial towns: he put its cemetery into *Doctor Startsev* (1898); its Yelizaveta Park and shore into *Lights* (1888); its grammar school into *A Hard Case* (1898).[7]

Chekhov loved and hated Taganrog, just as he came in time to love-hate Moscow and St. Petersburg; the visitors to his house whom he could neither be with nor without; the adored and detested world of the theatre; above all his literary work and the Russian literary milieu as a whole: source of so much satisfaction and irritation.

He was to become similarly ambivalent and seemingly contradictory in his attitude, now of self-identification, now of withering contempt, towards his native country as a whole. That vast, multiracial, autocratically ruled Empire, sprawling over a sixth of the earth's land surface, had long been struggling to fight its way out of cultural, economic and political backwardness. Many Russians of Chekhov's day strove to equip their country to compete with the most advanced western states by seeking either to reform its institutions or else to destroy them utterly as hopelessly antiquated. Others proclaimed that what seemed backward was merely different, and in some mysterious fashion vastly superior. But the great majority, consisting of peasants whose thoughts tended to bypass the intermediate territory between God and village affairs, adopted none of these attitudes. Still largely illiterate, the peasantry contributed four-fifths of a rapidly swelling population which was to surge well past the hundred million mark during Chekhov's lifetime. Within this population Russians such as the Chekhovs were merely the largest minority, for the Empire included a hundred-odd nationalities, large and small. As a reading of Chekhov's works reminds us, Ukrainians, Poles, Tatars, Jews, Georgians and Armenians were particularly numerous. Nor were the boundaries between all these peoples strictly drawn. In the nineteenth century the term "Russian" covered (as it no longer does) Ukrainians and Belorussians as well as those whose descendants are now called Russians but who were and are distinguished, in contexts where it is necessary to be precise, as "Great Russians". A southerner born in a town bordering on the territory of what is now the Ukrainian Republic, Chekhov was accustomed to refer to himself in later life as a *khokhol* or "top-knot": the denigratory Great Russian term for a Ukrainian. He thus describes himself dozens of times in his letters, whimsically and without feeling any less Russian for doing so.

Born in 1860, the year before the Emancipation of the Serfs, Chekhov would himself have entered this world as a serf had it not been for the energy of his paternal grandfather. That sterling character, whose Christian name was Yegor, hailed from Voronezh Province in central European Russia (about half way between Taganrog and Moscow), where he somehow saved 3,500 roubles to buy freedom for himself and his family. The deal with their owner, one Chertkov, was clinched in 1841, at 700 roubles a head; but that stretched only to Yegor himself, his wife and his three sons. It did not include his only daughter, Alexandra. But in the end, through impatience or good will, Chertkov threw her in for nothing, according to a story many times told in the family.[8]

Nearly all Anton's family connections were with trade. Though Grandfather Yegor's most notable coup was as serf-dealer, by obtaining a sizeable discount when purchasing himself and his own family, he had earned his money through some other sort of commerce; perhaps it was cattle-dealing.[9] In any case Yegor apprenticed one of his sons, Anton's Uncle Michael, to a bookbindery in Kaluga near Moscow. The other two boys, Anton's Uncle Mitrofan and his father Paul, worked as shop assistants before each started up his own small grocer's shop in Taganrog. By now they were all calling themselves "Chekhov" or (in Kaluga) "Chokhov", having been known during their serf period by the bald, barbarous monosyllable "Chekh". Paul had married Anton's mother Yevgeniya, daughter of a travelling cloth salesman called Morozov. Their marriage took place in 1854, early in the Crimean War, and the young wife's first pregnancy chanced to coincide with a British naval bombardment of Taganrog. Fleeing the town, she bore her first child, Alexander, in the safety of the near-by countryside. By the time her second, Nicholas, was born in 1858 the family had returned to a Taganrog sunk back into its peaceful slumbers under a new Tsar-Emperor, Alexander II. The new Tsar generated a less tyrannical atmosphere than had his predecessor, the little-lamented Nicholas I; and was soon embarking, as even Taganrogers noticed, on reforms designed to put Russia on terms with the industrialized West.

After Anton's birth in January 1860 three more Chekhov babies followed in 1861–5: Ivan, Mariya and Michael. And all Anton's siblings, the four boys and the one girl, have left memoirs of their famous brother's childhood. Those of Nicholas and Ivan are skimpy, but the other three form our most extensive but tantalizingly contradictory evidence on these early years.[10] The liveliest account is Alexander's: a detailed tragi-comic picture of the Chekhovs in the 1860s and 1870s.

Reading Alexander's story we enter a Dickensian world of terrorized infants cowering before a tyrannical father. Grocer Chekhov paraded his children at interminable church services, private prayers and choir rehearsals; he saw that they did their exacting school homework; made them mind his shop for hours on end. Any one of these occupations might have overtaxed a small boy, and the combination of the three made life a martyrdom, especially as any dereliction of duty provoked self-righteous rebukes, slappings, cuffings and strappings. Alexander shows the father rigorously imposing attendance at Russian Orthodox Church services and conscripting his sons into a church choir of which he was the dictatorial choir-master. Anton sang the alto parts; but, says Alexander, he had a poor ear and no voice. That did not save him from being turned out of bed at two or three o'clock in the morning to trudge through the mud or slush to church, where he also acted as bell-ringer and censer-holding altar-boy.[11] There were evening prayers at home too, with the family kneeling before the living-room icons and beating their heads on the floor from time to time, as ritually prescribed; wiggling his feet was the only way in which a boy could express his protests on these occasions.[12] The severe fasts of the Church were also imposed by a father firmly convinced that all these proceedings would ensure salvation in the life to come. And we note that they did at least help to equip Anton for earning his living on this earth, furnishing the knowledge of church affairs on which he was to draw in his stories. Surprisingly, in view of his childhood ordeals, his pictures of Russian religious life are usually sympathetic. They are outstandingly so in his penultimate story *The Bishop* (1902); but in the earlier *Murder* (1895) he evokes a religious fanaticism so much exceeding his father's that it provokes a sordid crime of violence.

From liturgical drudgery Paul Chekhov's grocery shop might have provided relief under conditions less burdensome. The place had much to fascinate a child. It was small, dirty and infested with flies; it smelt of paraffin and sardines, it was equipped with barred windows like a prison; yet was as much of a pub or a club as a shop, trading in wine and vodka, consumed on or off the premises by a varied clientèle including Greek merchants and monks. The shop opened at 5 a.m. and closed when the last customer felt like leaving, perhaps in the small hours of the morning. Often there were no customers at all, for trade was poor, and Anton would con his Latin verbs in the fly-infested gloom among shelves which groaned under stocks of unsold tea, penknives, lamps, wicks, curative herbs, vodka, wine, olives, olive oil, castor oil, hair grease, scent, grapes, paper, paraffin, macaroni, laxatives, rice, coffee, tallow candles, gingerbread, jam, sardines, herrings, soap, buckwheat, tobacco, sal ammoniac, mousetraps, camphor, cigars, brooms, sulphur matches, raisins, strychnine, salt, lemons, smoked fish and leather belts.[13]

Two local boys, Andryushka and Gavryushka, were the regular shop assistants. Serving for their board and lodging alone, receiving no wages, they were slapped and cursed if, for example, Paul Chekhov found his sugar, coffee and rice smelling of paraffin, fish or tallow. From time to time a fire inspector would arrive to "raid" the premises: that is, to receive a few bumpers of free vodka and a small bribe from grocer Chekhov before going peaceably on his way to certify that all was in order. Paul systematically cheated his customers (says Alexander) by giving short weight, palming off inferior wares and so on; and he insisted on his children doing likewise. Once a dead rat was found in a barrel of cooking oil. The copeck-pinching Paul would not throw away the contents, but fished out the corpse and persuaded the local archdeacon to "sanctify" the product by an exorcism service, after which the oil remained on offer to customers. Once this absurd tale had gone round Taganrog a decline in turnover naturally followed.[14] As this anecdote reminds us, Anton's eldest brother was, amongst other things, a professional writer of comic fiction. That his evidence is distorted by flights of fantasy is alleged by his more sober younger siblings, Mariya and Michael, who have both impugned his credibility. Both claim that Alexander wrote his reminiscences when "ill": that is, drunk.[15] This is not an unbelievable charge, for the unfortunate man was indeed an alcoholic.

It is, then, a more sympathetic picture of the father which we have from Michael and Mariya Chekhov. Here was no bristling disciplinarian or religious fanatic, but a complex, gifted man: the victim of circumstance. He was not even much of a religious believer, Michael rather unconvincingly maintains; and certainly religious ritual by no means excluded secular interests. Paul played the fiddle; he collected old newspapers; he liked discussing politics; he took part in local elections, attended public dinners and ceremonies; he even read light French novels. Always immaculately dressed, he was still sporting a top hat and starched linen when facing imminent bankruptcy.[16] In strong contrast with Alexander, Michael Chekhov says that the father only beat his children "in exceptional cases". Mariya says the same, speaking of the "occasional" application of the strap to her brothers, and expressly warning Anton's biographers against exaggerating the severity of Chekhov père. Life was not, according to her, the comic hell evoked by Alexander. "We lived in harmony and good cheer. Games, jokes, pranks, laughter always dominated our home."[17]

Always? That carries as little conviction as the possibly apocryphal rat in the oil barrel. Which version do we believe? The romancings, if such they are, of the drunken Alexander? Or the whitewashing job, if such it is, of Anton's sister and youngest brother? Many of their reminiscences were first published after the 1917 revolutions: not, we suspect, without some "guidance" from totalitarian literary officials charged with imparting maximum decorum to the record of such a respectable cultural asset as an Anton Chekhov.

That Alexander's is the more credible bias, that his effervescent annals are (to put it mildly) no more suspect than Michael's and Mariya's attempts, couched in their all-jolly-Chekhovs-together style, to cover the family chronicles with a varnish of seemliness: so much seems evident when we turn from their combined memoirs to the yet more important testimony of Anton himself. Though he wrote no memoirs as such, it was his adult practice to drop uninhibited comments on his childhood in conversations or letters. These references emphasize the unhappiness of his early years, and come down heavily against any other interpretation. "As a child [he wrote in March 1892] I received a religious education and upbringing, complete with church singing, readings of the Gospels and the doxology, regular attendance at matins and the duty of serving in the chancel and bell-ringing. The upshot is that my childhood seems a pretty gloomy business when I recall it nowadays. When my two brothers and I used to sing in . . . church . . . the congregation gazed at us with deep emotion and envied my parents, while we felt like little convicts at hard labour." Religious education, to the adult Chekhov, set up a screen impenetrable to the eye of the casual observer. "Behind that screen torture takes place, but in front of it all is smiles and emotional gush. No wonder seminaries and church schools have produced so many atheists."[18]

Writing to Alexander in 1889, Anton stated that "despotism and lying so distorted our childhood as to make it a frightful and nauseating memory. Remember the horror and disgust we used to feel at meal-times in the old days when Father read the riot act because the soup was over-salted? Or cursed Mother and called her an idiot?" As for the beatings, Chekhov once claimed that they had given him a faith in progress: how could he believe in anything else after the "terrific difference between the time when I was beaten and the time when I was beaten no longer"? Nor was it only his father who beat him in childhood; every day someone or other boxed his ears for stealing fruit.[19]

To cite Chekhov's imaginative work as a source, unsupported by other evidence, for his biography—this is an all-too-common error. But it would be perverse not to draw on his fictional writings in those occasional instances when they appear, by collation with the source material proper, to furnish especially vivid illustration of some aspect of his life. It is not surprising, for example, in the light of the material from Chekhov's letters quoted above, that the following passage from the story *Three Years* (1895) should be accepted in several earlier Lives of Chekhov (including my own) as authentically autobiographical.[20]

Father began teaching or, to put it bluntly, beating me before I was five. He birched me, boxed my ears, clouted my head, and when I woke up each morning I'd wonder whether I'd be beaten that day. My brother and I were forbidden to play and lark about. We had to attend matins and early mass, kiss the hands of priests and monks, recite the prescribed prayers at home. . . . I fear religion, and when I pass a church I remember my childhood and feel scared. When I was eight they took me into the shop. I worked as an ordinary shop-boy: which was unhealthy because there too I was beaten nearly every day. Then, after I'd started school, I would study up to dinner-time; and from then until night I'd be cooped up in this same shop.[21]

Such was Chekhov's own childhood, and as such it can be confirmed from the evidence in every detail save one: far from being effectively "forbidden to play and lark about", the boy developed into a great jester and practical joker. We shall find him fitting a surprising amount of such activity into a routine so exacting and in many ways humiliating.

Humiliating above all was that obsession with money which, all too understandably, afflicted the family of a struggling grocer with heavy responsibilities. At the age of twenty-eight Anton could still describe himself as "terribly corrupted by being born, growing up, studying and beginning to write in a milieu where money played a grotesquely large role".[22] Hurt and offended in so many ways, Anton also suffered from inadequate love and affection in his family life; and this despite the devoted care of a mother who was all kindness, yet never dared defend her children against the father's severity in their presence. And so little Anton would seek solace in some other friendly household. He was particularly fond of his Uncle Mitrofan: another top-hatted, church-going patriarch, but a kinder man than Paul. All in all, though, an absence of affection permanently stunted Chekhov's character, according to one not entirely convincing piece of self-analysis. "So little affection came my way as a child that I treat caresses as something unfamiliar, and almost beyond my ken, now that I'm grown up. That's why I just can't show fondness for others, much as I'd like to."[23]

Can this really be true? Despite his father's beatings, which he naturally resented, there were his mother, his sister and his brothers, with all of whom his relationship seems to have been close. Surely young Anton received as much, perhaps far more, affection than the average child? Perhaps he needed more. Or perhaps there was something about him which prevented him from absorbing the love which he craved. Could these be the roots of that extreme reticence which always distinguished the adult Chekhov in a society where *umileniye* (the ostentatious and self-congratulatory parading of emotion) was commonly regarded as a virtue? And yet this very restraint helped him to express emotions on paper more powerfully than any other Russian author.

Chekhov's was a very different upbringing from that enjoyed by members of the gentry: the privileged estate to the upper or lower ranks of which all his greatest predecessors as exponents of Russian fiction had belonged. "What gentlemen writers receive from life gratis, members of the lower classes buy with their youth", Chekhov reflected in January 1889. He went on, in the most frequently quoted passage of his correspondence, to describe himself as "a young man, a serf's son, a one-time shop-boy, choirboy, grammar-school pupil and student, brought up to worship rank, to kiss priests' hands, to defer to other people; who said thank you for every bite of food, who was often beaten; who had no galoshes to wear ... who fought, tormented animals, liked to eat with rich relatives; and who behaved hypocritically towards God and man for no reason at all, but purely out of consciousness of his own insignificance". After such an upbringing Chekhov had proceeded to "squeeze servility out of himself drop by drop", until he had woken up one fine day to feel that he had the blood of a real man, not of a slave, coursing through his veins.[24]

How thoroughly Chekhov did eventually cast off the influence of his father, and of "Taganrogism" in general, we can judge by his level-headed attitude in later life. His reactions were not intemperate or extreme. He respected in others the religious beliefs which he himself had given up, or had perhaps not held even as a child. Nor did his father's harshness create any violent hostility. Anton could never forget the beatings and the bullying, could never quite love his father as he loved his mother. But he did not bear an active grudge against an elderly man who was fundamentally kind, as even Alexander concedes, and who was only trying to do his best for his children according to the primitive traditions in which he himself had been reared. As we shall see, father and children were able to live amicably together when the children had all grown up. By that time Paul Chekhov was regretting his earlier tyrannical behaviour. He said that he could never forgive himself; and he asked his children to try and forget; times had changed, he told them.[25] Re-reading the memoir material, one wonders whether the mellowing of Chekhov Senior may not have begun earlier than is commonly allowed; if so it would help to explain discrepancies in the testimony of his children. Here we have the two eldest sons remembering their father as almost unremittingly stern, while his two youngest offspring insist that he was far less of a monster. Can it have begun to dawn on Paul Chekhov, while some of his brood were still in infancy, that to spare the rod is not necessarily to spoil the child?

Though Anton treated his father with outward respect, he could not fully respect him in his heart. Privately, in their correspondence, he and Alexander regularly referred to Paul by comic nicknames apparently derived from the storminess of his character. They treated him as a bit of a joke. And Anton's most considered pronouncement on the old man, delivered in a letter of January 1895, is devastating. "Father ... still remains what he has been all his life: a small-calibred person of limited range."[26] As for reflections of these father–son relations in Chekhov's writings, the most revealing are in the long story *My Life* (1896), which describes the clash between the wayward hero, Misail Poloznev, and his father, chief architect in a somewhat Taganrog-like provincial town. Like Paul Chekhov, Father Poloznev is indeed "a small-calibred person of limited range"; he is also a domestic tyrant who even whacks his adult son with an umbrella. Here is a tragi-comic, truly Chekhovian failure of communication between the generations, the general atmosphere and some of the details being drawn from life: speaking of the "unpleasant trace in Anton Pavlovich's soul" left by their father's regimen, Michael Pavlovich invokes *My Life*, noting its "many autobiographical traits".[27] And yet young Misail loves the preposterous and despised mediocrity of a father with whom he can establish no communication: not the least significant detail in the story, perhaps.

Yevgeniya Chekhov resembled her husband in having received little if any formal education. She was a simple, good-hearted, hard-working mother who lacked social pretensions and spent most of her waking hours cooking, sewing, laundering, keeping house and deferring to the domineering Paul. She taught her children to be kind to animals and to those less fortunate than themselves; she showed concern for prisoners in the local jail; she was quiet and gentle, her daughter tells us, and had a "poetic nature".[28] She was also a gifted story-teller, especially when she recounted her childhood memories. This faculty she bequeathed to her third son, who (says his brother Michael) was unfair to his mother when he claimed, as was his custom, that he and his siblings had received "our talents from Father and our souls from Mother".[29]

From his nurse Agafya and from Irinushka, the nurse in Uncle Mitrofan's house—for in those days even poor grocers could afford domestic servants—Anton also heard entrancing anecdotes and tales which, the child being father to the man, he was often found retelling in improved versions of his own.[30]

Early Schooldays

No choice affecting Anton's childhood had more impact on his development than that of his schooling.

His education began in a haphazard and ludicrous manner. After he had been taught to read and write by his mother, whose own spelling and punctuation were rudimentary, and also to calculate expertly on an abacus,[1] he was enrolled at the age of seven, together with his elder brother Nicholas, at the school for Greek boys attached to a local church of the Greek Orthodox persuasion. Since Greeks so dominated commerce in Taganrog, they must possess some special secret which might be communicated to Russian boys, if caught early enough: such seems to have been the logic behind this otherwise inexplicable choice of school. It catered for about seventy pupils, aged between six and twenty; they were all disposed on six benches, at one class per bench, in a single large room.

Instruction was in the Greek language, but was also carried out through

raps from the ruler of the headmaster, one Nicholas Vuchina. Other
stories were also told of the punishments imposed by this eccentric
pedagogue. One involved a form of crucifixion, being lashed to a window
shutter. Then there was "running the gauntlet", which meant being spat
at in turn by the entire pupil body as it paraded past the culprit in single
file. These details are probably apocryphal, coming as they do from
Alexander Chekhov, who was not himself a pupil of the Greek School.
But from what is known of Taganrog *mœurs* in general they should not
necessarily be dismissed out of hand. Certainly the school did little for
Anton and Nicholas but bring them in contact with Greek boys whose
main hobby was pilfering from the docks. Nor did the little Chekhovs
even learn any Greek, apart from a few swear words and the letters alpha,
beta and gamma: as became clear when they had been at school a year and
their father decided to display their prowess at an informal examination
held in his shop in front of his Greek customers. Not only had the boys
failed to acquire the tongue of millionaires; they had learnt nothing else
either, though favourable reports, describing Nicholas as "pious" and
Anton as "diligent", had been supplied by the enterprising Vuchina.[2]

After this wasted year the boys were sent to the Taganrog classical
gimnaziya or grammar school. Entering a preparatory class in 1868, Anton
embarked on the full eight-year course twelve months later, and finally
passed out in summer 1879, having been kept down in the third and fifth
forms for failing his mathematics, geography and ancient Greek. Though
his studies improved towards the end, he remained only an average pupil.
Even in Russian composition his marks were only "satisfactory"—by
contrast with another boy called Zelmanov for whom the masters predicted
a great future as a writer, but whose name is not found in the annals of
Russian literature.[3] And as for the decision to keep Anton down, twice,
this reflects less unfavourably on his prowess than it might seem, for
between 1872 and 1890 well over half the nation's grammar-school pupils
fell by the wayside; and the number of those who blithely traversed all
eight forms in eight years was astonishingly small: a mere four to nine
per cent.[4] These figures are an index of rigorous standards. As units in an
integrated Empire-wide educational network the grammar schools were
kept up to the mark by the Ministry of Education in St. Petersburg.
Official scrutiny was all the more intense since the schools' main function
was to prepare pupils for higher education; the Matriculation Certificate,
awarded to those completing the course, conferred the right to enter any
of the nation's universities without further examination.

To obtain a grammar-school place, to hold it, to pay for it: none of
these operations was easy, and all involved much heart-searching in the
Chekhov family. Fees were not unduly high, but to raise them sixfold was

not easy for a struggling and eventually bankrupt grocer. Still, paid they were by various shifts, with occasional intervals when the children were suspended from school at times of acute poverty. In the end all the young Chekhovs, the two youngest eventually supported by Anton, passed out of their grammar schools, and (except Ivan) went on to graduate from the University of Moscow or some other higher educational institute. Then they began earning their living by authorship, journalism, translating, medicine, teaching, painting and museum-keeping in various combinations. The family had passed, within half a century, first through serfdom and then through shopkeeping to the liberal professions. As an actor and producer who was active in western Europe and the USA and who died in Beverly Hills, California, in 1955, Anton's nephew (his brother Alexander's son) Michael Aleksandrovich Chekhov was to carry the social transformation of the clan into a milieu which can never have figured in Grandfather Yegor Chekh's wildest nightmares.

Though Russia's grammar schools indeed did provide a passport to the professions, a pupil might be forgiven if he did not always feel that unlimited vistas were open to him; rather did they seem blocked off by the dead hand of authority. This was a matter of official policy only comprehensible in the light of the general political situation of the 1860s and 1870s. These were decades of fundamental reform, decreed and imposed by the Tsar himself, the Emancipation of the Serfs being only one among a series of far-reaching measures which also affected the judiciary, local government and the army. But this was also a period of revolutionary ferment among those who believed that Alexander II's reforms did not go far enough. And though mutinous urges affected only a small section of the population, this section coincided fairly closely with those undergoing or anticipating higher education. The political dissidents of the period were above all university students, past and present, but also pupils of the grammar schools from which university students were drawn; hence the official policy of adapting grammar-school regulations and curricula to curb politically undesirable thinking. This policy was administered by the notoriously reactionary Minister of Education of the period, Count D. A. Tolstoy: as strong a supporter of regimentation as his more famous contemporary namesake, the author Leo Tolstoy, was of anarchy.

Given these conditions, the grammar schools almost resembled military establishments or prisons. There was a regulation uniform: a peaked cap and a blue tunic with buttons, which must be kept done up and brightly shining; it was compulsory wear, together with a grey cloak for winter, not only on the school premises, but also out of school and even during the holidays. Harsh discipline was imposed, with penalties ranging from reprimands and incarceration in a school lock-up to the ultimate sanction of expulsion. But corporal punishment was not applied, the grammar schools being partly intended for sons of the Russian gentry traditionally immune, at least in theory, from this humiliation.

In their anxiety to curb revolutionary ideas the authorities operated an espionage system in the schools. There were spy-holes in each classroom door so that patrolling disciplinary officers could check pupils' behaviour as if they were convicts in a prison cell. Officious masters would visit pupils in their homes and probe into any background thought undesirable. The laying of information with the authorities was also encouraged: a craft at which Taganrog Grammar School's Latin master, one Urban, was adept. Primed perhaps by too close a study of Tacitus, he would denounce the boys to the masters, the masters to the headmaster and the headmaster to the local authority. So unpopular did Urban become that someone tried to blow him up with a bomb made from a sardine tin.[5] As this episode shows, the winds of modernity could blow in remote Taganrog as well as in Moscow and St. Petersburg in these days when political assassination was becoming a fashionable pursuit.

In curbing political unrest the authorities made use of Latin and Greek. This represented a volte-face, for an interest in the ancient world had previously been discouraged. It had been feared, under the tyrannical Nicholas I, that wrong ideas might be put into the heads of the young by the study of an age when so many tyrants had been assassinated. In the newly reinforced classical syllabuses, therefore, little emphasis was placed on history. The main subject was to be Greek and Latin syntax, on the assumption that this subject was dull enough to blunt the sharpest juvenile intellect. And so, no doubt, it was for the majority: those who shared Anton's insensitivity to foreign languages.

Anton plodded through his ancient Greek and Latin without enthusiasm; doing what was required, never sensing the magic of the classics. Himself to become the most "classical" of the great Russian prose writers in the simple elegance of his style, he seemed blind to that or any other quality in the literatures of ancient Greece and Rome. They passed him by, to judge from the occasional references to the classics in his letters and literary works. These are almost all disparaging. When, in his story *A Hard Case* (1898), Chekhov wished to portray a preposterous, straight-laced pedant, he made him a grammar-school teacher of Greek whose sole pleasure in life was to roll the word *anthropos* round his tongue. Far from keeping an Odyssey at his bedside or coming out with the occasional Horatian tag, like an educated Englishman of his generation, Chekhov was more likely to speak of the classics with impatience and disrespect. The following passage comes from a work of fiction, the story *Who Was to Blame?* (1886), but probably expresses the author's general attitude. "In my day I had the honour to be taught Latin. . . . But when I chance to see some product of classical antiquity nowadays I don't feel any wild enthusiasm. Instead of that I remember the use of *ut* in consecutive clauses, my irregular verbs . . . the ablative absolute. I blench, my hair stands on end, and . . . I rush from the scene in shameful flight."[6]

By no means did intensively studied Greek and Latin grammar fulfil the hopes of authority. Juvenile drives to overturn contemporary society, far from being lulled into quiescence by ancient irregular verbs, only gained further ground as the schoolboys of the 1860s made way for their successors of the 1870s. But there were also many young people who remained immune from such urges. Chekhov was one of them. He was no more a revolutionary by inclination than he was a classical scholar. It was not that he supported the *status quo*; he just would not side with either left or right in the doctrinal rifts which divided some of his school-mates. Nor did he participate in out-of-school discussion groups dedicated to the study of such dissident Russian authors as Bakunin, Herzen and Pisarev.[7] The result is that we can steep ourselves in the material of his childhood, adolescence and young manhood without ever being forced to realize that this was an important period in the development of the Russian revolutionary movement. The attempts by young intellectuals of the early 1870s to stir up the peasantry by undertaking missionary crusades in the countryside, the assassinations of officials and political trials at the end of the decade, the slaughter of the very Tsar-Emperor in 1881, the period of oppression which followed—none of these events might ever have happened so far as any substantial impact on Chekhov's life is concerned. Politically speaking, he might as well have been living on the moon as in Imperial Russia. He could and very largely did ignore politics, which indicates how far the oppressions of the autocratic state were from the all-pervasive reign of terror as which they have been presented by the successor-regime.

Despite cumbrous attempts by authority to make Taganrog Grammar School unsafe for political nonconformists, there was an underlying relaxed, not to say corrupt, atmosphere which prevented the place from casting unrelieved gloom over Anton's spirits. He made friends with whom he kept in touch in later life, but it is typical of his reserve that none of these friendships was close. He was an easy-going, popular boy renowned for his skill in making fun of the masters, inventing comic nicknames for them, and telling funny stories. He would inscribe such anecdotes in an exercise-book and read them out in the classroom when his teacher was absent, until he was eventually caught and the offending material was confiscated. And yet, far from going in dread of the school authorities,

Anton was often seen walking down the corridors deep in conversation with the headmaster, Edmund Reitlinger, whom he would also visit informally at his house.[8]

The masters were not so much bogymen as eccentrics who excited the boy's mockery, both at the time and in two superb stories of his mature period, *The Russian Master* (1894) and the above-mentioned *A Hard Case* (1898). Some of his teachers were notorious for taking in pupils as boarders who paid an excessively high rent and then, by curious coincidence, always passed their examinations with ease. But Anton had a great regard for one of his pedagogues, Father Pokrovsky, who taught Scripture. This politically nonconformist priest subscribed to the radical journal *Otechest-vennyye zapiski* ("Notes of the Fatherland"); was versed in the dissident satirist Shchedrin; was even reputed to shelter hunted revolutionaries in his flat.[9] And Chekhov, who cared little in later life what a man's views might be provided they were that man's own views, probably appreciated the priest's independence of mind more than his radicalism. It must have made a welcome change, too, to be taught by one master who did not stick to prescribed routine but encouraged discussions of history, politics and current affairs in the classroom. Perhaps this was why Scripture became Anton's best school subject; especially as Pokrovsky, the enemy of all formalism, strongly disapproved of religious formalism as cultivated by Paul Chekhov. But the priest showed little insight into Paul's offspring when he predicted to their mother that Alexander was the only one of them who would ever amount to anything.[10]

Pokrovsky's chief claim to fame was to invent a nickname for his most famous pupil: "Chekhonte", a whimsical distortion of his surname. Combined with "Antosha", the affectionate form of his Christian name, this was to supply the chief among the many pseudonyms under which Chekhov published in the early 1880s.[11] For this reason the first phase of his literary career is often termed his "Antosha Chekhonte period". "Chekhonte" was not the boy's only nickname at school, where he was known as "Tadpole", and also as "Big Head": not because he was conceited, but because his large, round head was disproportionate to the size of his body at this time.

Anton's childhood was not all work and no play, for various outdoor pursuits were available. Fishing in the harbour—usually for the goby, a species common in the Black Sea area—laid the foundations of a lifetime's devotion to angling. Bathing was another childhood recreation which continued to delight Chekhov as an adult, despite the mishap which occurred when, diving into the sea on one occasion, he cracked his head on a rock and was left with a lifelong scar above his left temple. As a boy he also played *lapta*, the Russian form of baseball, besides becoming adept at the cruel sport of snaring goldfinches, which he would sometimes sell for a few copecks apiece. Other amusements included tobogganing in the town park, which made it necessary to protect his ears against frost-bite by smearing them with goose fat. Another amenity, the Yelizaveta Park, provided walks especially thrilling because it was sometimes possible to grub up human bones there, relics of a long-forgotten burial ground.[12]

Though opportunities for leaving Taganrog were rare, the Chekhovs spent some of their summer holidays as guests of Grandfather Yegor. He had for years managed the estates of Count Platov—seemingly endless acres of prairie to the north of Taganrog. These journeys to the grandfather's by horse or ox-cart took several days, and involved camping in the steppes with their intoxicating smell of wild flowers: a memory which Chekhov was to revive in his story *The Steppe* (1888). There would be no end of fun on the way, especially when Nicholas Chekhov insisted on wearing his opera hat; far from normal wear hereabouts, it ended up in a local river after many adventures.[13] The grandfather put the boys up in Count Platov's manor house, previously inhabited only by fleas, and drove them round the estate in his trap. The stern old man also forbade them to eat the Count's apples, but quickly relented when they did so. And old Yegor, a true Chekhov in his dislike of idleness, also set his grandsons to work, as Anton later recorded. "When I was a boy staying with Grandfather on Count Platov's estate I had to spend entire days from dawn to dusk noting the weight of the threshed grain. The whistles, the hissing, the deep whirring note of the threshing engine under full steam, creaking wheels, plodding oxen, clouds of dust, fifty-odd labourers with black, dusty faces: it all etched itself in my memory like the Lord's Prayer."[14]

During his later Taganrog years Chekhov found other steppeland hosts. His friend and pupil Peter Kravtsov, a Don Cossack boy a little younger than himself, had him to stay on his family farm. Here Anton enjoyed rough shooting, rode wild ponies. Here too he once chanced to hear an eerie, haunting noise caused by a cable snapping in a distant mine; it remained in his memory all his life and became the famous "sound of a breaking string" in *The Cherry Orchard*. The railway construction site described in *Lights*; the uncoupled goods wagon which plays such a devastating role in *Panic Fears* (1886); the backgrounds to two memorable later stories, *The Savage* and *Home* (both 1897)—these are some among the many literary echoes of Chekhov's boyhood travels through the steppes.

On one of these excursions the fifteen-year-old Anton bathed in a cold stream, after which he contracted acute peritonitis. He was cared for in a Jewish wayside inn, later to figure along with other memories of the southern prairies in *The Steppe*, before being nursed back to health in

Taganrog by the grammar-school medical officer, a Doctor Strempf. Anton liked this kindly physician, who is said to have inspired his own choice of a medical career.[15] This was Chekhov's second attack of peritonitis, from which he had suffered five years earlier. The lively boy, who was turning into a tall, well-built young man, had never enjoyed really good health. When, in the course of a serious later illness, he dictated notes on his early medical history, he described himself as a "rather weak, very stout" child. Between the ages of seven and nine he had suffered from coughs and catarrh, spitting up a great deal of phlegm. He had also suffered from chronic headaches ever since entering the grammar school, and both his attacks of peritonitis had been acute. Piles, migraine and scotoma (an affliction of the eye) had troubled him since the age of eight; and he had had a bout of malaria.[16] The combination of symptoms is consistent with a first infection with tuberculosis: overcome at the time, only to remain dormant until later life. And if this interpretation is correct, the tubercle bacillus, Chekhov's ultimate executioner, had a powerful ally in the regimen of his early days: the intensive shop-minding, the punitive ritual of church-going, involving much sleeplessness and braving the blizzards of Taganrog in the small hours.

To an extent which cannot be determined, Chekhov's premature death from tuberculosis, at the age of forty-four, must have been due to the physical and emotional strains of his childhood.

Alone in Taganrog

The most dramatic event of Anton's childhood and youth marooned him at the age of sixteen in Taganrog, the rest of his family having fled to Moscow.

The trouble had begun in 1874 with belated attempts by Paul Chekhov to improve his business. Hoping to benefit from the newly established railway line, he had set up a second shop near the station, some distance from the centre of Taganrog, and had put Alexander and Anton in charge of it during their summer holidays. But in vain did they gloomily attend from 5 a.m. to midnight each day; the shop had to be closed for lack of custom, and the stock was transferred to another new shop of Paul's which was not doing much better.[1] Meanwhile Chekhov Senior was building a house. His family had so far lived in rented quarters, and we can trace four such homes, from the humble shack in Politseysky Street where Anton had been born to the suburban house in Monastyrsky Street where he had lived from his tenth year. That had been more spacious, with shop, kitchen and dining-room on the ground floor, and with bedrooms and accommodation for two lodgers upstairs.[2] The new house built by Paul Chekhov in Kontorsky Street took all his savings plus a loan of 500 roubles from the local Mutual Credit Society. Meanwhile he had given up paying his dues to the Merchants' Guild, and had thus reverted to the status of *meshchanin*: "burgher" or town-dweller of the humbler sort. As this reminds us, all Russian citizens were officially assigned to various social estates, burghers being only a little less lowly than the peasants who formed by far the most numerous estate of all. At the top of the scale was the gentry, with clergy and merchants supplying the intervening grades.

The year 1875 was one of continuing difficulties for the Chekhovs. In that summer Anton learnt that he was to be kept down in the fifth form for doing badly in Greek, and soon afterwards he had his second, nearly fatal, bout of peritonitis. The family was also depleted by the departure of the two eldest sons to Moscow: Alexander to the University and Nicholas to the School of Painting, Sculpture and Architecture. They had no money, but blithely relied on coaching, copying, freelance journalism and hope.

As Paul Chekhov's business further deteriorated it became clear that he would never pay off the loan on his house. His main creditor, one Kostenko, therefore began legal action, threatening Paul with indefinite imprisonment for debt. And Paul had been swindled, it turned out, by the builders of his new house. Having contracted for payment at so much per thousand bricks, they had erected a squat, cramped structure with absurdly thick walls: a trick which seemed to matter less as it became clear that the family was likely to be dispossessed in any case.[3] Bankrupt, disgraced, fearing prison, grocer Chekhov could no longer sustain the role of top-hatted, starched-cuffed domestic Jehovah, but decided to flee to Moscow and join his eldest sons. Not daring to show his face at Taganrog station, where he might be arrested, he skulked out of town in a cart ignominiously covered by a mat; and sneaked into the Moscow train at a halt further down the line.[4]

Yevgeniya Chekhov did not know where to turn until a former lodger, one Gabriel Selivanov, offered his services. An employee of the local Commercial Court by day and a successful gambler by night, he had the resources to help his dear friend and former landlady keep possession of her new home, and she of course was delighted to find so sympathetic a listener taking an interest in her financial problems. But soon the two-faced Selivanov turned out to have bought the house himself and was telling Mrs. Chekhov that she and her children must clear out. Then their creditor Kostenko impounded most of their furniture in lieu of unpaid interest. Poor Yevgeniya was forced to take the two youngest children (Ivan being farmed out with a local aunt) and join her out-of-work husband and feckless eldest sons in Moscow. On 23 July 1876 they mounted the train from Taganrog, never to return as residents.⁵ Anton was left behind on his own. What he or the rest of the family would live on remained obscure.

By dispossessing the Chekhovs, Selivanov had supplied the future author with a theme, the loss of a family home, which was to inspire his play *The Cherry Orchard* a quarter of a century later.

Unless Anton was to renounce a respectable career he must somehow finish his grammar-school course. Fortunately he was able to stay in Taganrog through the offer of board and lodging in his former home in return for coaching Selivanov's nephew, candidate for a military academy. Thus began three years in which Anton supported himself in Taganrog: desperately poor, lonely and bored, but relieved of the father who had dominated his early life.

Meanwhile the rest of the family was living in a succession of damp, uncomfortable rented Moscow rooms—often hungry, often short of firewood in the bitter winters. When the mother was ill, all the cooking, laundering, sewing and other housework devolved on Anton's sister Mariya, who would also knit scarves and sell them for a few copecks. Paul Chekhov was out of work, having been discharged as incompetent after a spell as a clerk in a police station.⁶ Still asserting himself as head of his household, he posted orders in the home, signed "Father of the Family Paul Chekhov" and decreeing at what hour each of his children was to rise each morning, what domestic chores they were to perform, what church services they must attend.

This ludicrous document, headed *Schedule of Activities and Domestic Duties to be Carried out in the Household of Paul Chekhov, Resident of Moscow*, was made the judicial basis for punishing "Member of Family Michael, aged eleven" when he overslept reveille by eight minutes. Alexander Chekhov kept Anton informed of such things by letter, also describing—and no doubt embroidering—the unseemly spectacle staged in the yard of the Chekhov's lodging house when Father of the Family Paul rebuked Member of the Family Ivan (now newly arrived from Taganrog) for a misdemeanour involving some trousers, and "by Taganrog custom proceeded to institute the boxing of the culprit's ears". Member of the Family Ivan had screamed for help, rousing the landlords, who threatened to throw them all out. Trying to smooth the incident over, Paul Chekhov assumed an ingratiating manner, only to be yelled at through a window by Mother of the Family Yevgeniya, using an idiom harsher than is customarily attributed to her. "Take that bloody grin off your face, you bald old horror!"⁷ Alexander evidently relished such comic episodes, but refused to live at home, finding the atmosphere unbearable. Their mother was utterly demoralized and visibly fading away, he wrote to Anton; and their sister did nothing but cry these days.[8]

Hard up and far away though Anton was, he yet helped to ease the situation in Moscow by selling pots, pans and other oddments left behind when their furniture had been sequestered. Also earning a little from coaching younger boys, he sent small sums to the family, and dispatched olives, halva and tobacco. And he wrote to his cousin Michael Chokhov, formerly of Kaluga but now established in Moscow, asking him to visit his aunt (Anton's mother) and to give her moral support. He also tried to cheer his mother by filling his letters with endless jokes. But she was past laughing. "We've had two letters from you full of jokes [she complained in a typical missive innocent of punctuation] but we've been down to our last four copecks all this time and we've had nothing to buy bread with we've been expecting you to send money it's been very painful you obviously don't believe me Mariya hasn't got a coat and I have no warm shoes we're confined to the house and you haven't written for God's sake hurry up and send the money you got for selling my sideboard." So she rambled on, probably sensing in the object of these reproaches a better potential support than any of her other menfolk.[9]

At Easter 1877 Anton travelled to Moscow on money sent by Alexander, and spent the holidays with his family. It was the first time he had ever left Taganrog and the steppes. Escorted round the Kremlin, shops and boulevards by his adoring youngest brother Michael, attending the Bolshoy Theatre and soaking up atmosphere, the visiting provincial thoroughly enjoyed himself. He was less impressed, though, by Alexander Chekhov when that ebullient and top-hatted young student decided to demonstrate his high spirits or social aplomb on a Moscow boulevard, by belching into the face of a passing old lady. This appalling "Taganrogism" drew a well-deserved rebuke from the fastidious Anton. "I see you're as big a hooligan as ever." From Moscow Anton returned, his head buzzing with impressions, and disillusioned with Taganrog where (said he) the theatre was not a patch on Moscow's. He longed to leave the provinces and "take wing" for the big city.[10]

In November 1877 the Moscow situation eased when Paul Chekhov got a clerking job with Gavrilov's, a large clothing warehouse, at the recommendation of his nephew Michael Chokhov, who was already a trusted employee.[11] At Gavrilov's Paul earned thirty roubles a month: not enough to support his dependants, but far better than nothing. He now boarded at his place of work in the merchant quarter south of the Moscow River; this relieved his wife and children from living with a discredited martinet, while yet permitting him frequent visits to the home where they were still very fond of him.

Already in effect the most adult member of the family, the teen-aged
Anton behaved responsibly throughout the domestic crises of the late
1870s. Where was the slave mentality which he later claimed to have been
his in youth? We seek it in vain until we turn to his letters to that same
Cousin Michael Chokhov who had helped to secure employment for
Paul Chekhov at Gavrilov's. Conscious of the age gap of nine years
between himself and his cousin, conscious too of his cousin's role as
protector of the newly arrived Moscow Chekhovs, Anton strikes a note
strongly out of harmony with his mature character. There are passages
in his letters to his cousin which read like the effusions of some Uriah Heep
of the steppes. "How could I fail to seize the felicitous opportunity to
make the acquaintance of a person such as yourself? I have, furthermore,
considered it, as I continue to consider it, my duty to show respect for
the most senior of my cousins: to respect, that is, one so warmly respected
by our entire family. . . . Our mother sees in you more than a nephew,
she places you on the same level as Uncle Mitrofan, whom I know well
and of whom I shall always speak highly because of his kind soul and good,
pure, cheerful character."[12]

Things became easier between the cousins after they had been out on
the town together in Moscow during Anton's Easter trip of 1877. But
Anton still sent his cousin sententious letters, prosing on about how "there
is nothing in this vilest of worlds dearer to us than a Mother. Father and
Mother are the only people in the world for whom I shall never stint
anything. If I ever get on in life it will be their doing. They are splendid
people, and their unlimited love for their children is alone sufficient to
place them above all praise and conceal all the defects arising from a life
of poverty."[13] By this time Anton is practically writing his parents'
obituary notices. The point is not whether the Chekhov parents had done
well or badly by their young—at least they had never stood in the way of
the children's education—but that their son, later so fastidious, could
express himself so unctuously on this or any topic. Was young Anton a
hypocrite? It is tempting to think so when we collate his letters to his
cousin with his later scathing comments on Paul Chekhov in the role of
father. But we must keep a sense of proportion. The older Chekhovs
were in such dire straits that we need not condemn a loyal son for praising
them in a letter to someone whose help he urgently sought to enlist. It
was also very much in the idiom of the country and period for a young
person to adopt this sanctimonious tone when seeking a favour from his
elders and betters. To expect Chekhov, who later condescended and
deferred to no man, to have sprung, as an infant fully armed with his
mature virtues, from a Taganrog grocery: this is to inhabit a world of
fantasy. He began as a child of the age and milieu which he was to transcend.

Obviously the youthful Anton saw his fellows in terms of a "pecking order": a sure sign of the slave mentality, but an attitude of which he was to purge himself eventually. In youth he could be no less embarrassing when assuming a condescending role than when trying to ingratiate himself, especially when he condescended to someone who was trying to conciliate *him*. This happened when young Michael Chekhov described himself in a letter to Anton of early 1879 as "your worthless and insignificant little brother", only to receive the following broadside in reply. "Be conscious of your own insignificance if you like ... but where? Before God, Intellect, Beauty, Nature, but not before Man. Before Man one should be conscious of one's dignity. You aren't a scoundrel, I take it. You're a decent chap. So respect that decent chap within you and know that no decent chap is a nonentity."14 This may be good advice or bad; in either event the tone, here pompous rather than servile, is one which the mature Chekhov happily chose to discard.

Though the schoolboy Chekhov might abase himself at times, he could also defy authority, as he did over one ugly little scandal. A Jewish pupil of Taganrog Grammar School's eighth form, a certain Wolkenstein, had reacted to the sneers of a classmate, who had called him a "Yid", by slapping the other boy's face, only to be sentenced to expulsion for conduct pre-judicial to good order and discipline. But Chekhov, himself a seventh-former at the time, made Wolkenstein's cause his own. Bursting into the victim's classroom "like a bomb", he persuaded the pupils to unite in protest. Unless their Jewish comrade was reinstated, they would, he induced them to threaten, quit the grammar school *en masse*; whereupon the authorities, terrified, quickly countermanded the expulsion.15 This story has an apocryphal reek; but it may be true, and if so it foreshadows in miniature the position which Chekhov was to take over the Dreyfus Case twenty years later.

Responsible, fair-minded, reticent, occasionally pompous and priggish: the young Chekhov is all these things, but he is not unremittingly earnest. He has discovered a taste for drinking and jollification. What a pity he cannot attend his cousin Catherine Chokhov's wedding in Moscow, he writes to his cousin Michael in July 1877; and how dearly he loves "every kind of celebration and typical Russian orgy complete with folk-dancing ... and wine-bibbing". He attends dancing classes in Taganrog, given by an Italian and later portrayed in the story *The Crow* (1885); he also dances at the house of his friends, the Drossis.16 As for more intimate relations with the opposite sex, we enter a delicate area here. Chekhov himself once baldly stated, in 1892, that he had "mastered the secrets of love at thirteen". He may have been joking, for the context is whimsical. In any case we have no further details, except that his brother Michael refers cryptically to an early love affair of Anton's during a holiday at a local farm. Michael also reports Anton saying how he had enjoyed flirtations with Taganrog schoolgirls when in the seventh and eighth forms; all his romances had been happy.[17]

Though none of Chekhov's youthful activities seemed to promise an outstanding literary career, we can yet trace portents of the future in his love of pranks, practical jokes, mimicry and play-acting. A skilled comic actor with a strong entertaining instinct, he could imitate his elders' speech, walk and gestures. The targets ranged from eccentric grammar-school teachers and fatuous minor clerics to the Town Captain, Prince Maksyutov: in effect Taganrog's Governor. Buckling on Grandfather Yegor's old sabre, Anton would impersonate this dignitary inspecting Cossack troops outside the cathedral. He would also burlesque the cere-monious greetings exchanged when the brothers Paul and Mitrofan Chekhov met: a sequence of prayers and embraces which took some time to act out. Comic lectures by aged professors were also part of the boy's repertoire. He was so skilled with make-up that he once visited his Uncle Mitrofan disguised as a beggar, presented a letter soliciting alms, and retreated triumphantly with three copecks from the hoodwinked (or supremely tactful) old gentleman. Other early pranks included stealing a policeman's sentry-box, dragging it to the Police Chief's front door, ringing the bell and running away. In infancy Anton once constructed a device for touching off the bell at his front gate by remote control, thereby repeatedly waking an elderly baby-sitter who was trying to doze through his stint. There was also the skull, no doubt one of the relics dug up in the Yelizaveta Park, which young Anton decorated horrifically and illuminated with a candle to frighten a small girl.[18]

From such antics it was a short step to improvised charades and amateur theatricals. Anton would impersonate a dentist, solemnly laying out the tools of his profession until a fearful groan resounded from outside and in lurched brother Alexander, clutching a bandaged cheek and bellowing with "pain". After digging in the sufferer's mouth with the fire-tongs, Anton would triumphantly "extract" a cork. He would also impersonate an aged village sacristan seeking promotion to deacon from "Bishop" Alexander Chekhov. Craning his neck till the sinews stood out, altering his face beyond recognition, Sacristan Anton would intone extracts from Orthodox liturgy in the quavery voice of an old man trembling before his superior ecclesiastical officer; in the end, after much excruciating by-play, Alexander would solemnly pronounce: "Thou art received as Deacon."[19] More orthodox theatrical performances also took place, often at the house of Anton's school-friends the Drossis. Himself the main organizer and producer, the boy is said to have written many plays of his own, only to destroy them. He also acted in established plays. They included Gogol's famous comedy *The Inspector General*, in which he took one of the main parts, that of the Mayor, wearing cushions for padding beneath his school uniform. In another play, by an unknown author, Anton acted an aged crone whose mere appearance on stage aroused gusts of "Homeric laughter" from the Drossis' friends, so skilful was the boy's mimicry, so superb his make-up.[20]

Comic acting figures little in Anton's mature years, for he gradually lost the knack or the interest. But an allied childhood pursuit, theatre-going, was to remain with him for life. Taganrog's theatre gave him the opportunity to see the classics of the Russian stage, including Ostrovsky's plays; light opera such as Offenbach's *La Belle Hélène*; a stage adaptation of *Uncle Tom's Cabin*. Whatever the performance might be, Anton was liable to give his friends a spirited one-man reproduction of it on the next day.[21]

Theatre-going was itself a kind of theatrical performance, being forbidden to grammar-school pupils except with special permission rarely given. Since the school Inspector often attended in order to ensure that this regulation was not evaded, Anton would disguise himself in mufti, using make-up, a false beard and dark glasses; he would even approach the theatre by circuitous alleys, perhaps sporting a borrowed hat belonging to a friendly caretaker. Thus camouflaged, he would queue early for the gallery, where the unnumbered seats were cheap and popular. When the door was opened the narrow staircase would be taken by storm, after which there would be a long wait in the theatre's cavernous darkness, lit by a single gas jet, until the curtain went up. By then young Anton, himself a bit of a hooligan, might be shouting catcalls at the rich Greeks in the expensive seats down below. But despite such misbehaviour he was given a free run back stage through a school friend whose actor-father was a member of the company: in this way he met the well-known comic actor N. N. Solovtsov, to whom he later dedicated his one-act farce *The Bear*.[22]

With a public library opened in 1876 Taganrog acquired a second cultural asset vital to her most illustrious son. It was hard to find the two-rouble deposit required from readers as "caution money". But it was worth the effort, if only for the comic magazines which Anton and his friends leafed through, evoking by their chuckles the irritated shushes of more solemn readers. Here Anton encountered the humorous weekly *Oskolki* ("Splinters") and the stories of its prolific editor and his own future employer, Nicholas Leykin. But he also read more serious material. It included translations of foreign works known to every literate young Russian: *Uncle Tom's Cabin*, especially fascinating in a country recently emerged from its own form of slavery; the adventure stories of Mayne

Reid; Buckle's *History of Civilization*. The novels of Victor Hugo, Friedrich Spielhagen and Georg Born also attracted young Chekhov's attention; as did Friedrich von Humboldt's scientific treatise *Cosmos*, and even Schopenhauer's works. The youth also read some of the Russian radical "thinkers", Belinsky, Dobrolyubov and Pisarev. But the supply of that material suddenly decreased as the political atmosphere deteriorated: in 1878 a police raid on Taganrog library resulted in the removal of three hundred volumes, including Belinsky's and Herzen's works and the most celebrated dissident literary reviews, *Otechestvennyye zapiski* and *Sovremennik* ("The Contemporary").[23]

Of Chekhov's reading during his last Taganrog years a letter of April 1879 to his brother Michael provides evidence, as also of the condescension with which he continued to lecture that thirteen-year-old boy:

So Madame Beecher Stowe [authoress of *Uncle Tom's Cabin*] has squeezed tears from your eyes, has she? I read her once, and did so again six months ago for research purposes. Thereafter I suffered the unpleasant sensation familiar to those mortals who have indulged to excess in raisins or currants. . . . Now, you read the following books: *Don Quixote* (complete, in seven or eight parts). Not bad at all. It's by Cervantes, who rates pretty well on Shakespeare's level. I advise your brothers to read Turgenev's "Hamlet and Don Quixote" if they haven't already; you wouldn't understand it, lad. If you want to read an interesting travel book, try Goncharov's *The Frigate Pallas*.[24]

So much for Chekhov's first recorded essay in literary criticism. But what of imaginative writing? As a schoolboy he experiments in the area of his future career. He produces manuscript magazines, including *Zaika* ("The Stutterer"), specially written for his two eldest brothers in Moscow. He also sends to Moscow certain "anecdotes" which Alexander promises to submit to *Budilnik* ("The Alarm-Clock"), a comic magazine known to Anton from the public library. Alexander quotes the titles of two such "witticisms" as *Which Sex Adorns itself the More* and *God Granted*; these, he thinks, "will do", but certain other unnamed contributions are weak. Anton is to send along further material, as short and sharp as possible. The two items named by Alexander have never been traced. Nor has an early stage farce by Anton of which the bare title survives: *Deadlock* (literally "Scythe Strikes Stone").[25]

All this must have been facetious material, comparable to the earliest work which Chekhov was to publish in humorous magazines from 1880. But he also wrote, in his penultimate school year, a long, serious play called *Fatherless*. It was later "torn up into tiny fragments" by its author. Yet *Fatherless* may conceivably be equated with an item which has survived: the early, long, untitled, posthumously-published play usually called

Platonov, to be discussed in the next chapter. At all events *Fatherless* was obviously more important to its young author than any of his other schoolboy writings. Anton sent the play to Alexander, but received an unfavourable verdict. A couple of scenes had been "handled with genius", but the drama as a whole rang false; and that despite the great effort, energy, love and anguish which Anton had evidently invested in it. The treatment and dramatic skill were, Alexander added, worthy of an enterprise more substantial and far-ranging.[26]

Such strenuous efforts have been made to unearth Chekhov's every word that, unless *Fatherless* indeed can be equated with *Platonov*, we must presume all these schoolboy efforts irretrievably lost. This is unfortunate, but is by no means an artistic tragedy, for we can safely infer that the interest would have been largely documentary. Humanity was robbed of no masterpieces when Anton Chekhov tore up or mislaid his first experiments in belles-lettres. They amounted, as we know from allusions in contemporary documents, to at least twenty-four items in all.[27]

Each summer from 1869 onwards Anton had sat for the end-of-year school examinations which qualified him for promotion to a higher form. At times this harrowing event had nearly driven him mad, but the most nerve-racking ordeal of all was naturally that of the final examinations in summer 1879. They began on 15 May with an essay, "There is no Greater Evil than Anarchy", and they ended on 11 June with a mathematics oral. Anton secured a pass, helped by cribs of the Latin and Greek translation passages smuggled to the ill-equipped candidate by helpful cronies. He was placed eleventh in a class of twenty-three.[28]

After performing this last school ritual the young man stayed on in Taganrog for a few weeks to deal with bureaucratic matters. With admirable enterprise he secured a scholarship of twenty-five roubles a month, awarded by the city authorities and open to local lads bent on higher education. He also obtained essential documents, issued to the lapsed merchant's son by the burghers' corporation of Taganrog; these permitted him to leave his native town and reside elsewhere.[29] He intended to study medicine at Moscow University. But we know nothing of the background to this decision beyond a suggestion noted above: that the friendly Doctor Strempf, who had treated the fifteen-year-old boy for peritonitis, may have inspired the choice of a medical career. We also know that Anton sometimes snubbed those who asked what he was going to do when he left school. He intended to be a priest, he would tell inquisitive friends; but though Scripture was indeed his best subject they knew him better than to take the answer seriously.[30]

CHAPTER TWO

Early "Chekhonte"
1880-2

Domestic and Student Life

Leaving Taganrog, Anton joins his family in Moscow on 8 August 1879. His arrival has been described by his brother Michael in typical jolly style. After changing lodgings twelve times during three years in Moscow the family is now housed in a crowded, damp, squalid basement flat on Grachovka Street in the brothel district near Trubny Square. Michael, still a schoolboy, happens to be sitting outside sunning himself when a cab draws up. Out jumps a tall stranger who addresses the boy in an unfamiliar deep voice and with mock solemnity.

"Good day, Michael Pavlovich."

Realizing with a shock of delight who this is, Michael Pavlovich pelts inside squealing with joy, and tells his mother. Hugs, kisses, delighted exclamations are exchanged; the good news is wired to the father at his place of work south of the Moscow River. Anton has brought two Taganrog school-friends, also future medical students, who are to board and lodge with the Chekhovs. The three young men are soon out exploring the Kremlin, guided by Michael; returning exhausted, they sit down to supper with Paul Chekhov, now arrived from Gavrilov's.

The Chekhovs had never had so much fun in their lives, Michael reports.[1]

For the next twenty years Moscow and its environs were to provide Anton with a series of homes. At first he was enchanted with the city. "I'm terribly in love with Moscow [he wrote after a few months' residence]. No one who knows her will ever leave her. I'm a Muscovite once and for all."[2] But we shall later find him falling out of love, until he insists on moving to the country; only to return at the end of his life to his early passion for Moscow.

After many centuries as Russia's capital, Moscow had taken second place since 1712, when Peter the Great transferred the seat of government to the newly founded St. Petersburg. But Russians could not easily think of Moscow as less than a metropolis, and would speak of their chief cities as "the two capitals". Moscow was the cosier, the less smart, the less europeanized, the folksier, the more "Russian"; it was a vast, sprawling village of eight hundred thousand inhabitants rather than a nineteenth-century city. "Mother Moscow" was renowned for her taverns, her churches, for the din of her bells. Priests, merchants, shopkeepers, students, soldiers, domestic servants, officials, lawyers, school-teachers and prostitutes jostled each other on the streets, and rode about by horse-tram, droshky, cab or sledge. All were one day to be represented in the works of the Anton Chekhov who, in late 1879, seemed just an ordinary young man about to enter the university and begin a professional training.

However ordinary Anton might seem, the other Chekhovs already looked on him as their rescuer, for little could be expected from the older members of the family. Both parents seemed defeated by poverty and disappointment. Neither living *en famille* nor able to support his dependants, Paul Chekhov was abdicating as head of his household, but without leaving any obvious successor. His eldest son Alexander neither would nor could fill the gap. Still a student, he kept himself by free-lance journalism, copying work and coaching, giving the family what little money he could spare, but refusing to share their lodgings. This eldest brother of Anton's, with his quick mind, literary gifts and wide interests, was more at home on the Bohemian fringes of Moscow's artistic community. Having revolted against the world of small shopkeepers and against provincialism in general, he had not cut himself off from his family entirely, but hovered uneasily between the status of dutiful son and ne'er-do-well. Less still could be expected from the highly-strung, rowdy second son, Nicholas. A talented artist already much in demand by illustrated magazines, he was an unreliable youth, forever hobnobbing with undesirables, neglecting commissions, failing to deliver copy. Though he also kept himself by free-lance work, and was able to help his family a little, he was grotesquely ill qualified for the vacancy as its head. And he too was soon to leave home for cheap students' lodgings.

Reliability, so deplorably lacking in the first and second sons, was possessed in full measure by the fourth, Ivan. About a year after Anton's arrival he too left home, to take charge of a small elementary school in the town of Voskresensk (now Istra) about thirty miles west of Moscow. Ivan thus helped the family in two ways. His departure further reduced the number of Chekhovs to be fed and housed at Grachovka Street, and provided the others with a regular holiday home in his new quarters.

The Moscow activities of Mariya and Michael, the two youngest Chekhovs, demonstrate admirable initiative. Newly arrived in the city while Anton was still in Taganrog, and left to his own devices by his demoralized parents, the eleven-year-old Michael would have obtained little or no education—in fact he would have ended up drudging away at Gavrilov's with his father—had he not managed to fend for himself. He went from one Moscow grammar school to another, and eventually persuaded a headmaster to admit him. A similar feat was performed shortly afterwards by his sister Mariya.[3]

These three youngest Chekhovs—Ivan, Mariya and Michael—were dependable, sympathetic, conventional souls, much respected and beloved by Anton, whom all three idolized. He does not seem to have found them dull. But deadly dull they were by comparison with the two eldest boys Alexander and Nicholas: both so gifted yet so wayward, with their drunken habits, irregular love lives and financial unreliability. How fortunate, then, that there should be one member of the clan who combined in his person all the Chekhov virtues. The talent, the high spirits, the verve of the two eldest sons were Anton's, but so too were the resourcefulness and persistence of the three youngest children. No wonder that his arrival in Moscow seemed to promise delivery from evil. The financial benefit was immediate, for Anton brought a hundred roubles with him: the first four-month instalment of his Taganrog scholarship. It was intended to support only one person, and was soon swallowed up by the family's debts; yet it promised a small regular income nearly equal to the wages paid to the father at Gavrilov's. Then again, the two lodgers from Taganrog were soon joined by a third, which enabled the family to move to more capacious quarters: still very crowded, though, and still on the same disreputable Grachovka Street. Here Anton shared a room with Nicholas and Michael. And here they could afford better food, usually bought at the near-by market by Michael before he went to school in the morning.[4]

All the Chekhovs now busied themselves with survival. Even Michael could earn a few copecks from copying. The mother and Mariya sewed and cooked, while meagre sums trickled in from the father and two eldest sons. Soon Anton was adding modest earnings from contributions to periodicals. But his first concern was his training as a doctor. Soon after reaching Moscow he enrolled at the University Medical Faculty's gloomy, crowded, dirty offices on Mokhovoy Street. These depressed the keen young student, who had been expecting something grander, as he records by implication in his *Dreary Story* (1889), set in an unnamed university recognizable as that of Moscow.[5]

To choose medicine at Moscow showed serious intent, for this was not a subject like law or literature, which permitted pupils to coast along in idleness. It was a long, hard, five-year grind to which Chekhov now set himself, especially as he combined his studies with an active social life and the growing demands of authorship. One can only wonder that so little evidence of his arduous student activities survives. That he was punctilious in attending lectures and performing clinical duties we learn from a contemporary, N. I. Korobov, who has also noted that Chekhov showed no tendency to specialize. We see him attending a graduate student's defence of his medical doctorate thesis; writing up autopsies and individual case histories; gaining practical experience in summer vacations at Voskresensk. P. A. Arkhangelsky, doctor in charge of a local hospital, has described the young student as hesitant with patients, but calm, courteous and careful.[6]

Chekhov's letters contain few references to his medical studies, and those largely complaints about the many examinations, which he describes as a hindrance to progress. He was fed up with examinations; in fact, he was sick and tired of medicine altogether. And yet medicine provided a refuge from the tribulations of early authorship. "I shall immerse myself in medicine, it's my salvation."[7] But let us not regard these contradictory attitudes as evidence of a flaw in Chekhov's nature. It is no disadvantage to an author to possess this capacity for seeing things from more than one angle.

On one point Chekhov remained consistent throughout: his reluctance to be drawn into radical politics as cultivated at Russian institutes of higher learning. At Moscow he still kept in the background politically, as he had at Taganrog.[8] Meanwhile political assassinations and trials had dominated the late 1870s; but though this duel between a few revolutionaries and a few policemen became the talk of Russia, it made little direct impact on the population at large. Then the assassination of the ruling autocrat Alexander II, in St. Petersburg on 1 March 1881, provoked a further intensification of repressive measures under the more rigorous regime of Alexander III. And yet, as we have noted, even this bloody event might never have occurred so far as Chekhov's biography is concerned: except, that is, for troubles stemming from the severer literary censorship of the new reign.

The harsher regimen was also reflected in a contretemps at Moscow's Great Russia Exhibition of summer 1881. Chatting by a stand, Chekhov chanced to learn of a terrible railway accident: near the village of Kukuyevka a crowded train from Moscow had crashed down an embankment which had then subsided on to the wreckage and buried the victims alive. Only in so "swinish" a country as Russia was such a catastrophe possible: this was the opinion which Chekhov rashly voiced in the heat of the moment. Unfortunately he was overheard by a General resplendent with dark blue peaked cap and white epaulettes (and also, no doubt, encrimsoned face) as he pounced on the student who had dared express so unpatriotic a sentiment. "*What* did you say, young man? Repeat your words. 'Swinish Russia', I think. Your name? Who are you? . . . You may answer for this." Half expecting to be flung into Butyrki Jail and Siberian exile, Chekhov was shaken; but the incident luckily had no sequel.⁹ It is worth recording, however, since it reminds us that late Imperial Russia, though never the fully-fledged police state of popular misconception, was no haven of permissiveness either.

Rejecting radical talk, Chekhov did not shun other brands of self-indulgence. To the city's lurid night life he and his brothers were introduced by two provincial merchants, Lyadov and Gundobin, who would take them out on the town when up for a spree from their native Shuya. In the notorious Salon de Variété and other "restaurants, to call them by no worse name" (Michael Chekhov's phrase), these well-heeled Shuyaites would push the boat out in lusty merchant style. In a journalistic article of 1881, "Salon de Variété", Anton describes this clip-joint and whorehouse with its Hungarian orchestra, atrocious can-can, drunken quarrels and private rooms. Meeting the various Blanches, Mimis, Fannys, Emmas and Isabellas, we learn that no self-respecting tart would call herself by such a mundane Russian name as Matryona, Mavra or Pelageya; nor could any proper Muscovite take his vice seriously unless it bore a French label.¹⁰

That the youthful Chekhov shunned purchased love, as purveyed in such establishments, seems likely from his character and financial position. But he was no ascetic. As we have seen, he liked drinking, possessing a natural gift for this activity traditionally revered in Russia as an art form. He particularly enjoyed the annual celebrations of 12 January—St. Tatyana's Day, Moscow University's anniversary. A young guest of Anton's has recorded the shattering impression made on him by one of these chaotic undergraduate jollifications. There were cacophonous choruses of *Gaude-amus igitur*; tipsy professors clinking glasses with tipsy pupils; guests honouring other guests by tossing them in the air; a pile of writhing medical students on the floor promiscuously taking each other's pulses and babbling drunken obituary speeches. Above it rang the din of Moscow's youthful intelligentsia baying for broken glass. From the Hermitage Restaurant Anton's party moved on to a Tatar tavern where three young women, respectable and including a medical student, treated them to drinks and songs while Nicholas Chekhov strummed on a piano. Anton was last seen staggering after his guest's cab, pretending to be even drunker than he was and ostentatiously "swigging" cognac from an unopened bottle.¹¹

Chekhov's social life was not uniformly riotous. We also meet him with other students in a room full of smoke, samovar steam, salami, pens, exercise-books and paper. He is revising for examinations among heated arguments which he ignores except when directly addressed. The youth inspires confidence, and resembles a kindly grandfather. Free of affectation and conceit, he is good-looking with large, open face and smiling eyes. He sometimes looks you in the eye and throws his head back with an especially tender smile. "He positively exuded secretions of sincerity."[12] The tender smile, the sincerity, and above all, the secretions: we meet these again and again in Chekhovian hagiography. But the picture is not wholly misleading if we can ignore its unfortunate tone.

In his early student years Chekhov occasionally escaped from Moscow's bustling streets, with their clattering drays and yelling hucksters, to Sokolniki Park in the suburbs. Here we meet him one spring afternoon taking tea, rolls, smoked sturgeon and salami with two solemn medical students who bore him with tirades about their convictions and ideals; for all Russian students, except Chekhov, were by definition Men of Ideals dedicated to the High Goals of Existence. Chekhov tolerantly commented that these youths would make excellent doctors; he envied their ideals, he said, also remarking that there was something depressing about spring.[13] Here is a glimpse of the serious Chekhov soon to supersede the light-hearted student.

Besides brief trips to his brother Ivan at Voskresensk, Chekhov also visited Taganrog twice. In summer 1880 he stayed on the steppeland farm of his Moscow lodger and fellow-student Zembulatov; coached his host's younger brother in mathematics and Latin; dissected frogs and rats; decorated his room with a human skull. A year later he was back in Taganrog with Nicholas, attending a wedding in the family of their relatives the Lobodas. After the brothers had returned to Moscow Anton's comic sketch *The Wedding Season*, recognizably based on this celebration, was published in a magazine with caricatures of their hosts by Nicholas. This caused great scandal when a copy turned up in Taganrog, being resented as a poor return for hospitality.[14] The episode foreshadows certain works from Chekhov's mature period, notably his story *The Butterfly* (1892) and his play *The Seagull* (1895), in which he was to cause further dismay by exploiting his friends as literary copy.

Apprentice Author
(March 1880–November 1882)

Chekhov's literary career begins on 9 March 1880, when the St. Petersburg comic weekly *Strekoza* ("Dragonfly") brings out two cumbrously entitled items from his pen: *A Letter from the Landowner Stephen Vladimirovich N. of the Don Region to his Learned Neighbour Doctor Friedrich* and *What is Most Frequently Encountered in Novels, Stories and so on*. It was from this twin birth that Chekhov himself sometimes dated his début.[1] We have already noted that he had submitted certain earlier items to periodicals, that some may have appeared in print, and that none has been traced: a process complicated by pseudonymous publication, as normally practised by contributors to the comic magazines and by Chekhov almost invariably during his early years of authorship. For example, these first two items for *Strekoza* were signed ". . . v" and "Antosha".

How far Chekhov was from discovering an identity in 1880 is symbolized by the signatures to his ten short publications of that year, all in *Strekoza*. These have seven different pseudonyms distributed among them. Mostly variations on the Christian name "Anton" and the jocular school nickname "Chekhonte", they include the combination "Antosha Chekhonte", his best-known pen name.

Strekoza paid five copecks per line of about nine words, a copeck being one hundredth part of a rouble. The magazine was slow to settle up, as we note from editor I. F. Vasilevsky's letter to Chekhov of January 1881, enclosing 32 roubles 25 copecks for six contributions of July–December 1880.[2] These earnings amounted to less than a quarter of his scholarship from Taganrog Town Council for the same six-month period, and were more a boost to morale than a substantial contribution to the family budget. Meanwhile, far from acclaiming the budding genius, editor Vasilevsky had been abusing him in print. Instead of returning certain unwanted contributions of Chekhov's with a rejection slip, he gave his verdicts—as was customary—in a section of the journal entitled POST BOX, spurning several (untraced) items submitted by Chekhov with open contempt. "The hackneyed epistolary form is not redeemed by originality or humour." "A few witticisms cannot redeem impenetrably vacuous balderdash." "Very long and colourless like a paper ribbon pulled out of a Chinaman's mouth." Finally, on 21 December 1880, *Strekoza*'s editor pronounced one of the most erroneous literary diagnoses on record by printing the following lapidary words: "To Mr. A. Ch——v. You are withering without having flowered. A great pity."[3]

Such was the epitaph on his literary career which Mr. A. Ch——v found himself reading almost before it was launched. That he was discouraged we cannot doubt, for six months were to elapse before he resumed publication, and in a different journal. Obviously he was at least as fed up with *Strekoza* as *Strekoza* was with him.

Despite Vasilevsky's apparent folly in thus dismissing the brightest literary star of his age, the plain fact is that even Chekhov's items accepted by *Strekoza* merited these hostile criticisms. Here are ten contributions, covering forty-odd pages of what is indeed "impenetrably vacuous balder-dash". We have a long, would-be-funny pseudo-advertisement in which "Antosha Ch." seeks a wife. We have a facetious plaint in which "Prose Poet" laments having submitted 2,000 contributions to various editors without a single acceptance; and can we wonder, if this was a typical specimen? There is a crude parody of Victor Hugo, *A Thousand and One Passions*; and a facetious programme of homework set to "Nadenka N", pupil of a girls' boarding school. Only four items have a rudimentary plot and are therefore Chekhov's first extant essays in the short story. In one a jealous Major whips his unfaithful wife in a boat which capsizes, nearly drowning them both. Another has a father bribing a mathematics master to give his son higher marks: vintage Taganrog Grammar School material. A third portrays a girl whose fiancé achieves the remarkable feat of be-having as maliciously as her parents. Only in one work of 1880, *Because of Little Apples*, do we scent a whiff of literary talent. A sadistic landowner catches two young lovers stealing fruit in his orchard and forces them to beat each other, thus wrecking their romance. This story is derivative, the wicked landowner being a stock figure in Russian "populist" or peasant-fancying literature. Still, the plot is deployed not ineptly, while the young author's cumbrously expressed sympathy for victims of oppression strikes a note which will echo more effectively later.

In June 1881 Chekhov returned to literature, after a six-month interval, with *St. Peter's Day*, a comic sketch of quarrelling huntsmen celebrating the new sporting season with an alcoholic orgy. Disappointed with St. Petersburg as an outlet, he was now writing for the Moscow magazine *Budilnik*. Another, still humbler, Moscow journal carried eleven of his thirteen 1881 publications: *Zritel* ("The Spectator"). Its proprietor, V. V. Davydov, was an exuberant eccentric whose premises were more club than office, what with all the laughter, funny stories, smoking and tea-drinking. For a few months this publication was almost a Chekhov family business. Alexander acted as assistant editor; he and Anton wrote the words; Nicholas did the drawings; and Michael, our main witness, was after-school office-boy.[4]

The thirteen items of 1881 are again scurrilous sketches. They include bogus advertisements; jocular anecdotes; an item allegedly "translated from the Portuguese"; a romance about the Inquisition, "from the Spanish". There is a comic provincial train journey with one passenger's luggage thrown out of the window by another. As is common in Chekhov's earliest work, almost all the characters have comic names. There is a lawyer called Moshennikov (from *moshennik*, "shyster"), a Dr. Verflüchter-schwein; a Don Alfonso Zinzaga; and there will soon be a Lieutenant Zyumzyumbunchikov. Absurdly named or not, they exhibit no characteristics beyond silliness, self-seeking and a malice which seems to be shared by the young author, until we remember that he was merely conforming with the traditions of the gutter press to which he had attached himself.

Chekhov's most significant *Zritel* items are journalistic. One is "Salon de Variété", already mentioned. Two others discuss the visiting French actress Sarah Bernhardt. They testify to Chekhov's early interest in the stage, representing a serious attempt to assess this notable artiste, though in the disparaging manner of the comic press.

In 1882 Chekhov becomes more of an established writer, publishing over four times as much material as in the previous year. He also makes his début on 20 November in the St. Petersburg weekly *Oskolki*; but we shall leave that landmark to the next chapter, concentrating for the moment on the pre-*Oskolki* items of 1882. There are twenty-five, spread over five Moscow periodicals, chiefly *Budilnik* and *Moskva* ("Moscow"). The 1882 contributions include a little theatrical reportage and a dozen facetious sketches. There is a clutch of spoof supplementary questions "to be added" to a current census questionnaire, for instance: "are you (*a*) honest; (*b*) a swindler; (*c*) a hold-up man; (*d*) a blackguard; (*e*) a lawyer?" There are more comic advertisements, including one in mock-Jewish speech by a "Dentist Gvalter"; there are also imaginary pornographic books "for sale": "MEMOIRS OF A WOMAN'S STOCKING (1 rouble, 50 copecks)". There are eight *Problems of a Mad Mathematician*, culminating in the side-splitting "my mother-in-law is seventy-five years old and my wife is forty-two; what time is it?"

Besides such trifles there are nine items of fiction. The most popular was *Unnecessary Victory*: nearly ninety pages long, by far the most extensive published work of Chekhov's first three years of published writing. It parodies the prolific Hungarian romantic novelist Jokai Mor, and Chekhov wrote it after betting *Budilnik*'s editor that he could produce a full-length work with a foreign setting as good as Jokai's novels, then appearing in Russian translation. Describing the exotic adventures of Ilka, daughter of a gipsy violinist, the story pleased *Budilnik*'s readers; some believed it a genuine Jokai, but the editor tired of the joke as instalment succeeded instalment. *Unnecessary Victory* is less facetious than much of Chekhov's earliest work, but lacks serious merit. Four films were made of it between 1916 and 1924.[5]

Green Point is another early romantic story. Introducing the Georgian aristocracy in a castellated villa on the Black Sea, it is a romance un-Chekhovian in that the right boy ends up with the right girl. How different is the ponderously entitled "*Though the Assignation was kept, yet . . .*" where a young man prepares for a "date" by drinking six bottles of beer, arrives drunk, and behaves so badly that the girl throws him over: a mere trifle, the story yet pioneers the Chekhovian formula of romantic illusion shipwrecked on vulgar triviality. Another miscued love affair is *A Nasty Story*; here the heroine, after long expecting a proposal of marriage from her shy artist-suitor, is subjected to a protracted suspenseful romantic build-up before receiving the devastatingly unexpected proposition, "my darling, be my—model". No less deflated is the love intrigue in *A Living Chattel*: rich landowner purchases pretty young wife of poor official for 150,000 roubles, and all end up as a lugubrious *ménage à trois* in the depths of Chernigov Province.

That love inevitably betrays the illusions of bliss which it promises: this thesis, here so flippantly conveyed, is to obsess Chekhov throughout his life, figuring in the long series of inverted romances of which *A Marriageable Girl* (1903) is the last. Even in 1882 we find two stories, his least inconsiderable to date, in which *chagrin d'amour* is treated with a certain seriousness, sentimentality rather than facetiousness being the damaging factor.

The Mistress has a wicked, lascivious female landowner seducing her handsome peasant coachman, and so corrupting the poor man that he murders his pathetic wife abandoned in her village home.

Belated Blossom is Chekhov's most important published item of 1880–2, and foreshadows the clash in his last work, *The Cherry Orchard*, between the decaying genteel owners of that property and the self-made serf's son who buys it from them. Chekhov, who himself had recently experienced in Taganrog the loss of a family home, portrays in *Belated Blossom* the same fate as it befalls the feckless, titled, outstandingly un-grocerlike Priklonsky family: a mother with pretensions more suited to her former status than to her present reduced circumstances; the son a hopeless drunkard and ne'er-do-well; the daughter a sentimental, ailing half-wit. With these upper-crust "no-hopers" is contrasted the successful plebeian Dr. Toporkov (nephew of the young Prince's valet). At the last moment this monster of ruthless insensitivity suddenly takes pity on the hapless young Princess Priklonsky, who is suffering from hopeless love for him complicated by terminal tuberculosis. The story dissolves in sentimentality as the now compassionate doctor takes the poor girl abroad to die. Still, despite its obvious faults, *Belated Blossom* does conjure up a sort of Chekhovian mood. What was later to be handled so lightly and poignantly is here managed coarsely and heavily. Yet there is nothing in Chekhov's first three years of published writing which more closely anticipates his maturity.

Frustrated love and the loss of a family estate, two main themes of *Belated Blossom* and *The Cherry Orchard*, also figure in another work of the early 1880s: one which was not to be published until long after its author's death. This is the huge and immature play, discovered among Chekhov's effects and brought out by the Soviet Central State Literary Archive in 1923. Untitled by its author, the work is commonly termed *Platonov* (the hero's surname); as noted above, it might possibly be the same play as *Fatherless*, written in 1877-8 but destroyed by the schoolboy Chekhov, if we are to believe his brother Michael.[6] The manuscript of *Platonov* is undated, but has been assigned to 1880-1 on calligraphic and stylistic evidence combined with Michael Chekhov's witness. He has the second-year student Anton taking the play to a well-known actress, Mariya Yermolov, hoping to have it staged at the Moscow Maly Theatre. But *Platonov* was turned down: no surprise on grounds of length alone, for at 160 pages it would take about as long to run—uncut—as *Uncle Vanya, Three Sisters* and *The Cherry Orchard* put together. But a curtailed *Platonov* did achieve stage performances in at least four countries between 1928 and 1960.[7]

Platonov eschews Chekhov's usual hints, half-statements and eloquent silences, being as exuberant and outspoken as the later plays are evocatively reticent. Another contrast lies in the part played by action. Notoriously the writer in whose later works "nothing happens", the Chekhov of *Platonov* makes far too many things happen. One of his heroines tries to throw herself under a passing train on stage, being saved by a horse-thief who is later lynched by enraged peasants; the same young woman also saves her husband from being knifed and later tries to poison herself by eating sulphur matches. The play ends with a murder, its hero being shot in a fit of passion by one of three discarded or would-be mistresses. The only on-stage murder in any of Chekhov's plays, which were to move away from the direct presentation of violence, this concludes a sequel of intermeshed amatory and financial intrigues vaguely reminiscent of Dostoyevsky and revolving round a sexually irresistible village school-master.[8]

Continuing to contrast the Chekhov of 1880-2 with the mature writer, we are also struck by his early, seemingly perverse, avoidance of themes on which his Moscow experiences best qualified him to write: the academic and medical worlds. This was the serious background of his life. Is that why he barely invoked it at all in facetious sketches, but left it for such a mature masterpiece as *A Dreary Story* (1889)?

How did the mature Chekhov himself assess these earliest writings? We can judge that from the first "Collected Works" (1899-1902), chosen and edited by himself. Of the forty-eight items published in 1880-2, he excluded every single word as unworthy of preservation.

CHAPTER THREE

"Splinters"
1882-5

The Ascendancy of "Oskolki"
(November 1882–May 1885)

In the afternoon of a winter's day in late 1882 Chekhov and his brother Nicholas are walking down a Moscow street when a shout is heard and a sledge suddenly pulls up beside them. Two middle-aged men step out. One, whom they already know well, is Liodor Palmin, contributor to the comic press, poet and alcoholic. The other, to whom they are speedily introduced, is a minor celebrity: the lame, thick-set, full-bearded Nicholas Leykin, owner and editor of the St. Petersburg weekly *Oskolki* ("Splinters"), and as such uncrowned king of the humorous magazines. Palmin has long been eager to introduce Anton and Nicholas Chekhov to *Oskolki*; and Leykin, a keen recruiter of new talent, needs no urging. There and then he invites the two young men into the nearest tavern for a glass of beer and solicits their contributions to his journal.[1]

Thus occurred the first significant promotion in Anton's literary career. It was sealed on 20 November 1882 when his first contribution to *Oskolki*, the story *Running into Trouble*, appeared. From then onwards we can observe, over a period of five years, the rise and fall of Chekhov's first close relationship with a single editor and publication. It is only the first half of this five-year period, the thirty months ending in May 1885, which concerns us for the moment. During these months *Oskolki* serves as Chekhov's most favoured publication; by which we mean that it regularly receives his best work and has first claim on his attention. We shall later observe *Oskolki* being superseded by other preferred vehicles, while yet serving on into 1887 as an important reserve publication in which numerous items still continue to appear.

Oskolki's thirty-month ascendancy represents the second of the four phases into which we have divided Chekhov's immature (pre-1888) writings. This second stage is marked by a distinct increase in productivity, for it witnesses the publication of no less than 224 new items (excluding journalism), by contrast with the mere 42 published in the pre-*Oskolki* phases, as analysed in the preceding chapter. The material of both phases is, however, rather less bulky than the tally of titles might suggest, simply because so many of the individual items are very short. Of these 224 items, 162 appeared in *Oskolki* and 62 in other periodicals. Chekhov included only 34 of the former and 13 of the latter in his "Collected Works" of 1899–1902.

As the pre-*Oskolki* material has already shown, it would be misleading to think—simply because Chekhov is known as a short-story writer—that all these manifold early contributions can properly be called "stories". Nor can we even specify how many "stories" there are among them, since no hard and fast line can be drawn between the different genres which are involved. Though some of these early contributions may indeed be dignified as works of (usually facetious) narrative fiction, others are mere cartoon captions of one or two lines; some are sketches pure and simple; yet others are sketches with a thin narrative line. And though few items run to more than three or four pages, they also include, as we shall shortly show, Chekhov's only extant novel.

Oskolki both was and was not just one more comic magazine. Its material consisted, as did that of its rivals in which Chekhov had already been publishing, of certain topics deemed amusing irrespective of any context in which they might occur. A mother-in-law, *any* mother-in-law, was automatically funny. A man was slightly funny if he happened to be slightly drunk; and he was very funny if he happened to be very drunk. Armenians, Georgians, Tatars and other non-Russian citizens of the Russian Empire were funny because they could not speak Russian properly. So too were Frenchmen, Germans and other Western Europeans, with the added salt of their ludicrous inability to adjust to the Russian way of life. Jews were funny because they spoke Russian with a funny accent—and because they were Jews: all usurers or dentists, it seems. Russian merchants were funny because of their comic, old-fashioned turn of phrase, and so too were Russian peasants and shopkeepers and anyone else who could not read and write properly. High officials were funny because they bullied low officials, and low officials were funny because they crawled to high officials. Young men in love were funny because they were in love; young women were funny because they were all so desperate to get married; and both were funny because marriage, any marriage, was sure to begin with a brief idyll of romantic self-deception, only to collapse into quarrels and tiresome domestic trivialities—what with the wife's natural proneness to hysterical screeching combined with the husband's insistence on squandering her dowry, while fuel is constantly cast upon the flames by idiotic mothers-in-law and tyrannical, avaricious fathers-in-law. Both wives and husbands become even funnier whenever, as frequently happens, they find occasion to be unfaithful to each other. Cuckolded, abandoned, impotent, nymphomaniac or victims of satyriasis, all adults are funny in all their amatory involvements or non-involvements. Children are funny too because they are always being beaten for not knowing Latin irregular verbs, the amount of physical violence (all funny) recorded on the pages of the comic press being an eloquent indictment of contemporary Russian manners.

In conclusion, everyone, high or low, male or female, young or old, is funny because in the last resort all they care about is money, power, self-esteem and keeping up with the Ivanovs. Above all life itself is funny because of the ironical contrast between high-flown illusions and sordid reality, between hypocritical professions of devotion to persons or principles and unavowed contempt for those before whom one prostrates oneself for motives of self-seeking while privately cursing or abusing them.

In flogging these hoary themes to death once a week, Leykin and his contributors were creatures of their age and country, as they also were in their close adherence to seasonal topics. From the text of almost any contribution to Oskolki one may deduce the time of year at which it was written. The round begins with an orgy of food and drink on New Year's Day, and with the ritual visits which comic low officials are then required by convention to make in order to sign their names, as a form of obeisance, on the sheets of paper specially provided at the homes of comic high officials. In Lent there are lenten themes; at Shrovetide there are carnival themes, the gorging of pancakes with caviare prominent among them. Summer brings the funniest theme of all, that of the *dacha* season; a *dacha* being an out-of-town cottage, often part of a holiday colony, in which a harassed husband is apt to settle his wife and children between June and September, himself being absent or commuting to work in town. Angling tales, whether strictly piscatorial or depicting young women in their eternal search for husbands, are *de rigueur* during the *dacha* season, as are hunting stories, whether game in the normal sense or other men's wives are the prey; from this brand of venery the term "*dacha* husband"—by definition a cuckold, an adulterer or both—had gained currency. With autumn, and the return to town, the new theatrical season and the antics of actors claim their annual boost of attention: a prelude to Christmas with its roast goose, its sucking pig, its alcoholic excesses and its mummers (the Russian counterpart of carol-singers).

It was all, as Chekhov was apt to say in his later stories, great fun. And it was even greater fun, no doubt, because many more serious themes were banned by the censorship. One might abuse an official, even a high official, in the pages of a comic magazine—especially if, as was usually the case, he was given some such comic name as Krokodilov or Nikchemu-shensky. But one might not openly criticize the Imperial Government, the social system or the ruling autocrat. To the very considerable sufferings of the peasantry, who constituted four-fifths of the over-all population, to the no less considerable tribulations of Russian industrial workers—numbering less than three million at this time—no reference other than perfunctory might be made, and the censor was there to see that this restriction was enforced while benevolently passing material which disparaged pompous merchants, ludicrous civil servants and the like.

And yet, despite all these handicaps, the comic magazines flourished, for they were popular with the intellectually undemanding (the majority in any society) among the urban professional and business classes, especially in the two capitals, St. Petersburg and Moscow. They were often read on the move, in train, cab or horse-tram; or readers would leaf them through in the numerous taverns and beer-houses of the cities, knowing that they would find nothing to tax the brain. From the pages of *Oskolki* and its rivals no new thought was, to put it mildly, likely to leap at the eye; there were only variations on old and tried themes. The magazines were also popular for the very unedifying nature of their material. Such nasty, mediocre, self-seeking, squalid and generally amoral characters, all por-trayed by authors who contrived to insinuate that they themselves were on an equally unedifying level—it made comforting reading, this, for the average shop assistant, petty official or even mother-in-law. These could assure themselves weekly that there were other shop assistants, petty officials and mothers-in-law who behaved so contemptibly as to make the reader, however dissatisfied with his own performance, glow with the warmth of moral superiority.

Since *Oskolki* shared all these qualities with a score or so of similar publications, we may well ask what made it superior to these rivals. The answer lies in Leykin's strong personality, and in the firm control which he exercised over his magazine. Disliking the salacious near-pornography cultivated by all the comic magazines, but unable to dispense with it entirely, he imposed standards of comparatively good taste sadly wanting elsewhere. He also managed to assert an unusual degree of freedom from censorship restrictions, enjoying an advantage here over Moscow-based publications—subject, at this period, to especially pernickety interference. Leykin knew his local St. Petersburg censor personally, and would take tea with him, often persuading him to relax an unfavourable ruling or appealing successfully over his head to higher authority. Such negotiations were one of his most important duties as proprietor of a comic magazine, and the results justified his efforts, for *Oskolki* was notoriously more "liberal" in its complexion, and therefore more stimulating, than any other comic paper of the period.

That *Oskolki* was the best and deservedly the most popular of all the comic magazines Chekhov himself repeatedly stated, especially in the first flush of his new status as a contributor. Leykin was honest, he paid a fair fee (eight copecks a line), he settled up on the nail every first of the month. What a difference from the wretched Moscow *Budilnik*, where one sometimes had to call a dozen times to collect a measly three roubles. Still, Chekhov was in no position to jettison *Budilnik*, which remained his second-string outlet during the early *Oskolki* years. Nor did he abandon sporadic work for other comic papers. He would have been glad enough to give up the whole lot had it not been for the hard facts of economic life; and he often had to explain as much to Leykin, who would have liked to monopolize his work entirely. But *Oskolki* was not large enough to accommodate all Chekhov's writings during this very prolific period. "Don't be angry when you see me deserting *Oskolki*", Chekhov told Leykin in November 1884, referring to his work for yet another comic magazine, *Razvlecheniye* ("Entertainment"). This periodical was paying him ten copecks a line, Chekhov explained, and he was in no position to refuse, for "I must earn at least 150 to 180 roubles a month or I'll be bankrupt."[2]

In the following November we again find Leykin chiding Chekhov for continuing to publish in the despised *Budilnik*, and (what was worse) sending it contributions towards the end of the year: a sensitive season, for all the magazines were then busy trying to lure new subscribers by printing the most attractive items which they could obtain. Such diplomatic subtleties were above Chekhov's head, he told Leykin, while promising not to give *Oskolki*'s rivals a comparable advantage on future occasions. He would be glad enough to abandon *Budilnik* altogether, he continued, but it was bringing in thirty to fifty roubles a month, which was useful to "a proletarian like me". *Oskolki* was paying him a little more, between forty-five and sixty-five roubles a month;[3] but that was the upper limit of Leykin's resources, for which reason Chekhov was compelled to continue selling his literary favours on a promiscuous basis. Within a few years *Oskolki* itself would be relegated to the position of *Budilnik*: that of repository for items judged unsuitable for the new organs which were to take over as Chekhov's most-favoured vehicles.

Leykin was a fussy and exacting editor. He required from Chekhov as many items as possible, each containing as few words as possible. The staple length for a story was a mere hundred lines: that is, up to a thousand words or two-and-a-half pages. There were times when Leykin pressed for contributions of only half that length, but he was by no means inflexible, and there were other occasions when he permitted Chekhov to overrun the hundred-line limit.⁴ Further stipulations were the obligatory comic tone, whereby some of the inferior items seem to wear a perpetual frozen grin, and an ending with a comic and preferably unexpected twist.

Chekhov chafed against all these restrictions, not least against compulsory brevity. His *Tragic Actor* (1883) would have turned out not a bad story at all but for the "frame" put round it by Leykin. "I had to squeeze its very pith and essence, whereas I could have written an entire novella on the theme." The obligatory frozen grin also proved irksome, but when Chekhov began slipping in one or two serious items—for example, the stories *The Willow* and *The Thief*—among his contributions, Leykin was quick to object. In the second of these works Chekhov had gone out of his way to speak sympathetically of a condemned criminal's predicament: not at all the sort of thing which was expected from contributors to *Oskolki*. But Chekhov stuck to his guns. "However serious it may be . . . a short item does not preclude light reading [he told Leykin]. One must not be arid, God forbid, but a kind word spoken at Easter to a thief under sentence of exile: that won't ruin an issue. Actually it really is tough chasing after humour. In doing so you sometimes come out with something that positively turns your stomach, and you find yourself willy-nilly moving over into the serious area." As for the need to deal in one particular stock character, the comic drunken merchant: rather than take money for such base mockery Dr. Chekhov would, he said, much prefer to find himself "dealing with a dose of clap"!⁵

It was little use Chekhov complaining, for Leykin did not hesitate to return his most promising contributor's work if it failed to come up to scratch. Thus *Flying Islands* came back with a note pointing out, correctly, that it was no more than a parody of Jules Verne, besides being too long. Even a minor masterpiece, *The Bird Market*, met the same fate because it had what Leykin called a "purely ethnographic character";⁶ no matter that Chekhov had evoked, with a skill unparalleled in his other work of so early a date, the atmosphere of the old capital as richly displayed in its traditional market for domestic pets on Trubny Square. Prevented from publishing these two items, along with others, in *Oskolki*, Chekhov sent them straight off to *Budilnik*.

Complaints notwithstanding, Chekhov's apprenticeship to Leykin had its beneficial aspects, not least in the compulsory brevity which seemed at the time the most hampering restriction of all; for the fact is that Chekhov, the notoriously laconic Chekhov, could be appallingly verbose and repetitive in his earliest years. Indeed, it is precisely in the least trivial among his earliest items—*Because of Little Apples, The Mistress, Belated Blossom* and especially the monster-drama *Platonov*—that we find the future exemplar of masterly economy at his most diffuse and wordy. Leykin helped to cure him of that.

It was a few months before Chekhov began to get the hang of writing for *Oskolki*, and his first score or two of contributions include nothing approaching a masterpiece. But with *The Death of a Government Clerk* (published on 2 July 1883) we at last meet a story which, while conforming with Leykin's most stringent restrictions, is yet a minor *chef d'œuvre*. At a theatre performance a comic junior official chances to sneeze and bespatter the neck of a comic senior official. Attempting to apologize excessively for what was at first taken as no offence at all, the culprit pesters his high-placed victim, even visiting him at his home to repeat his apologies, and finally provokes by his importunity, not by the long-forgiven sneeze, an explosion of rage which proves fatal in the literal sense. "Going mechanically home, he did not take off his uniform, but lay down on the sofa and—expired!"[7] The skill of this work does not lie in the inevitably trivial plot, but in the ingeniousness, verbal felicity and playful panache with which the theme is developed. Like the somewhat similar *Fat and Thin*, published by *Oskolki* later in the same year, the story has become famous in Chekhov's own country. It is a perfect specimen in an admittedly lowly genre. Many similar pearls were to follow, including *The Daughter of Albion*, *A Chameleon* and others no less notable, all more or less conforming with the limitations imposed by Leykin.

As the years of Chekhov's work for *Oskolki* roll on the apprentice becomes more and more the master craftsman: but only in his best work of the period, and always within the restricted genre of the comic sketch or short story. Meanwhile the bulk of his contributions, far from being masterpieces, consist rather of what Chekhov himself, when posting one batch to St. Petersburg, does not hesitate to call "my literary excrement".[8] Captions to picture jokes, brief and often unfunny anecdotes, comic and less comic pseudo-advertisements, whimsical invocations of the months of the year—such trivial or scurrilous items are still tripping off Chekhonte's pen. Little indeed does he foresee a future in which all this material, however ephemeral, will be carefully collected and published in a series of increasingly scholarly editions. This is only as it should be, but there can be no doubt that Chekhov himself would have contemplated such a prospect with despair and bewilderment. At the time he had, he thought, sufficiently protected himself from being associated personally with his early literary trifles; he had, after all, regularly used pen-names, including "A. Chekhonte" for the better items and "Man without a Spleen" for the more trivial. And though the real identity of "Chekhonte" was an open secret in the journalistic world, the existence of this vast corpus of early pseudonymous work yet remained hidden from Chekhov's readership at large during his heyday as a writer publishing, from 1886 onwards, under his own name. Only through the efforts of bibliographers and editors active after his death did the bulk of Antosha Chekhonte's voluminous writings re-emerge into the light of day.

Items deriving from the period of *Oskolki*'s ascendancy, but not published in that journal, may be passed over in silence—all three score of them—as constituting the least forward-looking work of the period. But we must make a single exception in *The Shooting Party*, one of the greatest anomalies to be found in Chekhov's *œuvre*. It merits attention if only as a curio, being his only surviving work of narrative fiction long enough, at about 180 pages, to be described as a novel. Moreover, this sole novel of Chekhov's belongs to a genre which a majority of his readers cannot easily associate with him: it is a mystery thriller in which, after a series of melodramatic scenes and false trails, the murderer suddenly stands revealed at the end of the narrative as—the narrator. Extraordinary too are the circumstances of the novel's publication in a daily newspaper, *Novosti dnya* ("News of the Day"), which Chekhov sometimes called *Pakosti dnya* ("Filth of the Day"). Here *The Shooting Party* dragged on through thirty-two instalments between 4 August 1884 and 25 April of the following year. Split into so many segments, the work deteriorated as it progressed, for the early sections contain lyrical invocations of scenes and personalities which remind us of the mature Chekhov, though his early biographer Izmaylov has perhaps overpraised these particular passages.[9]

From the evidence which Izmaylov quotes it seems that the editor of *Novosti dnya* insisted on mangling the later sections of Chekhov's text, pruning the more elegiac passages and placing increasing emphasis on melodrama. This we infer from allusions to such interference which Chekhov has inserted in the text of the novel. We cannot otherwise document the matter, since his correspondence and other recorded utterances include no reference whatever to his longest imaginative work; and we thus have nothing from him directly bearing on its history or on the hopes which he may have attached to it. He simply preferred not to talk about *The Shooting Party*, just as he is never recorded as discussing the earlier *Platonov*: also an anomalous, botched, experimental item, and one rejected for the stage, whereas *The Shooting Party* was merely mangled by the press. These are both works in which the young Chekhov was trying, however ineptly, to find out what he should really be writing; and both differ markedly from the run-of-the-mill Chekhonte-type material which he was dashing off for *Oskolki* and other periodicals in order to earn money. Each of the two unwieldy experiments seemed to lead to a dead end, and it is not surprising that their author should have wished to bury them both in decent oblivion.

Chekhov did, however, attempt to rescue some of his flimsier writings at this time, less in the interests of posterity than with the aim of augmenting his income. In 1882 he had planned to issue in book form a collection of twelve previously-published sketches and stories. It was to have been called *Mischief*, and was to have appeared with illustrations by his brother Nicholas; but the project fell through.[10]

It is in June of the following year that we encounter Chekhov's first published book. Consisting of only six short stories—all based on the life of the theatre; all, once again, previously published in periodicals—it was entitled *Fairy Tales of Melpomene* and signed "A. Chekhonte". The slim volume was largely ignored by reviewers, but hailed in the Taganrog area for its "Dickensian humour" by *Novorossiysky telegraf* ("The Novorossiysk Telegraph"). These stories were too trivial to make any deep impression on public or critics, but at least the enterprise did not end in fiasco; both of which points were made by Chekhov himself in the following April, when he commented that "even such rubbish as *Fairy Tales of Melpomene* has caught on".[11]

Imaginative writings, whether masterly or "excremental", by no means exhausted Chekhov's literary contributions during the period of *Oskolki*'s ascendancy. There is also, lodged among his contributions to that magazine, a large block of humorous journalistic material: the column entitled *Splinters of Moscow Life*. This was contributed between 2 July 1883 and 12 October 1885 to a total of fifty items adding up to about a hundred and fifty pages, each contribution being split into several short paragraphs covering different topics. During most of this period the column appeared regularly, once a fortnight. Comment, not straight reportage, on local Moscow affairs for the St. Petersburg-published *Oskolki* was the purpose: comment from a characteristic standpoint, as laid down by Leykin in a letter of 10 June 1883 to Chekhov. The column is to deal with all outstanding scandals, the boss explains; it is to mock, it is to lash out; it is to praise nothing; it is to show enthusiasm for nothing. "Just you shoot out right and left; shoot everyone down without mercy."[12] From the start Chekhov felt uneasy and defensive about his column, protected though it was by a new pseudonym, "Ruver". Sending his first contribution to Leykin in late June 1883, he stressed his inexperience and ignorance as a journalist; and he invited Leykin, who never needed any such invitation, to prune out unsuitable material. Meanwhile Chekhov promised not to be too petty. He would not, he said, abuse restaurants for providing dirty napkins, and he would not make fun of minor actors.[13]

As this last comment reminds us, theatrical gossip plays an especially prominent role in the column. Besides discussing stage performances, Chekhov also denounces the ladies' lavatory in the Hermitage Theatre as the haunt of gossiping whores from Riga and Hamburg. Other targets for his sardonic derision include the scandalously neglected Moscow Zoo, a topic which was to rankle with him for another decade. The lash also fell on university graduates, for neglecting in prosperity to pay back loans once made to them by the Students' Aid Society; on his future publisher, Suvorin, for recommending in his paper that crayfish should not be plunged alive into boiling water when cooked, but yet more cruelly brought slowly to the boil; on Moscow undertakers, for tastelessly soliciting custom from the newly bereaved; on the drivers of wagons delivering Moscow's water, for having ideas above their station. Chekhov also slated the local railway system for a variety of misdemeanours and defects. But when two schoolboys, attempting to travel by train without tickets between Tver and Moscow, stowed away in the lavatory and refused all invitations to emerge, Chekhov took the side of the transport authorities; those boys should be soundly beaten, said he—speaking, for once, the language of his father—and made to learn lots of irregular verbs.

Train crashes, recent books, gossip about journals and newspapers, court cases, the weather, a mayoral election, the importunities of beggars: such were the topics which Chekhov evoked briefly and lightly, but often very pointedly, before passing on to others. It was, most of it, flippant in the *Oskolki* manner, with the accent on the fleeting sneer rather than reformist zeal. Yet Chekhov did occasionally emerge as a would-be custodian of morals. He trounced a Muscovite purveyor of pornography, the bookseller Leukhin. And he was surely thinking of the tribulations of his own childhood when he rose to defend Moscow shop-boys against the sweated-labour conditions imposed on them.

By now Chekhov had become an admirably fluent stylist in the off-hand *Oskolki* manner, and his column rippled on week after week without betraying to its readers what was in fact the case: that the author was bored stiff and longed to give it up, much as he needed the fifteen roubles a month which it earned him. He kept complaining to Leykin of the difficulty of obtaining material, and deprecated his own journalistic inadequacies: columnar journalism was like probing a chronic anal stricture or making a pharmaceutical preparation from a flea's sex organs, Dr. Chekhov lamented. But Leykin was pleased with the young doctor's probings and concoctions, and kept urging him to continue. Well might the proprietor rejoice, for the column was popular and much discussed in Moscow, where the identity of "Ruver" became a matter for speculation. Someone told Chekhov that he had traced the owner of the pseudonym as "a clever bastard" who lived in St. Petersburg and had his material sent over from Moscow.[14] Eventually, however, Ruver's true identity began to leak out and caused Chekhov unpopularity, for he had not spared his friends and acquaintances in his column. In view of this Leykin agreed, in February 1884, to change the pseudonym from "Ruver" to "Ulysses", and the column marched on; or limped, rather, for with the passage of time the number of Chekhov's contributions decreased before the enterprise finally petered out in October 1885.

Despite the verve with which Chekhov treated even the most hackneyed and trivial themes in his *Oskolki* contributions, whether imaginative or journalistic, he was inclined from the start to regard the work as an unwelcome chore. Forced to earn money as a comic journalist, he regarded that activity more as a hard-labour sentence than as the opening to a rewarding career. " 'Journalist' means at very least a scoundrel [he wrote in May 1883].... I share journalists' company, I work with them, I shake their hands, and I've even begun to look like a scoundrel from a distance, it's said.... The journalist is someone who smiles into your face while selling your soul for thirty fake pieces of silver; someone who, because you're better and bigger than he is, secretly tries to cause your downfall by proxy.... I'm a journalist because I write a lot, but that won't last for ever; I shan't die a journalist.... Writing gives me nothing but a twitch."15 How nerve-racking prolific authorship could be, especially in the disorderly Chekhov ménage, we learn from a passage in another of Chekhov's letters, dated August 1883. "I'm writing under atrocious conditions. I'm faced with my non-literary work, which nags mercilessly at my conscience. A visiting relative's baby is crying in the next room. In another room Father is reading [Leskov's] *Sealed Angel* aloud to Mother. Someone winds up the musical-box and I hear [Offenbach's] *La Belle Hélène*.... It's hard to think of an environment more odious to a literary man. My bed has been taken by a visiting relative who keeps buttonholing me on medical topics: 'My little girl must have a tummy ache, that's why she's crying.' I have the misfortune to be a medical man, so every Tom Dick and Harry thinks he's bound to 'discuss' medicine with me. And when they're tired of medical chat they start on literature."16

Chekhov was in fact more robust in sustaining the vicissitudes of early authorship than this extract suggests. It was as well that he should be. Not all editors were as prompt as Leykin in paying their contributors. One tried to settle up in kind, inviting Chekhov to order a pair of trousers from his tailors. Others kept fobbing the young author off until in the end he was reduced to sending Michael round with a chit certifying that the bearer had "been my brother since the year 1865"; and empowering him to receive payment from defaulting editors. Oppressed by the need to dun his employers, Chekhov was also harassed by the constant search for new ideas. He boasted that he could take a subject at random, an ashtray or even a wall, and make a story out of it; but such inspirations were not in practice so abundant that he could dispense with suggestions from other people. He offered fifty copecks to anyone in Moscow who could come up with a usable subject. Money, money, money! Was there nothing else in life, he must sometimes have wondered; and his correspondence abounds in intimations of immediate bankruptcy. "The hundred roubles a month I earn go into people's stomachs. . . . I have to pay out left right and centre; I have nothing left for myself. . . . If I lived on my own I'd be a rich man."[17]

After two years on *Oskolki*, though, the prospects were better. By now, Chekhov reckons, his family's position is assured, provided always that he himself remains alive and well. He has bought new furniture and a piano; he keeps two servants; he holds musical evenings at home; he is out of debt; he no longer has to buy food on credit.[18] But this was, alas, to prove a mere rift in the clouds, for money worries were to continue oppressing Chekhov until the end of his days; indeed, as is the way of things, the more he earned the more his financial anxieties seemed to grow.

The Young Doctor

After taking his final examinations the newly qualified Doctor Chekhov leaves the University in June 1884 and joins his family at Voskresensk, where they are as usual to spend the *dacha* season as Ivan Chekhov's guests. Soon after arriving, Anton is offered a permanent post on the medical staff of the District Council at Zvenigorod, the local county town, about twenty miles to the south. He turns it down,[1] but agrees to stand in as locum for two weeks at the end of July during the absence of one of the regular Zvenigorod doctors. Thus began Chekhov's career as a medical practitioner. It was to continue off and on until he settled down in Yalta in 1899, and was to involve him in prolonged and arduous work at times, though at other times he was capable of dropping it for many months on end.

During his fortnight at Zvenigorod he took regular surgeries, seeing between thirty and forty patients a day. They included an unfortunate five-year-old boy who suffered from paraphimosis (a retraction of the foreskin) combined with indications of incipient gangrene. An immediate operation was necessary, but what with the poor child screaming and kicking his legs about, not to mention the ghoulish interest displayed in the young doctor's methods by his brother Michael and a gawping ambulance man, Anton lost his nerve and summoned a more experienced local practitioner to take his place. The operation was soon done without fuss, much to the disappointment of onlookers who had been relishing the general air of crisis.[2]

Chekhov's temporary duties also included giving medical evidence in court and performing post-mortems. One of these involved driving a few miles out of town to dissect the victim of a violent crime; and since the superstitious peasants would not allow the corpse under their roof, this procedure had to take place in the open air. It left the officiating doctor with a memorable impression which he used in *A Dead Body* (1885) and *On Official Business* (1899). As the episode illustrates, he was soon exploiting the local colour which he was now soaking up in and about Voskresensk. We find further traces in *Surgery*, the tale of a clumsy medical student treating a sufferer from toothache by extracting a sound tooth; the theme came from Dr. Arkhangelsky of Voskresensk. *An Examination for Promotion* was suggested by conversations with a local post-office official, while *The Siren* was based on contacts with local officials.[3]

Chekhov's medical activities in the Voskresensk–Zvenigorod area happen to be better documented than those on which he embarked in Moscow after his return in autumn 1884. We know that he applied unsuccessfully for a post at a children's hospital in the city, and we also know that he sported the plate DR. A. P. CHEKHOV on the door of the flat in Yakimanka Street where he and his family were now living. Most of his patients were either personal friends or chance acquaintances; he was also generous in treating members of the Moscow literary-artistic fraternity, from whom he would never ask a fee, and who often exploited his good nature. For these reasons medicine showed no sign of rivalling literature as a source of income. He had only earned a single rouble from treating several hundred people during the summer, he wrote in September, and he was fed up with the sight of patients.[4] And though he did pick up the occasional three or five roubles in Moscow, most of that seemed to go in cab fares.

Among his first Moscow patients were a mother and three daughters, the Yanovs, who had contracted typhoid, a disease which Chekhov himself particularly feared. He was so assiduous in attending these stricken ladies, however, that one of the daughters was firmly clutching his hand as she died. Feeling helpless and guilty, seeming to sense the cold clasp of the dead girl long afterwards, Chekhov decided there and then to give up doctoring completely and devote himself to literature. So, at least, his brother Michael reports:[5] misleadingly, as we have seen, for Anton was to practise medicine extensively, albeit sporadically and as his second profession. Nor is his later career as a doctor marked by further examples of the very natural squeamishness which came over him occasionally when he was taking his first steps as a newly qualified practitioner.

Far from committed to a professional writing career in 1884–5, Chekhov was by no means committed to medical practice either; but rather, it seemed, to an academic study: a History of Russian Medicine. During these two years he devoted considerable energy to compiling an extensive bibliography and making extracts from relevant works.[6] And though the projected treatise never saw the light of day, the same urge towards scholarly work was to find an outlet in the one learned dissertation of his life: *Sakhalin Island*, to be completed in the following decade.

As these details confirm, Chekhov the writer cannot be understood in isolation from his close ally, Chekhov the doctor. That medical practice provided the young physician with literary copy we have already noted, and we shall find the theme gaining strength in later years, for not a few doctors are to be numbered among the most significant characters in the mature short stories. Medicine brought Chekhov into close contact with other human beings from all levels of society, and did so at times of crisis when they were often too distressed to wear their usual masks and project their usual images. For an author who specialized in delicately detaching people from their illusions about themselves the experience was invaluable.

Important to Chekhov as a source of copy, medicine was still more important in a philosophical sense: it reinforced his pragmatical, down-to-earth view of life. Of all the major Russian writers he was the one who kept his feet most firmly on the ground; who most consistently considered problems in the context of available evidence; who refused to leap to conclusions based on combined instinct and ignorance; who, in short, was more firmly addicted than many another creative artist to scientific method. This natural bias was confirmed and supported by his medical theory and practice. A doctor does not, or at least he should not, diagnose and treat illness solely on the basis of inspirational "feel". And though creative writing was a very different occupation, and one which even a Chekhov could never divorce from subconscious and ultimately mysterious inspiration, he yet remained scrupulous in his respect for evidence throughout his writing career. Never in his mature fiction would he knowingly incorporate material which ran counter to available data: a crime for which we shall incidentally find him severely censuring the great Tolstoy and lesser scribes.

Having made these claims, we must hasten to support them with the kind of hard evidence for which Chekhov himself always called. A carefully considered statement on his attitude to medicine is incorporated in a short *curriculum vitae* which he supplied on request in October 1899.

Medical study has exercised a serious influence on my literary activity. It has considerably widened the area of my observations. It has enriched me with knowledge of which the true value to me, as a writer, can be appreciated only by another doctor. It has also helped to guide me in the right direction, and it is probably thanks to my medical knowledge that I have avoided many mistakes. Familiarity with the natural sciences and with scientific method has always kept me alert, and I have tried wherever possible to take scientific data into account;

and where that has *not* been possible I have preferred not to write at all. Incidentally, artistic conventions don't always permit complete faithfulness to scientific data: you can't portray, on the stage, death from poisoning as it actually occurs. But, conventional though such a portrayal may be, one must yet feel that it is consistent with scientific data: in other words, the reader or theatre-goer must realize that ... he is dealing with a writer who knows his business. I am not one of those fiction-writers who take a negative view of science; nor would I wish to be one of those whose approach is always based on hunch alone.[7]

Scrupulously cultivating the scientific method in other walks of life, the young doctor for some reason neglected it signally in one particularly intimate area: that of his own health. It was in the December following his graduation that he first suffered a serious bout of blood-spitting: sufficiently serious to make him abandon a projected first visit to St. Petersburg. During the same year he also complained of being woken in the night by acute chest pains which made him feel as if his "lungs were being flayed"; these agonies would last a few minutes or seconds before passing.[8] Here, we presume, were the symptoms of tuberculosis: symptoms which the medically qualified sufferer was to ignore or push to the back of his mind for nearly thirteen years until this disease, which ultimately killed him, was to be firmly diagnosed by other doctors in spring 1897.

That many other creative artists, especially in the nineteenth century, have also been victims of tuberculosis, is no secret. Without wishing to claim that the disease somehow activated in Chekhov a leaning towards profounder creativity, we shall content ourselves with noting a striking coincidence of timing. His sickness, with its intimations of ultimate mortality, declared itself on the threshold of a major change in his evolution. It appeared, in other words, just as the jolly, carefree, joking Antosha Chekhonte was beginning to evolve into the wiser, the more serious, the more mature, the infinitely more talented Anton Chekhov.

As for another popular conception or misconception about tuberculosis, that it may predispose the sufferer to intensified sexual activity, we find no evidence suggesting that such may have been Chekhov's case. Even as a young man he considered love-making a threat to activities which he regarded as more important, and made this clear when discussing the misdemeanours of his brother Nicholas, that combined rake and toper. "The trouble isn't his boozing, but *la femme*. ... The sexual instinct is a greater hindrance to work than vodka."[9] As this comment reminds us, Chekhov tended throughout his life to speak as if men and women would greatly benefit if they could avoid making love altogether, or at least reduce that activity to a minimum. Though he did not hesitate to comment frankly on sexual topics, and though he most certainly cannot be described as a prude, the fact is that he generally invoked the theme in contexts which aroused his disapproval. He several times rebuked Leykin for permitting *Oskolki* to publish excessively "revealing" illustrations. And he was much offended by posters exhibited on Moscow's Tsvetnoy Boulevard outside the so-called "Museum" kept by a certain Winter. Anticipating London's Soho of the late twentieth century, the wretched proprietor had festooned the place with naked women: Three Graces who shocked one with their unbelievably broad pelvises; a Cleopatra with vast breasts and calves so gross as to disgust even an Armenian. The very policemen were embarrassed, said Chekhov.[10]

That Chekhov was particularly horrified by prostitution, a fairly obtrusive phenomenon in Moscow life, will not surprise us; especially as we have already noted the distaste aroused in him by one notorious Muscovite whorehouse, the Salon de Variété. But it was not his way to ignore social evils, and we find him in the year of his final examinations visiting another brothel with two young colleagues. Their purpose in penetrating the notoriously unsavoury Sobolev Alley is by no means the gratification of the flesh, but a serious scientific investigation into the motives and natures of the "unfortunate slave women". After asking one or two of them what a nice girl like her is doing in a place like this, the three young medicos repair to a tavern and compare their findings.[11] The episode left the Muscovite white slave empire untouched, but at least furnished material for *The Seizure* (1888), one of the most sensitive stories of Chekhov's early maturity. It portrays the pity combined with aversion evoked in a young student by the seamy side of Moscow's night life. Why on earth can't this miserable youth forget his scruples, his coarser comrades ask; why can't he let himself go and behave "like a real human being" for one night?[12] The irony of that "real human being" is quintessentially Chekhovian, and we have no cause to doubt that the sensitivity of his hero was, in this sordid context, fully his own.

To the unfortunate victims of Sobolev Alley Chekhov extended a degree of sympathy and understanding which he was not always prepared to accord to their more respectable sisters. In spring 1883 we find him projecting, semi-seriously, a History of Man and Woman. Woman, says Anton, is always passive, and her main function is to give birth to cannon fodder. Never is she man's superior in the sphere of sociology or politics. Women doctors have been active for the last thirty years without ever producing a single serious medical dissertation. Moreover, "in the field of [artistic] creativity Woman is a goose". As it turned out, Chekhov was drunk when he volunteered these sweeping generalizations.[13] Yet his sentiments are only an unusually outspoken version of views on the female sex which tend to recur throughout his life. Himself shunning or fearing passionate involvements, he treated women with amused and

ОСЬМНАДЦАТЫЙ ГОДЪ ИЗДАНІЯ

Удильникъ

ЕЖЕНЕДѢЛЬНЫЙ САТИРИЧЕСКІЙ ЖУРНАЛЪ СЪ РИСУНКАМИ И КАРРИКАТУРАМИ

№ 33   Москва, 20 августа 1882 г.   Томъ 36

Cover illustration to the comic magazine *Budilnik*, August 1882, by Anton's brother Nicholas

affectionate condescension which, in that submissive age, they were apt to repay with extreme devotion.

If, in the early 1880s, Chekhov's love life was as restricted as his many disparaging references to sensuality seem to imply—and in the absence of hard evidence we are reduced to speculating in a near-vacuum—the explanation may lie partly in sordid experiences which came his way through medical practice. Recommending, on one occasion, the procedure of subjecting wet-nurses and prostitutes to compulsory medical examination, he remarked that without such precautions they were liable to "treat one to a dose of something besides which even decomposing oranges, trichina-infested ham and tainted salami would pale".[14] In a man so subtle, obliged to take professional cognizance of topics so distasteful, we need not be surprised to find a degree of sensitivity greater than might otherwise have developed.

By no means excessively priggish or pernickety, Anton was to show throughout his life a strong dislike of domestic squalor. Clean, tidy, neatly dressed himself, he does not spare his relatives when they offend his admirable standards of decorum. In October 1883, for instance, he severely castigates the disorderly ménage maintained by his brother Alexander and that brother's common-law wife, Anna. "Clean and dirty underwear jumbled up together, organic remains on the table, nauseating rags, your spouse with her tits hanging out and a ribbon as dirty as Kontorsky Street [in Taganrog] round her neck"—such squalor could not fail to have a profoundly degrading influence on their baby daughter, thundered Anton.[15]

Horrified by domestic squalor, yet fascinated by the theme, Anton was to develop superlative skill in evoking it in his fiction, which he often uses as a platform for recommending his readers, in modestly oblique fashion, to cultivate decent, seemly behaviour in their domestic and social environment. They should, he delicately but eloquently implies, be unselfish and considerate; they should be polite to their servants; they should avoid the errors of overeating, getting drunk, making love, wearing dirty underwear, swearing at their wives, playing cards, talking scandal and spitting on the floor. Alexander Chekhov was, alas, guilty of most of these crimes. But though Anton might rebuke Alexander in a self-righteously censorious tone which he would never have adopted towards his readers, the fact remains that Alexander was the only Chekhov who could match, or even outdo, Anton in wit, intelligence and mordant irony. This Anton himself richly appreciated. Never did he lose his affection for his eldest brother, however much he might officiously or justifiably lecture Alexander on his disorderly way of life.

CHAPTER FOUR

"The St. Petersburg Gazette" 1885-6

The Ascendancy of "Peterburgskaya gazeta" (May 1885–February 1886)

In May 1885 Chekhov publishes his first story in the daily newspaper *Peterburgskaya gazeta* ("The St. Petersburg Gazette"); it thereby takes over, for a mere ten-month period, as the most-favoured outlet for his work. But he still continues to send frequent contributions to *Oskolki*, even though that magazine is no longer his preferred publication. Nor has he entirely abandoned *Budilnik* and the other comic journals.

Chekhov's introduction to *Peterburgskaya gazeta* had come about at the end of the previous year through a strictly journalistic enterprise of his own. An important bank had failed in the near-by provincial town of Skopin, causing widespread scandal which led to the prosecution in Moscow of a certain Ivan Rykov and others on charges of embezzlement. The affair was the talk of Russia, and Chekhov conceived the notion of covering the trial, which was to last sixteen days, for St. Petersburg in the role of court reporter. He accordingly persuaded Leykin, who was on the spot in the capital, to sell the idea to S. N. Khudekov, editor of *Peterburgskaya gazeta*; and it was agreed that Chekhov should receive seven copecks a line for a series of trial reports. He duly discharged this obligation, covering the entire proceedings from the act of indictment to the sentence condemning the ringleader and numerous accomplices to Siberian exile. Realizing that he was only a novice reporter, and unaccustomed to the compulsion to write "like one possessed", Chekhov came to regret an assignment which proved far more onerous than he had bargained for.[1]

Leykin was now going round the capital boasting about his protégé in Moscow: "Gentlemen, I have discovered a new Shchedrin." Soon he was persuading Khudekov to request contributions of belles-lettres from

Chekhov. They were to be published once a week, on Mondays, and must be posted to arrive regularly by the previous Saturday. Delighted with the offer, Chekhov wrote to thank Leykin, promising to be the soul of reliability.² It is with *The Last Mohican Woman*, on 6 May 1885, that he makes his fictional début in *Peterburgskaya gazeta*, thus entering the third of the four phases into which we have divided his pre-1888 writings. This new phase is to last until February 1886, when yet another periodical, *Novoye vremya* ("New Time"), takes over as Chekhov's most-favoured vehicle.

The *Peterburgskaya gazeta* phase is even more productive than the preceding, *Oskolki*-dominated, era. Within the ten months Chekhov publishes a total of 106 new items. Still consisting of stories, sketches, sketch-stories, story-sketches and miscellaneous rubbish, these include, as their more serious and important component, the 43 contributions published in *Peterburgskaya gazeta* itself. Of these 106 items, 20 of the 43 *Peterburgskaya gazeta* pieces were included by Chekhov in his edition of the "Collected Works", in which he also included 19 of the 50 items published in *Oskolki*; but none of the 13 which appeared in other publications.

Chekhov rarely expressed enthusiasm for *Peterburgskaya gazeta*. At seven copecks a line his fee was less than he was receiving from Leykin, and his new editor was maddeningly slow in settling up. The new periodical was earning him no extra money, Chekhov complained in October 1885; it had simply taken over extra writings such as he had previously been sending to *Budilnik*, *Razvlecheniye* and other humorous magazines.³ But this was one of his many exaggerations; never had he written so frequently and regularly for those two comic organs as he was now writing for *Peterburgskaya gazeta*. And however much Chekhov might from time to time rail against Khudekov and his paper, the plain fact is that they freed him from a double tyranny exercised by Leykin: the compulsion to be brief and the compulsion to be funny. Now enabled to write at greater length than hitherto and to abandon the frozen grin, the young author had taken an important step towards becoming Anton Chekhov while still using the pseudonym A. Chekhonte.

Of his new-found freedom to write seriously Chekhov makes striking use in three particular stories published by *Peterburgskaya gazeta* during its ascendant phase. In *The Huntsman* the jaunty hero spurns the pathetically loving wife whom he had married when drunk, and whom he has abandoned. In *Misery* an elderly cabby mourns the recent death of his son by pouring out his troubles, in which no one else is interested, to his horse. In *Sorrow* an aged, drunken village turner speaks tenderly to his dying wife (whom he has beaten regularly during forty years of marriage) while conveying her to hospital by cart: only to discover that she has given up the ghost *en route*, too soon to appreciate this one and only expression of her husband's all-too-well concealed devotion. These stories are tailored with superb skill, and are all deeply moving. Perhaps they are too deeply moving? Certainly the mature Chekhov never aims so directly at the emotions as the young contributor to *Peterburgskaya gazeta* had in these particular items. Here, after five years of the frozen grin, we suddenly discern a mask of anguish. All three stories are as far removed as possible from Chekhov's contributions to *Oskolki*, and they show him swinging to the opposite extreme.

To suggest that *The Huntsman*, *Misery* and *Sorrow* are typical of Chekhov's contributions to *Peterburgskaya gazeta* would be misleading. Chekhov could and did write sad stories for that paper on occasion, but on the whole he tended to stick to comedy. Many of his contributions are rollicking absurdities, whether with a bedroom flavour, as in *Boots*; or without such a flavour, as in *A Horsey Name*. There is also farce with a spicing of social criticism, as in the famous *Sergeant Prishibeyev*: much admired by Joseph Stalin, perhaps because it portrays the mentality of a potential concentration-camp guard. There is farce with a hint of tears in *The Cook's Wedding*; and there are tears with a hint of farce in *An Actor's End*. Then again, there are other stories which fit none of the above descriptions, such as *The Fish* and *A Dead Body*: portraits of peasant manners in the very different contexts of angling and sudden death. No less fascinating, and also foreshadowing a permanent interest of the mature Chekhov, are a few items in which he depicts the humiliation of some weak, pathetic, approved character by a vulgar, vicious bully. Such is *The Head of the Family*, where the repulsive father tyrannizes his seven-year-old son; and such is the eloquent *Upheaval*, where a spoilt rich woman, who has lost a brooch worth two thousand roubles, unceremoniously ransacks the belongings of a poor governess in the mistaken belief that she is the thief.

These are some of the main features of Chekhov's stories published in *Peterburgskaya gazeta* during the ten months of its ascendancy. And the same elements—the humiliation of the weak by the strong, peasant manners, laughter through tears, tears through laughter, social criticism and farce (bedroom or non-bedroom)—are also to be traced in contributions which he is still sending to *Oskolki*.

Most of these *Oskolki* stories are on an inferior level, but one of them, *Good-for-nothings* (*Svistuny*), is by far the most interesting item of its period. Chekhov was later to exclude it from his 1899–1902 "Collected Works", perhaps because it is so untypical a product of his pen: a mordant political satire *à la* Shchedrin on Russian intellectual patronizers of the peasantry. The main character is an unctuous landowner who displays his local yokels to his visiting brother as if they were animals in a zoo. Dilating on the muzhik's innate strength, natural sense of justice, instinctual wisdom and the like, Squire Vosmyorkin contrasts the feebleness of his own class: "all skin and bones . . . outsiders, rejects. How dare we consider ourselves *their* betters?" After intruding into a humble peasant hut and forcing its inmates to sing folk songs while their buckwheat gruel grows cold on the table, Vosmyorkin earmarks two lusty wenches, Dunyasha and Lyubka, and asks for them to be sent up to the manor for his own and his brother's after-dinner delectation. "Tell them it's for folk-dancing."[4] With *Good-for-nothings* Chekhov the baiter of Narodniks (intellectual peasant-fanciers) had been born. He was later to embroider the same theme many times in a very different, less overtly satirical, style; especially in his most controversial story, *Peasants* (1897).

The ascendancy of *Peterburgskaya gazeta* ends on 15 February 1886 with Chekhov's first contribution to another St. Petersburg daily newspaper, *Novoye vremya*: an item which makes history as the first serious work by Anton Chekhov to be published under his own name. We have now, therefore, come to the end of the almost exclusively pseudonymous period which had begun in March 1880 with his first publications in *Strekoza*. During those six years he had brought out the daunting total of 372 individual titles, all under assumed names, of which he later jettisoned two-thirds when editing his "Collected Works". In speaking slightingly of much of this material we have accordingly not treated it more severely than did the author himself.

Babkino

The 6th of May 1885, the date of Chekhov's début in *Peterburgskaya gazeta*, is also a landmark in his personal life, for it was on the very same day that he and his family set out to spend their first summer at a new holiday cottage on the estate of Babkino.

This change of routine had arisen through an episode which at first seemed to bode ill for their plans. After regularly making the family welcome in his capacious flat at Voskresensk, brother Ivan had now unfortunately been dismissed from his school-teaching post: not for any misdemeanour of his own, but through the antics of Nicholas Chekhov. That uninhibited artist had, while staying with Ivan at Voskresensk, strung up an ingenious array of pots on a rope in the school playground and played an obbligato on the improvised carillon, much to the delight of the children; but their elders, less impressed, had supposed the Chekhov boys to be practising the black art. Ivan, steadiest and most conventional of the five, had been forced to leave and pursue his teaching career in Moscow.[1]

It seemed lucky, then, that Anton had been able to find substitute holiday accommodation on the Babkino estate, especially as this was only a few miles distant from their beloved Voskresensk. In the small hours of 7 May he arrived with other members of the family after an adventurous journey culminating in hours by jolting peasant cart in total darkness. Leading the way on foot, Chekhov fell into the local river and nearly drowned while his mother's and sister's anxious cries rang out in the gloom. But when they at last stumbled into their cottage all these tribulations seemed worth while: the rooms were large and comfortable, a nightingale was singing, and at daybreak they saw that they had chanced upon a very paradise. In the distance loomed the Monastery of New Jerusalem, its gilded onion-domes shimmering in the blueish morning mist. The river, scene of Anton's recent ducking, was enchanting. It had a convenient bathing-hut; there were stepping-stones leading across to the mysterious Daraganov Forest with its masses of wild fruit, flowers and—most exciting of all—a profusion of edible fungi. "You never saw anything like it in your life", Anton wrote to Leykin. "The view's so delicious I could practically eat it."[2]

Besides mushrooming there was rough shooting, and Chekhov at once took a gun and embarked on a ten-mile tramp from which he returned with a single hare. Meanwhile he had set fish-traps in the river and brought out his rod and line: all with such success that a variety of fish, baked or in aspic, was soon being served at their table, as also was *bouillabaisse à la russe*. With a haul of twenty-nine crucian carp and an enormous perch, the Chekhovs soon felt sufficiently well-stocked to invite their landlords down from the big house for supper. These were the Kiselevs, Alexis and Mariya, who quickly made friends with their new tenants, not caring or noticing that these were their social inferiors. Alexis Kiselev's uncle had been a Count and a Minister under Nicholas I, but it was not so much through aristocratic pretensions that the squires of Babkino shone as through a wealth of cultural connections more exalted than those of the Moscow journalistic and artistic Bohemia in which Anton was accustomed to move. The great Pushkin had dedicated poems to Alexis's mother, while Mariya Kiselev was the daughter of V. P. Begichev, Director of the Imperial Theatres in Moscow; she was also a granddaughter of the long-deceased author and publisher N. I. Novikov, persecuted under Catherine the Great in the late eighteenth century.[3] Alexis Kiselev was active in local government affairs and held the post of "land captain": magistrate with jurisdiction over certain peasant affairs. His wife had been trained as a singer by the composer Dargomyzhsky, and was a published writer of children's stories. The composer Tchaikovsky was a friend of the family, and their household included M. P. Vladislavlev, a retired tenor from the

Moscow Bolshoy Theatre; a devoted pockmarked governess, Miss Yefremov, who was also a talented pianist; a small son and daughter.

This was not the sort of house in which one found *Oskolki, Budilnik* or any other such rubbish lying around. Far from it, for the Kiselevs subscribed to the Thick Journals: serious literary monthlies to which the facetious Antosha Chekhonte could not yet dream of gaining an entry. Still, Chekhov was already more than a mere routine comic journalist, and he was soon advising Mariya Kiselev on literary technique and helping her to place her work with editors. He also kept an album, which has been lost, for the Kiselev children; and wrote for them a comic sketch, *Soft-Boiled Boots*, which has survived. For their part the Kiselevs taught Chekhov to love music. Beethoven sonatas, Chopin nocturnes, Liszt rhapsodies, songs by Glinka—with the governess at the piano, with Mariya Kiselev and the tenor Vladislavlev in full voice, the evenings could never be dull. If spirits ever did seem to flag, the younger Chekhovs were there to put things right, aided by an eccentric friend and future notability: the landscape-painter Levitan, whom they had invited to share their cottage. A student friend of Nicholas's from the same Moscow art college, Levitan was at the centre of many of their pranks, including one portrayed in the memoirs of Mariya Kiselev's sister, Nadezhda Golubev. She was sitting in the dining-room with a few guests one evening when an enormous racket was heard and a gang of "Asiatics" burst in. "On a sort of box sat a terrifying Turk, carried by four Ethiopians, and—oh horrors!—they were making straight for me. The Turk snatched up a dagger and held it over me. I shrieked and jumped like one possessed on to the table, which creaked and would have collapsed if Father hadn't got hold of me in the nick of time. It was funny, silly and embarrassing." The intruders were as much put out as poor Nadezhda until the "Turk" adroitly leapt down from his box and gallantly introduced himself as "Levitan the artist", whereupon the Ethiopians removed their masks and announced themselves like a music-hall turn. "We are the four Chekhov brothers." One of them was Anton, of course. And when there was dancing at the Kiselevs it was he who would act as master of ceremonies, improvising so many amusing japes that the dancers would beg him to stop. "There was so much laughter and dressing up that they didn't even leave my old father and father-in-law in peace [Nadezhda Golubev reports]. They forced them into impossibly tight student uniforms and made them dance with their arms held out like wings."[4]

Rarely in their later life was there to be so much spontaneous gaiety and humour as at Babkino.[5] So enjoyable was the new holiday home that the Chekhovs spent three successive summers there, those of 1885-7. Anton must have passed about twelve months there, all told, in visits which cover not only the period when *Peterburgskaya gazeta* was his most-favoured periodical, but also that during which its successor, *Novoye vremya*, was dominant.

Though Anton relished the amenities of Babkino as much as anyone, he was not to be seen functioning as life and soul of the party during every single minute of the day. Sometimes a distant, withdrawn look would come over him. Lost in thought, he would sit by himself on the bottom step of the porch, preferring in such moods to be left alone with his thoughts.[6] Here, once again, we meet the stranger with whom we shall become more and more familiar: Anton Chekhov was taking a rest from the exhausting task of projecting Antosha Chekhonte.

But Antosha Chekhonte was still very much in evidence as a writer, not just as jester-in-chief to the Babkino ménage. Rising early, he would work on an improvised table, the stand for a sewing-machine; and maintained an impressive output of stories, in which Babkino themes now figure prominently. Some came from the theatrical director (Mariya Kiselev's father) who had given Chekhonte the plot for his superb *Death of a Government Clerk*, mentioned above and based on a real sneeze executed by a real minor official in a real theatre. From the same source too came the theme of a remarkable early masterpiece, *Volodya*. And the old gentleman himself was soon to serve as the model for the comic Count Shabelsky in the play *Ivanov*. *The Daughter of Albion* and *The Fish* derive from the angling annals of Babkino, while a lonely chapel near the Daraganov Forest furnished the scenes for *The Witch* and *A Bad Business*.[7] Wherever we find the countryside of Moscow Province evoked in Chekhov's work of the late 1880s we may always suspect the influence of his beloved Babkino.

Among other literary inspirations of the area an artillery battery, commanded by a Colonel Mayevsky and stationed at Voskresensk, helped to plant the seeds of the play *Three Sisters* (written some fifteen years later), while the same unit also provided Mariya Chekhov with an unsuccessful suitor. One of Mayevsky's officers, a Lieutenant Yegorov, wrote to her declaring his love, but she had no feeling for him; at her wish Anton replied, declining the proposal from a young man who may incidentally have given him the idea for Baron Tuzenbakh in *Three Sisters*. More flattering to Chekhov's sister was the flamboyant wooing of that notorious ladies' man and prankster Levitan. He fell violently in love with her; but then he tended to fall violently in love with someone or other on most days of the week. Sinking to his knees, the fiery young Jewish painter declared his passion to Mariya; and she reported the incident to Anton, of whom she always stood in considerable awe. He warned his sister off. She could marry Levitan if she wanted; but she should remember that Levitan, like Balzac, needed older women—which reminds us that it was to be Anton's fate to scotch, wisely or unwisely, all the budding romances in his sister's life. Dismissed as a suitor, Levitan remained a true friend to Mariya, and it was with his encouragement that she took up sketching and painting. Thus to the musical and writing scenes of Babkino we can also add artistic vistas, with Levitan working under a huge parasol in one part of the grounds, while elsewhere the moody Nicholas Chekhov lay on a rug, sketching in an album.[8]

Babkino is, all in all, perhaps the period in Chekhov's life in respect of which the routine idyllic picture—that of all jolly Chekhovs together, all having great fun yet all earnestly engaged on serious cultural activities— seems least remote from the truth.

CHAPTER FIVE

"New Time" 1886-8

The Hub of Empire

In December 1885 Chekhov first visited St. Petersburg.

Why had he been so slow to appear in the capital city? He had now been contributing to the St. Petersburg press for nearly six years; St. Petersburg periodicals had published well over two hundred items from his pen, totalling several hundred thousand words and including a regular journalistic column; he had long conducted an extensive business and personal correspondence with a variety of St. Petersburgers. But so far lack of funds, illness and the demands of a busy life had conspired to thwart his plans to visit a city which was situated nearly five hundred miles north-west of Moscow, but was reasonably accessible in about twelve hours by the Empire's best and most important rail link.

Even now, according to one of Chekhov's own conflicting accounts, it was not his own initiative which at last took him to St. Petersburg, but Leykin's. That bearded editor had turned up in Moscow, bought the young man a first-class ticket on an express train, and carried him off like an infant in need of an escort. Leykin then installed Chekhov in his comfortable St. Petersburg flat, where the guest was splendidly housed with his own pair of horses, magnificent food and free tickets to all the theatres. "I was never so pampered in my life.... I was praised to the skies, entertained in every way and given 300 roubles to boot." Thus Chekhov boasted of his first trip to the capital to his Taganrog relatives, whom he apparently sought to convince that authorship could be as lucrative a trade as the grocery business.[1]

Received "like the Shah of Persia" at *Peterburgskaya gazeta* on his first day in the capital, Chekhov met similar enthusiasm everywhere. All St. Petersburg had its eye on the Chekhov brothers, he told Alexander, tactfully including him in the family triumph. Anton was much better known in St. Petersburg than in Moscow, he discovered to his amazement, as eulogies and invitations reached him from the capital's literary notabilities. Daunted to find himself in the public eye, he felt ashamed to have written carelessly and hastily. "When I didn't know I was being read critically I wrote as casually as if eating pancakes, but now I'm afraid to write."[2]

Soon after returning to Moscow Chekhov sent an effusive thank-you letter to Leykin. "It was sheer paradise in your house. My life in St. Petersburg was one long round of pleasure. . . . Thank you ten thousand times over." Such was Chekhov the dutiful guest. That his private reactions to Leykin and Leykin's hospitality were startlingly different we learn from letters to Alexander Chekhov, also a contributor to Oskolki. Alexander was on no account to trust Leykin, Anton warned him. "The swine nearly choked me with his lies. . . . He's always trying to put me in the wrong with Peterburgskaya gazeta, and he'll do the same for you. . . . Don't you trust that lame devil. If the Bible calls Satan the Father of Lies we can at least call our editor their Uncle." It was not true that Leykin had dragged him off to St. Petersburg. "I went there of my own will against the wishes of Leykin, for whom my presence in the city was in many ways disadvantageous." Leykin was, said Chekhov, a "blockhead" and a "liar, a liar, a liar". Just how Leykin had so annoyed Chekhov does not matter. The important point is that, as these comments illustrate, Chekhov was apt to take one line when dealing with an individual directly, but a very different line when speaking of that same person to a third party. Such social hypocrisy came as easily to him as to most other human beings in similar situations; but it is worth noting as a corrective to the stereotype of Chekhov as too noble for ordinary mortals' petty subterfuges.[3]

That Leykin and Chekhov should disagree was now inevitable. Here was the rich, jealous, efficient proprietor of a successful comic paper watching helplessly as his most important contributor and favourite protégé prepared to soar away never to return. This became clearer than ever when, soon after this first visit to the capital, Chekhov was invited to write for the important St. Petersburg newspaper Novoye vremya ("New Time"). With the publication of his story The Requiem, on 15 February 1886 over the signature "An. Chekhov", this organ supersedes Peterburgskaya gazeta as his most-favoured vehicle. Its ascendancy is to last two years until he breaks into one of the serious literary monthlies, or Thick Journals, in March 1888.

Novoye vremya had the largest circulation of any St. Petersburg newspaper, and paid well: twelve copecks a line. Its proprietor, Alexis Suvorin, was now fifty-two: exactly twice Chekhov's age. Grandson of a serf (like Chekhov) and a self-made magnate, he owned a large publishing firm and five bookshops as well as his newspaper; he was later to acquire his own theatre in St. Petersburg; and he easily eclipsed the minor tycoon Leykin, hitherto Chekhov's main publisher. "I'm devilish rich; just think, I'm working for Suvorin", Chekhov boasted soon after starting to write for *Novoye vremya*. A single early story for Suvorin, *The Witch*, brought him about seventy-five roubles: more, he pointed out, than he could earn in a month from *Oskolki*. Soon afterwards he received a further 232 roubles from *Novoye vremya* for three short stories. He could hardly believe his luck, especially as he could still count on a hundred roubles a month from the "little" *Peterburgskaya gazeta*; nor, incidentally, had he yet abandoned *Oskolki*.[4]

Chekhov's association with *Novoye vremya* was not all gain, for that newspaper had an unsavoury political reputation. As a militantly right-wing organ it was suspected of being in government pay; wrongly, for Suvorin was by now too rich to need the government's money. When he supported government policy, which was by no means always, he did so from conviction:[5] a particularly heinous offence in the eyes of those "liberal" or otherwise oppositionist intellectuals of the period who are usually lumped together as "the Russian intelligentsia". Having himself held oppositionist views in youth, Suvorin was also detested by the intelligentsia as a renegade: one who had blatantly abandoned the "lofty ideals" and "high goals", of which they were always speaking, for outright commercialism. By now, though, under the stricter regime imposed by Alexander III, the intelligentsia itself was, with some honourable exceptions among personalities of particularly angular and stubborn temper, engaged in unavowedly shedding its own high ideals; it was ceasing to pursue oppositionist policies apart from mere verbal exercises continued through force of habit. It was, therefore, less for having sold out that the liberals abhorred Suvorin than for having sold out at a price so much higher than they themselves could conceivably command. Herein lay the main burden of their dislike of Suvorin, far more than in any objection of principle to such regrettable features of *Novoye vremya* as its aggressive anti-Semitism. This derived from the paper's general chauvinistic policy, which also involved discrimination against other minority peoples of the Empire: Finns and Poles as well as Jews. For these complex reasons Chekhov was compromising himself by writing for *Novoye vremya*, as he knew from the start. "After my début in *Novoye vremya* I doubt if I'll ever be admitted to a Thick Journal", he predicted in February 1886.[6]

Given this context we can perhaps understand why Chekhov's work for this notoriously "reactionary" (that is, arch-traditionalist) newspaper became in his own mind a manifesto in favour of freedom. Far from supporting either *Novoye vremya*'s politics or the autocratic regime bolstered by that organ, Chekhov was, we remember, opposed to political militancy of whatever complexion. But it happened that those who termed themselves liberals, and who denounced Suvorin's newspaper together with Chekhov's "lack of principle" in contributing to it, betrayed intolerance far more tyrannical than that of Suvorin and the autocratic state combined. Though the "liberals" of the day were indeed hostile to the Tsarist system (as also was Chekhov), they yet agreed with the State (and differed from Chekhov) in assuming a tutelary attitude towards humanity at large and towards individual writers in particular. And Chekhov disliked being told what to write and what to believe by either side.

He was more vulnerable to such personal attacks now that he was no longer protected by a pseudonym. From the start his work for *Novoye vremya* was signed with his true name, the discarded "A. Chekhonte" being reserved for his continuing publications in *Oskolki* and *Peterburgskaya gazeta*. It was only with great reluctance, in response to Suvorin's urgent representations, that Chekhov had agreed to sign himself "Chekhov". He had been reserving that name for projected, but never completed, medical research. How far he still was, at the age of twenty-six, from regarding literature as his main occupation we may see from a letter of early 1886. "I have assigned my surname and family crest to medicine, and I shall cleave to that until my dying day. As for authorship, sooner or later I'll have to give it up. Besides, medicine takes itself seriously, and requires a different label from toying with literature."7

Despite such characteristic self-deprecation literary promotions followed thick and fast in early 1886. Not least among them was an important letter from D. V. Grigorovich.

Grigorovich, whose name is hardly known outside Russia, was chiefly celebrated for two short stories of 1846–7 depicting the miseries of peasant life and anticipating Turgenev's *Sportsman's Sketches*. Though these and Grigorovich's later writings were not much to sustain a major literary reputation, the elegant, white-haired old gentleman was yet honoured as an important figure from the heroic literary past. Nor were his claims to be regarded, in the mid-1880s, as the acting, temporary Grand Old Man of Russian letters entirely ridiculous. He was still a keen follower of emerging Russian fiction now that he had survived into a period of apparent stagnation, his most famous contemporaries either being dead (Turgenev and Dostoyevsky) or seeming to have abandoned creative writing (Tolstoy and Goncharov). For a young author such as Chekhov, chiefly known through pseudonymous contributions to the comic press, to receive from this august source a long letter treating him as a potential major writer—it was a delightful, a barely credible surprise.

In this unsolicited testimonial to a man nearly forty years his junior Grigorovich describes how he had noticed Antosha Chekhonte's work in *Peterburgskaya gazeta*. He had made a point of reading every item appearing above that signature, irked though he was by an author so careless of his own merits as to hide behind a pseudonym. But that Chekhonte had "real talent . . . talent which sets you far above other writers of the younger generation"—of that Grigorovich had no doubt. Chekhov was destined to pen "truly artistic" works; and would commit "a grievous moral sin" should he disappoint these high expectations. He should respect his own gifts, and give up working under pressure. He should also avoid a "somewhat pornographic" note;[8] which, in this delicate age, meant any reference, even those as chaste and remote as Chekhonte's, to erotic topics.

By the standards of euphuistic utterance, traditionally cultivated in Russian discussions of the arts, Grigorovich's letter was a sober, practical missive. It offered excellent advice which Chekhov eventually followed, and it still reads well as an elderly craftsman's tribute to a promising apprentice. It is, curiously enough, the normally laconic Chekhov who strikes the more extravagant tone in their correspondence. "Your letter, my kind, my ardently beloved Harbinger of Good Tidings, struck me like lightning [he gushes in reply]. I almost burst into tears, I was overcome with emotion and I now feel what a deep imprint it has left on my soul." It was true indeed, Chekhov admitted, that he had undervalued his own gifts: as had those nearest to him by advising him not to neglect his career for mere scribbling. Onerous medical duties had also hampered the single-minded pursuit of literary excellence. Such, wrote Chekhov, were the only excuses which he could offer for the "grievous sin" with which Grigorovich had rightly taxed him. Yes, it was true: his attitude to authorship had indeed been casual and slovenly. He could not remember spending more than one day writing any of his stories; and had dashed off *The Huntsman*, praised by Grigorovich, in a bathing-hut. As for giving up writing to a deadline, Chekhov said that he himself was quite ready to starve, but indicated that others depended on him. Perhaps he might undertake more leisurely work in the summer when there would be fewer calls on his time. He promised to do his best: "after all, I'm only twenty-six". Meanwhile Grigorovich was to forgive so long a letter. "Don't blame a man, who, for the first time in his life, ventures to indulge in such a luxury as a letter to Grigorovich. . . . I have been so caressed and excited by you that I could have filled a whole ream of paper, not just a single sheet."[9]

That Chekhov was genuinely moved, genuinely grateful to Grigorovich, we need not doubt. But we also note that he chose to address the older man in terms more appropriate to one of Chekhonte's comic junior officials as he ingratiates himself with some domineering comic senior official. Thus, in his famous story *Fat and Thin*, might the pathetic second of those two characters have addressed the all-powerful first. The tone recalls those sycophantic letters once written by the seventeen-year-old Anton to his cousin Michael. A less pompous reaction to Grigorovich's missive is found in a letter to Bilibin, assistant editor of *Oskolki*. "The old boy wants me to write something substantial and give up working to a deadline. He demonstrates that I have *real talent* and quotes extracts from my stories to prove what an artist I am. He writes warmly and sincerely. I'm glad, of course, but I do think G. has rather laid it on with a trowel."[10]

The appearance, in spring 1886, of Chekhov's first *Novoye vremya* stories much enhanced his reputation. By early April he could boast of his increased vogue in the capital. "Leykin's out of fashion, I've taken his place."[11] On 25 April Chekhov arrived in St. Petersburg for a second stay, of three weeks, like a conquering hero. A fifteen-copeck cab ride took him to *Oskolki*'s offices, where the lady receptionist hailed him as the magazine's best contributor, and confided her opinion of Leykin: "a difficult man". After a glass of tar-thick tea with Bilibin, followed by a boat trip on the Neva and lunch at Dominic's Restaurant, Chekhov moved on to *Peterburgskaya gazeta* and thence to *Novoye vremya* itself. Here the great Suvorin granted him an eccentric audience. Chekhov has described the scene as follows.

"Do your best, young man," he said. "I am satisfied with you, but you must go to church more often and not drink vodka. Let me smell your breath."

I exhaled. Suvorin, detecting no smell, turned and shouted "Boys!" A boy appeared, and was ordered to serve tea and sugar without a saucer, whereafter the worthy Mr. Suvorin gave me some money.

"You must save," said he. "Pull in your belt."[12]

Despite this unpromising encounter, Suvorin was to become an intimate friend, a valued confidant and a close professional associate of Chekhov's for many years.

Soon after this Chekhov set off for a reception at Suvorin's house, where he was to meet "everyone, headed by Grigorovich". He was "on the closest possible terms with Grigorovich and Suvorin"; his first five stories published in *Novoye vremya* had created "a stupefying hullabaloo". Still, it was a relief to return to Moscow. "These St. Petersburg trips have a bad effect on me. I lose my bearings, and it takes a long time to clear my head of fumes."[13]

Yet another triumph in St. Petersburg followed in mid-May 1886 when Leykin's publishing house brought out *Motley Tales*, a collection, in book form, of seventy-seven Chekhonte-type stories which had already appeared in periodicals. This was a far more substantial volume than Chekhov's only previously published book, *Fairy Tales of Melpomene*. Appearing on the crest of his sudden popularity as St. Petersburg's favourite writer, the new collection was widely reviewed, evoking a lively response which included much hostile criticism. Chekhov's great solace was that the Thick Journals had been forced to notice his book. "*Nov* ['Virgin Soil'] abused it and called my stories the ravings of a lunatic; *Russkaya mysl* ['The Russian Idea'] praised me; *Severny vestnik* ['Northern Herald'] depicted my future lamentable fate on two sides of print." This last-mentioned review particularly galled Chekhov. It was unsigned, but identifiably by the well-known critic A. M. Skabichevsky. He wrote that Chekhov had "festooned himself with a jester's bells"; that he was "wasting his talent on rubbish and writing the first thing that came into his head". Chekhov's book, in sum, presented a spectacle sad and tragic indeed: the suicide of a young talent destroying itself with the slow death of enthralment to the gutter press. Skabichevsky further compared writers like Chekhov to squeezed lemons, predicting that they would one day be found dead in a ditch. To this review, with its gloomy prophecy, Chekhov was to refer again and again during the course of his life.[14]

And yet Chekhov's own opinion of *Motley Tales* was not far removed from Skabichevsky's. He told Grigorovich how much he disliked this "mish-mash, this jumbled hash of undergraduate sketches mauled by the censor and by editors of humorous publications. I'm sure it will disappoint many readers. Had I known I was being read, and that *you* were following my progress, I'd never have published it." Still, whatever might be said against *Motley Tales*, the book boosted Chekhov's growing reputation. That Chekhonte fans were enthusiastic is evident: the collection, radically pruned for its second edition of 1891, eventually ran into twelve editions in twelve years, being superseded in the end when Chekhov again re-edited its contents for his "Collected Works" of 1899–1902.[15]

When first reissuing this and later periodical-published stories in book form, and occasionally when reissuing a new edition of a published book, Chekhov was apt to revise the text. Some of these revisions were extensive, others merely superficial. In either event his general policy was to cut rather than to expand, while toning down the facetiousness associated with "Chekhonte".

At Home and on Holiday

In October 1885 Chekhov was living with his mother, his sister and his brother Michael in the Yakimanka, an inconvenient area south of the Moscow River. Their flat was damp, with mildewed walls, and they moved out after six weeks to other quarters across the street. These too had their disadvantages: the floor above was regularly rented out for balls, wedding celebrations, wakes and other rowdy entertainments. But the Chekhovs, hospitable as ever, were soon holding rival parties and musical evenings of their own downstairs.[1]

The second Yakimanka flat was a makeshift at best, and in August 1886 the Chekhovs did well to rent new quarters in Sadovy-Kudrinsky Street. At 650 roubles a year this was expensive. But it was conveniently central. It was in a "good neighbourhood"; it was relatively comfortable and spacious: a small, self-contained, two-storey house of a type unusual for Moscow and resembling, said Anton, a chest-of-drawers.[2] Painted red, it stood out from the other, larger, houses of the neighbourhood; and it is still there, now maintained as a Chekhov museum. For the young author, during these years of his rapid rise to fame, the house in Sadovy-Kudrinsky Street was to prove an admirable setting, and he retained it for four years. Never since leaving Taganrog had he and his family known anything so much like a home; never had they clung so long to a single Moscow base.

Less self-indulgent than his elder brothers, Chekhov yet retained his old talent for occasional drinking bouts. As during his student years, the celebration of St. Tatyana's Day on 12 January was still liable to leave him with a hangover after visits to the Hermitage Restaurant and the Salon de Variété. In 1886, on the morrow of this annual orgy, we find him with "an empty purse, someone else's galoshes, a heavy head, a fluttering in the eye and a feeling of desperate pessimism". On Easter nights he loved to stroll round Moscow from one church to another, listening to the bells. Thus engaged at Easter 1886, he fell in with two opera singers, both basses; he invited them home for drinks which inspired one of them to improvise passages from the Orthodox litany in the manner of an officiating priest.[3]

Young friends of the Chekhovs visited their flat every evening, says Michael Chekhov, adding that they included various "interesting young ladies". Singing and piano-playing were part of the entertainment on these occasions. Anton himself would make only sporadic appearances, and join in the fun between writing sessions in his study on the ground floor. On one such evening a tall, elegant, nonchalantly-cravatted, white-haired elderly gentleman appeared, became the life and soul of the party, flirted with the girls and took the bewitching Dolly Musin-Pushkin home afterwards. It was Chekhov's new ally and protector Grigorovich, who later boasted of enjoying "a regular orgy" at the Chekhovs' home.[4]

Of Chekhov's relations with the many young women who came and went at Yakimanka, and later at Sadovy-Kudrinsky Street, we know little except for one puzzling episode which breaks the rhythm of his bachelor existence. In January 1886 he became engaged to be married: a fact which

The Chekhov family at Taganrog.
Seated (left to right): Michael, Mariya (Anton's youngest brother and sister); their father and mother; Anton's aunt Lyudmila Dolzhenko, her son George. *Standing*: Ivan, Anton, Nicholas and Alexander Chekhov; their Uncle Mitrofan.

A view of Taganrog, Chekhov's birthplace, where he lived until the age of nineteen.

Portrait by the artist Nicholas Chekhov (1858–89) of his brother Anton, 1883.

Ilyinsky Street, a popular shopping district in central Moscow,
late nineteenth century.

The young Chekhov's literary patrons.
D. V. Grigorovich (1822–99), author and 'discoverer' of
Antosha Chekhonte.

A. N. Pleshcheyev (1825–93), poet and Literary Editor of
Severny vestnik.

Members of the Chekhov family with friends, in the yard of their rented home in Sadovy-Kudrinsky Street, Moscow, late 1880s.
Front row (left to right): Michael and Anton. *Second row*: Miss A. Lesov, Lika Mizinov; Mariya and Yevgeniya Chekhov; Seryozha Kiselev. *Third row*: A. I. Ivanenko; Ivan and Paul Chekhov.

Main street, Aleksandrovsky Post, the administrative capital of Sakhalin Island, visited by Chekhov in 1890.

Lydia Yavorsky (1871–1921), the actress
who was briefly Chekhov's mistress.

Lydia Avilov (1864–1942), memoirist
and fiction-writer.

Chekhov with two author-friends: D. N. Mamin-Sibiryak (1852–1912)
and I. N. Potapenko (1856–1929) during a visit to St. Petersburg in the
mid-1890s.

Melikhovo, where Chekhov lived between 1892 and 1899.
Above: Chekhov's house. *Below*: The village.

has emerged only recently through the publication of certain hitherto suppressed letters to his young St. Petersburg friend Bilibin. From this material we know that Chekhov's fiancée was Jewish; which makes it plausible to identify her as a Jewish friend of the family, Dunya Efros. To this Dunya he was accustomed to refer ungallantly as "Efros the Nose":5 a nickname in keeping with the allusions to his unnamed fiancée in the letters to Bilibin, which are far from conveying the romantic feelings of an ardent young lover. Moreover, barely have we learnt of Chekhov's engagement in January before we discover, in February, that it is about to be broken off for religious reasons.

Despite immersion in Orthodox church ritual during boyhood, Chekhov had neither embraced religious faith with fervour nor yet taken violently against it. We have no evidence that he was much of a believer at any stage of his life; and he was to become an outspoken but exceedingly tolerant unbeliever during his later years. Still, religious belief was one thing and the social-ritualistic background of Orthodoxy was another. To the extent of being thoroughly at home in that familiar atmosphere and setting, for all the miseries of his childhood as a conscripted choirboy, Chekhov felt himself fully Orthodox. His Jewish fiancée would therefore have had to change her faith if she was to become his wife, as Chekhov spells out clearly in his letter to Bilibin. "My girl is Jewish. If this rich little Yid has the courage to accept Christianity with all its implications, so much the better. But if she hasn't we shall call the thing off. Besides, we've quarrelled; we shall make it up tomorrow, but we'll be quarrelling again in a week. She's so vexed over the religious barrier that she keeps breaking pencils and photographs on my desk. It's typical of her, she's an awful shrew. That I'll divorce her a year or two after we're married is certain." By 28 February Chekhov has broken finally with his fiancée. "Or rather she has broken with me. But I haven't bought a revolver and I'm not writing a diary."6 And that is all we know of the affair.

Possibly there never was any such engagement, for Chekhov's letters so abound in flights of whimsy that it may have been a figment of his imagination from the start: a private joke between himself and Bilibin. As for Dunya Efros—whether briefly affianced to Chekhov or not, she later became a Mrs. Konovitser; and remained, with her husband, on friendly terms with the Chekhovs throughout the years.

For more details of the young man's intimate life we search in vain. Was he joking when, in May 1887, he improbably listed "excesses *in Baccho et Venere*" among the causes of piles, from which he suffered severely? And when he complained, from Babkino, that "I'm bored and sad and have no one to [. . .]", do we infer that he *did* have someone to "[. . .]" back in Moscow? There is no hint that he found Dunya Efros attractive;

nor yet that he "[. . .]ed" either her or any of the other girls who visited the house on Sadovy-Kudrinsky Street. But then he practically never, during his whole life, indicated that he found *any* woman physically attractive: rather did he harp on repellent female physical attributes. For instance, he now wants to jail both Leykin and one of Leykin's cartoonists for inelegantly, coarsely and odiously portraying a lady with an outrageously exposed bosom; not even in "a one-rouble knocking-shop" were any of the whores so "grossly corpulent". There is also his description of a blonde woman, wife of a Taganrog friend, as "a greasy, overdone hunk of Polish meat, beautiful in profile but displeasing *en face*, with bags under her eyes and hypertrophy of the sebaceous glands".[7]

The nearest Chekhov comes, during this period, to displaying any appreciation of feminine charms is in another letter to his confidant Bilibin. "Re your query about pretty women, I hasten to confirm that there are lots in Moscow. My sister's just had a whole bevy visiting her, so I melted like a Yid contemplating his ducats."[8] And the author of these lines could criticize others for falling short of his own standards of good taste in erotic contexts.

Living peaceably with his mother, sister and youngest brother, Anton now found the company of his father—a frequent visitor—easier to bear. It was on his two eldest brothers that domestic irritations focused. Still feckless and inconsiderate, Alexander and Nicholas were running up debts in Moscow shops on Anton's account. In early 1886 one store, Semyonov's, successfully sued him for 105 roubles on account of goods taken against his credit by this tiresome pair. Their offence helps to explain and excuse the habit, into which Anton had fallen, of sending them both magisterial rebukes and sermons on the art of living. Alexander was admonished to pay his debts and to respect his gifts as a writer by devoting more care to his stories:[9] the very reprimand which Anton himself had so recently received from Grigorovich.

These reprimands to Alexander were nothing to the homily on conduct delivered to Nicholas, a more spectacular wastrel, in March 1886. Accusing that wayward artist of a whole catalogue of misdemeanours, Anton drew up a schedule of features characterizing the Educated Man: a model as far removed as possible, we infer, from the hapless Nicholas. "The Educated Man must, in my view, satisfy the following requisites", fulminates Nicholas's younger brother, listing them at inordinate length. They are, much abbreviated, these.

Educated Men respect people's personalities, and don't read the riot act over a lost indiarubber. They are compassionate; they don't offend their loving parents by visiting them rarely, and then only when drunk. They respect others' property and pay their debts. They are honest; they do not lie; they are not puffed up, neither do they chatter unnecessarily. They don't embark on a course of self-destruction in order to gain sympathy. They don't go round name-dropping and pompously describing themselves as "representatives of the press". They respect their own gifts: to develop which they give up women, strong drink and other vanities. They cultivate good taste. Educated Men "can't sleep in their clothes, bear the sight of bug-filled cracks in the walls; breathe dirty air, walk on a floor covered with spit. . . . They strive to tame and ennoble the sexual instinct. To sleep with a female, to breathe into her mouth, to [. . .], to tolerate her brand of logic—what's the point of it all? Now, Educated Men are not so ill-bred. From woman they require not just bed, not equine sweat, not [. . .];—nor yet the kind of intelligence expressed in the ability to cheat their man by simulated pregnancy and constant lying. They, especially the artists among them, need freshness, elegance, humanity, the ability to be a mother, not a [. . .]. They don't swig vodka all the time . . . they need a *mens sana in corpore sano*."[10]

All this was water off a duck's back to Nicholas; but is significant in showing that Anton still believed, at this early stage of his adult life, in the possibility of influencing his fellows by direct exhortation. Perhaps the sheer hopelessness of poor Nicholas—who was to die of tuberculosis three years later—together with the incorrigible waywardness of Alexander, who was to remain an alcoholic all his life, helped to convince their brother that, as he seems to have concluded in later life, people are and tend to remain what they are. One may put up with them or not put up with them; one may depict them in stories and plays, or one may not depict them. But one cannot change them; for true communication between one human being and another is, the mature Chekhov seems to imply again and again, a virtual impossibility. Still, he did contrive in his imaginative works to recommend, by implication, his own fastidious standards of clean, orderly living, while never bombarding his readers with the kind of tirade occasionally directed at Nicholas and Alexander: and, by implication, at the various mistresses or common-law wives with whom each was usually cohabiting, and whose standards of housekeeping were so abysmal. "I'm staying with Alexander", Anton wrote from St. Petersburg in December 1887. "Filth, stink, tears, lying. One week in his place is enough to drive you mad and make you as dirty as a dish-rag."[11] Did contemplation of so much domestic squalor help to confirm the bachelor Anton in his celibate status during most of his adult life?

Though Anton's bachelor existence was assuredly less squalid than married bliss as cultivated by Alexander and Nicholas, his circumstances were far from ideal. He feared bankruptcy through his own and his brothers' debts: a prospect from which he once considered escaping by proposing—need we say, in jest?—to set up as a pimp. Nor was his state of health encouraging. He was still spitting blood occasionally, and wrote that he feared to submit to the examination of medical colleagues. He believed, though, that his lungs were not affected: an impression which was to grow and grow as tuberculosis of the lungs made ever greater inroads on his constitution.[12] Meanwhile he was complaining of toothache; of piles; of an abscess on his leg; of deafness due to catarrh. Such ailments, great and small, were to continue plaguing him increasingly throughout his life.

The young doctor who could not even diagnose, still less cure, himself was continuing to treat others. "I have lots of patients", he wrote from Babkino in May 1886. There were rachitic children, there were old women with skin rashes, including a sufferer from erysipelas of the arm with incipient abscesses which he dreaded having to lance. But though little satisfaction and less income flowed from his erratic medical practice, Chekhov continued to describe doctoring as his real business in life and writing as a hobby. Medicine was his "wife", he repeatedly claimed, and literature a mere "mistress".[13] Mistresses have, however, been known to supplant wives, and this is what was already happening in Chekhov's case.

What with the strains imposed by medicine and literature, as also by his poor health, his poverty, his brothers' fecklessness and by a general feeling of tedium, Chekhov was often thoroughly overwrought by the time Moscow's severe winter at last began to yield to warmer weather. To spend the summer in the city was "worse than pederasty and more immoral than buggery"—thus, most inelegantly, did he once express his revulsion against his Muscovite ambience. And it was in such a mood that, in early 1887, he planned an extended holiday in the countryside of his boyhood. Even an earthquake should not stop him leaving for the south, he said. "My nerves won't hold out any longer."[14] On 2 April he took the train out of Moscow, embarking on a six-week tour to be spent partly in his home town, Taganrog, which he had not seen since 1881, and partly in the steppelands of the Don and eastern Ukraine, where he had enjoyed so many holidays in youth.

In Taganrog Chekhov stayed with his Uncle Mitrofan, whose warm welcome he much appreciated; it was also agreeable to meet his four cousins and to renew acquaintance with many an old friend. But most of his impressions were unpleasant, perhaps because he was suffering from a new combination of ailments: to his persisting piles an inflammation of the left calf, and above all diarrhoea, had been added. This last affliction was particularly irksome owing to the danger of sudden death attendant upon nocturnal visits to Uncle Mitrofan's privy; located, as was the local custom, in a distant corner of the yard, it was often used as a doss-house by vagabonds with a reputation for violence.[15] We have already referred to the denunciations of Taganrog which Chekhov launched during this visit, in letters to his sister and to Leykin written at Uncle Mitrofan's: his strictures on this filthy, empty, lazy, illiterate, boring city of squat houses, peeling plaster, closed shutters, unpainted roofs, sticky mud and general inertia. Compared with Taganrog "even Moscow, with its mud and its typhus, now seems congenial". So squalid, so "Asiatic" a dump was Taganrog that Chekhov could hardly believe his eyes. And yet the town's situation was wonderful in every respect; the climate was superb and there were masses of the fruits of the earth. Why, then, were the citizens so "devilish apathetic"? They were musical, they were endowed with imagination and wit, they were highly-strung and sensitive, but all those virtues went for nothing: there were no patriots, no men of action, no poets; there were not even any decent bakers.[16]

After two uncomfortable weeks in Taganrog, Chekhov set out on a tour of the district, whereupon his health immediately improved. At Novocherkassk he helped to celebrate a Cossack wedding, officiating in borrowed tails as a groom's attendant, and was soon involved in such a medley of kissing and drinking that he could no longer distinguish girls from bottles or bottles from girls. Then he went on to the Cossack farm of his former pupil, Cornet Peter Kravtsov, where the goose soup resembled the dirty bathwater used by fat market-women and the coffee appeared to have been prepared from dried dung. A scene of constant carnage was this, owing to his hosts' habit of shooting anything which moved, engaged as they were in the day-long destruction of magpies, swallows, sparrows, crows and other dangers to the economy of their farm. They would wake Chekhov up at crack of dawn by firing rifles into the garden through open windows, and that often after a disturbed night; his looseness of the bowels had returned, but he had to rouse Cornet Kravtsov whenever he needed to cross the yard; otherwise he risked being torn to pieces by dogs.[17] Something of this atmosphere has percolated into Chekhov's *The Savage* (1897). A more specific echo of his continuing travels is also to be found in *Uprooted*, where he has exploited the excursion which he made that Easter, after leaving Kravtsov's farm, to Holy Mountains Monastery on the Northern Donets River. Here he spent two nights among a throng of pilgrims fifteen thousand strong; that there were so many old women in the world he had not suspected, or he would have shot himself long ago.[18]

This extensive journey revived Chekhov's consciousness of the southern countryside, a memory temporarily overlaid by impressions of central Russia in the Babkino area. That the landscapes of his boyhood were in many ways the more potent image he now realized as he travelled through the seemingly endless expanse of the steppe, with its hillocks, its water towers, its oxen, its kites, its top-knotted Ukrainian peasants and its Cossacks.[19] Most reluctant, throughout his literary career, to locate a story in a named and specific place, he yet tends to make it clear, through a few unobtrusive details, whether a given rural locality is to be conceived as situated in southern or central Russia. Among the better-known works set in the south is the first which he was to write for a Thick Journal: The Steppe.

Metropolitan Triumphs

Once established as a regular contributor to Novoye vremya, Chekhov found his literary reputation growing faster than ever. By the end of 1887 he had visited the main scene of his triumphs, St. Petersburg, five times; he was becoming a national celebrity. Fingers were pointed at him wherever he went, public readings of his stories were organized on all sides. "There is only one recognized writer in St. Petersburg: myself", he claimed after one such visit in March 1887. Soon afterwards a new book of his collected short stories further boosted his reputation, putting Motley Tales in the shade and being widely reviewed. Entitled In the Twilight, it was dedicated to Grigorovich, consisted of fourteen items previously issued in Novoye vremya, and bore the imprint of Suvorin's publishing house. For the record we also note yet another book of previously-published stories, Innocent Chat, which came out in autumn 1887. Pestered by a tiresome brace of publishers called Werner Brothers, Chekhov grudgingly yielded them a clutch of twenty-one early comic contributions for 150 roubles, feeling that he had sold his soul to the devil. After deliberately picking all the worst items, he was dismayed to see them issued in an incongruously elegant volume, and could only hope that reviewers would ignore it.[1]

Reviewers now had much weightier Chekhov material than Innocent Chat to discuss. It was no longer surprising to see his work considered at length in the literary monthlies. Vestnik Yevropy ("The European Herald") carried a long article on it in December 1887, while other Thick Journals were already bidding for his contributions and even inviting him to name his own fee: in vain, for the moment.[2]

Not allowing these triumphs to go to his head, as might have been excusable in so young a man, Chekhov reacted with modesty, reserve and anxiety. There was no true satisfaction for him in all this fuss. He was meeting too many people; he felt overpraised; above all he was over-burdened with work which made him nervous and tense because it was carried on in the public eye and suddenly seemed so fraught with responsibility. Every reference to himself in the press upset both him and his family, he was on tenterhooks all the time. After dashing round St. Petersburg day after day and hearing nothing but compliments, he found himself as modish as Zola's novel *Nana*; yet, while the entire capital was reading "my clap-trap", a serious writer like Korolenko went almost unrecognized. Chekhov was embarrassed by a public which ran after literary lap-dogs only because it couldn't recognize literary elephants. "I'm quite sure that when I do write seriously not a soul will acknowledge me." And again: "Being a Great Writer's not much fun—work, work, work, morning noon and night, with precious little sense to it and not a copeck to my name." But though money and renown might mean little to the young man, there was satisfaction in contemplating an achievement unique in the annals of Russian letters: never before had a contributor to the comic press caught the attention of highbrow critics without publishing one word in any Thick Journal.[3]

Under these circumstances Chekhov was naturally wearying more and more of *Oskolki*, the main comic paper in his life. He was looking forward to abandoning the hunchbacked Leykin—"that Quasimodo", who was now accusing him of treachery and duplicity. The feeling was mutual, and by January 1887 Chekhov was talking of his comic work as a thing of the past; he now disliked all the comic magazines, found them simply unreadable.[4] Henceforward, obviously, nothing would ever convert Chekhov back to Chekhonte. Only exceptionally would a Chekhonte-like item of fiction emerge from his pen after 1887: the last of his five years' close association with Leykin.

Despite brushes with Leykin, Chekhov remained on friendly terms with that "lame devil", continuing to meet him during visits to St. Petersburg while also cultivating more stimulating and recent friendships. With his new employer, Suvorin, no quick rapprochement developed; but a four-hour discussion during an evening of March 1887, recorded by Chekhov as "extremely interesting", must have helped to prepare this, his most substantial future friendship. Meanwhile Chekhov was "almost deluged with scorn" for contributing to the despised *Novoye vremya*. Suvorin was now more loathed than ever: not only for his pro-government policy and commercial success, but also for his press vendetta against the dying poet Nadson and alleged sharp practices over his firm's publication, then under way, of Pushkin's *Collected Works*.[5]

Among Chekhov's less happy St. Petersburg experiences was a visit to Grigorovich in March 1887. "The old boy kissed me on the forehead, embraced me and wept tears of emotion which caused him to suffer an acute attack of angina." Chekhov stayed with the sufferer for two and a half hours, cursing the helplessness of medicine, while his host was groaning in agony. "Luckily Bertenson [Grigorovich's doctor] turned up and I could escape."[6] In this dry comment on his dearly beloved benefactor, whom Chekhov also (incorrectly) described as on the point of death, we find a characteristic distaste for emotional involvement. There is a reflection too, perhaps, of Chekhov's inability, as noted by several memoirists, to tolerate a relationship on the level of effusive intimacy which Grigorovich and others found acceptable.[7] More likely Chekhov was, as so often, ambivalent: genuinely grateful to Grigorovich for his help and patronage, while somewhat embarrassed in the role of client to an older man usually more demonstrative in his sentiments than himself.

If Chekhov experienced genuine rapport with anyone in St. Petersburg at this time that person was certainly his eldest brother, Alexander. After various adventures, including a spell in the customs service back at Taganrog, Alexander had now settled down to what was to prove his life's work: as a journalist on *Novoye vremya*. The post did not do justice to his talents, but enabled him to live and support a family despite the crippling effects of his sad addiction to alcohol. Anton greatly appreciated Alexander. If only his brother could write stories as good as his letters (said Anton, with reason) he would long ago have been a Great Man, a Colossus. As it was, "you [Alexander] are not a genius, and so we have nothing in common". Such was the tone of the banter between the two. Meanwhile Alexander was generous in acting as Anton's literary agent in the capital; helping to see his books through the press; claiming payment on his behalf; and, as we have seen, having him to stay from time to time in his intolerably squalid flat. Anton advised Alexander on problems of fiction writing, encouraging his brother while lamenting that all the women in Alexander's stories were like wobbly pieces of blancmange. He also gave medical treatment to Alexander's first common-law wife, Anna, who was soon to die of tuberculosis.[8]

The Ascendancy of "Novoye vremya"
(February 1886—January 1888)

After beginning with *The Requiem*, on 15 February 1886, *Novoye vremya*'s ascendant phase ends on 25 January 1888 with *Sleepy*, the last story to be published before his début in a Thick Journal in March of that year. With his subsequent fictional contributions to *Novoye vremya*, which were to continue until the end of 1892, we are not for the moment concerned.

Novoye vremya's ascendancy was the most prolific phase of Chekhov's life, with a slight falling off in 1887 after the peak year 1886, in which he brought out over six hundred pages of fiction. Altogether the new phase saw the publication of 156 new items totalling over 1,000 pages. This phase was also distinguished by a continuing improvement in quality, as we can monitor through our usual index: no less than 100 (exactly) out of these 156 titles were later to be judged worthy by Chekhov of inclusion in his "Collected Works" of 1899–1902.

Virtually all this material, apart from a few trifles tossed to Moscow comic magazines, was appearing in one or other of the three St. Petersburg periodicals with which we are already familiar. Of these, *Novoye vremya* itself took serious items considerably longer than Chekhov had previously been in the habit of writing; moreover, as we have seen, he was discriminating in favour of his *Novoye vremya* stories from the start by signing them with his true name. To readers of *Peterburgskaya gazeta*, which continued to carry his shorter serious work, and of *Oskolki*—still the staple vehicle for short, comic items—he remained "A. Chekhonte".

The distribution of titles between these and other vehicles was as follows during *Novoye vremya*'s ascendant phase: 29 in *Novoye vremya* (of which 27 were included in the "Collected Works"), 65 in *Peterburgskaya gazeta* (43 included), 50 in *Oskolki* (28 included), and 12 in other periodicals, of which only 2 were included in the "Collected Works".

The range of this material is wider than ever. A dozen or so of the best items are more impressive specimens of the short story than anything of Chekhov's which had preceded them, yet fall short of his greatest mature achievements. At the other end of the scale we find slapstick and facetiousness; and we still meet the comic officials, ludicrous mothers-in-law and other fauna familiar from Chekhonte's earliest years. In one such item the brightest rising star of Russian literature records the lascivious musings of a tom-cat after a night on the tiles. In another he launches on *Oskolki*'s readers a prize competition for the best love letter; it provoked only two entries, both in barely literate doggerel.[1] Between the extremes of low facetiousness and high seriousness there are other items which stand poised at all possible intermediate points. Some have roughly equal proportions of Antosha Chekhonte and Anton Chekhov; others incline more to the one, while admitting an admixture of the other.

Though this two-year phase saw much of Chekhov's best work appearing in *Novoye vremya* itself, we should err in dismissing all his contributions to other periodicals as necessarily inferior. For instance, the outstanding *Typhus* and *Volodya* both went to *Peterburgskaya gazeta*; and so did other minor masterpieces: *Boys* and *Sleepy*. Even *Oskolki* could not be written off so long as it could still command items as good as *An Incident* and *Grisha*. As the five last-mentioned contributions remind us, Chekhov had now become adept at portraying children. These might be playfully described: like the kitten-loving infants of *An Incident* and the juvenile heroes who run away from home in *Boys*. Or the subject-matter might be harrowing, as it is in *Vanka* (1886); and as it is even more in *Sleepy*, where an exploited thirteen-year-old nursemaid, permitted no rest by her employers, ends by strangling the infant which will not stop crying.

Now free to indulge in pathos, Chekhov broadcasts it without discrimination of age or sex. *The Dependants* presents an old man forced to have his only friends, an aged horse and dog, destroyed at the local knacker's yard. *The Father* shows a pathetic dipsomaniac scrounger battening on his respectable sons. In *A Gentleman Friend* the victim is a whore with toothache and no customers, while *A Nightmare* limns the sufferings and humiliations of a poverty-stricken rural priest. Ecclesiastical life, in a variety of aspects, also figures in *The Requiem, The Letter* (1887), *Easter Eve* and *Uprooted*. Knowledgeable in church matters and sympathetic towards Orthodoxy, the unbeliever Chekhov was delighted when an acquaintance reported that he had seen a bishop reading the last-named story aloud, and with evident relish, to two other bishops.[2]

Sharply contrasted with such serious material are those stories of 1886–7 in which Chekhov continues to purvey uproarious farce. Still, in the work of the fast-maturing young author, *dacha* wives betray absentee husbands, while absentee husbands savour metropolitan sin unimpeded by *dacha*-marooned wives. And still, among the rollicking slapstick, we find an occasional gem to remind us that Antosha Chekhonte, however much Anton Chekhov's inferior, was yet a minor artist in his own right: even when handling farcical themes. *The Orator*, surely the finest of all Chekhonte's comic stories, depicts a specialist in graveside rhetoric deploying his art at a funeral after being misinformed about the identity of the deceased. He pronounces a moving obituary oration which becomes more and more embarrassing as it slowly transpires that the object of his misdirected (and increasingly tactless) eulogies is by no means the occupant of the coffin, but an infuriated mourner who had little thought to hear himself—and even his fondness for the bottle—so condescendingly commemorated on the occasion of a friend's interment.

Another noteworthy feature of the 1886–7 stories is the didacticism traceable in many of them and extremely marked in a small number. Nothing, it might seem, could be more un-Chekhovian than to use fiction as a vehicle for edifying messages. And yet that is exactly what we now find, notably in certain stories bearing strong evidence of Leo Tolstoy's influence.

That Chekhov had become a disciple of Tolstoy's we might hardly suspect were it not for his reference, in a letter of March 1894, to Tolstoyan philosophy as having "deeply affected and obsessed me for six or seven years".[3] Just which years these were Chekhov annoyingly fails to specify. In any case he had so thoroughly rejected Tolstoy's teaching by the time he wrote these words that we shall find some of his finest mid-1890s stories inspired by a strong aversion to Tolstoyism. For the moment, though, in the mid-1880s, we meet the exact reverse: a Chekhov inspired by Tolstoy's example and doctrines to write some of the worst stories which ever came from his pen.

Thou shalt not be angry; thou shalt not go to law, resist evil by force, indulge in extra-marital or (in a later version of the doctrine) any other form of sexual intercourse: these were the cardinal elements in Tolstoy's creed. It also involved the renunciation of civilization's more elaborate trappings in favour of a simple, hard-working, peasant-like way of life. All in all, Tolstoy's teaching constituted a variety of Christianity stressing the ethical element and fairly thoroughly purged of supernatural ingredients. Besides preaching these virtues, in theoretical form and at inordinate length, Tolstoy had also done something more difficult: made them the basis, in his *Popular Stories* and elsewhere, for fictional sermons contravening the law or tendency whereby overt didacticism is, or often seems, incompatible with a high level of artistic achievement. On Chekhov these works had evidently made a strong impression, for we now find him aping Tolstoy's didactic virtuosity.

In Chekhov's *An Encounter* an itinerant alms-gatherer is blatantly robbed by a travelling companion; but runs true to the doctrine of non-resistance, neither showing anger nor attempting to invoke the law, until in the end the shamed thief repents and returns what is left, after a drinking orgy, of the stolen money. In *The Beggar* a tramp is hired to split logs. He proves too feeble and demoralized to tackle the job, and so the household cook rolls up her sleeves and does it for him: a display of good will which transforms the wastrel into an effective member of society. *In Trouble* (*Beda*; 1886) presents a petty official who loses his job after a drunken orgy; reaching home and expecting a tantrum from his wife, he is greeted with such loving tenderness that he finds the strength to turn over a new leaf.

Such works are best understood as part of an experiment which failed: failed, that is, except in helping to teach the author that overt fictional sermons were to be avoided as disastrous to his art. Tolstoy could carry off this sort of thing, but Chekhov most emphatically could not; as he himself later recognized by implication when he excluded the egregiously Tolstoyan *An Encounter* and *In Trouble* from his "Collected Works". He was kinder to *The Beggar*; and also to *Excellent People*. This portrays a brother and sister: a journalist and a doctor respectively, they are representatives of the professional classes whose activities Tolstoy deplored wholesale as incompatible with the Simple Life. Over this issue, and also over the problem of non-resistance to evil, a quarrel develops between the Tolstoyan sister and the more conventional brother; in the end she leaves him in his ivory tower to go and work among the peasants. Here we find reflected the tug in Chekhov's own mind between his two professions of writer and doctor: should he too give up the trappings of civilized existence as a rising literary star in order to work among the poor and downtrodden?

These are the most outspokenly Tolstoyan works in Chekhov's writings of the 1880s. They are recognizable as such from their themes and manner; not through overt references to Tolstoy, of which we find none, in the text. Nor did Chekhov frequently invoke Tolstoy in his voluminous correspondence of the period during which he wrote these stories. In Chekhov's letters up to the end of 1887 the sage's name figures only three times, and his philosophical views are not mentioned once. We do have one recorded conversational comment by Chekhov on one cardinal Tolstoyan doctrine, but it is emphatically not that of a fanatical disciple. "Chekhov maintained that the theory of non-resistance to evil required to be properly studied, and that in the meantime one couldn't decently pronounce either for or against it."[4]

How far advocacy of Tolstoyism was from obsessing Chekhov exclusively we may see in his uproarious *A Story without a Title* of early 1888. Here an isolated community of fifth-century monks is visited by an aged itinerant prophet. In his lurid denunciations of the nearest city, an atrocious sink of lust and debauchery, we find echoes of Tolstoy the advocate (less commonly the practitioner) of sexual abstinence. Execrating this local Sodom or Gomorrah in horrific detail, the touring sage of *A Story without a Title* most shocks the monks with his account of a strip-tease performed at a banquet by a beautiful young girl. So profoundly, indeed, are they moved that, one fine day, they are discovered to have packed up and left their monastery *en masse* in order to investigate the horrors of the wicked city at first hand! This is not, to put it mildly, the sort of thing that we find in Tolstoy's *Popular Tales*.

All in all, then, the Tolstoy connection of the late 1880s adds up to precious little. We are inclined to suspect Chekhov of exaggerating considerably when, in the passage from a letter of March 1894 quoted above, he claimed that Tolstoy's philosophy had "deeply affected and obsessed" him for about six or seven years. "Vaguely interested and superficially attracted" might have been nearer the mark. In any case the problem of Chekhov–Tolstoy relations still remains obscure in patches.

So far we have discussed works didactic in the sense of offering models for imitation and making positive recommendations: to be kind, to show sympathy, to sacrifice oneself for the poor and unfortunate. But though such explicit messages could be disastrous to Chekhov's art, it could yet profit immensely on occasion from didacticism of a more negative, less strident variety: that which involves denouncing wrong behaviour without proceeding to recommend right behaviour. Particularly successful are the numerous stories in which Chekhov studies man's or woman's inconsiderateness to man or woman. To the medical student in *Anyuta* his pathetic mistress is a teaching-aid, not a person; as he shows by making her pose naked, with the position of her ribs marked in charcoal, to help him prepare for an examination in anatomy. In *A Trifle from Life* a jealous lover outrageously betrays a confidence by informing his mistress that her small son has been secretly visiting his father: her estranged husband. In *Enemies* a bullying landowner buttonholes a doctor, whose son has just died, and browbeats him into making a long and unnecessary journey to attend a "sick" wife; her malady proves to have been feigned as a means of getting her husband out of the house so that she can elope with her lover.

To these examples of grossly inconsiderate figures we can add many a bullying, bad-tempered, treacherous husband; and many a bullying, bad-tempered, treacherous wife too, for Chekhov shows no bias in favour of either sex when portraying these powerfully drawn negative characters. Women seem particularly hateful to him when their misdemeanours are amorous. One such villainess is Nyuta (in *Volodya*), who allows an over-wrought teen-aged boy to seduce her, but treats him so cruelly that he eventually commits suicide. Another villainess is the two-faced Sophia of *A Misfortune* (*Neschastye*), who hypocritically rejects her lover's advances out of pretended devotion to her husband and the sanctity of married life, only to go to her seducer in the end. "She was gasping, she was burning with shame, she barely noticed where her feet were carrying her, but that which pushed her onwards was stronger than her shame, her reason and her fears."[5]

In Chekhov's works only the naughtiest girls ever feel physical desire: a lesson driven home especially effectively in *Mire*. Here a jolly Jewess, Susanna, has formed the habit of borrowing money from the more attractive men of the locality. But whenever one of her IOUs is presented for payment she will impudently confiscate it from the bearer while disclaiming any intention of meeting the debt amid roars of laughter and struggles which end with her settling up in a manner not envisaged by the original contract.

Depraved indeed, but no monster of depravity, Chekhov's Susanna is among his most effective character studies of the period, but her saga much offended Chekhov's Babkino landlady, Mariya Kiselev. She objected less to his handling of the theme than to his choice of it. "Rummaging in a dung-heap", she called it. But Chekhov was not taking this from an authoress of children's stories. He replied with a harangue admirably championing the artist's right to treat any subject under the sun: a passage which incidentally shows how wrong we should be to deduce, from his various above-mentioned strictures on the "cheesecake" pictures in *Oskolki*, or from his other protests against sexually titivating "suggestiveness", that he was *au fond* a prey to prudish inhibitions in this or any area.

"I don't know who's right [he fulminated]. Was it Homer, Shakespeare and Lope de Vega, was it the Ancients in general: they who did not fear to rummage in this 'dung-heap', but who were far more stable, morally, than we? Or is it modern writers: so strait-laced on paper, so coldly cynical in their hearts and lives?" It was no use Mrs. Kiselev talking about the potentially corrupting effect of these topics. There were, after all, people who could corrupt themselves by reading "the spicy bits" in the Psalms and the Book of Proverbs; or even (a dig at Mariya Kiselev) in children's books. No literature, in the last resort, could be so scabrous as to outdo actual life, and in any case "the reason we call literature an art is that it describes life as it actually is. Its aim is unconditional truth and honesty.... To the chemist nothing in this world is unclean. The writer must be as objective as the chemist; he must ... know that dunghills play a very respectable role in the landscape, and that evil passions are just as much a part of life as are good ones." Literature would be in a bad way indeed if Mrs. Kiselev should ever succeed in emancipating it from the quirks of individual writers' different approaches. And who, in any case, was to police the kind of regimented literature for which she hankered? Critics and the authors' own consciences—these were the best, the only possible, "literary police".[6]

From the way in which Mariya Kiselev and Chekhov both discuss the topic one might deduce that the offending story was a piece of hard pornography; in fact, however, the erotic aspects of the plot are handled by discreet allusion, not by techniques of full frontal exposure such as would have been unacceptable in so sheltered an age. Even so, *Mire* is outspoken compared with Chekhov's other love stories of the period. Most of these avoid the sensitive issues which dominate *Volodya*, *A Misfortune* and *Mire*, merely chronicling the antics of deceived wives and cuckolded husbands as they execute their endless mechanical variations on the theme of the bedroom farce. But we must also note, at the other end of the scale, such pathetic studies of hopeless yearning for an unattainable love-object as *A Trivial Incident* and *Verochka*.

As Chekhov's work approaches the threshold of maturity we find an increasing tendency for elaborations of plot to disappear. To be more precise, we find that the more elaborate the plot of a given story is, the less effective it tends to be as a work of art. Some of the most admired stories are mood-pieces in which the element of action is barely present at all: for example, *Panic Fears* and *Happiness*, the latter being Chekhov's own favourite among his entire works of 1880-7.[7]

Sparsely plotted too are the three works which, with many hesitations, I would nominate as his finest of the period: *Typhus*, *The Kiss* and *The Schoolmaster*. In the first of these a young army officer catches typhus and recovers to find that his sister has died of the disease in the meantime. The hero of *The Kiss*, also an army officer, chances to be embraced in the dark by an unknown woman while attending a ball at a country house. *The Schoolmaster* depicts a dying teacher at a party attended by his colleagues. In these, and in many another example of Chekhov's finest work, precious little happens. And in any case it was not "what happens", or even "what does not happen", but "how it felt" which more and more constituted the essence of Chekhov's stories. To call these "biographies of a mood" or "studies in atmosphere" is therefore legitimate; but only provided that we do not allow such critical commonplaces to obscure the important but varying role which plots, however muted they may occasionally seem, do continue to play in much of his work.

When invoking the "atmosphere" of a scene or a person Chekhov was increasingly brief, simple, concrete.

In my view [he told his brother Alexander] nature descriptions should be extremely short and to the point. One must throw out such clichés as "the setting sun, bathed in the waves of the dark sea, was flooded with purple gold", or "swallows merrily twittered as they skimmed the surface of the water". In nature descriptions one must cleave to minor details and so group them that the reader sees a picture when he closes his eyes. For instance, you can put across a moonlit night by writing that a fragment of broken bottle gleamed like a bright star against a mill-dam; and that the black shadow of a dog or a wolf flashed past. . . . Nature seems to come to life if you don't jib at comparing its manifestations with human actions and so on. In the psychological area too it's details that count. Heaven preserve you from clichés. Better not describe your heroes' mental state: try to make that clear from their actions.[8]

Chekhov dispensed similar advice to Mariya Kiselev. He tended to patronize her, as he did all women writers: seriously trying to help them, but evidently believing that they laboured under a considerable handicap as members of an artistically inferior sex. "Splendid; you write quite like a man," he told this lady pupil. One of her stories was a bit rough in patches, he told her. "But its brevity and the masculine tone of the story make up for all that."[9]

Stage Début

In November 1887 Chekhov suddenly puts himself on the map as a playwright with the successful but controversial staging of the four-act play *Ivanov* in Moscow.

His previous excursions into drama had been discouraging. We remember the lost *Fatherless*, written during his schooldays and torn up by himself; we remember the mammoth four-acter *Platonov*, rejected for performance during his first years as a student and put into cold storage. Since then Chekhov had written two one-act plays, both of which have survived. Each was based on a published short story of his own. *On the High Road* is an adaptation of *In Autumn* (1883), and was presented for censorship on 29 May 1885—only to be rejected as too "gloomy and sordid" for performance and to remain, like *Platonov*, unpublished during the author's lifetime. *Swan Song*, the second of these one-acters, derives from *Kalchas* (1886), and was written "in an hour and five minutes" in January 1887.[1] Its first publication, later in the same month as part of an illustrated symposium, was not, to put it mildly, a major event in Russian theatrical history; nor was its first performance on 19 February 1888, three months after *Ivanov*'s première, as a minor item on the bill of the same Moscow theatre (Korsh's).

Doomed to failure or extinction though they may have seemed, these early plays all had one feature in common: their artistic purpose, their contents, were serious—perhaps over-serious. This is even true of the two one-acters: *On the High Road* presents the plight of a dipsomaniac squire abandoned by his wife; *Swan Song* features a drunken, senile actor brooding in an empty theatre over a lifetime's wasted opportunities. Minor tragedies or somewhat embarrassing "tear-jerkers"—the two one-acters are skilfully or unskilfully enough executed to be seen in either light.

To lost or discarded full-length juvenile dramas, and to sentimental playlets adapted from early stories, we must add the short comic monologue *Smoking is Bad for You*. This rambling lament by a hen-pecked husband was written in two and a half hours in February 1886 and immediately published in *Peterburgskaya gazeta*; after which it underwent a series of six recensions spread over sixteen years, only attaining its final form in September 1902. By that time Chekhov had made so many changes, infusing this comic sketch with increasingly sombre elements, that he himself regarded the *Smoking is Bad for You* of 1902 as "a completely new play" which happened to bear the same title as its superseded predecessor.[2] An exercise in the vein of "laughter through tears", with the tears increasingly predominating over the laughter as version succeeded version, this endlessly improved soliloquy remained at all stages essentially what it had been at its inception: an amusing trifle.

Ivanov was to eclipse all these juvenilia. As Chekhov's first dramatic work ever to appear on a public stage, it immediately established its author as a figure to be reckoned with in the Russian theatre. No less serious in conception than his earlier plays, it was far more effectively executed.

Playbill advertising the first public performance of any Chekhov play: the première, on 19 November 1887, of *Ivanov* at Korsh's Theatre, Moscow

To the best stories of 1886–7 *Ivanov* certainly yields in importance, but it does so only if those stories are taken as a group: and it therefore remains the most important single work to have come from Chekhov's pen during his first eight years of authorship. The play retains a modest but honoured place in the repertoire of the world's theatre, even though its techniques are conventional when compared to those of Chekhov's mature drama as pioneered in *The Seagull* and brought to fruition in *Uncle Vanya*, *Three Sisters* and *The Cherry Orchard*. *Ivanov* is, in my opinion, a finer play than *The Seagull*, which has been overrated in general esteem.

And yet *Ivanov* arose somewhat casually and as the result of a misunderstanding. It was commissioned by F. A. Korsh, founder of a well-known Moscow theatre specializing in farces, and soon to become the impresario of Chekhov's one-acter *Swan Song*. Korsh, then, had requested from the city's most popular humorous writer a play suitable for light entertainment *à la* Antosha Chekhonte, only to find that he had provoked a tantalizing problem-drama from the pen of Anton Chekhov. The initial draft of *Ivanov* was dashed off with astonishing speed between 20 September and 5 October 1887 in the house on Sadovy-Kudrinsky Street, each act being rushed away to Korsh with the ink barely dry, so that he could present it to the dramatic censor and put it into rehearsal.³

On 19 November, exactly two months after Chekhov had first set pen to paper, *Ivanov* received its Moscow première at Korsh's Theatre.

Ivanov's first night became one of those many scandals "without precedent in theatrical history" of which we are continually reading in Russian stage annals. Theatre people had never seen such a to-do on the stage, Chekhov told his brother Alexander. Never had there been such a hotch-potch of clapping and hissing. Never before had any author had a curtain-call after the second act in Korsh's theatre. Nor, during thirty-two years in the theatre, had the prompter ever known more excitement in the audience and off-stage. What with people clapping, hissing and nearly coming to blows in the bar, there had been a most fearful racket. The students in the gallery had tried to chuck someone out, whereupon the police had chucked two of them out. Everyone was very worked up, and sister Mariya had nearly fainted.⁴ That Chekhov was not exaggerating much we know from other sources. The theatre critic of *Novoye vremya* spoke of "a storm of applause, curtain-calls and hissing", claiming that no author of recent times had made his bow to such a medley of praise and protest. These hissings and protests were partly due to the defects of the performance. The play had been grossly under-rehearsed by actors who barely knew their parts and either ad-libbed or followed the prompter. Others, by contrast, took their roles over-seriously. So devoted to their art were the "extras" playing the drunken guests, at the wedding in Act Four, that they appeared on stage in a state of all too genuine intoxication; Chekhov decided to ban them from future performances.[5]

It was not so much the quirks of the performance as Chekhov's controversial script which stimulated a response polarized between wildest enthusiasm and wildest disapproval. *Ivanov*'s plot is easily told. The play's main character, a landowner in his thirties called Nicholas Ivanov, has a Jewish wife, Sarah. She has been cursed and abandoned by her family for giving up her religion and marrying him; and she is now, as the play begins, dying of tuberculosis. Ivanov should have taken the sick woman to a warmer climate, thus giving her some hope of recovery, instead of which he is busy seducing Sasha, daughter of a rich neighbour. For this caddish behaviour he is repeatedly denounced by his wife Sarah's plain-speaking young doctor, Eugene Lvov. Sarah dies and Ivanov marries Sasha, but is subjected by Dr. Lvov to an especially severe final denunciation. This occurs on the very wedding day, when the young doctor turns on Ivanov: "You are the most unmitigated swine, sir!" The outburst causes the bridegroom to expire, most implausibly, from shock on stage; or, in the final version of this much-revised ending, to shoot himself.

Running an estate, coping with peasants, farming scientifically, falling into debt, marrying a doomed wife of alien faith—it had all been too much for Ivanov, whom we observe subsiding beneath the strain throughout the play's four acts. That his conduct is highly reprehensible must be admitted. But what on earth was there about it to tax an audience's comprehension? Or to provoke such violent reactions in the theatre? Only this: that the author himself, in so far as his attitude seemed to emerge from the dialogue of his characters, came nowhere near condemning Ivanov outright. Far, indeed, from pillorying that spineless individual as an arrant scoundrel, Chekhov seemed rather to sympathize with him, while displaying marked hostility towards the well-meaning young doctor who so persistently attempts to persuade Ivanov to do his duty by the unfortunate dying Sarah.

Could the wicked Ivanov conceivably be Chekhov's hero? And could the priggish, self-righteous Dr. Lvov be his villain? Indeed they could, as we discover beyond all shadow of doubt from lengthy passages of exegesis in the author's correspondence.[6] From these we also learn that the riddle of *Ivanov* did not lie in any obscurity of the script, but simply in Chekhov's failure to adopt a conventional moralizing attitude.

Unable to follow the workings of a brain so gloriously untrammelled by clichés, some baffled theatregoers took refuge in the hoariest stereotype of Russian literary criticism by relegating Ivanov to the category of Superfluous Men, as found in Pushkin's *Eugene Onegin*, Lermontov's *Hero of Our Time* and elsewhere. But Chekhov would have none of that. Ivanov differs markedly from the Superfluous Men (said his creator) because he does not blame society for his predicament. His hero's other distinction was, Chekhov added, that of being more closely observed from life. "I conceived the daring ambition of summing up everything so far written about such Dismal Desmonds and of putting an end to these writings with *Ivanov*."[7] Indeed, the play's chief claim to originality was simply this, according to its author: there were a great many of these Ivanovs around, but no one had yet made them a model for an imaginative study. Here, then, was Dr. Chekhov analysing a psychological malaise hitherto ignored by all literary clinicians. No wonder, then, that he was piqued to receive little or no recognition for so brilliant a diagnosis. He was irritated above all to find himself censured for failure to generate precisely the kind of facile moral indignation which he had hoped to discredit in his portrayal of Lvov.

Not content with mere diagnosis, the author-doctor also ventures into the area of prescription, for the play has an ironical, characteristically Chekhovian and devastatingly anti-Tolstoyan, moral: do not moralize. Do not be too ready, that is, to ape the stuffy Dr. Lvov by condemning a man, that all too complicated mechanism, on the basis of his behaviour. An immoral scoundrel may be a better human being than a self-righteous prig. Himself, in his early and middle twenties, often censorious and sometimes priggish, Anton was perhaps castigating the self-righteous element in his own nature when he went to such pains to make his Lvov as odious as possible and to present his feckless hero as sympathetic. Not for the first or last time we suspect Chekhov the artist of drawing on an inner conflict which troubled Chekhov the man during the period of a work's genesis. It was the creative tension between the author's own censoriousness and tolerance which helped to make *Ivanov* so tantalizing, so controversial, so stimulating a play. And *Ivanov* remains a highly didactic work: but only if that label can be applied where the message is, simply, do not be didactic. "We all have too many wheels, screws and valves to judge each other on first impressions and one or two pointers"—these words, spoken by Ivanov to Lvov in Act Three of the play, arguably represent the maturing Chekhov's counsel to the younger Chekhov who, Lvov-like, so outspokenly denounced his Ivanov-like elder brothers on occasion.[8]

By comparison with Chekhov's later pioneering drama, *Ivanov* now seems old-fashioned. One reason is the concentration on a single hero round whom all the action revolves; another lies in the emphasis placed on carefully orchestrated dramatic crises. Chekhov gave the audience "a punch on the nose" at the end of each act.[9] So he himself pointed out at the time, not realizing that, later in his dramatic career, the cunningly sprung dramatic climax would give way to something far more impressive: the yet more cunningly sprung anti-dramatic anti-climax. From crises to let-downs: such, in brief, is Chekhov's evolution as a playwright from start to finish.

While remaining comparatively conventional in structure and technique, the thematically startling *Ivanov* is yet a triumph of craftsmanship. The scenes are well put together; the dialogue is subtle and lively; the background is suitably light, and throws the sombre elements of the main drama into effective relief, introducing several comic minor characters who might have stepped straight from the better pages of *Oskolki*.

CHAPTER SIX

Growing Pains
1888-90

"The Steppe"

In March 1888 Chekhov published his long story *The Steppe* in the St. Petersburg monthly *Severny vestnik* ("The Northern Herald").

This was Chekhov's first appearance in a serious literary review or Thick Journal. It marks the end of his apprenticeship and the beginning of his mature period, being the last and most significant of the four promotions which punctuate his early career. After *The Steppe* he no longer rates as a light-weight writer, for he has now penetrated the sort of periodical in which major works of Russian literature have traditionally received first publication. Never, while his best work was going to *Oskolki* and St. Petersburg daily newspapers, could a Chekhov be the potential heir of Pushkin, Turgenev, Dostoyevsky and Tolstoy. But now such a claim need not sound ridiculous.

It is on the first day of 1888, as if to emphasize the start of a new era, that *The Steppe* is first mentioned in Chekhov's correspondence. The thought of writing this "trifle" for a Thick Journal makes him self-conscious: "jogs my elbow as the devil jogs a monk". The sheer size of the work, at least ten times as long as a typical pre-*Steppe* story, created its own problems. Unfamiliar too was the process of writing "unhurriedly, as a gourmet eats snipe".[1] So he remarked while work was in progress, evidently not foreseeing that this story of ninety-odd pages was to be completed within a month. When writing *The Steppe* Chekhov was thus hitting an output rate double that of 1886, the most prolific year of his life. So much for his claim that the story was written at leisure.

Strictly speaking, *The Steppe* is hardly a story at all. It has no plot, but sketches a journey through the Ukrainian countryside as seen by a nine-year-old boy, Yegorushka. Written by one who had himself traversed these regions so often as a child, the material was avowedly autobiographical, consisting of "my own steppe experiences". The inn and its Jewish landlord Moses, for example, were based on the wayside hostelry in which the fifteen-year-old Anton had succumbed to peritonitis.[2] Such memories had recently been revived by his excursion of spring 1887 to Taganrog.

While working on The Steppe Chekhov wrote a brief summary of the story. "I depict the plain, the mauve distance, sheep farmers ... priests, thunderstorms at night, inns, wagon-trains, steppe birds and so on. Each separate chapter is a story on its own, and all the chapters are intimately linked like the five figures in a quadrille." On the work's merits the author is ambivalent as ever. Here is no artistic, integrated description of the steppe, but rather a steppe encyclopaedia, a prospectus, a dry catalogue of impressions piled one on top of the other. Still, the work is at least original, Chekhov claims: if only in treating a subject long neglected by the Thick Journals, though once handled extensively by that Tsar of the Steppes, Gogol. Perhaps The Steppe would open contemporaries' eyes to the neglected beauties of their landscape? Or inspire some minor poet? Successful or unsuccessful, The Steppe was "my masterpiece, the best work I can do".[3]

Severny vestnik's literary editor A. N. Pleshcheyev agreed. "I read it eagerly ... couldn't put it down ... am in mad ecstasy." Never mind the lack of plot, for there was an inexhaustible spring of inner content; poets and artists with a feel for poetry would be driven mad; there was a wealth of subtle psychological touches. Descending from poetry to prose, Pleshcheyev sent Chekhov an advance of 300 roubles, asking him to name his over-all fee.[4] This, now that he had penetrated the Thick Journals, was no longer to be calculated by the line, but by the "printer's sheet": about sixteen pages of a book. At 150 roubles per sheet the eventual fee came to 750 roubles. Never had Chekhov earned so much from fiction in a month.

His decision to contribute to Severny vestnik had political implications. Within the limits imposed by official censorship the review followed a liberal and Narodnik ("populist" or peasant-fancying) line contrary to the conservatism of Chekhov's previous most-favoured publication, Novoye vremya. That paper and its tycoon-proprietor Suvorin were abominated by Chekhov's new associates on Severny vestnik, who assumed that their latest discovery would drop Novoye vremya flat now that he had been received with open arms by so much more respectable a publication. Chekhov was urged to send all his fiction, including the shortest items, along to Severny vestnik. Why (Pleshcheyev asked) did Chekhov's reputation still lag behind that of many another writer unworthy to latch up his shoes? Simply (Pleshcheyev answered himself) because Chekhov had hitherto published in "lousy rags fit only for wrapping paper".[5]

The venerable, grey-haired minor poet Pleshcheyev was, like Chekhov's other protector Grigorovich, an almost legendary figure from Russia's literary past, but he carried the added glamour of political martyrdom. In 1849 he had been sentenced to hard labour, later commuted to army service, along with Dostoyevsky and others, for expressing opinions uncongenial to Imperial authority. Pleshcheyev was also famous throughout politically disaffected Russia as author of the rousing revolutionary hymn "On, on! Put Fears and Doubts behind You!"

What such a man must have thought of the traditionalist Suvorin we can imagine. But Pleshcheyev was mildness itself compared with his younger associate, the great radical critic N. K. Mikhaylovsky. He too belonged to the *Severny vestnik* set, and he too read *The Steppe* before publication. He at once tackled Chekhov by letter, addressing him in the censorious manner and theological language which permeate literary discussions of the period. There was no worse school (wrote Mikhaylovsky) than that which Chekhov had been through as contributor to *Novoye vremya*, *Oskolki* and the like. What a sin the young man had committed by "tearing himself up into shreds"; and how irredeemable that sin would be if he should continue to write for those journals after producing *The Steppe*. Chekhov must eschew Evil and cleave to Good. He must not dare to be a literary dilettante, but must consecrate his whole soul to letters. "God has given you much, Anton Pavlovich, and of you much shall be required." Brooding on Chekhov's lack of discernible ideological convictions, Mikhaylovsky wrote that, reading *The Steppe*, "I seemed to see a giant walking down a road, not knowing where he was going or why. . . . Unconscious, simply unaware of his great strength, he pulls up a seedling or uproots a tree: both with equal ease, not even sensing any difference between these acts."[6] To this harangue Chekhov replied coolly that he would not abandon *Novoye vremya* or Suvorin, to whom he was grateful. But Mikhaylovsky roundly rejected Chekhov's view that his *Novoye vremya* items were "harmless", repeating that they "directly serve Evil".[7]

Appearing in *Severny vestnik*'s March number, *The Steppe* was extensively reviewed, being widely recognized for the original, talented work as which even its modest author had claimed it.[8] But though it indeed forms the most important landmark in Chekhov's evolution, it yet accomplished no miraculous transformation. The story symbolizes rather than exemplifies the transition from apprenticeship to mastery, suffering as it does from the limitations implied by its subject: the Ukrainian prairies as seen by a nine-year-old boy. Evoking that scene most adroitly, *The Steppe* yet falls below its creator's most distinguished later writing. Beside *A Dreary Story*,

Ward Number Six and other fully mature works, the earlier study is just a sequence of charming sketches.

The Steppe's importance therefore lies less in what it is than in its status as Chekhov's first Thick Journal contribution; in the enormous interest which it immediately aroused; and above all in what was to follow—a period of fiction-writing far more impressive but far less prolific than the early period. During the sixteen years of life remaining to him Chekhov was to publish a mere three score stories, totalling some fourteen hundred pages. With this we may contrast the relatively short period of eight years (1880–7) during which the youthful Chekhov had been about four times as productive a bulk supplier of fiction, churning out the many hundreds of items—528, to be precise—which occupy twice as much space as do the infinitely more valuable mature stories introduced by *The Steppe*.

Having launched *The Steppe* in March 1888, Chekhov left for St. Petersburg on the fourteenth of the month and arrived to find everyone discussing his story. He was put up in style in Suvorin's flat. It was comfortable and almost self-contained, but the guest did not like to return drunk or bring his own friends back. Meanwhile he was basking in his glory, savouring the smell of incense, riding in a landau, drinking champagne. Altogether, he was behaving like a Great Writer; which meant, he said, that he was beginning to feel something of a "mountebank".[9]

Chekhov had no illusions about the Thick Journals. These arbiters of excellence paraded preconceived notions hatched within small, complacent coteries. They generated an atmosphere of constraint and parochial bigotry, an intolerance of contrary opinion, which made him gasp for air. They were enemies of freedom, their editors were nonentities beside such great editors of the past as Belinsky and Herzen. The Thick Journals, said Chekhov, offered only one real advantage to a writer: they were thick enough to print a long item *in toto* without any need for serialization.[10]

One Thick Journal particularly galled him: the well-known Moscow monthly *Russkaya mysl* ("The Russian Idea"). More militantly and intolerantly "liberal" than *Severny vestnik*, this organ so exasperated Chekhov that he could only speak of it with contempt. He described its "Grand Vizier", V. A. Goltsev, as pompous, and said that he knew as much about literature as a dog knows about radishes. Goltsev and Company were dreary mediocrities, desiccated and lifeless as gnawed crows' bones. So obsessed were they with their ultimate political aim of achieving constitutional in place of autocratic rule in Russia that they thought everything else beneath their notice, including ordinary courtesy. No, Chekhov had never published in *Russkaya mysl*. He had not submitted to its "lugubrious censorship"; nor would he do so except as a last resort, though he had been invited often enough.[11] Chancing when drunk to meet a member of the journal's staff at a party in early 1888, Chekhov denounced the *Russkaya mysl* set as honest, well-meaning hacks without a scrap of talent between them. His words were reported to editor Goltsev, and *Russkaya mysl* shortly afterwards retaliated by publishing a hostile unsigned review of *The Steppe*. Here Chekhov's story was condemned as void of ideas, vivid imagery, psychology, plot, and even of mere ethnographic interest.[12]

Just why was Chekhov so annoyed with *Russkaya mysl* in early 1888? We do not know, but the fact is that he was exasperated by practically all his literary contacts at this time. Much as he respected Suvorin, he was irked with Suvorin's firm for failing to promote the sale of his books, and for losing his friends' manuscripts.[13] Then again, the clumsily patronizing Leykin was still irritating Chekhov. So were virtually all other contemporary writers, whom he called nonentities concerned with literature only because it offered scope "for boot-licking and easy pickings". Chekhov was much distressed when an author whom he did admire, Vsevolod Garshin, killed himself by jumping down the well of a staircase in a high building: and that shortly after being allegedly "driven out of his mind" by his ecstatic response to *The Steppe*. But Chekhov was also incensed by tactless attempts to commemorate the unfortunate suicide. Who on earth was this "little ponce" Leman, known only as a billiard-player, who yet took it upon himself to pronounce a funeral oration on Garshin "in the name of authors of the younger generation"? Who was this Babikov or Bibikov who dared publish his memoirs of Garshin? "What a conceited, sickly, sloppy, boastful, blundering little twit!" May not this same Bibikov or Babikov one day be found publishing inane memoirs about a deceased Chekhov? And may not the egregious Leman be destined to pronounce the funeral oration by his, Chekhov's, grave? As for critics and reviewers in general, they were toadies and cowards the whole lot of them.[14]

Nor did Chekhov's own work escape denigration by its creator. He was bored stiff with *Lights*, his second story for *Severny vestnik*, and he feared to become a purveyor of literary ballast like other writers once hailed as "promising". Commenting on his unusually bad temper and new habit of writing rude letters, he concluded that his character was deteriorating.[15]

Such were the effects of solid literary success, achieved in a fairly short space of time, richly merited and far beyond the attainment of any other young writer of the day.

Southern Travels

Exhausted by years of intensive writing, weary of the literary circles of Moscow and St. Petersburg, embarrassed by his own success as an author, Chekhov needed a change of scene by mid-1888. He accordingly rented a summer cottage much further from Moscow than his family's usual holiday haunt at Babkino. This latest *dacha* was taken "at random" at 100 roubles for the season, and was at Luka on a bend in the River Psyol (a tributary of the Dnieper) near the Ukrainian town of Sumy. Chekhov's desire to holiday in these southern regions was shared by his parents: particularly his father, who was talking pompously about bidding farewell to his native land before he died.[1]

Though haphazardly prompted and planned, the expedition rescued Anton's morale: as witness his ecstatic letters from Luka, which he reached in early May. With the cottage itself, with its surroundings in the grounds of an old manor, he was delighted. There were prospects for fishing and picnicking, there were facilities for entertaining visitors. But there was no privy; "one has to relieve oneself . . . in the gullies and under the hedges. My entire [. . .] has been bitten by gnats."[2] Undeterred, guests turned up in quantity. A visiting flautist and cellist combined with a local pianist to supply the musical evenings without which Chekhov's life, Muscovite or *dacha*-based, was never complete. Among writers who sampled his hospitality were K. S. Barantsevich and the recently-bereaved Alexander Chekhov; his wife had died in May.[3] The venerable Pleshcheyev was also welcomed and fêted by the young ladies of the locality, especially when he declaimed his famous revolutionary call to action: "On, on! Put Fears and Doubts behind You!" Other visitors included the actor P. M. Svobodin, who organized comic fishing expeditions; resplendent in top hat, tails, white gloves and white tie, he would solemnly plant himself with his rod and line on the banks of the Psyol. A Kharkov professor, V. F. Timofeyev, would imitate comic German academics and get drunk with Chekhov, much to the distress of his kindly but high-minded landlords up at the big house.[4]

Luka, like Babkino, had its local squires: the Lintvaryovs. Chekhov has described the elderly mother and her five grown-up children in his letters. The youngest girl, Natalya, was one of those hearty, laughing, healthy young women favoured by Chekhov in real life: as opposed to the wilting damsels whom he portrays so sympathetically in his fiction. Natalya's two elder sisters were both qualified doctors, and thus professional colleagues of their newly arrived tenant. One, Helen, was the soul of kindness and sensitivity. The other, Zinaida, was even more impressive; having lost her sight through a brain tumour, she showed great courage in supporting her affliction and could speak equably of her imminent death. One of the two Lintvaryov boys, Paul, had been sent down from the university for political reasons and was under police supervision; the younger, George, was training as a pianist, and it was he who took part in the improvised trios at the Chekhovs' *dacha*. The Lintvaryovs were thus worthy successors to the Kiselevs of Babkino. These new landlords also had the spice of radical political views. Even the dashing Natalya, whose dream it was to achieve a conventional bourgeois marriage, had yet read her Karl Marx. And so seriously did the massed Lintvaryovs take the politics of opposition that when Suvorin (that *bête noire* of dissidents) came to stay at the Chekhovs' cottage, the entire household of radical landowners combined to make him unwelcome. They even put up the manor shutters during his stay until such nerve warfare—but also, we suspect, the lack of even the most primitive amenities—drove the daunted tycoon to a near-by hotel.⁵

Besides serving Chekhov as an admirable base from May to September 1888, Luka also became the springboard for extended trips in southern Russia. One of these took Anton, his sister and Natalya Lintvaryov on a delightful 250-mile excursion south of Sumy to Sorochintsy, heart of the Gogol country, and to the near-by farm of the Smagin brothers, relatives of the Lintvaryovs. Chekhov has said, without being specific, that there were no end of adventures and comic misunderstandings during this expedition, which also had a practical aim, for he had decided to buy a small farm in the area; and he would have gone ahead, had the price, at 3,000 roubles, not seemed a little steep. He was now thinking of giving up authorship entirely in order to settle on the banks of a Ukrainian river and practise medicine. With Moscow he felt no links of sympathy at all. And the intellectual fads of St. Petersburg seemed "pale and stunted" when viewed from the Ukrainian steppe at haymaking time. Chekhov therefore proposed to turn his farm, had he purchased it, into a hostel where literary colleagues could live and recuperate from life in the capital.⁶ If this plan had been realized, Chekhov would have been importing into his country retreat the very element of metropolitan literary fuss from which he so urgently sought relief; but he was by no means unique in thus combining the two seemingly contradictory traits of gregariousness and love of solitude.

In July Chekhov took the southbound train from Sumy to Sevastopol, whence he sailed eastwards along the Crimean seaboard, casting a jaundiced eye at Yalta—where he docked—and at the other coastal resorts which he could observe from the steamer, until he disembarked at one situated in the east of the peninsula: Feodosiya. Here he was a guest at Suvorin's *dacha* for ten days, and here the first real rapprochement took place between the two men, who had first met over two years earlier. Suvorin and Chekhov got drunk together; they would talk all day and half the night; first they solved all existing problems and then they marked out a whole host of new ones. Suvorin was a great man, Chekhov solemnly concluded. He was also amused by Suvorin's young wife, the eccentric Anna Ivanovna.

With her habit of speaking in a bass voice, imitating the barking of dogs, singing, quarrelling and endlessly gossiping, this creature was irrepressible, flighty, imaginative, an original to the marrow of her bones. She earned Chekhov's two highest expressions of appreciation: "not boring" and "doesn't think like a woman". Indeed, of all the women he knew, Anna was "the only one who has her own independent view of things".[7]

The other amenities of Feodosiya included bathing in a sea as tender as a virgin's hair; glasses of Chartreuse and other liqueurs; an excursion to the near-by estate of the aged painter Ayvazovsky, a one-time friend of Pushkin's famous for his pictures of naval battles. All this Chekhov evokes in his correspondence with the additional verve which enters his letters in 1888, coinciding with his attainment of literary maturity, and makes him one of Russia's liveliest, wittiest correspondents.

On 23 July Chekhov sailed out of Feodosiya with Suvorin's son Alexis, bound for a tour of the Caucasus. They put in at Sukhum, which so enchanted Chekhov with its eucalyptuses, cypresses, cedars, palms, donkeys, swans and bullocks that he reckoned himself capable of writing fifty delightful folk-tales if he could only stay there for a month;[8] instead of which he sailed off to Batum, city of soldiers, merchants, foreigners, night-clubs, brothels. Taking the train to Tiflis, the administrative capital of the entire Caucasus, he admired mountains, tunnels, waterfalls. He went on to Baku, the oil metropolis on the Caspian Sea; but not for a million roubles would he have settled in this tarantula-infested city of greasy puddles. From Baku the two travellers intended to cross the Caspian, with Bokhara, Samarkand or Persia as ultimate destinations. But a telegram reached Alexis Suvorin announcing the death of a brother, and the decision was taken to return. Re-established in Sumy by mid-August, Chekhov retained unforgettable exotic memories of liana-veiled trees, dolphins, oil gushers, mountains. But he was glad to be back in his *dacha* after so strenuous a journey. The banks of the Psyol seemed more charming than ever, albeit less spectacular than the canyons of the Aragva and the Terek at which he had recently marvelled.[9]

And yet Luka never rivalled Babkino as an inspiration for Chekhov's works. Some features of *The Cherry Orchard* derive from the Lintvaryovs' estate, Chekhov's brother Michael tells us; the Smagin farm near Soro-chintsy contributed to the setting of *Gooseberries* (1898), and a near-by village, Mezhirichi, figures in *Home* (1897).[10] Chekhov's Caucasian expedi-tion also helped to furnish the background for another notable story, *The Duel* (1891). Otherwise we may search his imaginative work in vain for traceable echoes of these southern travels.

The *dacha* at Luka had been such a success that Chekhov rented it again in the following year. By now, though, the shadow of tragedy lay over his family, for his elder brother Nicholas was known to be suffering from advanced tuberculosis. Anton brought the sick Nicholas back home from his Bohemian haunts to Sadovy-Kudrinsky Street, and decided to take him down to the Ukraine in the hope that the southern climate might do him good. Having settled Nicholas at Luka, and knowing that his case was hopeless—but not suspecting that the end was quite so near—Anton set off on an excursion over now familiar territory: to the Smagin farm near Sorochintsy. But barely had he settled in after an appalling journey through dense rain and mud when a wet muzhik handed him a wet telegram announcing Nicholas's death, on 17 June, and Anton had to embark on a yet more lugubrious return trip to comfort his mother and arrange the funeral. This was his first experience of death in his own family; it profoundly grieved him and set the tone for a summer dominated by misery and boredom, yet not without its compensations.[11]

Chekhov left his cottage as soon as he decently could. He intended to join the elder Suvorin in western Europe, but allowed himself to be side-tracked to Odessa, where the Moscow Maly Theatre was on tour. Chekhov put up at the same hotel as the company and spent much of his time with actresses. He took tea with them, dined with them, escorted them on walks; but "didn't seduce a single one and didn't even try", according to his own confession.[12] Presented with a cravat and given a rousing send-off from Odessa harbour by his theatrical friends, he sailed away to the Crimean resort of Yalta on 15 July. He put up in a comfortable cottage near a beach with excellent bathing, yet found the place "hellishly boring". Yalta's famous cypresses were stunted, dark, hard, dusty; the women smelt of ice-cream; students kept bringing him bulky manuscripts to read. Here were too many clean-shaven actors and Jews:[13] on which latter point the Imperial authorities must have agreed, for soon afterwards Jews were officially banned from the resort. All this confirmed the bad impression which Chekhov had received in the previous year when briefly docking at Yalta on his way from Sevastopol to Feodosiya. Yalta was, to him, a mixture of the western European and a squalid Russian market town. The box-like hotels in which miserable consumptives languished, the impudent faces of the Tatars native to the area, the ugly mugs of rich holiday-making idlers in search of trivial adventures, the smell of cheap scent drowning that of cedars and sea, the wretched, dirty harbour, the chatter of girls and their escorts—it was all intolerably depressing.[14]

Domestic Trials

Distressed though Chekhov was by his brother's death in summer 1889, this was only the most acute among various factors which depressed him in the closing years of the decade. Irritations seemed to grow along with his fame, as if success and exasperation were linked. And though many of these frustrations were literary, there were other nuisances: increasing financial, domestic and health worries.

"By and large my life is boring [Chekhov writes at the end of 1888]. And I'm beginning to feel hatred at times: something new to me. Long, stupid conversations, guests, people who want something out of me ... money wasted on cab journeys to patients who don't pay me a thing: such bedlam, in other words, it's enough to make you leave home. People borrow money from me and don't pay me back; they run off with my books; they waste my time. All I need is an unhappy love affair." As usual he felt pestered by the guests whose presence he shunned; yet also sought, even as they prevented him from working. Would that he could emigrate to the North Pole. And yet this is the very period of which Michael Chekhov writes, in his usual jaunty style, that "Anton Pavlovich could not bear being on his own. Young people were always jostling elbows in our house; there would be piano-playing, singing and jocular talk upstairs, while he would be sitting and writing at his desk downstairs. But these noises only encouraged him. He could not live without them, always participating eagerly in the general jolly mood."[1]

Anton was not only earning more than ever, but could now see himself relieved of maintaining his youngest brother and his sister, for both were completing their education and about to become self-supporting: Michael as a provincial tax official, Mariya as a Moscow schoolmistress. But comparative affluence seemed to bring no real improvement. Anton's literary income had increased, since book and play royalties were now coming in; but these new sources were unpredictable, and his expenses seemed to keep pace. After his first stay at Luka he felt trapped "like a fish in ice" by his debts, and was visiting a pawnbroker. In the first few weeks of 1888 he had earned and spent 1,500 roubles.[2] That sum would have been far beyond his range a few years earlier; but so too would the new expenses incurred by living more comfortably.

Anton still suffered from poor health. His brother Michael, when sleeping in the next room, could often hear him coughing hour after hour through the flimsy wall.[3] These bouts were most worrying when he spat blood, as happened about twice a year. Commenting on such an attack in October 1888, he gave an account sinister in two ways: for the worrying nature of the symptoms, and for the medically qualified sufferer's wilful refusal to interpret them, Reporting that he had a chronic cough except in dry summer weather, Chekhov added that this frightened him only when he spat blood. Still, the fact was (said he) that neither tuberculosis nor any other serious lung affliction could be diagnosed on blood-spitting alone: only on a combination of that with other symptoms. Such a combination was not present in his case, pronounced Dr. Chekhov. There was nothing serious about bleeding from the lungs, natural though it was for the sufferer's family to be horrified by such portents. "Anyway, take it from me that if *someone known not to be suffering from tuberculosis* suddenly starts bleeding from the mouth, that's nothing to be scared of." Had his initial attack of December 1884 been a symptom of incipient tuberculosis, Chekhov would long ago have departed this world. "Such is my logic."[4] And pathetic logic it was. That Anton could care for the dying consumptive Nicholas a few months after writing these lines, but without revising his faulty self-diagnosis, is a striking example of a physician's perverse blindness towards his own health. "It can't happen to me": that, in essence, was the "logic" of which Chekhov boasted in October 1888. And yet there was perhaps some method in this seeming madness; was there any point in his admitting to himself that he had contracted an affliction for which there was then no effective cure?

Nicholas's death was not the only tubercular fatality in the family. When Alexander Chekhov's common-law wife Anna also died from the same disease, leaving him with two small sons, Alexander applied for help to Anton. His reply sheds light on his environment in Sadovy-Kudrinsky Street. There was no room for his small nephews there, he pointed out. The house was already crowded with adults: his mother, Mariya, Michael; the doomed and drunken Nicholas (abandoned by his latest woman); their Aunt Fedosiya Dolzhenko (Yevgeniya Chekhov's sister) and her son, Cousin Alexis; besides which Ivan and Paul Chekhov were generally there in the evenings. They were charming and amusing people, Anton told Alexander; but they were also self-centred, demanding, talkative, impecunious and heavy-footed. To add two little boys and the nanny whom—in these days of readily available domestic service—even a struggling widower such as Alexander could take for granted: it would mean Anton having to wear wax ear-plugs and dark glasses. If he had had a wife and children of his own, things would have been different, he explained. As it was he suggested that Alexander's boys could be housed separately; Aunt Fedosiya had agreed to head such a ménage, but Alexander must guarantee a regular fifty roubles a month for their upkeep.[5]

This transfer of Chekhov's nephews to Moscow proved unnecessary because Alexander soon found himself a new wife, Natalya, in St. Petersburg. Unfortunately, though, her advent did not purge his household of its traditional squalor. Far from discouraging his drinking, the second Mrs. Chekhov was apt to join in, and both spouses seemed reconciled to lice and bugs as an ineradicable feature of their home. No less deplorable were Alexander's manners. That scruffy domestic tyrant lounged about in his underpants, yelling swear words at his wife, screaming at the maid: "Gimme the piss-pot, Kate!" He would also tell scabrous stories liable "to corrupt a woman and alienate her from the God in whom she believes". At night a husband might sleep with his wife, Anton conceded, provided that he preserved all the decencies in his tone and manner; in the morning he should rush to put on his tie lest he offend her by his unseemly appearance. Such minor details had an important formative influence on people; and Alexander should remember that "between a woman who sleeps in clean linen and one who dosses down on a dirty sheet, lustily guffawing when her lover [. . .]s, there is the same difference as between a drawing-room and a public bar."[6]

Once again we note that Anton could refer to sexual matters so frankly only in distasteful contexts. Never dwelling in detail on the physical charms of an attractive woman, he preferred to stress the disgust aroused in him by a certain female doctor whom he met in Feodosiya: "a fat, bloated lump of meat; strip her bare, paint her green—and you'd have a marsh frog". That Chekhov became friendly with a young actress, a former ballerina called Glafira Panov, in Odessa, we know from his brother Michael; but if we seek Chekhov's view of ballerinas at this time, all we find is that they "smell like horses" after their performances. He was still harping on the indelicate illustrations to Leykin's *Oskolki*, with "all that naked navel and naked leg stuff". And whatever he meant by the bustles (worn by holidaymaking ladies in Yalta) being "the frank expression of something very nasty", we are once more reminded that the physical attributes of women tended, even when simulated, to inspire his revulsion rather than his desire.[7]

This material seems less significant for what it is than for the virtual absence of any counter-balancing material. The man could be revolted by the sight of an ugly woman, yes. But did he never set eyes on any desirable representative of the sex? If so he usually kept quiet about it. Exceptional indeed is his boast of having met "such girls that if I corralled the lot in my cottage the result would be a glorious medley pregnant with consequences".[8] As for specific reference to any woman whom Chekhov found physically attractive, there is only the miller's daughter at Luka, a plump little piece "like an Easter cake with raisins", whom he encountered during his fishing trips on the river. This young person aroused "such feelings of lust that I wanted to scream for help":[9] a more direct expression of desire than we find elsewhere in nearly four thousand pages of admittedly censored correspondence. But here too we note that Chekhov lacked, even in his fantasies, the element of male sexual aggressiveness. What are we to say of a young man whose first reaction, however whimsical, on seeing an attractive girl is to summon aid from a third party?

Despite such reactions Chekhov continued, throughout his young manhood, to toy with the idea of marriage. That many of his references to the prospect were jocular will not surprise us. He would designate as his future bride the infant daughters of his friends, the little Misses Suvorin and Kiselev; or proclaim his intention of wedding a girl from a rich merchant family and then stripping her as bare—of her property, of course—as a lime-tree barked by peasants. Feeling in need of a change, he said that he wanted "to fall in love, get married or go up in a balloon", not greatly caring, it seems, which of these possibilities might materialize. More seriously he reflected that even a bad marriage was better than loafing around. "I'd be glad to shackle myself with wedlock; but it's circumstances which control me, alas, not I them." He did remain sufficiently in control to take evasive action when Mrs. Lensky, an actor's wife, tried to promote his marriage to the Glafira Panov whom he was squiring round Odessa in summer 1889. Anton proved impossible to pin down, and successfully frustrated these well-meant designs.[10]

A significant comment on marriage occurs in Anton's response to a letter received from his brother Alexander during the latter's brief wifeless period of summer 1888. The widower had written to ask Anton to further his suit with Helen Lintvaryov, the kindly doctor whom he had met when staying at Luka. But Anton realized that Alexander barely knew Helen, and that he only wanted to marry her because he was lonely. Alexander was not a "Chokhov", Anton pointed out in reply: that is, he did not resemble his shopkeeping cousins who pronounced the family name in that way, and who regarded such arranged marriages as normal. "You're no Chokhov, and so you know very well that a family, harmony, affection and kindness don't come from marrying the first comer, however decent she may be, but from *love*. If there's no love why speak of affection? And you aren't in love; you can't be because you know Helen Lintvaryov less than you know the man on the moon." Alexander should get to know Helen better before considering uniting his life with hers; perhaps the two might indeed fall in love in due course.[11] In fact, however, this projected union came to nothing; as we have seen, Alexander soon found himself another life partner in St. Petersburg.

But what of Anton? Did he fall in love at this time? We have no evidence that he did, though not for lack of opportunity. Liking rowdy, jolly, boisterous girls, he whimsically threatened to throw himself under a train for love of the ebullient Sasha Selivanov, a childhood friend from Taganrog. He also appreciated the noisy laugh and radiant good health of Natalya Lintvaryov. And Natalya was "pretty keen" on him, Mariya Chekhov tells us, unaware that Anton had long ago dismissed this heartiest of the Lintvaryov girls as too ugly to get married.[12] There were other maidens in the offing, though. There were the Maly Theatre actresses; there was the young authoress and actress Helen Shavrov whom, with her two sisters, Anton "picked up" in Yalta. And there were the other young women whom Mariya brought to the house in Sadovy-Kudrinsky Street.

Supreme among these was Lydia Mizinov. Lika, as the Chekhovs called her, was a colleague of Mariya's at the Rzhevsky Grammar School in Moscow. This stunning eighteen-year-old schoolteacher was intelligent, witty, with a gift for sharp repartee. Accustomed to men staring after her in the street, she was yet deliciously shy. When she first appeared in the hall of the house in Sadovy-Kudrinsky Street the Chekhov brothers gathered on the landing above her, gazing at the lovely girl with such frank admiration that she hid her face in the fur coats on the hall-stand. Here, surely, was the most eligible woman of Anton's early manhood, and Lika is the potential wife with whom posthumous matchmakers among his biographers would most like to have seen him united. Anton's sister at first believed that his feelings for Lika were stronger than hers for him,[13] and many years were to elapse before this impression was revealed as profoundly erroneous.

The Theatre

In 1888–90 Chekhov's involvement with the stage increased. Often seen with actors, actresses and producers, he became a familiar figure in theatrical circles of both capitals. He advised on the production of his own and others' plays; he wrote a new four-act play, *The Wood Demon*; he branched into a new dramatic field with four one-act farces: *The Bear*, *The Proposal*, *A Tragic Role* and *The Wedding*.

These one-act "vaudevilles" were unpretentious essays in slapstick. They form a sharp contrast with the serious short stories which he was now turning out, being more in the spirit of Chekhonte; indeed, the two last-mentioned are adaptations of stories which had appeared over that now-discarded signature: *One among Many* (1887) and *A Wedding with a General* (1884). We thus note a paradox in Chekhov's evolution as combined fiction-writer and dramatist. During the early years, when his fiction had been largely comic, all his known dramatic efforts except the anomalous *Smoking is Bad for You* had been serious in conception, however badly some had fallen down in execution. But now that he was writing more serious stories he was also writing less serious plays. When composing *The Bear* in February 1888 he reflected on this phenomenon. He had used up all his juices and energy on *The Steppe*, he said; and, however much he might cultivate a serious approach, "with me the serious always alternates with the trivial".[1] And the vaudevilles are indeed vintage Chekhonte material, being all based on some grotesque misunderstanding which leads to an absurd climax. Skilfully scripted for laughs and sparkling dialogue, they were not the dramatic equivalent of run-of-the-mill Chekhonte, but of Chekhonte at his best. As such they have enjoyed great success on the stage, beginning with the première of *The Bear* in Korsh's Theatre on 28 October 1888. On that occasion the audience laughed non-stop and the soliloquies were interrupted by applause.[2]

As was his way, Chekhov disparaged his vaudevilles. He called *The Proposal* "a wretched, vulgar, boring little skit . . . a lousy little farce"; and referred to *A Tragic Role* as "a stale farce which falls flat", being based on "a stale and hackneyed joke". Still, he appreciated the boost to his income. He was "living on my dole from *The Bear*", he wrote; it was his "milch cow". Any author of ten tolerable vaudevilles could regard his future as assured, he said, for they were as profitable as sixty acres of land. He planned to write a hundred such farces a year; "vaudeville subjects gush out of me like oil from the Baku wells." Yet he completed only one further vaudeville after the quartet of the late 1880s: *The Anniversary* (1891).[3]

December 1888 finds Chekhov revising *Ivanov* for its first St. Petersburg production, at the Alexandrine Theatre, while simultaneously supervising the production of Suvorin's play *Tatyana Repin* at Korsh's Theatre in Moscow. Agreeing to negotiate the casting of that drama, Chekhov finds himself dealing with rival Muscovite prima donnas. "Actresses [he ungallantly concludes] are cows who see themselves as demi-goddesses. To visit them is to adopt a suppliant posture; at least that's what they think." Observing the tussle between Nadya Nikulin and Mariya Yermolov over the title role of *Tatyana Repin*, Chekhov called them "Machiavellis in skirts. These wretched females loathe each other and are all-out intriguers." Still, *Tatyana Repin* was staged in the end, and Chekhov complimented Suvorin by writing a short "play" of his own with the same title. Not intended for production, but as a private joke between himself and Suvorin, Chekhov's *Tatyana Repin* is a whimsical continuation of the original four-acter. Suvorin returned the compliment by publishing the play in an edition so exclusive that it consisted of two copies only.[4]

Meanwhile, in St. Petersburg, Suvorin was trying to do for Chekhov's *Ivanov* what Chekhov was doing for *Tatyana Repin* in Moscow: interpreting the author's intentions by proxy. For more than three months, from October 1888 onwards, Chekhov tinkered with a work originally dashed off in a bare fortnight. His main efforts were concentrated on Act Four. It was, we are reminded, nearly always the endings of his works, whether narrative or dramatic, which caused him most difficulty; but seldom was this terminal agony so intense as that caused by *Ivanov*. Successive revisions have left more variants to the play than we have to any of Chekhov's other imaginative writings. They account for nearly fifty pages in my *Oxford Chekhov*; even then only the most important items have been selected from a mass of more extensive material.[5]

Not content with bombarding the Alexandrine Theatre with advice and fresh drafts routed through Suvorin, Chekhov descended on the capital in person on 19 January 1889 to attend rehearsals and to coach the actor V. N. Davydov, who was having difficulty with the revised title role.[6] And when *Ivanov*'s St. Petersburg première at last took place on 31 January, all these efforts were rewarded. The author received an ovation in the theatre; his critical notices were enthusiastic; he returned to Moscow "crowned with laurels" after a "terrific reception": and therefore, being Chekhov, in a mood of intense dissatisfaction. He had escaped from St. Petersburg in a state of poisoned befuddlement, worn out and ashamed. "When things go badly I'm always more buoyant than when I'm in luck. Success panics me, makes me long to hide under a table." In early March he reports himself "frightfully bored" with *Ivanov*. "I can't read about it, and I'm really put out when people offer ingenious explanations of it."[7]

Thus Chekhov, far from becoming stage-struck through closer involvement with the theatre, only seemed to experience increasing irritation. After calling actresses cows, he was no kinder to actors; they should never, said he, be permitted to air their views since these were inevitably so boring, whatever the subject. And why could neither actors nor actresses bother to study ordinary citizens such as landowners, merchants, priests, officials? Why could they only play such off-beat creatures as billiard markers, kept women, emaciated card-sharpers: the sort of people they met on pub-crawls? "The modern theatre is a skin rash, a sort of urban venereal disease." It was no use calling the theatre a school of life when it was on a lower level than the public. Nor was it any use blaming audiences. "The public always was a flock of sheep in need of good shepherds and sheep-dogs." Still, Chekhov did feel sufficient resentment against his public on one occasion to wish that *it* was capable of writing a play, collectively; just so that he and Suvorin could attend and hiss it off the stage. Wearying of *Ivanov* in the throes of pre-production chaos, he had found himself hankering for the peace and quiet of fiction-writing. "Narrative is my legal wife [he wrote, varying one of his favourite metaphors] and drama a flamboyant, rowdy, impudent, exhausting mistress." He gratefully reckoned, in November 1889, that he had not put in more than one month's work for the stage during his whole life: a gross underestimate. And he added that he would as soon brood on yesterday's porridge as on matters theatrical. In any case there were far too many rival playwrights in the offing. "I'm not keen on competing with the 536 dramatists now writing for the stage."[8]

His views on the themes and techniques of these 536 rival playwrights, all of whom he was to eclipse in due course, are apparent from advice sent to one of their number: brother Alexander, now pregnant with a drama of his own. "Declarations of love, wives' and husbands' unfaithfulness, widows' tears, orphans' tears, everyone else's tears—all that's been portrayed long ago. Your theme must be new and you can dispense with a plot."9 Chekhov also warns his brother to avoid recondite speech. His dialogue should be simple and elegant. Servants should use straightforward language, not that of comic flunkeys. "Red-nosed retired captains, boozy reporters, starving writers, overworked consumptive wives, noble young men without a blot on their escutcheon, idealistic girls, kindly nannies: that's all been done before and should be shunned like the plague."10 In these recommendations we find clues to Anton's own practice in the playwright's craft, at which he had not yet fully served his apprenticeship.

Just how immature a dramatist Chekhov still was we learn from his major dramatic creation of the period, the four-act *Wood Demon*. The play occupies a special position in his career since it was later to be used as raw material for a more mature work, *Uncle Vanya*. That drama contains large chunks of dialogue quarried directly from *The Wood Demon*, and several characters with the same or similar names; yet it differs so markedly in tone and content that one hesitates to call the earlier play a draft of the later. For the moment, though, we are concerned solely with *The Wood Demon*, which underwent many tribulations of its own long before Chekhov was thinking of it in terms of *Uncle Vanya*.

Chekhov originally intended to write *The Wood Demon* in partnership with Suvorin, to whom he sent a long letter on 18 October 1888, outlining the main characters as he then envisaged them. Suvorin soon dropped out, but Chekhov continued to brood on *The Wood Demon*. It would be incomparably subtler than *Ivanov*, he wrote; it would net him six or seven thousand roubles next season.11 But to the close student of Chekhov these favourable forecasts seem to bode ill for his latest play, since he was given to such small gusts of complacency only when considering inferior products; towards his best work he was almost always severe.

Forging ahead in spring 1889, Chekhov completed a draft of *The Wood Demon* in May. Then he destroyed it and suspended work during the summer, when we remember him preoccupied with his brother's death and with trips to Odessa and Yalta. In September he resumed work on the play in Moscow. He proclaimed it "a long romantic comedy"; it presented "good, healthy people who are half likeable; there is a happy ending; the general mood is one of sheer lyricism". A happy ending! That seemed a sinister augury. Could *The Wood Demon* be shaping as one of those exceptional life-affirming works such as the Tolstoyan moral tales which figure so disastrously in Chekhov's fiction of a few years earlier? Fortunately no. The play was to turn out the romantic comedy which Chekhov had claimed it to be: yet with a considerable infusion of implied moralizing. After contemplating the negative, feckless, world-weary, demoralized Ivanov, we now meet types more positive: a very nest of Lvovs or potential Lvovs. In the "Wood Demon" himself (Michael Khrushchov) Chekhov seems to commend the virtues of charity, contrition and commitment to a good cause: nature conservation. Then again, the beautiful Helen Serebryakov seems to be applauded for her kindness in "sacrificing herself" to her elderly gout-ridden husband. Another character, Ivan Orlovsky, is apparently pioneering the techniques of Moral Rearmament on the occasion when he describes himself as having made ostentatious public confession of his sins.[12]

That one should repent of one's sins, behave tolerantly, eschew malicious gossip: these are no bad guides to conduct. Yet to preach a worthy cause is not necessarily to compose a great work of art. With Chekhov, as we have seen, such implied exhortations were often aesthetically counter-productive. That he himself later found those of *The Wood Demon* unsatisfactory we know because he threw out all this moralizing material lock, stock and barrel when converting the play into *Uncle Vanya*. As for *The Wood Demon*'s cloying ending, in which two pairs of young lovers ardently arrange to unite their fates: for that he substituted the pathetic resignation with which Uncle Vanya and his niece Sonya face a future of drudgery. *The Wood Demon*'s world is not, perhaps, the best of all possible worlds. Yet we do receive the impression that such a Utopia might easily come about if only people would just be kind to each other and stop cutting down trees. No such affirmations or certainties bolster the world of *Uncle Vanya*. Its characters move among shadows; the ground is nowhere firm beneath their feet; virtue goes wholly unrewarded.

By October 1889 the completed *Wood Demon* had passed the censor and was promised to two actor friends of Chekhov's for benefit performances: to Lensky of the Moscow Maly Theatre, to Svobodin of the St. Petersburg Alexandrine Theatre. But then a difficulty arose. A committee, specially appointed to consider the play for the St. Petersburg theatre, rejected it outright: there was not enough action; there were boring passages; above all, the author contravened certain preconceived notions about the nature of comedy. This blow was all the more unexpected after the enthusiastic reception of Chekhov's *Ivanov* at the same theatre earlier in the year. Furthermore—unkindest cut of all—the individual committee member most hostile to *The Wood Demon* turned out to be Chekhov's old friend and "discoverer" Grigorovich.[13]

Svobodin apologetically reported all this from St. Petersburg to

Chekhov, who was furious—most of all with Grigorovich. "This means one of two things. Either I'm no playwright, which I readily endorse, or we must regard certain gentry as hypocrites: I mean those who love me like a son and beg me in God's name to be myself in my plays, to avoid stereotypes and to present a complex conception."[14] The trouble was, though, that Chekhov had not "been himself"; he had not avoided stereotypes; he had not presented a complex conception. Those are the qualities of *Uncle Vanya*, not of *The Wood Demon*.

To soothe the ruffled author, Svobodin wrote that he could at least bank on *The Wood Demon*'s success on Lensky's benefit night at the Moscow Maly Theatre. But Lensky was soon returning his copy of the play with a remarkably offensive letter: Chekhov should stick to short stories; scorning stage conventions, he could never manage a play, especially as drama was a more difficult form than narrative fiction; he was too spoilt to learn the ABC of the stage.[15] To this outburst Chekhov replied peaceably, accepting his defeat with dignity.[16]

Robbed of prestigious performances in two leading houses, Chekhov resignedly sold *The Wood Demon* to a Moscow theatre, Abramov's, which was on the verge of bankruptcy. Here the play received an inadequate first performance on 27 December 1889. One of the actresses, who played a young girl, was so corpulent as to defy attempts by her lover to embrace her. This absurdity, and the ineptly reproduced glow of a forest fire in Act Four, helped to provoke the wrong sort of laughter from the audience and hostile notices from the critics.[17] The play was taken out of production after only three performances,[18] but was published in a lithographed edition. For a time Chekhov also thought of publishing it in *Severny vestnik*, but received so discouraging a reaction from Pleshcheyev that he abandoned the idea.[19] Henceforward he rejected requests, of which several reached him over the years, to stage or publish *The Wood Demon*. Ten years later he remarked that he hated the thing and was trying to forget it; "it would be a real blow to me if some unknown force were to drag it from obscurity and revive it".[20] By that time, of course, Demon had already been converted into Uncle.

Uncle Vanya—so different from, yet so extensively based on, the earlier play—is a pioneering dramatic masterpiece; from which it by no means follows that the relatively conventional *Wood Demon* is a resounding failure. Chekhov, in his disillusioned later phase, was far too harsh to the earlier play—still eminently stageable, as shown by the fine production with which the British Actors' Company toured Britain and the USA in 1973–4. At the time, though, the disappointment aroused by *The Wood Demon* was so acute that Chekhov abandoned serious dramatic writing during the six-year period which elapsed between the completion of that play in late 1889 and the writing of *The Seagull* in late 1895. He abandoned it, that is, with the exception of any work on the conversion of *The Wood Demon* into *Uncle Vanya*: an operation, conducted in total secrecy, which may fall within this period.

Stories

Chekhov's début in a Thick Journal heralded other literary triumphs. In October 1888 his book of stories *In the Twilight*, published by Suvorin in the previous year, earned an award from the Imperial Academy of Sciences—the Pushkin Prize. This honour was grudgingly bestowed, for the author received only five hundred roubles (half the total available) together with a condescending reprimand for contributing hastily written work to the gutter press. Here was success of a kind, but Chekhov's main reactions were ironical. He compared the award to "the dread thunder of Immortal Zeus", and reported that the news had sped round Moscow like wildfire. It had delighted his parents; it had been broadcast everywhere by his sister, "who watches over our reputation with the meticulous severity of a Lady of the Bed-Chamber". Yet Chekhov felt that all his writings, including those which had earned the Prize, would surely be forgotten within ten years.[1]

The prize-winning *In the Twilight* of 1887 was followed during each of three successive years by a further book of stories put together from Chekhov's work as previously published in periodicals: *Tales* (1888); *Children* (1889); *Gloomy People* (1890). When preparing these collections Chekhov changed some titles and revised the text, shortening it usually, and toning down facetiousness. The resulting volumes were popular and went into many editions over the years. Their proceeds, together with play royalties, both increased the author's income and changed its general character. Previously dependent on current earnings from periodicals, and often embarrassed when they arrived late, he now finds income accruing even when he does not put pen to paper. He is "living on my books and plays"; *Ivanov* and his books have "turned me into a rentier"; had he no dependants, he could "live on them for two or three years free of care, lying on a sofa and spitting at the ceiling".[2]

Yet financial worries still oppressed Chekhov, as in the days of his poverty. Money seemed to bedevil his relations with his new friend Suvorin. Chekhov could never forget that Suvorin was rich, and felt their friendship compromised by the patron-client relationship as which St. Petersburg gossips interpreted it. This even reached the point of imputed homosexuality, Chekhov being described as Suvorin's "kept woman". Irritating too was Chekhov's old friend and "discoverer" Grigorovich, who insisted that *The Wood Demon*'s preposterous "Professor Serebryakov" was modelled on Suvorin. How pleased Grigorovich and the rest of "them" would be, Chekhov commented, if he were to put arsenic in Suvorin's tea, or to be unmasked as a spy of the political police.[3]

As noted above, the post-*Steppe* Chekhov is no longer the prolific author of earlier days. During the two years which end with his departure for Sakhalin in April 1890 he contributes only eleven new narrative works, totalling under 250 pages, and is thus turning out less than a quarter as much fiction as during the peak years 1886–7. This modest production rate is to continue throughout the 1890s.

Of these new items the three longest appeared, as we would expect, in *Severny vestnik*: the superb *Dreary Story*; the disturbing *Party*; the unsuccessful *Lights*. *The Seizure* was sent to a symposium published in commemoration of the writer Garshin, who had committed suicide, while six shorter items went to *Novoye vremya*: *An Awkward Business*, *The Beauties*, *The Bet*, *The Princess*, *Thieves*, *Mediocrities*. A single item, *The Cobbler and the Devil*, appeared in the now neglected *Peterburgskaya gazeta*, while the even more neglected *Oskolki* received nothing at all.

These stories were all included by Chekhov in his 1899–1902 "Collected Works", with the sole exception of *Lights*. That he was right to reject so inept an effort we do not doubt. It belongs, with certain "Tolstoyan" stories already discussed, to the small group of didactic works in which the Chekhov of the late 1880s so embarrassingly demonstrated that what may be good moralizing may also be bad art. *Lights* has a jolly engineer countering the pessimism of a student acquaintance with a story from his own youth: he had cynically seduced one Kisochka, a pathetic, waif-like young woman; had callously abandoned her after a single night of sin, sneaking out of town on the first train; but had then slunk back, much ashamed, had begged her forgiveness, and had turned over a new leaf. Didactic too are *The Bet* and *The Cobbler and the Devil*: both show the vanity of earthly goods, thus resurrecting another familiar Tolstoyan theme, and do so fairly well in their light-weight fable style. But *The Princess*, the fourth work of the group which we may consider didactic—at least in the sense of showing Chekhov's readers how *not* to behave—reveals more effective missionary zeal. The kindly philanthropic lady of the title is skilfully unmasked in the course of the narrative, and the unspoken lesson vividly drawn: if you wish to bestow charity on the deserving poor, find some less callous and complacent way of doing it than this.

That this moralizing vein was experimental, that it formed only a small part of Chekhov's creative mentality, is richly demonstrated by *Thieves*. The dashing hero, a picaresque character who seems to belong to Gorky's pages rather than Chekhov's, adroitly steals the horse of a travelling hospital orderly. Though Chekhov could point a lesson when he wished, he signally failed to do so here, seeming to condone the theft rather than condemn it. So at least Suvorin told him, accusing him—like a very Mikhaylovsky—of not distinguishing between Good and Evil, and of lacking ideals. But Chekhov would have none of this. "When I describe horse-thieves you want me to say that horse-stealing's a bad thing. But that's surely been known long enough without my having to say so. Let juries decide their guilt, my only job is to decide what they're like." To combine art with sermonizing would be "nice", Chekhov added. But it was not technically feasible.[4] Such was his epitaph on his own experiments in didacticism of the late 1880s.

In another item of the period, also published in *Novoye vremya*, Chekhov reverts to the plotless sketch. This is the widely admired *Beauties*. It describes the emotions, recollected in tranquillity, of a youth who had once encountered two surpassingly lovely girls during travels in southern Russia. In accordance with the canons of feminine beauty accepted by Chekhov in his writings, but less so in his life, the physical frailty of both heroines is stressed as their most delicious quality.

The least effective among these stories is *An Awkward Business* (*Nepriyatnost*). It describes what happens when an angry doctor slaps a drunken male nurse; describes, rather, what does not happen, for seldom did even Chekhov write so inconclusive a study of inconclusiveness.

Another, very different, work published in *Novoye vremya* has an amusing history: *Mediocrities* (*Obyvateli*), which depicts the idyllic courtship and wedding of a provincial young couple. Having happily married off his bride and groom, Chekhov was girding himself to wreck the idyll by blowing his ecstatic newly-weds "to smithereens", but committed the tactical error of reading the uncompleted story to his family and explaining what was in store for the young couple. Begging him for mercy, they persuaded him to publish the work with the happy ending which it chanced to have in its unfinished form. This, said Chekhov, was why *Mediocrities* had turned out so "sloppy".[5] But he was to atone for his unwonted sentimentality five years later with a revised version of the story. Here, in a sequel such as he had all along planned, the marriage founders, as all true Chekhovian marriages must, on the rocks of domestic triviality. Re-entitled *The Russian Master* (*Uchitel slovesnosti*) and rendered suitably astringent, the work is one of his finest.

Of the stories published between *The Steppe* and April 1890 the three best and most important remain to be discussed. All portray mental or physical-mental malaise, being examples of what is known in Chekhov criticism as the "clinical study".[6]

The Party describes late pregnancy as experienced by a hostess compelled to smile hypocritically at guests whom she finds irksome; she is provoked into a pointless quarrel with her husband, himself also an exponent of social hypocrisy, after which she gives birth to a stillborn child. Here we again find a Tolstoyan theme: the vanity of upper-class social conventions in collision with such basic human realities as birth and death.

Chekhov's next story, *The Seizure*, describes a sensitive young man, Vasilyev, touring the brothels of Moscow with fellow-students not disqualified by inhibitions such as his from "having a good time". When Vasilyev moralizes about prostitution, lamenting the effect of intercourse with, say, five hundred strangers on a typical whore, his art-student friend flares up. "You look at me with hatred and revulsion, but I say you'd do better to build a score of brothels than to go round looking like that."[7] There is more real vice in Vasilyev's facial expression than in all Moscow's "red-light" Sobolev Alley! But these rough words do not console poor Vasilyev. He suffers a nervous collapse brought on by his brothel experiences—which do not, incidentally, include sampling Sobolev Alley's wares. For this omission the great Tolstoy, a keen reader of Chekhov, mocked the story, claiming that the squeamish Vasilyev should have "had a go" at one of the girls.[8] But despite this robust objection on a point of detail, there was no fundamental difference of opinion between Chekhov and Tolstoy on prostitution. Both regarded it as the social evil which it was and is; for which reason *The Seizure*, like *The Party* before it, can be grouped among Chekhov's "Tolstoyan" works. But it is not one of those stories—such as the earlier *An Encounter*, *The Beggar* and *Lights*—in which Chekhov makes positive recommendations and furnishes Tolstoyan models for behaviour. Considering prostitution "an atrocious evil" and Sobolev Alley "a slave market", Chekhov had contented himself with ventilating the issue. As he pointed out himself, he had not "drawn any conclusions". But he did claim to know what he was talking about. "I used to be a great expert on tarts in the old days." That this expertise partly derived from an informal sociological survey of the Moscow red-light area we remember from an earlier chapter. Whether Chekhov always confined himself to the role of observer during such expeditions we do not know; but he was certainly entitled to claim, as he did, a special status in writing about Vasilyev's condition, since this had its clinical aspects. "As a doctor I think I've described mental illness correctly and in terms of all psychiatric canons."[9]

Linking his two clinical studies of 1888 together, Chekhov also claimed that "My *Party* has satisfied the ladies. My praises are sung wherever I go. Really, it's no bad thing to be a doctor and know what you're writing about. Ladies say my description of childbirth is *true*. In my story for the Garshin symposium [*The Seizure*] I describe mental suffering."[10]

These two stories thus continue the tradition—previously pioneered in *Typhus, Volodya, Sleepy* and *Ivanov*—of evoking illness, or conditions akin to illness, whether physical or mental. But it was left to a long story of 1889 to surpass all Chekhov's other clinical studies put together. With *A Dreary Story* he attains a higher level than in any other work, narrative or dramatic, written during his first ten years of authorship. Here is a masterpiece worthy to rank with his major contributions in the genre. *A Dreary Story*'s appearance in *Severny vestnik* in November 1889 therefore confirms his attainment of maturity as a writer, as already marked by the noteworthy but overpraised *Steppe*. The new work firmly establishes him as the finest active Russian fiction-writer of his age: over-shadowed still by the towering Tolstoy, but only in respect of novels written in the distant past, not of current fictional production.

By a strange paradox *A Dreary Story* is both the most pessimistic and the most exhilarating work yet to have come from Chekhov's pen. To summarize it is, alas, inevitably to emphasize the first of these characteristics. Here, in an almost plotless tale, are the reminiscences of an old man, ill and on the point of death, who reviews his past life in a chain of querulous harangues. And yet that lamented past life, far from being inglorious, has represented all that any conventional person might desire: an outstanding career, public recognition, the rewards of professional success, domestic satisfaction. A husband and father, a professor of medicine, Chekhov's hero has taken up options discarded or postponed by his young creator: only to discover, in the evening of his life, that all his experiences, good, bad and indifferent, have been dust and ashes. The Professor's wife, his colleagues, his students—all provoke the bitter and weary complaints of one who has nothing left to do with his life except to leave it. Chekhov's Professor still believes, as did Chekhov himself, in "science"; but—again like his creator—lacks any unifying creed which would put his science, his many achievements, and his domestic circumstances into acceptable perspective. All this was "dreary" enough, but Chekhov drives home the lesson yet more forcefully in his portrayal of the Professor's ward Katya. Where the Professor is old, ugly, ill and poor, Katya is young, beautiful, healthy and rich. His life is behind him, hers has barely begun. And yet she is even unhappier than he. When she goes to him for help in the poignant last scene he can offer her no consolation at all.

This masterpiece was largely written at Yalta in August 1889, and the theme of impending death must have been deepened by the death of Nicholas Chekhov two months earlier. Anton recognized as much when he wrote—how incorrectly!—that "the entire story has been ruined by the revolting mood which I couldn't shake off all summer". Characteristi-cally reserving his most severe self-criticism for his best work, he alluded to *A Dreary Story* as "a piece of crap" and "a great load of turgid balder-dash". "To write the memoirs of an old man one should be old oneself", the twenty-nine-year-old author lamented. So one might have supposed, were it not that *A Dreary Story* triumphantly refutes this typical self-deprecation.

With his collection of ten stories published in March 1890—and including *A Dreary Story*—Chekhov continued to disparage his work by calling the volume *Gloomy People*. Also containing the "clinical studies" *Volodya*, *Sleepy* and *The Seizure*, it was dedicated to his favourite composer, P. I. Tchaikovsky: but with trepidation, since it consisted "of particularly gloomy, psychopathological sketches and has a gloomy title, so that my dedication will be most distasteful to Peter Ilyich and his admirers".[11]

Despite obvious differences between the demoralized, ailing, elderly hero of *A Dreary Story* and his young, successful, still vigorous creator, the impression arose that this was a self-portrait. Surely the pessimistic views ascribed to Chekhov's Professor must be Chekhov's own? But the author scouted such suggestions, and harangued one source of them, Suvorin, as follows. "When you're served coffee, don't complain it's not beer. And when I offer you my Professor's ideas, do trust me; don't go searching them for Chekhov's ideas, pray. There's only a single idea in the whole story which I share: one lodged in the head of that scoundrel Gnekker, the Professor's son-in-law. 'The old man's off his rocker.' Everything else is invented and contrived. Where have you found this 'preaching tendency'? Do you really set such store by *any* ideas, whatever they may be, as to see the centre of gravity exclusively in those ideas, and not in the manner of their expression, their origins and so on?. . . For me as author none of these ideas has the slightest value in itself. . . . If I should describe St. Vitus's dance, you wouldn't approach my description from a choreographical point of view, now would you?" When Suvorin still did not seem to take the point, Chekhov repeated that ideas could not possibly be made the be-all and end-all of *A Dreary Story*. "What matters isn't the content of those ideas but their form. To hell with the bloody story, it may not be worth tuppence."[12]

These sentiments are a warning to critics and biographers who unjusti-fiably quarry Chekhov's imaginative work, not for illustrations of his views (as is legitimate), but for direct evidence on those views. All too often we find the sentiments of his fictional characters lifted out of context as proof that the author was an "optimist", a "pessimist", a this, a that, a the other. And yet we cannot wholly agree with Chekhov when he so drastically dissociates himself from the entire body of opinions voiced by his elderly hero in *A Dreary Story*. In the Professor's disparaging remarks about the theatre we shall find, if we collate what is said in the story with the strictures on the Russian theatre made by Chekhov himself over his own signature, a remarkable harmony of tone and matter. Nor is it fanciful to equate Chekhov, or at least the Chekhov whom we shall meet in the 1890s, with his imaginary Professor in respect of another quality: defeatism or elusiveness in face of other people's emotional quandaries. Chekhov once described his Professor as casual in this respect; he added that, had his hero been a different sort of man, his daughter and ward might not have come to grief. In Chekhov's future evolution we shall find certain episodes which show him comparably unhelpful, evasive and selfish when confronted with the emotional dilemmas of sister, women friends and wife. There will be times when we shall find these ladies levelling at Chekhov, and with some justification, much the same reproach as he has directed at his own fictional Professor. "While those around him are shedding their tears, making their mistakes and telling their lies, he's laying down the law about literature and the theatre with sublime imperturbability."[13]

The Professor's lack of any unifying philosophy of life was, as we shall now demonstrate, also Chekhov's own.

Unsolved Problems

"So far I have no political, religious and philosophical views [Chekhov wrote in 1888]. I change them every month, and so I shall have to limit myself to describing how my heroes love, marry, give birth, die and speak." Not that he wished to exclude all mention of political, religious and philosophical problems from his writings; what he claimed the right to avoid, rather, was the suggestion that he had solved any of those problems. In the most celebrated of his many glosses on this dilemma he agreed that Suvorin was right to require from the artist a conscious attitude to his work. "But you confuse two concepts: *the solution of a problem and its correct presentation*. Only the second is incumbent on the artist." Neither in Tolstoy's *Anna Karenin* nor in Pushkin's *Eugene Onegin* was any single problem solved, Chekhov went on. "But they fully satisfy one just because their problems are all presented correctly."[1]

In comments on *Lights*, which ventilates the issue of pessimism, Chekhov further elucidates his attitude.

You write that neither the discussion of pessimism nor my heroine's experiences shift or solve the problem of pessimism to the slightest extent. In my view it's not the writer's job to solve such problems as God, pessimism and so on. The writer's job is only to show who, how, in what context, spoke or thought about God and pessimism. The artist must not be the judge of his characters and of what they say: merely a dispassionate observer.... It's time that writers ...

realized that nothing in this world makes sense, as Socrates and Voltaire acknow-ledged in their day. . . . If the artist, in whom the rabble believes, ventures to declare that he understands nothing of what he sees, then that fact alone will form a substantial theoretical contribution and a great step forward.[2]

This insistence that a writer should not claim omniscience reminds us of Chekhov's refusal to use his story *Thieves* to condemn the rustling of horses. The writer, he was now more and more convinced, was not a judge, not an arbiter, not a teacher. Chekhov was persuaded that "it's only fools and charlatans who know everything and understand every-thing". Hence the frequency with which those characters in his works who "know the purpose of life" appear to incur his disapproval. We can imagine, then, how irritated he must have felt if he ever heard his youngest brother Michael talking as he writes in his memoirs, of his, Michael's, "convictions as a man and a citizen" being formed "firmly and for all time" during visits to Voskresensk as a student.[3]

Sceptical about politics, religion and philosophy, Chekhov was no less sceptical about his literary work. In the Russian cultural hierarchy he occupied the ninety-eighth place, according to himself; Tolstoy, Tchai-kovsky and the painter Ilya Repin being numbers one, two and three respectively. Despite having published "a couple of hundredweight of stories", Chekhov still claimed not to know where his strength and weakness lay. Did it matter, anyway? "There's no escaping death, and I haven't long to live. I therefore attach no serious importance to what I write, to my reputation or to my literary errors." What on earth was the point of writing, anyway? For the public? But the public was ignorant and uneducated, and Chekhov somehow couldn't believe that it really existed. For money? To that he was almost indifferent. For praise? But praise only irritated him, especially in the absence of true criticism to tell him whether he was on the right lines.[4] "Sketches, articles, stupidities, vaudevilles, Dreary Stories, a vast mass of mistakes and inconsistencies, oodles of bescribbled paper, the Pushkin Prize, living like a lord—yet with all that not a single line of serious literary importance in my own eyes. . . . I yearn to hide somewhere for five years or so and tackle serious, meticulous work. I need to study, to learn everything from the very beginning because I'm a complete ignoramus as a writer. I need to write conscientiously, with feeling and sense: to write sixteen pages in five months, not eighty pages in one month."[5]

It was some time, incidentally, since Chekhov's output had approached eighty pages a month, but he was apt to get carried away by these out-bursts. They are less records of progress than expressions of a mood which, in these years of early success, was more harshly self-critical than at any other period of his life. "For two years I've disliked seeing my works in print. I couldn't care less about reviews, literary chat, gossip, success, failure, high fees. In other words, I've become a complete idiot." Laziness, apathy, idleness: these were the qualities which he ascribed to himself, also commenting on what he felt to be a lack of panache. "My flame burns low and steady without flaring and crackling. That's why I never dash off fifty or sixty pages in a night, or get so absorbed in work as not to go to bed when tired. And that's why I never do anything outstandingly stupid or remarkably brilliant."[6] To regrets about the past Chekhov's fictional characters often unite illusions about the future, and such comforting illusions sometimes visited their creator. "I think that if I lived another forty years and spent all that time reading, reading, reading and learning to write well—which means economically—then . . . I'd bombard you all from a vast cannon which would shake the heavens. But as it is I'm a pygmy like everyone else."[7]

Claiming to despise the entire corpus of his published writings, Chekhov invested his illusions in work which was never to be completed and which must be presumed irretrievably lost: his "novel". To write a novel was a natural ambition for a young Russian author, since this was the main genre of his great predecessors from Tolstoy, Dostoyevsky and Turgenev downwards. That his novel was no passing whim Chekhov's correspondence between October 1887 and May 1889 shows. Sizeable sections of a novel or novels did take shape on paper. By October 1887 he has written about forty pages, and his setting is to be a military district court. By the following February he is wishing that he could afford to complete his unfinished novel under a Crimean cypress. Six months later, in August, he plans to take several more years over his work; which has bifurcated, by October, into two novels. In his head is an army of characters, all awaiting his word of command. "Everything I've so far written is rubbish compared with what I'd like to write." *The Party*, *Lights*, his vaudevilles: all that was boring, mechanical, dull stuff. Annoyed with any critic capable of taking such nonsense seriously, Chekhov records yet again his dislike of his own literary success. That success seems ludicrous to one who is secretly storing up and jealously preserving all his favourite ideas, while refusing to waste them on such ephemeral material as *The Party*.[8]

By March 1889 the novel is acquiring political undertones and seems liable to fall foul of the censorship since it portrays a police chief who is ashamed of his uniform and a young man sentenced to Siberia for armed mutiny, together with a host of characters who do not believe in God. The work now has a title, *Tales from the Lives of My Friends*, and is to form a sequence of self-contained short stories, each with its own title, but with common elements (plot, characters, ideas) to give the whole sequence unity.[9] This prospectus happens to describe the "trilogy" of three interlinked stories, all illustrating the theme of freedom, which were to be written by Chekhov in 1898 and will be discussed below.

How alien a form the novel must have been to a writer who, after brooding on the problem so long, could only plan his first serious essay in the genre as a chain of short stories! Yet Chekhov had made sufficient progress with the work by May 1889 to talk of selling it at 250 roubles a printer's sheet in St. Petersburg. Soon afterwards, though, he writes that it will take two or three years to finish.[10] Never in fact did he publish such a work, though technically he already was the author of a novel—his juvenile thriller *The Shooting Party*. After writing and presumably destroying several drafts of the new "novel", he reverted to the short story: the genre which he had made his own. That he failed to achieve the novel or novels on which he was working seems regrettable, until we remember his knack of saying more in a few hundred lines than many another writer could express in the Russian novelist's traditional six hundred or more pages.

We have seen Chekhov experiment with didactic fiction, and we have seen him turn against those experiments. Meanwhile he was still plagued by critics and colleagues who thought commitment to a cause essential to any right-thinking man of letters. This imputation derived from the Russian tradition, already well established by the mid-nineteenth century, that an imaginative author must be more than a mere entertainer. His role was not to amuse his readers, but to show them how to live. Yet here was Russia's most promising young writer openly boasting that he had no idea how to live, and explicitly refusing to instruct his readers in the matter. As for *The Wood Demon*'s pathetic moral, as for the few oddments of the late 1880s in which Tolstoyan ideas on Christian forbearance are advocated: such items were highly exceptional and artistically weak, forming no discernible ideological pattern. So sceptical and philosophically uncommitted that he was not even a committed sceptic, Chekhov much resented the suggestion that he should harness himself to a cause or write "tendentiously", this being a term of praise in the context. Far from yielding to these pressures, he feared those "who look between my lines for tendentiousness, and are determined to see me as a liberal or conservative. I am not a liberal. I am not a conservative. I am not an advocate of moderate reform. I am not a monk. Nor am I committed to non-commitment. I should like to be a free artist, that's all."[11]

Freedom is the one abstract idea to which the pragmatical Chekhov returned again and again, the ideal which he pursued and seemed to seek in vain throughout his life: "freedom complete and absolute, freedom from oppression and falsehood in whatever form these may be expressed". But it was not the oppressions of the Imperial state which he chiefly had in mind when he expressed this longing for freedom, much as he abominated censorship restrictions, passport regulations, and other bureaucratic or police controls. Rather did he still seek liberation from the proprietorial and paternalistic interventions, from the officious tutelage, from the sententious advice, from the watchful, beady eyes of those liberals and other political dissidents who proclaimed themselves—proudly, but with some discretion, as incumbent in so authoritarian a state—enemies of the Imperial system. Nearly always, when this subject came up, it was the liberals of the *Russkaya mysl* set in Moscow, with the review's joint editors Lavrov and Goltsev at their head, who still evoked his most virulent abuse. He hated political despotism wherever it might raise its head: whether in the Imperial Ministry of Internal Affairs or in the editorial offices of *Russkaya mysl*.[12]

That these two theoretically opposed institutions might even be acting in collusion seemed possible in summer 1888, when *Russkaya mysl* was thought to be intriguing with the censors against Chekhov's current vehicle, *Severny vestnik*. Could *Russkaya mysl* somehow have got the censorship in its pocket? Could Goltsev and company be bribing the censors? Chekhov's patience exploded.

Just you wait [he told Pleshcheyev]. This is nothing to the dirty tricks *Russkaya mysl* will get up to in time. Under the banner of learning, art and persecuted freedom of thought Russia will one day be ruled by such toads and crocodiles as were unknown even in Spain under the Inquisition. Yes, you just wait! Narrow-mindedness, enormous pretensions, excessive self-importance, a total absence of any literary or social conscience: these things will do their work. All these Goltsevs and their ilk will spawn an atmosphere so stifling that every healthy person will be bloody well nauseated by literature, while every charlatan and wolf in sheep's clothing will have a stage on which to parade his lies and hypocrisy.[13]

Unfair to Lavrov, Goltsev and company though it surely is, this outburst yet forms what some might think a clinically accurate prognosis of Russia's intellectual future.

Matters came to a head in March 1890 when Chekhov found himself described, by an anonymous reviewer in *Russkaya mysl*, as "a devotee of unprincipled writing". Seriously offended, he despatched the angriest letter in his correspondence. Never, he told Lavrov, had he been an unprincipled writer, "in other words a scoundrel". Never had he written anything morally reprehensible, however objectionable his work might be on aesthetic grounds. Nor had he ever set himself up as a judge of his fellow-writers. He believed that "in the present dependent condition of the press every word spoken against a magazine or a writer is not only cruel and tactless, but downright criminal". In placing his own work for the press, Chekhov had (he claimed) always sent it to those organs which most needed his contributions, which was why he had earned only half as much as he might. Here he let moral indignation run away with him, for he had come nearer than he implies to pursuing, however modestly and inefficiently, the maximization of his literary earnings: a practice no more reprehensible for a writer than for the member of any other profession. *Russkaya mysl*'s accusation was, Chekhov continued, an outright libel. And since that libel had clearly been uttered deliberately by decent, intelligent men who knew just what they were about, he did not propose to ask for it to be retracted. Meanwhile all business relations between himself and *Russkaya mysl* were terminated forthwith; besides which Chekhov even announced an intention to "cut" the hated Lavrov and his associates should he chance to meet them in the street.[14]

What so grotesquely inflated Chekhov's natural resentment against *Russkaya mysl*? One doubts whether the charge of being an "unprincipled writer" was solely responsible. Again and again in the past he had been abused, and in terms far more strident, by other journals, yet without countering so viciously. It was, very likely, less the specific accusation which provoked the outburst than a build-up, over the years, of prejudice against all those "liberals" and others who had expressed towards him and his work that high-minded, interfering, condescending tone which he so much detested. Moreover, furiously though Chekhov reacted at the time, he was not one to bear a grudge. Two years later we shall find the breach between himself and *Russkaya mysl* healed very easily; after which that organ was to supersede *Severny vestnik* as the premier Thick Journal in his life. And editors Lavrov and Goltsev were to become friends of the "unprincipled" author who so pompously denounced them in April 1890.

This quarrel with *Russkaya mysl* was only the most dramatic episode in the continuing war against critics and reviewers which Chekhov kept up in his correspondence throughout his life. Even the favoured *Severny vestnik* published no book notices worth a glance, he said. All criticism filled him with horror. Were there then so few intelligent people in this world? Was there no one capable of assessing works of art? All attempts to do so—why were they so astoundingly stupid, petty and trivially personal? If you lumped all the critics together they wouldn't be worth a brass farthing. Then again, if reporters of criminal trials could show common courtesy when describing an accused felon, why on earth must critics lambast writers, who were neither highwaymen nor burglars, with such charming expressions as "riff-raff, puppies, street urchins"?[15]

He particularly detested the mindless labels and cant phrases which came so easily and mechanically from the pens of critics and reviewers.

When D. S. Merezhkovsky spoke of Chekhov, a prose writer if there ever was one, as "a poet"; when he referred to Chekhov's characters as Superfluous Men or Failures, their creator was disgusted. Merezhkovsky was peddling clichés. It was time, Chekhov told Suvorin, "to give up these Failures, these Superfluous Men and so on, time to think of something original. . . . To divide people into Failures and Successes is to look at human nature from a narrow, biased angle. Are you a success or not? What about me? Or Napoleon? . . . Where's the criterion? One would need to be God to distinguish successes from failures unerringly. I'm off to a dance." A similar attitude emerges when Chekhov rejects the charge of betraying (in his *Party*) a fear of being considered a liberal. "I think I could be accused of gluttony, drunkenness, frivolity, frigidity or of any crime in the calendar rather than of wishing to seem to be or of wishing not to seem to be something."[16]

So far we have examined Chekhov's attitude to his own writings and his reactions to other people's reactions to those writings. But he was not exclusively preoccupied with his own work; he often had time to spare for that of others. And however bitterly he might denounce the irritations of the literary life, he always felt part of it. These other authors, whom he would abuse behind their backs one day, but praise, help and encourage on the morrow; whose company he fled, yet sought: they formed a loose community of which Chekhov considered himself a member. We are not surprised, then, to find him joining a professional organization, the Society of Russian Playwrights and Opera Composers, in March 1889; he is elected to its committee, and serves conscientiously for a year before declining to solicit re-election on the eve of his departure for Sakhalin. He also joins a well-known Moscow organization, the Society of Lovers of Russian Literature, attending one of its masked balls and collecting subscriptions in aid of a memorial to Gogol.[17]

Meanwhile Chekhov was still busy advising other writers who sent him their material for criticism. Assuring Suvorin that he would ask to be a fiction editor on *Novoye vremya* if he happened to live in St. Petersburg, he in fact discharged that task informally through the post by reporting on stories forwarded to him by the paper. This activity ministered, according to Chekhov, to a streak in his nature of which little other evidence survives: a craving for power. "It's nice to think that one has some power over other men's Muses: that one can tear them into strips or eat them with porridge according to the whim of the moment."[18]

Besides supervising minor scribes, Chekhov also offered casual literary judgements, in his letters, on the work of his great predecessors in Russian literature. To two of these he was outstandingly uncomplimentary. Reading an unnamed work of Dostoyevsky, he described it in March 1889 as "all right, but very long, immodest and full of affectations". Soon he had moved on to Goncharov, whose renowned novel *Oblomov* Chekhov called "a pretty poor piece of work": its hero was overrated and not worth basing a whole book on, while the minor characters all carried "a whiff of Leykin". He therefore proposed to scratch Goncharov's name from his "list of demi-gods".[19]

These references show how far Chekhov was from the automatic postures of reverence often considered incumbent on those who contemplate a generally admired literary figure. But he did not fall into the opposite posture of automatic irreverence, for the same period also sees him praising Tolstoy, Shchedrin, Korolenko and other senior authors. Whether favourable or unfavourable, whether concerned with giants or pygmies, Chekhov's allusions to the arts tend to be pragmatical and down-to-earth. So far was he from the obscurantism and self-importance cultivated by lesser beings when discussing matters cultural that he proclaimed himself scared of the very word "art". "When I'm told of what is artistic and inartistic, of what is stageworthy and unstageworthy, of commitment, realism and all that, I am baffled, I tentatively nod agreement, and I answer with banal half-truths not worth a brass farthing. I divide all works into two kinds: those I like and those I don't like. I have no other yardstick, and if you ask me why I like Shakespeare and don't like Zlatovratsky [a minor Russian novelist] I shall have no answer. Perhaps I shall grow wiser in time and acquire a criterion, but meanwhile all aesthetic discussions just exhaust me and seem like continuations of the scholastic disputes with which people wearied themselves in the Middle Ages."[20]

CHAPTER SEVEN

Sakhalin
1890

In 1890 Chekhov completely breaks the pattern of his life. Hitherto a man of letters, a town-dweller and a *dacha*-renter of sedentary habit, he now bursts these barriers to become an explorer and adventurer, undertaking a hazardous one-man expedition to Russia's Devil's Island: the dreaded Sakhalin.

Prelude to a Mission
(January–April 1890)

Chekhov's friends were baffled when they learnt that he intended journeying to so remote and atrocious an area. How could anyone choose to maroon himself in that cold, dank, inhospitable penal settlement, the abode of convicts, exiles, prison warders, officials and squalid, smelly, aboriginal tribes? Sprawling off the eastern coast of southern Siberia, the elongated land mass of Sakhalin was compared to a sturgeon in its general shape, being over 500 miles long from north to south, and varying in width from 15 to 120 miles. At one point, the Straits of Tartary, the Sakhalin coast is a bare five miles from the Siberian mainland.

Sakhalin was a recent adjunct to the Russian Empire, by contrast with mainland Siberia. Not until the expedition of a Russian naval officer, G. I. Nevelskoy, in 1849–55 had the place even been identified as an island rather than as one more dreary, neglected Siberian peninsula. Then Sakhalin had remained partitioned between Russia in the north and Japan in the south for twenty years; it had only become fully Russian in 1875, when southern Sakhalin was ceded by Japan in exchange for the Kurile Islands. By the time Chekhov set off for Sakhalin it had been a Russian convict settlement for a bare three decades, whereas the Siberian mainland had served as a dumping-ground for Russian criminals and political undesirables for over two centuries.

Sakhalin was the sort of place to which a writer, if considered a political trouble-maker, might conceivably have been exiled against his will by the Imperial government, as Chekhov's friend Korolenko had been sent to remote Yakutia in the previous decade. But here was a writer proposing to go to this Island of the Damned of his own free will. And the very journey from Moscow to Sakhalin was as forbidding as the destination. It would take two or three months to cross more than five thousand miles of inhospitable territory. Rail travel was possible only in the early stages, for not a verst of the great Trans-Siberian line yet existed: its first sod was to be turned by the Tsarevich Nicholas in the year following Chekhov's expedition. Parts of the journey could be accomplished in comparative comfort by steamer. But the middle section, of three thousand miles by horse-drawn vehicle, would expose the traveller to the legendary axle-breaking pot-holes and mud bogs of the *trakt* (the ill-famed "road" which spanned Siberia); to verminous post-stations at which he would be rudely informed that there were no horses; to flooded rivers, rickety bridges, drunken ferrymen; and, it was rumoured, to bears, tigers and murderous escaped convicts. This was not a trip to be undertaken lightly by a healthy man. Yet here was the ailing Chekhov proposing to subject himself voluntarily to all these hazards and discomforts.

The idea of visiting Sakhalin first occurred to him by accident. Michael Chekhov had chanced to be revising lecture notes on criminal law and prison management for his civil service examinations in autumn 1889, when Anton picked up the material, read it, and then and there decided to go to Sakhalin. At first it was hard to tell whether he was serious, but he soon made that clear through the elaborate preparations which preceded his departure for the island in April of the following year.[1]

What possessed Chekhov to undertake this bizarre expedition? He has explained his reasons frankly, repetitively and at length in his letters of early 1890; but the more closely we scrutinize this material the less does any single, overriding purpose emerge. The complex, self-contradictory motives which he discusses, often only to belittle them, are literary, scientific, humanitarian and personal.

The least important motive was the literary, Chekhov explained: he was not going to Sakhalin for copy. "Please don't invest any literary hopes in my Sakhalin trip. I'm not seeking observations and impressions." On the scientific motive he was more hesitant. Denying that any serious contribution to literature or science would come from his expedition, he added that he was not in competition with Humboldt or even with Kennan.[2]

The distinguished German explorer and naturalist Friedrich Humboldt had penetrated Central Asia, but was less closely associated with Siberia than George Kennan. That enterprising American journalist had extensively toured the penal establishments of Siberia, but not of Sakhalin, only a few years previously (in 1885–6) with official permission granted in the hope that his findings would vindicate the Russian prison system. They had not. In magazine articles, soon assembled as a book, Kennan had exposed that system as scandalously inhumane and inefficient. His material remains a valuable historical source; and though banned by the Imperial censor at the time, it was known in Russia through smuggled Russian translations published abroad. It was known to Chekhov too.[3] When he said that he had no Kennan-like plans for his own Siberian visit, he was therefore dissociating himself from the combined publicistic and humanitarian aims of his American forerunner. In fact, though, Chekhov was eventually to reinforce and develop Kennan's findings by publishing material on Sakhalin which further alerted Russian and international public opinion to the plight of Imperial Russia's convicts and exiles.

That scientific research indeed was a motive behind the expedition Chekhov's systematic preparations of early 1890 made clear. He was reading everything available on Sakhalin; making long extracts from this literature; hiring his sister to do the same. He also compiled a sizeable bibliography,[4] commenting that he needed to be a geologist, a meteorologist and an ethnographer combined. What with mugging up the price of Sakhalin's coal in 1863, rummaging in *Morskoy sbornik* ("The Marine Journal") back through nearly forty years, ferreting in libraries and coping with numerous works on the island sent to him by Suvorin, he was beginning to feel that he had beetles in his brain; he was going off his head, he was suffering from *mania Sachalinosa*.[5] He also claimed to have done more work in a month than any of his young colleagues could manage in twelve.

On the way to Sakhalin and on the island itself Chekhov intended to learn and study; even before starting out he had already discovered things which everyone ought to know on pain of forty lashes. Sakhalin was the only place in the world, apart from Cayenne and formerly Australia, where one could investigate the penal colony as an institution. Then again, certain Russian explorers had performed miracles of enterprise in and around Sakhalin about thirty years earlier, and Chekhov intended to rescue them from neglect. He planned to write "one or two hundred pages" to commemorate them; to report his other findings; "to repay my debt to medicine which . . . I have treated like a swine".[6] Here we meet the young man's recurrent obsession with his "treachery" in not practising regularly as a doctor and in failing to complete his medical research thesis of the mid-1880s.

To the scientific purpose behind the Sakhalin journey we may therefore add that of producing a scholarly study or research thesis. What of the third motive strand, the philanthropic? Here again we find a characteristic hesitation. Chekhov was no doubt sincere when he wrote, as he did, that he was not going to Sakhalin for the convicts alone, and added that he had no special reason for going at all. But at other times this humanitarian drive looms larger. "From the books which I have read and am reading it is clear that we have let *millions* of people rot in jail, and have done so pointlessly, irrationally and barbarously. We have driven them thousands of miles through the cold, in fetters; we have infected them with syphilis; we have debauched them; we have increased the number of criminals; we have put all the blame on red-nosed prison warders. Now all educated Europe knows that it isn't the warders who are responsible, but all of us."[7]

So much for the literary, scientific and humanitarian promptings which helped to send Chekhov to Sakhalin, but which all seemed to recede at times by comparison with a fourth, more private, motive: the need for a change. How strongly he craved a new environment is understandable in the light of the dissatisfaction which literary success had brought in the preceding years. That the cultural life of the two capitals, with its gossip, backbiting and malice, was essentially trivial Chekhov had often reflected; besides which a specific resentment against Moscow had begun to obsess him as he approached the end of a decade's residence in that city. Moscow theatrical news was like diarrhoea; how much better to live in Kiev, Odessa or the country than in Moscow; how he hated having to return to Moscow; how sick of Moscow he was now that he had returned; there was no one to talk to in Moscow; in Moscow he was a stranger and unrecognized: these are some of Chekhov's many complaints against the city from the period immediately preceding his Sakhalin expedition.[8] When we add all his other griefs and irritations of the period—his brother's death, the unsolved riddle of existence, the monstrous behaviour of *Russkaya mysl*—we sense that Chekhov may conceivably have been heading for a nervous breakdown.

Was the journey to Sakhalin the young doctor's prescription against such an eventuality? Was his main aim to escape an intolerable environment and enter another habitat: dangerous, unhealthy and uncomfortable, admittedly, but at least guaranteed to be totally different? There are passages in his correspondence bearing out such an interpretation. He wants "to expunge a year or eighteen months" from his life. He calculates that the journey will plunge him into six months' non-stop physical and mental hard labour which he badly needs, being a typically "lazy Ukrainian": that whimsical description, inaccurate in both particulars, which he often applied to himself. Then again, "my only reason for going is to spend six months differently from the way in which I've lived so far. . . . Even if I get nothing out of the expedition at all, it will surely provide two or three days which I shall remember with joy or sorrow all my life."[9]

It is, then, as one committed to penetrating the uttermost ends of the earth that Chekhov proceeds, in early 1890, with the complicated preparations for his journey. He arranges to receive mail *en route*, telling his friends that anything posted in central Russia before 25 July will find him still on the island, where letters will be invaluable in view of the intense boredom awaiting him in that abode of fetters. From Suvorin he obtains an advance of 1,500 roubles to tide himself and his family over a period when his earnings are bound to be reduced. He also asks Suvorin to send an extensive selection of periodicals to be picked up in transit, and arranges to dispatch travel articles of his own to *Novoye vremya* from points on his route. When his sister shows signs of missing him before he has even quitted Moscow he arranges for her to have a fortnight's holiday in the Crimea. Meanwhile he is equipping himself to face the worst weather and other hazards of the far east. He buys a fur coat; an officer's leather greatcoat; high boots; a knife for cutting salami and hunting tigers—until, in the end, he can describe himself as "armed cap-à-pie".[10]

Finally, on 21 April, at eight o'clock in the evening, Chekhov takes the train from Moscow to Yaroslavl on the Volga, accompanied by members of his family, by his friends Olga Kundasov and Isaac Levitan, by Levitan's mistress Sophia and her complaisant husband Dr. Kuvshinnikov. In Yaroslavl Dr. Kuvshinnikov presents Chekhov with a bottle of cognac, to be drunk on the shores of the Pacific Ocean,[11] and Miss Kundasov keeps him company during part of the steamer trip down the Volga which begins the second leg of his tour.

Outward Bound
(April–July 1890)

After leaving Moscow on 21 April, Chekhov covered more than five thousand miles to arrive at his destination, Aleksandrovsky Post on Sakhalin, eighty-one days later on 11 July. He had travelled by train, steamer and horse-drawn vehicle on a journey which fell into three main sections—Moscow to Tyumen; Tyumen to Sretensk; Sretensk to Aleksandrovsky Post.

After arriving in Yaroslavl by train, Chekhov proceeds down the Volga by steamer, passes Nizhny Novgorod (now Gorky) and steams on up the Kama to Perm, which he reaches at 2 a.m. on 27 April. He there entrains for Yekaterinburg (now Sverdlovsk) in the Urals, where he stays three nights at the Hotel America and meets a distant relative, editor of a local newspaper. So far his impressions are depressing. The Volga had been gloomy; and the Kama, with ice-blocks still floating down it, extremely cold and boring. A diet of cheap sturgeon had palled, but the caviare had

been delicious. At Perm there had been rain, mud and cold; at Yekaterinburg there was rain, sleet and snow. That Urals metropolis was just like
any other Russian provincial town—Perm, Tula, Sumy or Gadyach—
apart from the ill-favoured breed of native who inhabited the place:
"Asiatics with bulging foreheads and protruding cheek-bones, cross-breeds
of sturgeon and local pig-iron."[1] After a brief rest Chekhov was glad to
press on into western Siberia by train from Yekaterinburg to Tyumen.

After Tyumen he must manage without the railway. Leaving the town
on or about 3 May, he embarks on the difficult and hazardous middle
section of his Odyssey: the stretch of some three thousand miles to Sretensk.
All of this, apart from a steamer crossing of Lake Baikal, involved negotia-
ting the "road", or string of pot-holes and mud bogs known as the *trakt*,
during the spring thaw (worst season of the year), by tarantass. This was a
large, sturdy, four-wheeled, flat-bottomed type of conveyance in which
the traveller could lie full-length on a layer of straw. Lacking springs or
seats and open to the weather, apart from a small canopy, it was by no
means intolerable to those possessed of a rugged constitution and an abundance of furs. The horses which drew it were hired in pairs complete with
driver, as and when available, from the notoriously unhelpful and
uncomfortable post-stations. So inhospitable, so bug-ridden were these
hostelries that travellers would press on as fast as possible round the clock,
sleeping on the move. This Chekhov did, except when held up by various
hitches. "By evening [he wrote of the *trakt* near Tomsk] the puddles and
the road start to freeze, and by night they're frozen hard. . . . Brrr! It jars
you because the mud solidifies into lumps and turns your soul inside out.
By dawn you're horribly tired from the cold, the jolting, the harness-
bells; you long for warmth and a bed. While the horses are changed you
have a smoke in some corner and straightway fall asleep. But a minute
later your driver's tugging your sleeve with a 'get up, mate; time to be
off'."[2]

Among the major obstacles were Siberia's rivers, small and great,
including several even vaster than the Volga. Many were so broad that one
could not see across to the other side, especially as all were now in flood:
the giant Irtysh and Ob as well as the smaller Tom on the approach to
Tomsk. The river crossings were served by atrocious and unforgettable
ferries. "You approach the river at night. You and your driver start
shouting. It's rainy and windy, there are ice-blocks in the river, you hear a
splashing. . . . A bittern booms. . . . An hour later a huge barge-like ferry
looms up in the darkness with vast oars like a crab's claws." Clamouring
for tips in filthy language, the ferrymen would convey them across with
painstaking slowness: all of which evoked a feeling of acute loneliness.[3]
The bridges were no better, especially when their approaches were so

extensively flooded that the tarantass had to be manœuvred towards them through acres of shallow lakes, and then hauled on to the span over planks kept available for this purpose. "God, I never knew anything like it in my life. The sharp wind, the cold, the repulsive rain, and you're expected to get out of your tarantass (uncovered) and hold the horses which have to be led one at a time over every bridge. Where have I landed up? Wherever am I? All round is wilderness and anguish. ... By now one would be glad to turn back, but that's not so easy. ... Here I sit at night in a hut in a lake by the Irtysh, lonely at heart as I feel the damp pierce me to the marrow. I hear the river, which seems to be banging coffins. I hear the howling wind. I wonder where I am and why I'm here."[4]

In the small hours of 6 May Chekhov came near to sudden death. He was sleepily observing the snaking fires in the darkness—for the peasants had set fire to last year's grass—when suddenly out of the gloom ahead of him careered a convoy of galloping troikas belonging to the imperial postal service. Chekhov's tarantass was overturned, he and his baggage being flung into the mud and nearly run over by yet another troika even as he floundered there. Soon all the drivers were cursing each other with the special expertise of the Siberian coachman. "You can't think how lonely one feels in that wild, swearing horde, in open country before dawn, with the near and distant fires devouring the grass and warming the cold night air not one jot. Oh, how it makes the heart ache."[5]

At Tomsk, half-way between Tyumen and Irkutsk, Chekhov was able to take a five-day rest (16–20 May) from the *trakt*. He wrote up the notes which he had been keeping on the way—his first travel articles for Suvorin's *Novoye vremya*, where they appeared as *From Siberia*. Totalling nine contributions in all, of which the last was sent from Sretensk on 20 June, they were published between 24 June and 23 August. Chekhov was only writing them for money, he said;[6] but then, what published work did he ever write, according to his own account, except for money? These Siberian articles usefully supplement the yet more fascinating material contained in letters to his sister, Suvorin and others. At Tomsk Chekhov found his farce *The Proposal* advertised on all the hoardings, but otherwise the city was a disappointing bore. He was alarmed to learn at his hotel that the local Assistant Police Chief wanted to see him. Could he have stumbled into political trouble? No, for the police officer turned out to be a lover of literature anxious to pay tribute to a distinguished writer with a tour of the local brothels; whence the author of *The Seizure* returned feeling "disgusted" at 2 a.m. In Tomsk Chekhov also took stock of his future travel requirements. Dissatisfied with hired vehicles, he bought a Siberian-type springless "carriage" for 130 roubles, meaning to sell it further along the route. For 16 roubles he also purchased a monstrous floppy leather bag;

it could be spread on the capacious floor of his conveyance, thus enabling him to doze protected from the incessant jolts.[7]

On 21 May the traveller resumes his journey along the grotesque *trakt*, and heads for Irkutsk. Here was the ugliest road in the world: a sort of black pox. At every stop he was regaled with horror stories of wayfarers marooned in seas of mud from which the local muzhiks would rescue them only for an exorbitant ransom. Was this civilization's sole artery from western Russia to barbarous Siberia?[8] It was. But the more Chekhov saw of Siberia the less he felt inclined to call it barbarous. The Siberians were clean in their personal habits, he had observed. They were not forever belching or picking lice out of their hair. When serving a glass of water or milk, your Siberian was less likely to have his thumb stuck in it than was his Ukrainian opposite number; not to mention the yet more squalid Russian. Siberian huts did not stink. Siberians baked excellent bread: some compensation for the nauseating duck broth which they also fed him. "My God, how rich Russia is in good people," Chekhov reflected, also impressed by the pockets of Jewish and Polish colonists. "Were it not for the cold which steals Siberia's summer, were it not for officials corrupting the peasants and exiles, this would be the richest and happiest land in the world." But he also reflected that "your Russian really is a pig. If you ask why he doesn't eat meat and fish he'll put it down to lack of imports, of transport facilities and so on. But there's any amount of vodka to be had even in the remotest villages. And yet you'd think meat and fish would be far easier to obtain than vodka, which costs more and is harder to transport."[9]

Pressing on with all speed, Chekhov abandoned his customary mild manner: it got you nowhere on the *trakt*. To cultivate a rougher style was easy now that he was fed up with his dirty boots, fed up with his fur coat stinking of tar, fed up with his greatcoat having hay stuck all over it, fed up with the crumbs in his pockets and his dirty underwear. Even Siberia's notorious tramps looked at him askance as he fought his way on through flood, cold, mud, hunger, sleeplessness; and now, in the later stages, through heat and dust.[10]

At Krasnoyarsk, on the River Yenisey, the scenery suddenly changed. Now Chekhov entered the spectacular mountain ranges of central Siberia. Krasnoyarsk itself was a fine, civilized town where he would be glad to settle down. And so too was Irkutsk, which he reached on 4 June, and where a steam bath, plenty of sleep and a week's relaxation soon had him feeling "like a European" again. By now he had good cause for satisfaction. His worst two thousand miles were behind him; his health was standing up to the ordeal; he had a terrific appetite; he no longer had piles. Forgetting earlier regrets at embarking on the mission, he was soon claiming to have "seen a lot and experienced a lot. It's all fascinating and new to me: not as a writer, but simply as a man. The Yenisey, the taiga, the post-stations, the drivers, the wild scenery, the game, the physical sufferings caused by the inconveniences of travel, the pleasures of resting: the whole business is better than I can say. Just being in the open air day and night for more than a month is an interesting experience and good for one's health. For a whole month I've seen the sun come up in the morning and go down at night."[11] One blemish alone marred the idyll of Irkutsk: Siberia's women were inferior to those he had left behind. He had been dreaming of Lika Mizinov, he wrote to his mother on 7 June; which meant, he supposed, that he must be in love with her. As for these ugly, tub-like, Siberian cows, these Yakut and Buryat monstrosities who didn't know how to dress, sing or laugh, these frozen female fish: only a walrus or a seal was fit to engage in "hanky panky" with them.[12]

After selling his carriage in Irkutsk, Chekhov proceeded by hired vehicle on 11 June and was soon crossing Lake Baikal by steamer. He gazed into waters so limpid that, it was said, one could see down into them a whole verst. To behold great mountains and cliffs drowning in depths of liquid turquoise: it sent shivers down your spine.[13] And the scenery beyond Baikal had everything the heart could desire. It was the Caucasus, the Psyol valley, Zvenigorod district, the Don, Switzerland, Finland—all rolled into one.

Sundry hitches so delayed Chekhov in the Baikal country that he barely reached Sretensk in time to catch the steamer *Yermak* and begin the last and most comfortable stage of his journey along the River Shilka and then the larger Amur to Nikolayevsk, the port for Sakhalin. Not that the *Yermak* was excessively comfortable; it vibrated maddeningly and then got stuck on a rock. At Blagoveshchensk Chekhov transferred to a more salubrious vessel, the *Muravyov*. By now he had Russia to port and China to starboard. He was seeing many Chinese, and sharing his cabin with one for a time. But one of his reflections on this people was to be expunged from the 1944–51 *Works*: he suggested that Suvorin's infant children would find a few Chinese, those "charming tame animals", even more enchanting as pets than their beloved donkeys.[14]

In this frontier region Chekhov could hardly believe that he was still in Russia. What with girls smoking cigarettes and all the uninhibited chat, this was more like what he had read of Texas or Patagonia.[15] The air was "red-hot" with liberal talk here, everyone feeling free to discuss politics in terms which would have earned them Siberian exile had they not been in Siberia already. An escaping political prisoner could pass openly through the area without fear of being denounced to the police. And on the Amur the least regarded exile could breathe more freely than could the most important general in "Russia"; which was how Siberians spoke of the European part of the Empire, alluding to it as a foreign country and caring not a jot for its affairs. All this was so exhilarating that Chekhov no longer feared death. "I've seen so many treasures and enjoyed myself so much."16

On 5 July he docked at Nikolayevsk. Three days later he embarked on the steamer *Baikal*, and on 10 July he anchored off Aleksandrovsky Post, Sakhalin's capital, a log-cabin town of some 3,000 inhabitants.17

Devil's Island
(*July–October 1890*)

Before Chekhov could put ashore he was visited on the *Baikal* by the administrative head of the local district, who arrived by launch and soon showed that he had heard nothing and cared less about the new visitor. Forced to spend the night in his cabin, Chekhov had good cause for alarm. He was seeking entry to a highly sensitive area of the world's most bureaucratized country, and that with no documents apart from a chit proclaiming him a correspondent of *Novoye vremya*. He had sought to regularize his position back in January by applying to M. N. Galkin-Vraskin, chief of the Empire's prison administration, who had promised or seemed to promise to notify the Sakhalin authorities of his arrival in advance. Could this undertaking have been dishonoured? It seemed likely at the moment. But Galkin-Vraskin, as it later turned out, had sent a secret instruction categorically forbidding Chekhov access to Sakhalin's political prisoners. The important thing was, though, that this very restriction in effect conferred on Chekhov permission to pursue his investigations in every other direction.1

Early in the morning of 11 July he ventured ashore to beard officialdom in Aleksandrovsky Post. He first paid his respects to the Commandant of the island, General V. A. Kononovich, who received him affably and displayed his liberal views by benevolently deploring the practice of flogging prisoners for disciplinary offences. A week later Kononovich's immediate superior happened to arrive on an official visit: Baron A. N. Korf, Governor-General of the Amur Region. He too treated Chekhov courteously. Things had much improved on Sakhalin since his last visit five years previously, Korf blandly pronounced: a statement which Chekhov found complacent in view of the continued prevalence of hunger, mass prostitution and floggings. The Baron was, he noted, unfamiliar with the true conditions of prison and exile. Still, it was useful to meet so lofty a functionary together with many of Sakhalin's other administrators at a banquet given by Commandant Kononovich on 22 July.2

Settling down to lodge with the local education officer, Chekhov was ready to begin operations. He had now received permission to collect statistical data, and instructions had gone out to the island's various district commissioners, asking them to afford him every possible help subject to the proviso about political prisoners.[3] Such was the authorities' attitude: "we have nothing to hide".

Sakhalin is a sizeable island of more than three times Sicily's area. Owing to its atrocious climate and recent incorporation in the Russian Empire it was sparsely populated: the census of 1897 was to give the total number of inhabitants as 28,113 persons (20,472 male, 7,641 female), among whom prisoners and exiled settlers totalled just under half. These fell into various categories, the most serious offenders being convicts at hard labour, some of whom were confined in grim dungeons scattered through the island. The most unfortunate of the prisoners, those who had committed serious additional offences while in custody, were permanently chained to wheel-barrows. Others were confined by foot-fetters, but would leave their jail on working parties. The rhythmic clanking of their shackles, the mists, the smoke of forest fires: these were some of the most haunting impressions of Sakhalin.

Chain-gangs from the jails were employed chiefly on coal-mining, timber-felling, road-building and dock labour. But there were also convicts who lived *en famille* outside the prisons and engaged in agriculture. Under the island's grim conditions this might mean an even harder life, and was shared by the less serious category of offenders—exiled "settlers", obliged to remain on Sakhalin and free only in being permitted to scrape a living as best they could. In most parts of Sakhalin the basic occupation, agriculture, gave only a bare subsistence owing to the unfavourable climate and soil; the main crops were cereals and vegetables.

Exiled settlers, and also released convicts (after a ten-year stint as settlers), could hope eventually to receive "peasant status". This conferred the right to leave Sakhalin and settle in certain parts of mainland Siberia. But never could they expect to return, except illegally, to homes in European Russia. A sentence to Sakhalin, whether as convict or settler, was therefore a life sentence; and it was this provision, above all other features of the penal system, against which Chekhov most eloquently campaigned. Believing that punishment should lead to rehabilitation, he found this principle contravened by the denial of an ultimate return home.[4]

Besides prisoners and exiles, the island's population also included free wives, and a few free husbands, who had availed themselves of facilities for joining a sentenced spouse. There were also children, officials, warders, prison guards and soldiers. All these people owed their presence on Sakhalin to the fact that the island was a penal colony. As a cross-section of the multiracial Russian Empire, in which Russians themselves were a minority, they were ethnically mixed, including, for example, many Tatars and others of the Muslim faith, for whom a mosque was under construction in Aleksandrovsky Post when Chekhov arrived. Sakhalin also boasted two indigenous tribes, the Gilyaks and the Aynos (there were about two thousand of each), into whose lives the triumphant march of civilization had brought such amenities as syphilis, alcoholism and colonial exploitation.[5]

All in all, the population came to about one person per square mile, and was scattered in settlements along the coasts and rivers. To visit all the convicts and settlers, to talk to them all, to record their particulars on a simple, locally printed census card devised by himself—to do all this within three months was the daunting task which Chekhov now tackled. It might have seemed impossible had he not in fact accomplished it. The real purpose of his census was less the quest for statistics, useful though these were, than to provide an excuse for meeting all prisoners and exiles. Even with the political prisoners, not in any case a very numerous category, Chekhov did establish some degree of contact in spite of the official ban.[6] Sending an interim report to Suvorin on 11 September, by which time he had left the more populous north of the island and was sailing southwards, Chekhov claimed to have carried out a census of the entire northern population. He had toured all the settlements, he had entered all the huts, he had spoken to everyone, he had collected about ten thousand cards. There was not a single convict or settler who had not spoken to him;[7] and since the number of interviews averages out at over 160 a day we can judge how busy he must have been.

Trudging round the prisons, the barracks in which some of the exiled settlers were housed, and the huts of the settlements, Chekhov found less evidence of deliberate cruelty than of neglect, inadequate resources and official apathy. It was harrowing to push through the dark, damp, stinking, overcrowded cells infested with cockroaches; or to see a party of seasick convicts, their faces green and twisted, as they unloaded into lighters the cargoes of ships anchored far from the island with its inadequate harbours. The convicts were treated as beasts of burden, they were at the beck and call of every official, being issued as servants or concubines and having no redress against abuses. They were humiliated, too, by a regulation requiring them to salute free citizens by removing their hats at a distance of fifty paces; when Chekhov first received this obeisance from a group of fifty convicts he ironically reflected that he must be the only writer who had ever been accorded such an honour.[8]

The most forbidding place on Sakhalin was Duë, site of the first Russian settlement on the island in 1857. An abode of deathly silence apart from the sinister background noise of jangling fetters, droning telegraph wires and breakers crashing on the bleak cliffs, this had a coal-mine, scandalously mismanaged (said Chekhov) by a commercial company on exploited convict labour. There were two prisons here, those of Duë and Voyevoda, this last being the grimmest of the Sakhalin jails. And there was a yet more appalling barracks for the settler workers; this, and another prison at Derbinskoye, were the only places on the island where Chekhov claimed to have witnessed the ultimate in human degradation.[9]

Among the convicts were certain celebrities whose acquaintance Chekhov made. As one might have supped with Crippen, he accepted invitations from notorious convicted criminals exiled to the island with the status of settlers: he dined with the murderer Karl Landsberg, a former guards officer, and was invited into the kitchen of an illustrious arsonist, ex-Baroness Heimbrück. Another celebrated convict, whom Chekhov did not meet, since the man had escaped from Sakhalin to disappear without trace a few months earlier, was a certain Lagiyev, renowned as the slaughterer in 1886 of the Rector of Tiflis Orthodox Theological Seminary, where Joseph Stalin was to become a pupil in 1894.[10]

Such escapes, and endless anecdotes about them, relieved the legendary boredom of Sakhalin. To get away from prison was easy enough, for only a minority of the convicts was held in close confinement. The real difficulty was to reach and traverse the Siberian mainland. Unsuccessful escape attempts were savagely punished. And yet, according to Chekhov, no less than three in five convicts had tried it at one time or another. About two-thirds were caught or found dead. The rest disappeared without trace: some to freedom, many to perish unrecorded in the wilderness. There was also, among the convicts, one aged pseudo-escaper whose habit it was to enlist a partner purely in order to kill him and take his money and stores as soon as the two were alone in the wilds; he was said to have carried out sixty such murders.[11]

For attempted escape, for murder, for attacking a prison officer, for other serious offences harsh punishments were awarded, of which hanging was the most severe, followed by chaining to a wheelbarrow. Floggings were particularly common, and Chekhov forced himself to witness one, administered by a triply thonged whip. The experience gave him night-mares during the next three nights; but he survived to describe it in his own characteristic spare and, when necessary, spine-chilling manner. His spirit revolted against the barbarity of such punishments, and against their arbitrary nature. Flogging, consignment to the mines, imprisonment: these penalties could be handed out by local administrators without trial, without even perfunctory investigation.[12] Chekhov was also appalled by the prevalence of prostitution on an island where, he said, life was so monotonous that "the gratification of the sexual instinct is often the only entertainment available".[13] Prostitutes were at a premium owing to the scarcity of women, whom the men outnumbered by more than two to one. For specially imported whores a few settlers could afford to pay shippers a hundred pounds of tobacco per head. There was also the home-grown article: tales reached Chekhov of nine-year-old prostitutes and of young girls sold off at puberty by their drunken, corrupted mothers. Aleksandrovsky Post was famous for its brothels: institutions well developed throughout Siberia as a whole.

Despite the scarcity of women, more permanent relationships were common on Sakhalin, only a minority of cohabiting couples being legally married. There was also the problem of allocating the female convicts and exiles periodically freighted in bulk to Aleksandrovsky Post. These ladies were distributed on arrival according to the whim of officials of that log-cabin metropolis, the youngest and best-looking being retained on the spot, and often entering the "harems" (Chekhov's word) of local clerks and prison warders. Brutalized by the horrors of transportation, they were glad to start life anew as the "housekeeper" of some Sakhalin bureaucrat, especially as these did not all live in indescribable squalor. Settlers, and even convicts with means and "pull", could also hope to benefit from the general shareout of females. Chekhov has described the arrival of such a party at Aleksandrovsky Post. "The women, bent under bundles and knapsacks, trudge along the road: apathetic, still affected by seasickness, followed like buskers at a fair by crowds of peasants, urchins and hangers-on of govern-ment offices. It's like the herring swarming in the River Aniva, pursued by regiments of whales, seals and dolphins lusting for a dainty morsel of roe." The women are locked up for the moment, but are discussed throughout the night preceding the shareout.[14]

Chekhov has also described the apportionment of a batch of women filtered through, as less desirable, to the southern district headquarters at Korsakovsky Post, his headquarters during his last month on Sakhalin. At the appointed time local settlers who were on the list for a wife would deck themselves out in red shirts, planter's hats and flashing jackboots obtained from some unknown source; and would make for the local female barracks where the women, eyes lowered, were waiting to be picked.[15] There were few so old or ill-favoured that they were not soon cohabiting with some man. Haphazardly contracted, many of these unions turned out happy, Chekhov tells us. The newly allotted wife might have been sentenced for murdering a husband or lover on the mainland, but often settled down contentedly with a more congenial protector on Sakhalin. The shortage of women gave her the whip hand, for she could easily leave one mate and take up with another. Women's status varied a lot. There were self-respecting housewives; there were domestic drudges treated worse than animals.[16] This latter condition was in any case all too often that of the Russian peasant woman of the mainland.

For many the solaces of domestic life tempered the rigours of exile, such happiness being far more usual when there were children. Chekhov described them as the most important and pleasant people in Sakhalin. "Into the coarsened, morally harrowed Sakhalin family they bring an element of tenderness, purity, gentleness and joy. . . . Children's presence gives the exiles moral support, and . . . children are often the only link attaching exiled men and women to life, saving them from despair and ultimate disaster."[17] Such aspects of the children's role on Sakhalin helped to counterbalance the gloomier picture of starving babies, of infant concubines, of pregnant fifteen-year-olds in a place where Church and schools existed only on paper; where the young were educated solely by their surroundings, and by the conditions of prison and exile. Chekhov recorded an interview with an illegitimate barefoot boy who knew neither his father's name nor that of the step-father with whom his mother was living on the island after murdering her mainland husband.[18]

Like many men intensely interested in their surroundings, Chekhov had always been more prone to boredom than duller spirits, and boredom was the leitmotiv of Sakhalin life in his assessment. Wearied by two months' investigations based on Aleksandrovsky Post, he sailed off in September to the yet remoter Korsakovsky Post in the south, which lacked a telegraph and postal service and was visited by ships only once a fortnight. He was still working, but his initial drive and enthusiasm had spent themselves. As the end of his stay drew near he wrote to his mother that he was bored stiff and fed up with Sakhalin. "I've seen nothing for three months but convicts and people who can talk only of hard labour, convicts and the lash. What a dismal life!"[19]

Mission Completed

From the Island of the Damned Chekhov sailed away on 13 October in the liner *St. Petersburg*, bound for Odessa. He was delighted to flee the menace of a cholera epidemic, fearing the disease itself less than quarantine regulations which threatened to maroon him on Sakhalin for the winter. Since cholera was also raging in Japan he had to abandon a proposed visit to that country and the intended purchase of a naked Japanese girl, in ivory, for a friend's delectation.[1]

His first call was at Vladivostok, where he mourned the plight of the eastern Siberian Maritime Region, of which that thirty-year-old port was capital; here was a sink of poverty and criminality, with only one honest man to every ninety-nine thieves. Putting in at Hong Kong next, Chekhov brooded further on the colonizing incompetence of his fellow-countrymen. This British possession boasted wonderful roads, horse-trams, a mountain railway, museums, botanical gardens. "Wherever you look you see the Englishman's most tender solicitude for his servants; there's even a sailors' club; I rode in a rickshaw ... bought all sorts of gew-gaws from the Chinese, and was indignant to hear my Russian travelling companions cursing the British for exploiting the natives. 'Yes,' thought I. 'The British do exploit the Chinese, the Sepoys, the Indians. But they also give them roads, running water, museums and Christianity. *You* exploit people too, but what do you give them?'"[2] From Chekhov's *Works, 1944–51*, this passage has been omitted as lacking the degree of chauvinism deemed incumbent on a major Russian writer by his editors.

Further adventures included a storm which threatened to capsize the *St. Petersburg*, and two burials at sea. Singapore depressed Chekhov to the point of tears, but Ceylon was a paradise. He rode on the Sinhalese railway, he "glutted himself" on palm jungles and dusky women. So he told Suvorin, adding that he had made love to "a black-eyed Indian girl ... and where? In a coconut grove on a moonlit night."[3] This passage, which has also been excluded from *Works, 1944–51*—for recording an impropriety inappropriate to a Russian writer—does not read as a joke. It seems to represent the only occasion on which Chekhov is ever recorded as making such a boast.

After this mid-November orgy thirteen days at sea followed until Chekhov and his two travelling companions—a Midshipman Glinka and Father Hercules, a Buryat priest—felt themselves going berserk with boredom. This was most extreme in the Red Sea, though Chekhov was at least glad to find himself capable of tolerating its intense heat. He put in at Port Said; was moved by the sight of Mount Sinai; caught a cold in the Aegean, after enjoying excellent health so far throughout his whole expedition; "dined with the Dardanelles"; feasted his eyes on Constantinople; and docked at Odessa on 1 December with his card index, a mass of other papers, "eleven hundred thousand memories" and two tame mongooses, as well as Father Hercules and Midshipman Glinka.[4] On their way to Moscow by train they got out during a halt at Tula, arousing astonishment in the station buffet. The slant-eyed, flat-faced Buryat was thought by the goggling muzhiks to be something yet more exotic by Russian standards, a Hindu; while the mongooses, sitting up on their hind legs and begging for food, were taken for monkeys. On Tula station Chekhov was greeted by his mother and his brother Michael, who escorted him back to Moscow by train and introduced him to the family's new headquarters: a rented house in Malaya Dmitrovka Street.[5]

Trying to sum up the Sakhalin expedition, as he did in letters written soon after returning to Moscow, Chekhov sounded his usual conflicting notes. On the one hand he felt healthy and in good fettle to the marrow of his bones; he had brought back a trunkful of material; he had endless topics for conversation. "I'm so utterly satisfied, so sated, so enchanted that I want nothing more, and wouldn't complain if I had a stroke or was carried off by dysentery. I can say this: *I've lived, I've done enough!* I've been in the hell of Sakhalin and in the paradise of Ceylon." Yet, despite these satisfactions, he had also brought back a "bad sensation": the island had made him feel queasy, as if from eating rancid butter.[6]

Though Chekhov claimed to have returned with enough conversational material to last a month, the topic palled during a St. Petersburg visit of January 1891, when he had to describe his expedition to all and sundry. But one theme he was always ready to discuss: the supply of school text-books, so woefully lacking on the island. Seeking help from everyone he knew, he began to despatch batches of this material; there is a reference, for example, on 13 March, to his sending 2,200 more books to Sakhalin.[7]

The main thing was to put his impressions of Sakhalin on paper before they faded. He therefore settled down to a routine three days' work a week on the material: to such effect that he was prematurely claiming to have a whole book "ready for publication" by May. Work persisted through the summer, as did complaints that it was a millstone round his neck; he was fed up with ferreting through papers for an hour "for a single lousy reference". But there were satisfactions too. So well had he described Sakhalin's climate that one could actually feel the cold, he boasted. He also claimed to have written well on the subject of escaping prisoners. Here was a book to "outlast me a hundred years". Coming from an author whose best efforts were commonly accompanied by self-disparagement, these boasts augured badly for the current progress of his work. In any case he was in two minds about his Sakhalin dissertation. Should he give it up entirely? Should he devote another three or five years to it?[8]

It was the latter course which Chekhov eventually pursued. After publishing a single chapter, that on the escapers, in a charity symposium of late 1891 (*Aid to the Starving*), he suspended systematic work on Sakhalin for nearly two years, deterred largely by fear of censorship. His apprehension persisted when the completed treatise at last began to be serialized in the once hated *Russkaya mysl* of October 1893, appearing in a total of eight issues between then and July of the following year. This serialized material formed the bulk of the work—its first nineteen chapters. The last four were banned by the censor, and did not appear in the journal. The whole work, now complete with its last four chapters, was published as a book by *Russkaya mysl* in 1895. It was later revised and issued in its canonical form as Volume Ten of Chekhov's "Collected Works" of 1899–1902.[9] An early draft, containing numerous legible excisions, also survives. The variants are accordingly far bulkier than those to any of Chekhov's other writings; but then *Sakhalin Island* is far and away his longest work: nearly twice as long as its nearest rival, *The Shooting Party*.

The revision process consisted of pruning arid statistical material and cutting other matter through considerations of censorship or prudence. For example, kindly prison warders sometimes secretly unchained Sakhalin convicts sentenced to be shackled to wheelbarrows; but it would have been thoughtless to publish the fact when the result might have been a reversal of this humane concession on the spot. Chekhov also took out or softened some of his more scathing remarks on the island and its administrators.

It was satisfying to see *Sakhalin Island* in print. "My *Sakhalin* is an academic work [he wrote in January 1894].... Now medicine can't reproach me with treachery: I've paid my tribute to learning and to what writers of the old school call pedantry. And I'm glad that this rough convict's smock will hang in my fictional wardrobe." But Chekhov still felt ambivalent about Sakhalin, for we soon find him complaining of having wasted more time and money on the escapade than he could recover in a decade.[10] And yet despite such regrets Chekhov had every right to be proud of his *Sakhalin Island*. Together with Dostoyevsky's *Notes from the House of the Dead* and Tolstoy's *Resurrection* it occupies an especially honoured place in Russia's vast corpus of penological literature. It differs from those two better-known works in being wholly factual. And yet, free from fictional elements though it is, Chekhov's study is not quite an academic thesis, as he claimed. It contains too many personal reminiscences for that. Part dissertation and part travelogue, it is a harmonious work despite the mingling of genres. The style is cool, light, objective, admirably controlled, free from pomposity and jargon: a model for thesis-writers everywhere.

The work had considerable influence on Chekhov's contemporaries; it raised Sakhalin from obscurity, bringing the settlement, and Siberian penal conditions in general, to public notice. This interest was reflected in reviews of *Sakhalin Island* in the metropolitan press, as also in discussions published in Siberian newspapers. Contributions came in towards schools, libraries and children's homes in Sakhalin; Russian and foreign investigators paid more attention to the island; and one young woman was inspired by Chekhov's treatise to devote her life to welfare work on Sakhalin. During the 1890s the Russian government commissioned two officials to visit and report on the island.[11] As for the penal provision which Chekhov most deplored, that whereby return to European Russia was permanently prohibited to all those "sent to Siberia"—it was somewhat relaxed in a manifesto of Alexander III in May 1891. This was good news to Chekhov, though his Sakhalin expedition is unlikely to have influenced the Tsar. Gratifying too was another imperial manifesto of the same year: that embodying the historic decision to span the Russian east with the Trans-Siberian Railway, thus relieving future travellers from the horrors of the *trakt*.[12]

Thus was the humanitarian aim of Chekhov's expedition crowned with modest success. As for its reflections in his imaginative work, we remember him specifically denying in advance that he was going to the island for literary copy. He did, however, make use of Sakhalin impressions in three stories of the 1890s. His outward journey inspired the desolate Siberian river scene of *In Exile*. Sakhalin itself figures only once, in the closing pages of *Murder*; here the sentenced killer Jacob Terekhov, now an inmate of "the grimmest and most forbidding prison on Sakhalin", Voyevoda Jail, is one of a party of convicts detailed to load coal into lighters, on Düe's desolate wharf. Finally, death at sea, so superbly described in *Gusev*, was based on Chekhov's experiences when crossing the Indian Ocean in the *St. Petersburg*. Besides these reflections of specific experiences we also find, in *Peasant Women* and *In the Hollow*, descriptions of crime and criminals presumably inspired by what Chekhov learnt of such topics during his expedition of 1890.

Sparsely reflected in the subject-matter of Chekhov's fiction, his Sakhalin expedition yet remains a literary landmark. It rounds off a decade in which we have watched him develop from an unpromising début into early maturity: a decade largely experimental, prolific alike in rubbish, in middling material and in excellent original work. And it heralds more than a decade of superlative achievement, including a score of stories on his highest level and his fully mature four-act plays. How far this transformation from barely achieved to thoroughly exploited maturity was the direct result of Chekhov's 1890 experiences we cannot tell. But that so spectacular and taxing an eight-month change of scene did have a profound effect seems a safe assumption. After Sakhalin, as before it, Chekhov will often be found complaining: about himself, his work and his role in life. But the doubts and the irritability never again seem to cut so deep as in the harrowing years at the end of the 1880s. Far from merely fulfilling his ambition, expressed before setting out on the expedition, to live "two or three days . . . which I shall remember with joy or sorrow all my life", Chekhov had experienced two or three hundred such days on his far eastern trip. We may congratulate him, then, on organizing in mid-career, at a time of distress and bewilderment, as beneficial a holiday as could have been devised. But the contrary opinion, that the expedition was a tragic mistake and fatally undermined his health, has also been expressed.[13]

CHAPTER EIGHT

Between Sakhalin and Melikhovo

1890-2

We now consider the fifteen months which separate Chekhov's return to Moscow in December 1890 from his move to Melikhovo in March 1892. This period sees the publication of his outstanding *Duel* and *Butterfly* together with three other short stories of high quality.

Reluctant Metropolitan
(December 1890–March 1891)

In December 1890 the returned explorer resumes residence with his family in the new quarters in Malaya Dmitrovka Street—two-storeyed and detached, but cramped. He also reassumes his earlier dislike of Moscow, which soon develops into a violent aversion. Less a home to him now than a mere base, the city has become a place to escape from when possible: we shall see him spending about half his time elsewhere during these pre-Melikhovo months.

Far from settling down to recover from Sakhalin, Chekhov showed disquiet almost from the moment of his return. "It's not boring *yet*," he proclaimed on 10 December, using a favourite formula. But by 5 January Moscow life seemed "so vulgar and tedious that I'm ready to bite". As often, he felt "pestered" by the friends whom he would beg to pay the very visits which so irritated him. It was irksome too, now that he was itching to write on Sakhalin, to have to earn ready cash by turning out stories.[1] These were, to him, a more trivial product; even though they included the brief, masterly *Gusev*, now polished off after being drafted in

Colombo and sent to *Novoye vremya* on 23 December. Above all he was plagued by illness, for his health was failing after standing up to Siberian and tropical rigours. His severe cold, imported from the Aegean, persisted in wintry Moscow. He complained of headaches, piles, a cough. There was also a new malaise: his heart was functioning irregularly, he said, and had taken to stopping for a few seconds every minute; a rubber ball seemed to be bouncing in his chest. And he had acquired "a little paunch".[2]

He consoled himself with the thought of further travels, having "the hell of a lot of plans", which included a trip to the Arctic. But when he did leave Moscow, on 7 January, it was only for St. Petersburg, where a three-week stay showed that Sakhalin had added further lustre to his name. Fellow-writers, high officials and sundry busybodies harried him from morning till night, turning his room into an office and burdening him with "boring invitations to boring dinners". On his feet from 11 a.m. to 4 a.m., he was "eating and drinking endlessly; I'm sure to burst". Far from having left his depression behind in Moscow, he only found it intensified in the capital.[3]

That Chekhov could not bask in his new fame as an explorer will not surprise us when we remember his recent reluctance to wallow complacently in his popularity as a writer. Disliking adulation even when kindly intended, he loathed it more than ever now that it seemed so heavily laced with malice: the tribute, one feels, of mediocrity to genius widely recognized but not yet well enough established to stimulate sycophantic fawning. Breathing a dense atmosphere of impalpable and mysterious ill will, Chekhov was accepting dinner invitations from "friends" who, even as they intoned "vulgar dithyrambs" in his honour, were "ready to gobble me alive, the devil knows why. Were I to shoot myself I should give the greatest satisfaction to nine-tenths of my friends and admirers." There was V. P. Burenin, a fellow-contributor to *Novoye vremya* who was always attacking Chekhov in that newspaper, thus infringing literary etiquette. Even his friend Shcheglov was spreading gossip about him. These were not human beings, but "a sort of mildew". Tending to overreact—even perhaps to relish overreacting—to such slights, Chekhov may have enjoyed St. Petersburg more than he would allow: the trip at least brought a windfall of five hundred roubles in royalties.[4]

Restored to Moscow and good health, Chekhov was busy with an early draft of *The Duel* during February and early March. He also revised *Motley Tales* for a new edition, throwing out a multitude of inferior items. He was complaining of growing old, but was now only "slightly bored" as anticipation of the coming summer, his favourite season, and of fishing prospects alternated with apprehensions.[5] Would he find a suitable *dacha*? Meanwhile a more immediate prospect buoyed him up: a visit to Italy with Suvorin and Suvorin's son Alexis. Having decided on this expedition, he left for St. Petersburg on 11 March in high spirits.

Chekhov goes West
(March–April 1891)

Few subjects more obsessed nineteenth-century Russian intellectuals than "Europe": that is Europe-outside-Russia. Some, the Westernists, were avid devotees of the West: of its cultural, economic, political or religious institutions. Others, the Slavophils, asserted the supremacy of home-grown products. That neither "Slavophil", "Westernist" nor any other label could be applied to the elusive Chekhov does not need saying. Still, he could easily oscillate between admiration and dislike of Europe. Even before quitting Russian soil he had been put in a pro-Western mood in St. Petersburg by a performance of Shakespeare's *Antony and Cleopatra*, in Italian, starring the Italian actress Eleonora Duse. "I was thoroughly depressed to think that we [Russians] have to educate our temperaments and tastes through wooden actresses ... whom we call 'great' only because we've seen no better. Watching Duse, I could see why the Russian theatre's so boring."[1]

Similar invidious comparisons were suggested to Chekhov by Vienna, his first European city. Arriving on 19 March by luxurious sleeping-car, he admired magnificent architecture which went on for miles in undiminished splendour; fine buildings were not dotted about at random, as at home. The food was excellent, the women elegant; there were milliards of ties in the shop windows and he could make himself understood in German despite having studied it at school. It was exciting, too, to find that he could buy foreign-published Russian books—such as a *Secrets of the Winter Palace*—which would have been banned at home. "It's odd that one can read and say what one likes here";[2] he had made a similar discovery in the Russian Far East, we recall.

These delights were eclipsed by Venice, which the travellers reached on 22 March. Here was the most wonderful city which Chekhov had ever seen. Gliding along the canals by gondola at night, he watched other gondolas and boats festooned with lanterns, while the air throbbed with music. "Guitars, violins, mandolins, men's and women's voices rang out in the darkness. ... The hot, brilliant sunshine beating through open windows and balcony door, the shouts below, the splash of oars, the tolling of bells, the thunder-peals of the noon-tide cannon, the sensation of complete and utter freedom": these were his memories of Venice as evoked in the dénouement to *An Anonymous Story* (1893).[3] Distant sounds, especially music, always tended to move him, and he invokes them repeatedly in his writings. He also wrote, in a letter from Venice, that "in this world of beauty, wealth and freedom your poor downtrodden Russian can easily go off his head. You feel like staying here for ever, and when you stand listening to the organ in church you feel like becoming a Catholic." Venice was ten times cheaper than the Crimea, he claimed; and yet the Crimea was to Venice as a cuttle-fish to a whale.[4]

But then, abruptly, everything changed. Heavy rain sent the travellers scuttling to Bologna, Florence and Rome, where the weather, continuing inclement, did not raise their spirits. Chekhov's long, exuberant letters home now give way to curt notes which show that there is more to this disillusionment than rain. For Chekhov, never one of nature's tourists, is thoroughly ill at ease now that "Baedeker and bad weather have taken over". Too many museums, too many architectural *chefs-d'œuvre* soon pall. Florence is a row of picture and statue shops, and Rome turns out no better. Of the Vatican's eleven thousand rooms he has plodded through thirty or forty, and he feels so sick of it all that he is soon comparing the Eternal City to the ludicrous Kharkov (the Wigan or Pittsburgh of the Ukraine) and saying that he feels like marrying a Dutch girl. Wearying of the alien cuisine, he hungers for good old Russian cabbage stew and buckwheat gruel. And the sheer expense of foreign travel further depresses him. Since Suvorin Senior insists on living "like a doge or a cardinal", Chekhov looks like spending a thousand roubles on a six-week holiday which might otherwise have cost a mere three hundred.[5]

The seamy side of Italian tourism is reflected in Chekhov's story *Ariadne* (1895). "Rains and cold weather set in. . . . We stopped in Venice, Bologna and Florence . . . invariably found ourselves at expensive hotels . . . charged extra for lighting, service, heating . . . ate an enormous amount . . . dashed round museums and exhibitions, haunted by the fear of being late for lunch or dinner. . . . Like gorged boa-constrictors, we only noticed things that glittered. Shop windows mesmerized us, we were fascinated by cheap brooches and bought a lot of useless junk."[6] Such thoughts oppressed Chekhov as he continued to trudge round Rome. He dutifully visited St. Peter's, the Capitol, the Colosseum, the Forum and a night club, only to proclaim himself disappointed, footsore and suffering from backache. But his morale recovered in Naples. The view of the bay reminded him of Hong Kong; he marvelled at the sharks and octopuses in the Aquarium. The 6th of April found him in Pompeii, praising the ancient world (a compliment rare indeed from him) for combining simplicity with comfort and beauty. Emboldened by the local red wine, he rode to the foot of Vesuvius on horseback, toiled up the volcano on foot and sent his sister a masterly description of the crater. "Acrid white smoke surges forth, sparks and red-hot stones spatter out, while Satan lies snoring below.

There's quite a mixture of sounds: beating surf, thundering skies, a clattering train, crashing planks. It's absolutely terrifying, yet you feel like leaping into its very maw. Now I believe in hell."7

Returning north by way of Rome, Chekhov and the Suvorins halted at Nice and visited the tables at Monte Carlo. Here, too, early enthusiasm quickly gave way to disillusionment. A modest flutter on 13 April caused Chekhov to lose forty francs, to praise the casino's magnificent appointments, and to plan an entire year's gambling. But two days later he had lost five hundred francs after devising an "infallible" system, and Monte Carlo was looking like a luxurious water-closet. By now Chekhov the puritan was taking over again, and he reported himself "terribly fed up with lunching, dining and sleeping". Siberian travel had been better, offering none of these cloying amenities. "There you don't get anything to eat, and so you feel as if you had wings." Sated with too much food in Nice, he commented that "every morsel is liberally garnished with artichokes, truffles, nightingales' tongues and the like. Lord above us, how contemptible and loathsome this life is with its artichokes, palms and smell of orange-trees. . . . There's something in the air which, you feel, offends your sense of decency while vulgarizing nature, the roar of the sea and the moon."8 As these remarks remind us, the activities of eating and drinking are, in Chekhov's fiction, almost a monopoly of characters who appear to have incurred their creator's disapproval. In *An Anonymous Story* the French Riviera is described as "all so alien, so impassive . . . all such a clutter", with its over-dressed, heavily perfumed women waiting to be "picked up", while demi-mondaines and females in their dotage swarm round the gold at the tables like flies round honey.9

Before returning to Russia, Chekhov managed a few days in Paris. They included the first Easter which (he said) he had ever spent away from his relatives; and coincided with street riots during which the distinguished Russian sightseer, mistaken for a trouble-maker, was briefly manhandled by a gendarme. Undeterred, he went to a picture exhibition which persuaded him that his friend Levitan was a "king" by comparison with French landscape-painters; in the short-sighted Chekhov's defence it must be added that he was without his pince-nez at the time. His general verdict on Paris and its entertainments was as follows. "Persons girding themselves with boa-constrictors, ladies kicking their feet up to the ceiling, flying people, lions, night-clubs, dinners and lunches begin to nauseate me. It's time to go home; I want to work."10

In view of so many adverse reactions so frankly expressed in so many letters, Chekhov should not have been surprised to find, on returning to Russia, that rumours of his disillusionment with Western Europe were being bandied about. But surprised he was, and no little irritated, to learn how he had remarked, in the Piazza San Marco in Venice, that he would rather be lolling in the grass somewhere in the countryside near Moscow. Then again, the philosopher Merezhkovsky, who had chanced to meet him in Italy, was reporting his general attitude as inadequately exalted; instead of gushing away in the prescribed fashion about how wonderful it all was, Anton Pavlovich had been absorbed by such trivialities as the intriguingly bald head of a local guide. What on earth, asked Chekhov, did they want him to do? Go round bellowing with delight? Breaking shop windows? Embracing the natives? Why, he had never uttered one word expressing this supposed dislike of foreign countries which was now being bruited about the universe! So he protested. In fact he had uttered many hundreds of such words; and many another hundred expressing his pleasure.[11]

"Dacha" Life
(May–September 1891)

Increasingly weary of urban life, Chekhov had decided to spend the whole summer of 1891 in the country, but without going as far afield as his previous rural refuge at Luka. He therefore applied to his brother Michael, now newly-appointed tax inspector to the small town of Aleksin, about ninety miles south of Moscow. Michael obediently rented a local *dacha* by the River Oka, and Anton moved in on 3 May, only to find the accommodation unsuitable. The cottage was too small, too far from the river, too near the railway station. Despite good angling and mushroom-picking prospects, despite the ever-entertaining pranks of the mongooses, it was clearly going to be "boring and sad" here. How insipid it seemed to one who had tasted the delights of foreign travel! Pining for Venice, Florence and Vesuvius, Chekhov remained prey to his usual money worries. The European trip had left him eight hundred roubles in debt to Suvorin, and when he sat down to write in order to meet this and other obligations he found himself torn between his work on Sakhalin and the more profitable *Duel.*[1]

From the rigours of the *dacha* at Aleksin the Chekhovs were rescued by a lucky accident. A certain Ye. D. Bylim-Kolosovsky—a neighbouring landowner previously unknown to Chekhov, but an admirer of his work— chanced to hear of his predicament, and offered to rent him the first floor of his magnificent eighteenth-century mansion at Bogimovo, about eight miles away. This involved extra expense: justified in the event, for there seemed no end to the amenities of Bogimovo with its river, pond, park, church, piano and billiard table. But all paled beside the house itself, so large that your voice echoed from one side of the ballroom to the other. Chekhov has described that room exactly in his *Artist's Story* (1896), where he speaks of a "huge colonnaded ballroom with no furniture except the wide sofa on which I slept and the table where I played patience. Even in calm weather the ancient pneumatic stoves were always droning away and in a storm the whole house shuddered as if shaking to bits." Unconducive to work though this palace sounds, it did not prove so in fact. Chekhov would rise at four in the morning and start writing, often on a window-sill, as he pressed on with *The Duel* and *Sakhalin Island*.[2]

In *The Artist's Story* Chekhov depicts the helpful squire of Bogimovo in an unflattering light, as "Belokurov", described as affecting peasant dress and talking in a tiresomely argumentative tone. Chekhov also introduced his landlord's wife or mistress into the story, portraying her as "podgy, stout and solemn, not unlike a fattened goose".[3] As people were beginning to discover, there were penalties for becoming associated with the major active Russian fiction-writer of the age. Not usually an inconsiderate man, Chekhov did occasionally include in his work portraits, inadequately disguised and uncomplimentary, of his friends and associates.

Tedious though the landlord might be, he had other tenants whom Chekhov appreciated: especially V. A. Wagner, a young zoologist. Still keenly interested in science, Chekhov engaged in long debates with this future professor, a Darwinist, on the survival of the fittest and natural selection. While Wagner maintained that the decline of a species was irreversible once degeneration had set in, Chekhov held that the human spirit could triumph over inherited defects through will-power and educa-tion. In *The Duel*, which he was now completing, Chekhov attributes Wagner's views on natural selection to one of the characters, the zoologist von Koren.[4] This puritanical, self-righteous, fanatical scholar sets himself to exterminate the story's other main figure: the slovenly, sloppy, sexually casual, slipper-shuffling, beer-guzzling, thoroughly degenerate Layevsky. Their conflict culminates in the fiasco of an abortive duel, being the most superb quarrel ever to have come from the pen of an author who, unquarrelsome himself, is a masterly evoker of mutual animosity. That Chekhov indeed did seek, somewhat feebly, to champion the power of the human spirit to overcome degeneracy is confirmed by the story's dénoue-ment, in which a suddenly reformed Layevsky is shown reconciled to a mollified von Koren and dedicated to reversing the course of a hitherto misspent life. But this newly achieved concord is insipidly described, rather in the manner of *The Wood Demon*'s jolly last act. Here, in the finale of *The Duel*, is perhaps the worst writing to be found in any of Chekhov's mature work: a reminder that endings always came hard to him, whether in plays or in stories. Significantly, *The Duel*'s successful first ninety-odd pages are those in which he confines himself to presenting his problems. The trouble comes when, in the last ninety-odd lines, he tries to solve them: a mistake never to be repeated in so crude a form.

Contact with the zoologist Wagner also involved Chekhov in public controversy under an assumed name. Primed by his new friend, he wrote for *Novoye vremya* a pseudonymous article, "Tricksters", exposing with vehemence more typical of his nature than is generally allowed the scandalous mismanagement of the Moscow Zoo. This was, to judge from Chekhov's article, being run on the lines of the hospital in his own future story *Ward Number Six*: with rubbish, slop buckets, bits of cages, discarded galoshes, broken crockery and animal bones strewn all over the place. Indignantly denouncing such squalor, Chekhov makes clear his overriding concern for scientific integrity by arguing that a properly run zoo should above all be an arena for serious scholarly endeavour.[5]

During the Bogimovo months Chekhov seems to have worked as hard as at any other period in his career. But there were also relaxations in the usual fishing, bathing, picnicking and mushroom-picking. To these were added amateur theatricals; torchlight processions in the park; roulette with one copeck as maximum stake; the antics of the mongooses as they hid slippers, peed in hats, and on one occasion even slew a snake. Once again we have the picture of a lively, happy, active, industrious family. Mariya is busy with her painting; Mother bustles round the house; Father discusses the latest doings of ecclesiastical dignitaries; brothers Ivan and Michael make themselves useful;[6] guests come and go, including Suvorin.

Though Chekhov's personal relations with Suvorin remained excellent, publication of *The Duel* put an unforeseen strain on their professional dealings in autumn 1891. Only with reluctance had Chekhov consigned this work to *Novoye vremya*, feeling that he had no alternative after accepting from Suvorin advances which had not been paid off. Otherwise he could have obtained better terms elsewhere; besides, a story so lengthy was far less suitable for a daily newspaper such as *Novoye vremya* than for a Thick Journal, where it would not have had to be published in instalments. That necessity gave other contributors to *Novoye vremya* a grudge against Chekhov, for they considered that his serial was monopolizing "their" space by appearing on each Tuesday and Wednesday with no sign of ever coming to an end. Incensed by such petty jealousy, Chekhov asked his brother Alexander to see that *The Duel* was published on one day a week only. "Ask Suvorin to let them have the Wednesdays. What do I need with them? I have as little use for them as for my entire work on *Novoye vremya*, which has done me nothing but harm as a writer."[7]

Despite several earlier complaints by Chekhov about Suvorin and his paper, these harsh words come as a shock. Obviously *Novoye vremya* was due to fall by the wayside before long, just as *Oskolki* and *Peterburgskaya gazeta* had fallen before it. But Chekhov did follow *The Duel* with another, shorter, story written at Bogimovo for Suvorin's paper: *Peasant Women*.

It was, the author claimed, inspired less by a yearning for sweet sounds than by a longing to squeeze money out of someone quickly. Here is the last of Chekhov's peasant stories to be written before he began living among the peasants of Melikhovo in 1892. But it was boring to write about muzhiks, he said. Generals would make a more interesting subject.[8]

Moscow and Famine
(September 1891–March 1892)

In September 1891 Chekhov returns from Bogimovo to his Moscow base and remains there, apart from a few brief excursions, until he moves to his country estate at Melikhovo six months later. During September he works on *An Anonymous Story*; but puts it aside at the end of the month through fear of censorship, since "the Narrator is a former Socialist".[1] His other main literary achievements of late 1891 are two notable shorter stories: *My Wife* and *The Butterfly*. The latter is particularly outstanding, and both have significant links with his non-literary evolution. *The Anniversary* also belongs to this period, and is his last completed one-act farce.

Chekhov has described *My Wife* as "a topical story about famine victims",[2] the famine being that which ravaged southern and eastern European Russia in winter 1891-2. He showed concern over this in October, planning to visit the stricken areas at once. He also supported a literary symposium, *Aid to the Starving*, to which we remember him contributing a single chapter from his future *Sakhalin Island*. Then he wrote *My Wife*, only to contract severe influenza in mid-November. Compelled to postpone his tour of the famine provinces, he started a subscription in aid of the victims in co-operation with a former suitor of his sister's, Ye. P. Yegorov, a retired artillery officer who now held an administrative post in a remote corner of Nizhny Novgorod Province. Yegorov and Chekhov planned to discourage the local peasants from slaughtering their starving horses by buying up these beasts, keeping them fed through the winter, and then giving them back in the spring so that the next year's ploughing could take place. Their idea was, in other words, to forestall a potential famine in the winter of 1892-3 rather than to relieve the actual famine of 1891-2. The two friends faced many difficulties. These included governmental policy, for the authorities were incapable of taking effective measures themselves and were busy pretending that the crisis did not exist. Meanwhile they were thwarting private relief initiatives as involving the administration in loss of face.[3]

On 15 January 1892 Chekhov at last reached Nizhny Novgorod. He and Yegorov sledged through the backwoods on their errand of mercy; losing their way in a blizzard one day, they risked becoming snowbound and freezing to death. Then Chekhov, as befitted a touring celebrity, was regaled with a farewell dinner by the provincial Governor, and driven off to Nizhny Novgorod railway station in that dignitary's own carriage. The impact of his activities on famine relief had been slight. Nor did his second relief expedition, to Voronezh Province in early February, produce significant results. It was Nizhny Novgorod all over again, with another banquet at the Governor's and the usual swapping of famine stories. But a little more was being done for the peasants here, though Chekhov himself spent every evening at the theatre.[4]

As these excursions showed, it was the food-producers who suffered most from Russian famines. Members of the gentry, officials, other professional men and privileged persons were less likely to go hungry than to be found arguing amiably about the horrors of the famine over a multi-course dinner. The point is underlined in Chekhov's *My Wife*, where the wealthy landowning hero, much concerned with the peasant's plight, is seen dining with a fellow-squire. While the muzhiks are dropping dead of starvation in the village around them, these guzzling philanthropists dispose of sucking pig, horse-radish, sour cream, cabbage stew, pork, buckwheat gruel, pie, home-made liqueurs, pigeon, tripe, duck, partridge, cauliflower, fruit dumplings, curds and whey, jelly, pancakes and jam.[5] But here was an instance of life imitating art: the orgy cannot have been inspired by the Governors' dinners at Nizhny Novgorod and Voronezh, for these were held after the story's publication on New Year's Day 1892.

Kind-hearted by nature, Chekhov could yet treat his friends inconsiderately on occasion, as we have seen. In *The Butterfly*, written in November 1891, he again tactlessly exploited a real-life relationship. We remember the three people concerned as accompanying him on the train from Moscow to Yaroslavl at the beginning of his journey to Sakhalin: the painter Levitan; Levitan's mistress Sophia Kuvshinnikov; Sophia's husband, a police doctor. Their situation is mirrored in the story, where the artist Ryabovsky corresponds to Levitan, the flighty Olga Dymov to Sophia and the cuckolded Dr. Dymov to Dr. Kuvshinnikov. *The Butterfly* appeared in an illustrated weekly, *Sever* ("The North"), in January 1892, provoking great scandal in Moscow and causing Chekhov, that disliker of fuss, to "choke from boredom and various bothers. Believe it or not, an acquaintance of mine (a 42-year-old woman) has recognized herself in my *Butterfly*'s heroine, aged twenty, and all Moscow is accusing me of libel. The main incriminating factor is external similarity: the lady paints, her husband is a doctor and she lives with an artist."[6]

Chekhov might bluster, but he had not even tried to camouflage the original models for his characters. He described Olga Dymov's dining-room as decked out in folksy Russian style with sickles and ornamental towels; he showed her silent husband, who did the housework, coming in to tell the guests when supper was ready. These and other details were directly drawn from the Kuvshinnikov ménage, no matter that he had docked twenty-two years off his heroine's age. That he had suffered belated twinges of author's conscience is shown by minor changes made to the proofs of *The Butterfly*. But it was no use giving his Olga "lovely flaxen hair" when Sophia's hair was dark, and making Ryabovsky's eyes blue whereas Levitan's were black. It was still abundantly clear whom he had in mind. So offended was the fiery Levitan that he nearly challenged Chekhov to a duel. The two men were not on speaking terms for three years, after which they were reconciled by their mutual friend Tatyana Shchepkin-Kupernik. Her own very reasonable view of the quarrel was that the victims should have forgiven Chekhov more easily since the story is a masterpiece.[7]

Chekhov's health and morale sank even lower in the winter of 1891-2 than in the previous year. His severe bout of influenza hung on for six weeks, from mid-November until the end of the year, and there was now reason to suspect lung complications. He feared that his "former good health" might never return; he complained of deafness, headaches, back-ache, sneezing, coughing. He looked like the corpse of a drowned man. He no longer wanted his usual night-cap—two glasses of spirits. Was this old age? Or was it "something worse"?[8] And his irritation with Moscow had increased. He sent Suvorin a bilious and disparaging article on Musco-vite affairs: "In Moscow". Pseudonymously published in *Novoye vremya*, it briefly revived, in a sense, his column on Moscow life once contributed to Leykin's *Oskolki*.[9]

By now Chekhov no longer wanted to quit Moscow for a few months; he wanted to abandon the city permanently and make a new home else-where. He even turned against his one surviving mongoose: "Ah, friends, how bored I am. As a doctor I need patients and a hospital. As a writer I need to live among peasants, not in the Malaya Dmitrovka with a mongoose." As for being cooped up within four walls, without Nature, without people, without health, without a country to call his own, without appetite: it was no life, that, but a "sort of [. . .]": something so unmention-able that the word has been censored out of his *Works*.[10] And yet, despite these complaints of leading an inadequate social life and of knowing no "people", he was as irritated as ever by the importunities of visitors and guests whom he would surely have put off had he not, at some level of his consciousness, needed their company as much as he resented it.

Chekhov saw three major advantages in a country home: it would benefit his health; drastically curtail his expenses; enable him to practise medicine among the peasantry. This last urge had become a fixation. But why was medical practice so much more attractive in rural surroundings? Probably because the need for doctors in the Russian villages was especially acute.

In January 1892 Chekhov nearly bought, at long last, a farm near Sorochintsy in the Ukraine. We remember this project first cropping up four years previously. But he was no longer interested in a mere holiday home: he was planning to move to the Ukraine permanently. Having got word of a suitable property, he sent his sister to inspect the place, announced his intention of moving in March, and had even begun packing when the vendor, one Yatsenko, backed out at the last moment.[11] Perhaps he was doing Chekhov a good turn, for however much that reluctant metropolitan might dislike the big cities, he still needed easy access to Moscow and St. Petersburg. Isolated in the depths of the Ukraine, he would have found his professional and social life grievously impaired. And yet he had been eager to acquire this remote Ukrainian property, which he had not even seen, as his permanent residence: an indication of the haste and imprudence which he very occasionally showed in arranging his affairs.

It was in the same frenetic mood that Chekhov pursued, this time successfully, the purchase of another property which came on to the market at the time: the estate of Melikhovo, conveniently situated in Moscow Province. By early March 1892 Melikhovo's new owner was ready to move house.

CHAPTER NINE

Melikhovo 1892–7: Patterns of Life

With the move to Melikhovo Chekhov embarks on his most important phase as a short-story writer.

We can easily say when his Melikhovo period began: on 4 March 1892, which was when he took up residence. But it is harder to decide when it ended. Was it with his breakdown in health of March 1897, the crisis which was to make him a permanent invalid or semi-invalid? This is the solution adopted here, though Chekhov was to reside at Melikhovo off and on for a further two and a half years before departing for good in July 1899.

During Chekhov's Melikhovo years the Emperor Alexander III was to die and give way to his son Nicholas II. This replacement of a bluff, herculean conservative by a diminutive and less effectual conservative disappointed those who had hoped for the official unscrambling of traditional controls, yet somehow provoked a general feeling of relaxation. From now on Russians were to take their autocratic government less and less seriously, while it still tried to take itself as seriously as ever. On Chekhov, so detached from politics and public affairs, the advent of his third sovereign was to make as little impact in 1894 as had the assassination of the first and the accession of the second in 1881.

Landowner, Family Man and Host

Melikhovo provided stability. Only there did the adult Chekhov ever possess a true home, a base conceived neither as temporary nor as a place of exile from some more desired locality. Conscious of his peasant ancestry, he was now at last settled in the countryside which he loved; he was living and working among the peasants, whom he served without ignoring their faults. We shall find him practising as their doctor, and building them schools. We shall also find him surrounded by his family, and by the countless guests who still irritated and entertained him. Thus did Chekhov—the townsman, the urban nomad, the dweller in rented property—suddenly put down his roots. At a stroke he had become property-owner, farmer, squire, gardener, estate-manager, country doctor, architect, employer of labour, head of an established household.

So casual, so sudden—so frantic, almost—was the purchase of Melikhovo that the enterprise seems to have owed more to luck than judgement. By early 1892 Chekhov had become desperate to leave Moscow for the country, and haste now transcended all other considerations. That the Melikhovo property chanced to be a sizeable agricultural holding was a mere detail: seldom did anyone drift more accidentally into the role of gentleman farmer. Anton saw the estate advertised in a newspaper and gave his family an ultimatum: either they went straight out there and arranged to purchase the property on his behalf, or he would go and live abroad. He completed the formalities without setting eyes on the place, paying his first flying visit on 26 February, only six days before moving in. Nor, when previously viewing the property, had Mariya and Michael managed to conduct an adequate inspection in the deep snow of late winter, a season when no sane man bought a Russian estate.[1]

How accessible was Melikhovo from Moscow, nearly fifty miles away to the north? Even this point was obscure when Chekhov moved in. That there were five or six train services a day between the city and Lopasnya (now called Chekhov, the nearest small town) he was aware. But what of the six-mile journey by horse and trap between Lopasnya and his manor? It was easy to sledge through on snow, but what of the thaws? Many Russian villages were cut off from the world by the atrocious mud swamps of spring and autumn; and for all Chekhov could tell he might be marooned on his estate in rainy summer weather as well. What if the "road" to Lopasnya should turn out another *trakt*? In fact the journey was to prove manageable, though uncomfortable. Chekhov kept his own horses and traps at the manor, and would send a man over to fetch his visitors; or a vehicle and driver could be hired at Lopasnya station for one rouble per trip.

Precise information on the new property, a farm of 575 acres, was hard to come by at first. Just where were its boundaries? How much of it was woodland? As the snow melted Chekhov was amazed to find himself owner of a lime avenue and a straw rick. Arable land and a park, orchards and a garden, woodland and scrubland, emerged. There were too many fences; there were sturdy outbuildings. But it soon became clear that the place had been neglected by its previous owner, the artist Sorokhtin. Fields and livestock, especially the horses, were in poor shape; so was the house, with painting and wallpaper-hanging to do, with stoves to rebuild and floors to re-lay.

Chekhov's farm-house may still be inspected, now as a museum dedicated to his memory. Restored to a condition approximating to that which he knew, it is a charming, unpretentious, wooden, iron-roofed, one-storey structure: a large L-shaped bungalow rather than a mansion. The biggest room, the drawing-room, opens on to a terrace. The second largest room, on a corner with three windows facing south, was Chekhov's study. He had a small bedroom of his own, as also did Mariya, his mother and his father. There was a dining-room, a larder, a hall, a corridor; there were two lobbies; there was the "Pushkin Room", so-called from the poet's portrait which hung there.[2] At times, especially in summer, guests slept all over the place, including the corridor; it was fortunate that the servants' quarters and the kitchen were in separate premises.

Chekhov's financial position, never clear, was complicated by this purchase. The estate cost 13,000 roubles, to which incidental expenses added another thousand, the operation being triply financed: by a personal loan from Suvorin; by a bank loan; by a mortgage from the vendor. It was a large debt, but could be repaid from current earnings now that the rent for Moscow flats and holiday cottages no longer had to be found. There would be a new income, too, from farming. And expensive though seeds of clover and oats might seem, the business was favoured by amazingly cheap local labour. With a mere five roubles a month to pay for a gardener or odd-job-man, Chekhov was appreciating "the charms of capitalism". No wonder, for he could cover a day's work by one man by writing ten words. What author might not be a model farmer and estate-owner under those conditions?[3]

On this rural backwater the Chekhovs descended with the zest of hereditary peasants long cut off from the land. "A creative life of arduous toil" began at once,[4] with a rigorous division of labour among the residents, permanent and temporary. Michael handled the field work, so neglecting his local tax-inspecting duties that he had trouble from his superiors. Yet he somehow made time for ploughing. He would rise at three in the morning; direct the muzhiks; ride round supervising operations. With his help the Chekhovs raised rye, wheat, clover, oats and buckwheat. Like an American frontier community of the period they were—or at least felt that they could become—self-sufficient. They ate bread baked by Chekhov's mother from wheat grown by his brother, and in old age Mariya Chekhov still retained a linen towel made from their own flax.

Mariya grew the vegetables, including aubergines, peppers, gherkins, tomatoes, artichokes, peas, potatoes, cabbages, pumpkins, marrows. We see this "fragile, tender girl" striding about in hulking men's boots.[5] She also marshalled painters, decorators, tilers, stovemakers and the like. But the busiest Chekhov was perhaps the mother. She rose first, she went to bed last; she presided over her kitchen, having an aged cook and two maids under command, but working hard herself. Her hospitality, the abundance of excellent food at her table, were renowned: never mind the disparagement of good cheer implied in much of Anton's fiction. Rising early, the family was ready for the main meal at noon sharp: a special bell, mounted on a post and audible for many a verst around, would summon toilers and strollers from the distant fields.[6] As for Paul Chekhov, now retired, he was no longer a domestic tyrant, having accepted his third son's role as provider and effective head of the house. Paul too worked about the estate, clearing the paths of snow and weeds. Installed in his small room, he would read folio lives of the saints; burn incense; chant the Orthodox litany. He also logged all the comings and goings in a diary.

Anton himself appreciated his crops as embellishments to his landscape and supplements to his income. But he was no true farmer: more of a *dachnik* (holiday visitor to the country). And though he could sell much of his produce, he soon decided that no Russian landowner could show a profit from his estate unless himself prepared to roll up his sleeves and work like a peasant: a remark which reminds us of Alyokhin in *Concerning Love* (1898). Chekhov was a horticulturalist rather than a farmer. He bought young trees in quantity: fifty cherries, a hundred lilacs, eighty apples; some were destroyed by hares, but restocking proceeded apace. He also asked his sister to bring seeds of fir, pine, larch and oak from Moscow, and cultivated these. He lopped dead branches, felled dead trees, developed muscles suitable for a circus strong man. Pruning roses was also among his skills, and he planted tulips, lilies, daffodils, hyacinths and irises in quantity. Never had his friend Tatyana Shchepkin-Kupernik known a man so devoted to flowers as Chekhov; or, she might have added, to fish. For Chekhov, that compulsive angler, was stocking his ponds with tiny tench and other fry brought from Moscow in jars.[7]

This was all good copy for the heavily horticultural background of Chekhov's horrific story *The Black Monk*, written at Melikhovo. And it all sounds most idyllic, what with dear old Mother busily pickling mushrooms while dear old Dad, that mellowed former tyrant, pores over the lives of the saints in his incense-impregnated den. Sister Mariya, employed on socially useful labour as a Moscow schoolmistress during the week, spends all her weekends and holidays beavering away at Melikhovo: cleaning, painting, furbishing, instructing maids and workmen, until everything shines like a new pin. Unheedful of his tax-inspecting job, brother Michael sturdily ploughs up the neglected acres. While the two dachshunds, Bromide and Quinine, successors to the mongooses which have now passed from the scene, are merrily distributing everyone's galoshes all over the premises,[8] the master of the house bravely stifles his tubercular cough, writes his stories, doses his peasants, builds his schools, prunes his roses, catches his tench, keeps his guests in constant fits of laughter. "Anton was up and about at crack of dawn"; "Anton was an inexhaustible fount of merry jokes and wisecracks": such is the atmosphere conjured up by Mariya and Michael Chekhov, by Tatyana Shchepkin-Kupernik and by many another memoirist of Melikhovo. What with everyone so usefully, so happily employed at so many varied occupations during their entire waking hours, what with all the jolly teasing, explosive laughter, wholesome country food, adoring muzhiks, admiring neighbours, what with the high spirits, the bustle and the enthusiasm, we seem to have stumbled on some Golden Age.

However true or false this picture may be, no one familiar with Chekhov's works can contemplate it without recalling one of the master's favourite formulae as applied to writing which creates a false tone. "Things do not happen like this in real life."

That the atmosphere of Melikhovo was not in fact so uniformly hearty and euphoric we learn from many indications in Chekhov's letters. For instance, his father irritated him more than is commonly allowed. That Paul Yegorovich remained a figure of fun Anton and Alexander agreed; between themselves they still referred to him by comic nicknames deriving from his former tempestuous and imperious temper. And though this had indeed mellowed with age, the dear old chap was ordering the workmen about in tones suggesting that he was taking them off to be flogged. Nor could Anton forget the cruel beatings which his father had so freely administered in the old Taganrog days—from the best of motives, of course. But correct though relations between father and son now were, Chekhov secretly despised the old man. When friends claimed to recognize Laptev, the craggy old merchant in *Three Years* (1895), as a portrait of his father, the author protested. His father was no Laptev, said he; and it was now that he described Paul Chekhov as having remained until the end of his days the pedestrian mediocrity which he had always been. As for clashes of opinion between mediocrity-father and genius-son, the most eloquent incident occurred over a meal, when Paul began abusing educa-tion. He said that uneducated people were to be preferred to educated. Perhaps he had been reading Dostoyevsky? In any case this expression of opinion was bound to offend a son so concerned with progress and intellec-tual advancement that he was busy building village schools. Anton got up from table and silently left the room, thus cutting short his father's flow of reactionary eloquence.[9]

Though Chekhov made no similar complaints about other members of his family, there were difficulties with them too. These are most vividly invoked in an astonishing letter to him from his brother Alexander.

Alexander had arrived for a short stay at Melikhovo on 3 June 1893, only to storm out in a huff several days later in the wake of a family quarrel. The details of this clash of Chekhovs do not matter; they revolved around disagreements about feeding dogs and harnessing horses. The main point of Alexander's letter is the complete lack of understanding, as he sees it, between Anton and all the three members of his family—mother, father and sister—for whom the Melikhovo house was a permanent home.

> I'm very sorry for you [Alexander writes]. . . . I suffered constantly from what I saw of you and your hideous way of life. . . . They all wish you well, every one of them, but it all adds up to total absence of rapport. These misunderstandings, these mutual insults . . . these unavoidable sufferings, these hollow sighs and bitter tears: they can only be reconciled by your departure. Mother comprehends you not at all, and she never will. She suffers deeply . . . but only because you're unwell and therefore irritable. She'll never rise to understanding your mentality. . . . At all costs you must keep your soul alive. Throw it all up: your dreams of country life, your love of Melikhovo, the labours and emotions expended there. Melikhovo isn't the only place in the world. What good will it do if these monsters consume your soul as rats devour tallow candles? . . . As for Our Father, the less said about Him the better.[10]

Lack of rapport with the father need not surprise us in view of the old man's character and past treatment of his children. With the mother too, despite her greater kindness, no high degree of communion could be expected: fond as the old lady was of Anton, his deeper concerns transcended her limited horizons. What more astonishes us is Alexander's scathing verdict on Anton–Mariya relations. According to her own and many other accounts these were a model of brotherly and sisterly affection. And why not? It was not just that Mariya adored her brother; she was also an educated woman who could appreciate his subtler writings and enter his more complex preoccupations. So one might have thought. But Alexander will have none of it. "I'm sure of one thing: your relationship with Mariya is false," he tells Anton. "One kind word from you ringing with conviction, and she's completely at your feet. She's afraid of you and she looks at you with such humble and sincere eyes."[11]

False! This idyll of brotherly-sisterly love *false*? Since Alexander found Mariya's emotional dependence on Anton so excessive, a modern biographer is compelled to ask at this point whether any potentially incestuous element can be discerned in the relationship between Chekhov and the sister who shared his home. Anton was certainly the main man in Mariya Chekhov's life, and when he eventually married in 1901 she was to show jealousy and resentment of the woman who ousted her as part-time mistress of his household. But though these facts may alone suffice to persuade enthusiastic Freudians that Mariya must, if only subconsciously, have been sexually attracted by her brother, available evidence does nothing whatever to support such a speculation. Nor, to put it mildly, are there indications of such an attraction in the opposite direction—an attraction which might, had it existed, help to explain Anton's long delay in taking a wife. Whatever deterred him from wedlock it was surely not an emotional attachment to his sister, let alone one sufficiently strong to make other women seem undesirable. Far from it, for all indications show his attitude to Mariya as off-hand rather than passionate. He tended to take her for granted, being what many sisters might call a typical brother, and treating her more as a convenient housekeeper than as the object of clandestine desire. It is true that he was several times instrumental in preventing her from marrying, but his motive—in so far as it was selfish—seems to have been her value to him as a domestic asset, not as the target for a guilty passion. Chekhov was not, as we have often indicated, a sensual man, and the idea of him secretly lusting for his sister is preposterous. It runs contrary to everything which is known of his character as well as to all the available evidence.

We remember Anton detaching his obedient sister from two somewhat unsatisfactory suitors of the 1880s: Ye. P. Yegorov, then an artillery officer, and the painter Levitan. Now, during the Melikhovo years, she received a more attractive marriage offer. It came from Alexander Smagin, Ukrainian landowner and friend of the Chekhovs since their first visit to Luka in 1888. Liking him enough to consider him a possible husband, Mariya told Anton that she intended to accept this proposal: not because her mind was indeed made up, but because she wanted to sound his reactions and needed his counsel. His response was total silence—and silence combined with a mien strongly eloquent of disapproval. During the next few days he made no allusion to the matter whatever, beyond adopting towards poor Mariya a manner markedly less jocular and more aloof than was his wont. Subjected to this nerve warfare, she decided in some agony of spirit to turn Smagin down. Her motives were love for her brother and reluctance to disrupt the excellent working routine which she had always tried to create for him. To this extent Mariya sacrificed marriage and motherhood to look after her beloved brother.

Anton, says Mariya, "obviously did not guess what complicated emotions obsessed me at the time".[12] Perhaps not. But a better brother— that rarity—surely would have guessed. Deliberately or not, Anton had imposed his will by evading an issue crucially important to the sister who had sought his guidance. Was his carefully disseminated air of disapproval a deliberate stratagem—was it indeed designed to retain her services as a convenient housekeeper? And without compromising himself by making so selfish a claim explicit? If so, this episode was exceptional, for it must rate as the unkindest single act in a life happily marked by few instances of comparable inconsiderateness.

In any case the conventional picture of Melikhovo, as an unalloyed idyll of domestic harmony, must be firmly rejected. But we need not leap to the contrary conclusion that Melikhovo was a hell on earth. Nor was it as bad as Alexander hastily described it, on a single occasion, in an incoherently written letter composed when he was distressed and possibly drunk. As for the alleged disharmony between Anton and his family, such a failure to achieve communion—and not least between close relatives—is a major theme in his work. Why, then, should it not have been a theme of his life? Even without Alexander's testimony it is obvious that neither Mariya nor Michael could vibrate in sympathy with Anton. Their flat, cliché-peddling reminiscences lack the sparkle generated by the two elder brothers. Not that the memoirs of the younger siblings should be judged too harshly, for both may be presumed (especially those of the later-published Mariya) to have undergone "ghosting" designed to infuse them with the high degree of decorum appropriate to a major Cult Figure as processed by the literary officials of a totalitarian state. Still, when all allowances have been made for possible interference it is abundantly evident—if only from their unghosted letters—that neither Mariya nor Michael could ever have been a soul-mate to Anton. Of his irony, subtlety, resonance and independence of mind these poor creatures had about as much as a stagnant pond; and the sardonic Alexander, of all people, was best equipped to appreciate this—much as he liked his sister, and in some ways admired her.

Melikhovo offered other amusements besides family quarrels: fishing, bathing, mushrooming, picnicking. There were outings to the near-by onion-domed monastery of St. David's, there were visits to neighbours. One local lady, a relative of the poet Fet, was an accomplished pianist and would entertain Chekhov with performances of Beethoven's "Moonlight Sonata".[13] Austere and unsentimental in his literary tastes, Chekhov did not apply such standards to music, where he was a romantic. At Melikhovo too there was piano-playing and singing. Besides listening to such performances directly, Chekhov also liked to hear music in the distance when working in his study; which recalls the theme of distant music so frequently evoked in his stories and plays.

Visitors were both the joy and the curse of Melikhovo. Was Chekhov a solitary man who craved company? Or a gregarious man who craved solitude? He would have answered these questions in different ways at different times. A mixture of inconsistencies like most human beings, he was more divided in his attitude to hospitality than to almost anything else. We remember him leaving Moscow in order to avoid the visitors who pestered him day in day out; "it was guests that drove me out of

Moscow". And yet, once established in his rural retreat, he writes letter after letter begging his friends—even as he complains of the importunities of other guests—to come and stay at Melikhovo. Pestered by guests at Melikhovo in turn, he builds a small cottage a little distance from his house expressly so that he can work in peace: and then has to use that to accommodate the overflow of visitors. Melikhovo stood on a fairly main road between Serpukhov and Kashira, and Chekhov complains that "every passing intellectual feels in duty bound to call and to warm up, sometimes even to stay the night. . . . It's nice to be hospitable, of course, but there are limits." Yet on another occasion we find him pleased at having become so accepted in the neighbourhood that "people spend the night here when they're passing through".[14]

On the identity of these guests we are exactly informed because they are logged in the diary kept by Paul Chekhov with occasional entries in Anton's hand. They included literary associates: Leykin (who presented Chekhov with his two dachshunds); Suvorin (who found the surroundings inadequately magnificent for his rich man's tastes); the eccentric journalist Gilyarovsky, the novelist Potapenko, the editor Menshikov, Tolstoy's disciple Sergeyenko; the actor Svobodin; Chekhov's brothers Alexander, Ivan and Michael, with or without their wives and families; young women, many of them friends of Mariya's; Cousin George Chekhov from Taganrog. There were hosts of others, too, including an occasional total stranger who somehow established a foothold in this hospitable house. Besides writers, editors, girls, female admirers, local government officials, neighbours, doctor colleagues and distant relatives, a posse of hunters and dogs was liable to "lurch in" at any moment. From such importunities Chekhov suffered torments which he concealed with his usual tact. No doubt, though, he shared the sentiments of his father, who occasionally relieved the bald narrative of his diary with such entries as "glory be to the Almighty, the two fat ladies have left".[15]

Some of Chekhov's comments on this theme are unintentionally comic. "Thank God we have guests from Moscow, or else one might grow petrified with boredom." And this from the man who had fled to Melikhovo precisely in order to escape from Moscow, from Muscovite guests and from Muscovite boredom! Rarely did he show himself aware of his own oscillations in the matter, for at any given moment he was usually pro-guest or anti-guest. Yet there were occasions when he saw more clearly into his own nature as one who could be neither whole-heartedly gregarious nor wholeheartedly solitary. "There are crowds of people at my place and I long for solitude, but when I'm left alone I'm bad-tempered and feel disgusted by the day which has passed. Nothing but food and talk, food and talk all day long."[16]

We find similar ambivalence in the newly established countryman's general morale. He was bored, he was not bored, he was not bored *yet*. He had never been so bored in his life, he had never enjoyed himself so much in his life. Country life was boring in the evenings (but not in the daytime); in winter (but not in summer); for those not engaged on intellectual work (but not for the intellectual). Country life was a hundred times better than city life. He felt old, old, old; he felt so young that he wanted to play around for another couple of years before settling down.[17] But the fact was that he already had settled down, though still often lured by exotic quarters of the globe. Tahiti, Australia, Ceylon, South Africa, Kamchatka, Riga (for the beer), Chicago (for the Exhibition): he wanted to visit all these places at one time or another during his Melikhovo years. Or he would like to become a monk, if only unbelievers were eligible. Meanwhile life was flowing past to no purpose, his friends had all reached senior grades in the civil service, while he had picked up no money, no decorations, no rank: nothing but debts.[18]

And yet, however carefully we may log expressions of regret and disappointment, it is clear that his decision to move into the country had justified itself on balance. Irritated with Melikhovo though he often became, he never spoke of that rural retreat with the vehement exasperation and even hatred which Moscow (so often) and St. Petersburg (sometimes) had provoked in earlier days; which Yalta was to stimulate in yet fuller measure in the years of his decline; and which provincial towns headed by Taganrog inspired throughout his life.

Peasant Benefactor and Chronicler

By making his home in the country Chekhov was reviving and strengthening an important theme which had already appeared sporadically in his life and work: the peasantry.

The peasants formed the largest and most primitive of the social "estates" among which the citizenry of Imperial Russia was distributed in law. As noted above, there was no such thing as a Russian citizen pure and simple. There were Russian gentlemen, Russian clerics, Russian merchants; there were Cossacks, there were military persons; there were officials and students; there were townsfolk of various brands. And there were, above all, peasants. One or other of these classifications would be inscribed in the "passport" which, in a country highly bureaucratized by nineteenth-century standards, every travelling citizen was required to carry for identification purposes. That these regulations were—like almost all nineteenth-century Russian regulations—laxly enforced, Chekhov's own case illustrates, since he himself jogged along for years without being assigned to any official estate. But the majority of his new neighbours were registered as peasants. Those of Melikhovo were just a few score among about a hundred million in the country as a whole, for this was by far the largest social category: 81·5 per cent in a population of about 126 million, as recorded in the 1897 census.

After sheer weight of numbers, the peasantry's second most striking characteristic was primitiveness. Of the rural population aged between nine and forty-nine only 22 per cent were recorded by the same census as able to read and write, the proportion of illiterates being particularly high among women. Still more depressing was peasant health. Chekhov himself once informally reckoned village infant mortality as 60 per cent up to the age of five. And he even claimed that not one single healthy woman might be found among the many millions in the villages, in the factories and in the back streets of the towns:[1] a comment horrifying indeed, since it came from so detached and highly qualified an observer. To illiteracy and poor health we must add desperate poverty, overwork and inadequate nourishment. The atmosphere did not encourage a high standard of morality and social virtue. To call the typical Russian peasant a drunken brute who regularly beat his wife and children might be going too far, but certainly violence and bestial cruelty were common features of village life. Too poor to get drunk very often (the Empire's *per capita* consumption of alcohol was surprisingly low), the peasant was liable to become violently intoxicated when vodka did chance to be available in quantity, as on feast days or at weddings. With him an orgy was an orgy. To these unseemly features may be added a deep-seated, all too understandable, hatred and mistrust of landowners and officials. Yet the peasant was still apt to revere the Tsar— conceived as a remote, semi-divine, vaguely benevolent figure. And the peasant also prized Orthodox Church ritual, which brought colour, music, mystery and consolation to the drab, monochrome, mud-surrounded or snow-bound huts of the village.

It was with some apprehension that the Chekhovs took up residence among these "dark people" with their well-known propensity for murdering landowners and burning down manors: but also, as the event was to prove, for affection and gratitude. Barely established in his new house, with the snow still on the ground, the author-squire accomplished a brilliant stroke of public relations. Melikhovo had a village church, half abandoned and lacking a priest. With Easter, the chief and most beloved event in the Orthodox calendar, just upon them, he had the happy idea of hiring from near-by St. David's Monastery a cleric who agreed to officiate at services in their new parish. Chekhov's father now resumed under happier circumstances his old role as choirmaster, while the entire family, with guests, sang matins and evensong. "The peasants were delighted, and said that none of their services had ever been celebrated with such solemnity."² The episode established the cordial relations which the Chekhovs were to maintain with the local community throughout the Melikhovo years.

The new squire soon sealed this good impression by his work as a doctor. "I have the muzhiks and shopkeepers under my thumb, I've conquered them. One had a haemorrhage from the throat, another had his arm crushed by a tree, a third has a sick little girl. I turned out to be their last hope. They bow to me respectfully, like Germans to their pastor. I treat them kindly and all is well."³ That doctors and hospitals were in desperately short supply in the Russian countryside Chekhov had already been well aware when buying his Melikhovo house; indeed, he had gone to the country expressly to practise medicine "really fundamentally", having so far confined himself to treating the peasantry during occasional holidays. Inevitably the sick of the district soon found their way to his door. Arriving in carts from up to fifteen miles away, they queued at the manor to see Dr. Chekhov, who was assisted by Mariya when available. Treatment and medicine were free, the cost of a dispensary being met by the new doctor, though a grateful patient might reward him for his services with a pig or six pairs of gloves.⁴

Chekhov also did his rounds in the neighbourhood. Like his own Doctor Astrov in *Uncle Vanya*, he travelled at all hours and seasons by horse and trap over the abominable roads of his district. He had learnt, when lying in bed at night, to fear the barking of dogs and the knock on the gate which marked a call on his services. When a peasant was found lying on a near-by road, his body pierced by a pitchfork, he was brought and dumped in Dr. Chekhov's house, the only place where help was available. Then there was the three-year-old boy who had terribly injured himself by sitting in a cauldron of boiling water: thus, perhaps, suggesting to his doctor the murder by scalding of Lipa's baby (*In the Hollow*, 1900). And there was the urgent summons from a newly married factory-owner whose bride of a week was suffering from worms in the ear, diarrhoea, vomiting and syphilis. "Ugh! Sweet sounds and poetry, where are ye?" remarked the doctor-author, himself accustomed to portray in more delicate terms the clash of romantic illusion and harsh reality.⁵

Chekhov's comments on his medical practice are as ambivalent as on most other topics. By contrast with literature, a mere "mistress", he was still calling medicine his legal wife. But this was no honeymoon. "Doctoring is tiresome and sometimes involves much fuss over trifles. Some days you're called out four or five times. No sooner are you back from Kryukovo than there's a messenger from Vaskovo already in your yard. And I'm sick of women with babies. In September I'm giving up medical practice once and for all." Chekhov uttered this threat in July 1893, but did not of course carry it out.[6]

Committed to their idyllic picture of the doctoring squire of Melikhovo, most memoirists pass over his occasional bouts of impatience with the medical calling. A different view is given by the Ukrainian writer Ignatius Potapenko, one witness who does not portray the traditional dedicated Chekhov. Potapenko says that Chekhov was not at all keen on doctoring; nor was he well qualified to practise, having done so only sporadically in the past. He did not dose the peasants because he wanted to, but simply because they had no one else; approached by a landowner who could afford better treatment, Chekhov would have sent him straight to a competent specialist. That he had no vocation for medicine Potapenko asserts as indisputable: a little ungenerous, this, from one whom Chekhov had once cured of a skin complaint contracted at a Moscow barber's.[7] Here Potapenko, irked by the routine picture of Chekhov the saintly and dedicated healer, went too far in the opposite direction. Both with his "mistress" (literature) and his "legal wife" (medicine) Chekhov maintained an oscillating love-hate relationship. Such an attitude is, we suggest, not uncommon among competent professionals; it is the bunglers, amateurs, dilettantes, ignoramuses and other romantics who have invented the conventional stereotype of the dedicated genius unremittingly devoted, without qualm, tremor or hesitation, to his sacred life's vocation. Such paragons have existed. Chekhov was never one of them.

In the summer and early autumn of 1892 Chekhov was especially busy as a doctor and hard-worked medical administrator. Russia was now threatened by cholera. That danger Serpukhov County, to which Melikhovo belonged, was no better equipped to meet than any other rural area; and Chekhov agreed to serve the county council by supervising a sector which included twenty-six villages, seven factories and St. David's Monastery. His first task was to prepare the area to meet the epidemic, should it indeed materialize. It was an exacting three-month job for which Chekhov refused remuneration, wishing to preserve his independence; and which temporarily cut off his literary income.[8] For such frivolities as writing these new obligations left neither time nor energy. The entire responsibility for administrative precautions against the epidemic had been foisted on the doctors, for the local council could furnish neither premises nor materials. When Chekhov began work not one bed was available anywhere to take a cholera victim, so that he had to beg accommodation from rural factory-owners and landed proprietors. As for equipment, not a single thermometer had the council supplied: only a jug and half a pound of carbolic acid. Chekhov went round begging for such commodities as lime and oil of vitriol. During his tours of the locality he also gave "the local barbarians" lectures on elementary hygiene.[9]

He had some unpleasant encounters on his rounds. A local countess addressed him condescendingly, as if he was applying for a job; she might have been a near relative of the odious heroine of *The Princess* (1889). There was a second countess, too, with "vast diamonds in her ears, a bustle and a lack of poise; a millionairess. With such people you feel that stupid schoolboy urge to be cheeky." Ruder still was the Abbot of St. David's, who refused to allot any room for potential cholera patients. The doctor need not worry about visitors to the monastery's high-class guest house, this dignitary loftily informed him: they were all rich enough to pay his bills, should they have to call him in! At this suggestion that his interest in the epidemic was commercial, Chekhov lost his temper; he was a man of means himself, he told the Abbot, and would require no such fees.[10]

Meanwhile cholera was bearing down from most points of the compass: from Moscow in the north, from the east along the River Oka, and from the south. Melikhovo seemed seriously menaced; but by 15 October, when the approach of winter removed the danger, no single case of the disease had occurred in Chekhov's jurisdiction. The state of emergency was suspended and he could stand down. In the next year the same sequence recurred. Again Chekhov served as cholera doctor, cursing the weakness of will which prevented him from refusing; again the Melikhovo area was seriously menaced; again it was spared, and again he had lost time which he could ill afford. Time-consuming too was his membership of the county council's Health Committee, of which he frequently attended the "hellishly boring" deliberations.[11]

Chekhov's extensive doctoring experiences at Melikhovo find little traceable reflection in his imaginative work. And yet doctors loom large in his mature fiction and drama. They include, in *Ward Number Six*, a minor villain (Khobotov) and a discredited major figure who becomes a victim of his own mistaken philosophy (Ragin). There are the doctors victimized by selfish women (*The Princess, The Butterfly, His Wife*); there is that yet more memorable victim of old age and ill health, the Professor of Medicine in *A Dreary Story*. There is even a doctor (Dorn in *The Seagull*) portrayed as wholly contented with his life: an attribute distinguishing him both from Chekhov himself and from the general run of Chekhov's characters. And there is another doctor described as lapsing into complacent, portly, provincial, materialistic middle age after first appearing as a romantic, hard-working, idealistic young man: Doctor Startsev in the story of the same name (1898). Then there are occasional doctors who mirror aspects of Chekhov's own thought or activities: Blagovo of *My Life*, who expresses Chekhovian views on progress; Astrov of *Uncle Vanya*, a tree-planter and conservationist like his creator; Korolyov of *A Case History* (1898), who comes close to functioning as his creator's mouthpiece, and who judges social problems, Chekhov-like, "from the angle of a doctor accustomed to making accurate diagnoses of chronic ailments".[12]

Concerned with the peasants' mental as well as their physical welfare, Chekhov was active in local education. In November 1894 he became Visitor to the small school in the village of Talezh. Finding the premises inadequate, he built Talezh a new school, submitting his own plans and meeting much of the cost himself. The building was ready by autumn 1896 and Chekhov attended the inauguration ceremony, being presented with the traditional bread and salt by grateful villagers. So successful was this enterprise that the villagers of near-by Novosyolki were soon begging Chekhov to build them a school too. And he "had not the guts to refuse", though he would again have to pay most of the expenses himself.[13] Architect, financier and works supervisor, he visited the sites almost daily; ordered materials, hired carpenters, roofers, caulkers, glaziers and the like. He extracted contributions from his friends, he raised money through amateur dramatic performances: an activity usually deprecated when it figures in his fiction. The third and last school to be built in the area by Chekhov was in Melikhovo itself. The work anticipates our narrative, since it took place during his wanderings (1897–9) between his two homes in Melikhovo and Yalta. His sister was the moving spirit now. For two years she collected money—from selling apples, holding charity concerts and raffling landscape paintings donated by Levitan. But she could not have managed without a large subvention from Anton, combined with the practical help which he was to give her during his last month at Melikhovo in summer 1899.[14]

Chekhov also became Visitor to the school at Chirkovo and sponsored the school library at Khatun, besides functioning as Assistant Inspector of Elementary Education for Serpukhov County as a whole. He punctiliously conducted the customary oral examinations; took a keen interest in the local children; bought them gifts; planned a trip to Nizhny Novgorod for a hundred of them.[15]

The only systematic census ever held in Imperial Russia was conducted in January and February 1897, owing a little of its success to the squire of Melikhovo. Already an experienced one-man census-taker on Sakhalin, he now accepted responsibility for the group of villages to which Melikhovo belonged, having fifteen subordinate officials under his direction. He toured peasant huts, banging his head on the lintels while suffering from migraine and influenza. The officially issued ink would not write and the officially issued brief-cases were too small for the officially issued documents. A plague epidemic was feared at the time, and Chekhov reflected that this affliction (which in fact never materialized) would convince the peasants that the doctor and gentry were poisoning them so as to gain possession of their land. This was not quite a joke, for the benighted though often benevolent muzhik was indeed prone to sudden acts of violence based on such flights of fantasy.[16]

Though most of those whose details Chekhov filed were peasants, thus belonging to a legally defined social category, the chief census-taker of the area himself remained an anomaly. As the son of a failed petty merchant he would have rated as a *meshchanin* or petty burgher, the category for townsfolk of the lower orders, had he followed in his father's footsteps. In fact he had rated for many years as nothing at all. When asked to show his papers he would wave his Moscow University diploma, which usually sufficed as proof of respectability in a country which took its own elaborate bureaucratic regulations so casually. But he was repeatedly inconvenienced because this document was not considered quite adequate. At the same time he was ineligible for a proper passport as not belonging to a recognized estate of the realm.

So easygoing and immature was global bureaucracy of the late nine-teenth century that we have observed Chekhov—blithely undeterred by inadequate documentation—visiting places as remote as Hong Kong, Singapore and Naples; not to mention Russia's own most notorious and far-flung penal island. Still, the lack of proper papers was always a potential embarrassment, even if he wished to go no farther than Moscow or St. Petersburg. In 1893 the difficulty was at last overcome by a ruse. Chekhov secured appointment in the state Health Department as a "Junior Super-numerary Medical Officer";[17] then, immediately after assuming this lowly rank, he resigned it and lived out his last ten years, in the eyes of his government, as a junior official, retired. The episode emphasizes how essentially *déclassé* Chekhov was. The serf's grandson from the south, the failed merchant's son, the newly fledged landowner and farmer of central Russia, the doctor, the writer, the future husband of an actress—he seemed to touch the social structure of Imperial Russia at all points while adhering to none. In an age of shifting barriers he was a truly modern man, untypical of modernity in one vital feature: though well aware of class differences, which are richly illustrated in his work, he was not obsessed with "class" as a phenomenon. To him no social or other category ever transcended something which he discerned in all men irrespective of their origins: their common humanity and their none too uncommon inhumanity.

Though Chekhov's medical experiences at Melikhovo found little reflection in his imaginative work, his more general contacts in the locality provided ample literary copy and stimulus. He packed many impressions of the villagers into a single, very famous short story suitably entitled

Peasants (1897). For reasons independent of literary merit this was to become, as we shall shortly relate, his most controversial work in his own country and during his lifetime. But *Peasants* is also a literary *tour de force*. Having little plot, it presents a series of brief, lightly drawn sketches grouped around the family of an ailing middle-aged ex-waiter, Nicholas Chikildeyev, who returns from Moscow with his wife and child to die in Zhukovo, his native village. These details have Chekhov's usual socio-logical precision, since registered peasants such as his hero often spent decades working in a city without renouncing their peasant status and links with their villages; in such sad cases as that of the dying Nicholas they would return to a long-abandoned country home, where relatives were expected to support them.

When the three Chikildeyevs reach Zhukovo they find the parental hut dark, cramped, dirty, sooty, fly-blown and empty except for one unwashed, bored, fair-haired eight-year-old girl (Nicholas's niece, as it turns out) and one cat. Nicholas's small daughter beckons to the cat, after which the following brief dialogue or non-dialogue between the two little girls and the cat puts Zhukovo straight on the page with a brevity and force superlatively Chekhovian.

"'Puss, puss! Come here, pussy.'

"'It can't hear,' said the other little girl. 'Deaf.'

"'Why?'

"'Someone 'it it.'"[18]

From this all else follows. Returning to their hut, Nicholas's aged parents, brother and sisters-in-law resent the sick man and the three extra mouths to feed. They have little to eat themselves, and that of the poorest quality. The tea, their only luxury, tastes of fish, and even tea has to be renounced when the village Elder impounds their samovar because of unpaid taxes. Mariya (Nicholas's sister-in-law) trembles when approached by her drunken husband (Nicholas's brother) who beats her savagely. The other sister-in-law, Fyolka, is an absent soldier's wife; this strapping wench often swims across the local river at night, and swims lustily back at dawn, well swived by her paramours on the other side. Vicious Granny whips little Sasha Chikildeyev for admitting geese into the kitchen-garden. A village hut catches fire and has to be extinguished by the women and local gentry while drunken muzhiks reel out of the local pub, goggling helplessly at the flames. This is all very unedifying and it is no surprise when a peasant proclaims that they "were better off as serfs". The peasants lived worse than beasts. "They were awful people to live with: rough, dishonest, filthy, drunken. Holding each other in mutual disrespect, fear and suspi-cion, they were always at loggerheads, always squabbling."[19] Whose fault was all this? Society's? That of "the system" or the exploiting classes?

Without discounting such explanations, Chekhov makes it clear that the worst of all the peasant's exploiters is—the peasant. "Who keeps the pot-house and makes the peasant drunk? The peasant. Who squanders his village, school and church funds on drink? The peasant. Who steals from his neighbours, sets fire to their property, perjures himself for a bottle of vodka? Who's the first to run down the peasant at council and other meetings? The peasant."[20]

Such features of *Peasants* make parts of the story read like an indictment. What had become of Chekhov the kindly squire, the philanthropist, the healer, the promoter of education, the friend of his peasants? Was he inconsistent in helping the villagers on the ground while offering so sombre a picture of them in his fiction? Not at all, for it would never have occurred to him that to sympathize with the peasants was to become obliged to misrepresent the evidence of his eyes when it came to portraying village life on paper. Nor is there a jot of hostility in Chekhov's diagnosis of the peasant's condition as framed with the objectivity of so experienced a literary clinician. Nor yet is his picture of rural life all gloom. Difficult as the villagers might be to live with, they were human beings, as Chekhov also pointed out in *Peasants*. "They suffered and wept like men and women, there was nothing in their lives for which an excuse might not be found: back-breaking work that makes you ache all over at night, cruel winters, poor harvests and overcrowding, with no help and nowhere to turn for it."[21] Chekhov stresses the reverence, albeit superstitious, which peasants feel for their religion; and notes the touching respect in which they hold the mysterious ability to read and write. These details relieve the general impression of hopelessness. But they cannot remove it.

When Chekhov spoke of peasants in his own name he treated them more gently than is usual in his fiction. One of the few unedifying real-life village scenes recorded in his letters occurred in April 1895. "Yesterday a drunken old muzhik took off all his clothes and bathed in our pond while his decrepit mother beat him with a stick and everyone else stood round roaring with laughter. After his bathe the muzhik went home in the snow barefoot, followed by his mother. Then the old woman came to me to be treated for bruises: she'd been beaten by the son." These undignified proceedings presumably suggested the yet more ludicrous beating scene at the end of Chekhov's *New Villa* (1899); but his true attitude is revealed less by his account of such degraded antics than by the following comment which he appends. "To postpone indefinitely the education of the dark masses: what baseness!"[22] It is one of the few generalizations ever made on peasant affairs by a man who would rather build schools or teach his servants to read than theorize about education.

Chekhov held his peasant neighbours in respect and affection without treating them as shaggy, imperfectly house-trained, sometimes dangerous pets: an all too common habit among those whom we here term "peasant-fanciers". For years Russian intellectuals had been patronizing their peasants. The left-wing Narodniks, who sought or talked about radical reform or bloody revolution, tended to take this line. So did the very different Slavophils, right-wing on the whole, with their emphasis on native Russian traditions. There had thus arisen a general consensus among theorizing townees who would not have known one end of a peasant from the other: that the muzhik, dirty, drunken, primitive and brutal though he might seem to the superficial observer, was yet the repository of mysterious, imperfectly defined virtues visible only to the eye of faith. Beneath that grime-encrusted husk there beat a heart of gold. Such a view had been preached by two titans of the Russian novel, Tolstoy and Dostoyevsky, the one an anarchist and the other a fervent monarchist. It had also, in some odd way, become virtually compulsory for any intellectual wishing—as who except Chekhov did not?—to assume the posture of a humane and enlightened individual. In daring to portray a yokelry so unidealized, Chekhov was therefore breaching a hallowed unspoken taboo. Hence the tremendous fuss provoked when *Peasants* appeared in April 1897. It was a long time, claimed *Severny vestnik*, since any new work of fiction had made such a sensation: a stir like that once created by new works from Turgenev or Dostoyevsky. A more recent comment is that *Peasants* went off "like an exploding bomb".[23] Chekhov had expressed an attitude contrary to that deemed prescriptive by conformists who so strangely united authoritarian impertinence with the pretence of championing free speech. And to violate a sacred cow is naturally to offend the herd as a whole.

The cries of execration led to a vigorous press controversy over *Peasants* which soon made it clear that Chekhov had certain unsuspected allies: Russia's Marxists, now first finding their identity as a movement. The political, social and cultural backwardness of bucolic Russia was an article of their faith and they therefore spoke out in Chekhov's defence while the yokel-idolizing Narodniks, with Mikhaylovsky at their head, called down anathema on his story. It was sheer coincidence, this alliance between Chekhov and the Marxists, for he knew nothing and cared less about their creed. In any case he had no zest for such a politico-literary controversy. He blandly ignored it while it smouldered on in the Narodnik review *Russkoye bogatstvo* ("Russian Wealth"), which took a strong anti-Chekhov line, and the Marxist *Novoye slovo* ("New Word"), which stoutly defended Chekhov's views on rural backwardness.[24]

How far removed Chekhov's mentality was from both the Marxist and the Narodnik point of view we may learn from an unduly neglected passage in a letter of August 1892. Discussing attempts by political agitators to use the cholera epidemic of that summer as a means of inflaming peasant feeling against the government, he also makes other characteristic points on his attitude to the peasantry. "If our Socialists really are going to exploit the cholera for their own purposes I shall despise them. To seek good ends by foul means is to befoul those very ends. . . . . Why must they lie to the peasants? Why assure the peasants that they're right to be ignorant, and that their crude superstitions are Sacred Truth? Can any Glorious Future redeem such filthy lies? If I was a politician I'd never dare vilify the present for the sake of the future: not if I was promised two tons of bliss for every dram of filthy lies."[25]

Reverting from Chekhov's peasants to his *Peasants*, we find him making a puzzling comment, in June 1899, on this most controversial of his works. "From the fictional point of view Melikhovo is exhausted and has lost all value after *Peasants*."[26] Anyone might think that he had originally settled down in his village as a dedicated documentary realist, and had exploited the place for its value as copy before moving on to other, more promising pastures. Nothing could be more misleading, for Chekhov was much more than a documentarist—even when at his most documentary, as in *Peasants*. That story reflects the general atmosphere of Melikhovo, but has only the sketchiest links with the details of the place. To start with, the name "Zhukovo" appears to be fictitious, as are most village place names in Chekhov's fiction as a whole. But the Zhukovo fire was inspired by an actual fire which broke out in Chekhov's Melikhovo home, fortunately without doing much damage. Nicholas Chikildeyev was modelled on a certain waiter at the Moscow Grand Hotel; while the village Elder, with his quaintly mannered speech, was suggested by some local worthy.[27]

Far from concluding a chain of village tales set against a Melikhovo-inspired background, *Peasants* was practically the first such study. Among preceding stories of the Melikhovo period several had been set in the countryside: *Neighbours, Terror, The Black Monk, At a Country House*. But they lacked obvious Melikhovo references, being in any case concerned with the gentry and ignoring peasant problems. Not until *The Artist's Story* (1896) does the peasantry make any significant appearance in a work written at Melikhovo; and even then the peasants only function as the background to a clash among gentlefolk.

As noted above, *The Artist's Story* was specifically inspired by a locality other than Melikhovo: that of Bogimovo, where Chekhov spent the summer of 1891. And yet this work reflects his Melikhovo experience too, since he portrays in it a fellow-philanthropist, the handsome and determined Lydia Volchaninov, who is a great doser and educator of peasants. Lydia thus mirrors the activities of her creator. But far from making her his heroine, he portrays her as the villainess of the piece, a complacent, priggish, albeit beautiful busybody who cruelly destroys her young sister's happiness by officiously ending the girl's romance with the visiting artist. A philan-thropist à la Chekhov the non-approved Lydia might be, but Chekhov clearly gives his preference to her enemy the Artist, a lazy, moony individual who tells Lydia that to dose and teach her villagers only means adding to their existing burdens. Nothing could illustrate more vividly how unsenti-mental Chekhov was towards the peasants than this fictional rejection of a girl who took them so seriously in favour of a man who would not lift a finger to help them. Can Chekhov have been mocking or criticizing himself, subconsciously or consciously, in his portrait of the unsympathetic Lydia? Not only was she a teacher and healer, like her creator, but she also succeeded in preventing a sister's marriage. And that was the very operation which Chekhov himself so unkindly performed at about this time at the expense of his devoted Mariya.

Chekhov's refusal to sentimentalize the peasantry is a yet more prominent feature of the long study My Life, published shortly after The Artist's Story and also set (partly) in the countryside. Here he dips more obviously into his Melikhovo experiences, for he has his hero and heroine building a school for their peasant neighbours. But what a fiasco the enterprise proves! The peasants' first reaction to this offer of help is to demand the communal keg of vodka traditionally exacted from any landowner who sought their co-operation. Agreeing reluctantly to cart building materials from town, they make a practice of gratuitously hauling the huge beams into the slithering mud of the manor yard; swearing atrociously; uttering menaces; refusing to leave until once more bought off with a keg of vodka. The carpenters and sand-haulers extort payment before they will work, and altogether "there was no end to the muddling, swearing and cadging".[28]

So vividly are ignorance, ill-will and squalor invoked in the school-building sequences of My Life that it is hard to remember their author as one who wished his own local peasants nothing but good; who had already built them one school; who was building another as he wrote the story; and who was not to be deterred from proceeding to a third. If experiences such as those recorded in My Life came his way when he was putting up the Talezh, Novosyolki and Melikhovo schools, we find little evidence of them in the sources. Once again, then, we note the same paradox: Chekhov the stern, implacable author pillories the feckless muzhik in fiction, while Chekhov the man is tolerant and helpful towards his humble neighbours. Critics, reviewers, philosophizing ladies, hangers-on of culture, verbalizing idealists, rich and titled snobs, peasant-fanciers: to these, when speaking in his own name to third parties, he could and did refer with blistering con-tempt; to the muzhik never. His scorn for the trendy peasant-fancier of his age is most witheringly expressed in his diary entry for 19 February 1897, where he describes a dinner held at the Continental Hotel in Moscow to celebrate the thirty-sixth anniversary of serf emancipation. "Boring and silly. To dine, to drink champagne, to make a hullabaloo, to give speeches on peasant consciousness, on the peasant conscience, freedom and so on, while all the time tail-coated slaves [the waiters] scurry about the tables, as much serfs as ever they were; and while coachmen wait out in the freezing air of the streets. This is to lie to the Holy Spirit."[29]

Chekhov had the right to make these reproaches since he lived up to his own standards by avoiding lofty generalizations about muzhik virtues. While others were grinding out their tedious clichés about the Peasant, the master of Melikhovo would be treating a villager for gonorrhoea, or taking delivery of joists to build a new belfry. Nor would he join in choruses solemnly invoking the "ideals of the 1860s": facile sentiments associated with the Emancipation of the Serfs and other reforms of that period. His relations with the Melikhovo peasants are well expressed in a letter written a few months after he had moved in. "The peasants are rough, mistrustful and dirty in their habits; but the thought that our [medical] labours will not be fruitless makes all that hardly noticeable."[30] A remorseless analyst in fiction of the dubious, self-deceiving motives underlying much philanthropic activity, Chekhov emerges by any possible test as one who unsentimentally gave practical help to his fellows, and for their sake, not in order to see himself in some romantic or saintly image. He was a doer, not a talker.

My previous biography of Chekhov (1950) records as a curiosity the information, received at second hand, that Chekhov was still remembered with affection and gratitude by a surviving peasant of Melikhovo.[31] Ten years later I confirmed this on the spot in conversation with an aged collective farmer who smiled while recalling Anton Pavlovich and his work as doctor and benefactor to the community. These reminiscences were unfortunately cut short by his and my official custodians. This had all been put on tape long ago, they explained; and there seemed to be some fear that my informant might be on the point of changing his script. Still, it was a piquant encounter, and a link with a past happily free from the grotesque protocol of modern politico-cultural custodianship.

Traveller

Chekhov by no means remained cooped up at home during his Melikhovo years. Visiting near-by Moscow and, less often, St. Petersburg for professional and social reasons, he also undertook other, largely recreational, journeys inside and outside Russia.

His peak year for exotic excursions was 1894. Early March sees him established in the Hotel Russia at Yalta, where we last met him in 1889. Wearing new trousers with large grey checks, he had arrived at Sevastopol from Moscow by train and then taken the steamer *Tsesarevna* to Yalta in dense fog. With the visibility at nil and the ship's hooter sounding non-stop, he had derived comfort from the memory of worse marine ordeals off Sakhalin; he could afford to despise a mere Black Sea.[1] Now an established celebrity, Chekhov became one of the sights of the resort as he promenaded with a giant friend, the singer V. S. Mirolyubov, on the Esplanade which was to serve as the opening scene of his *Lady with a Dog* (1899). He ate kebabs at Bolotnikov's restaurant, drank coffee at the Central Hotel,[2] and made some of the usual tourist trips. He also wrote a very short story, *The Student*, which he later described as his favourite among all his works, besides claiming it as a manifesto in favour of optimism.[3] Neither assertion does much credit to his judgement as critic of himself.

Chekhov was excruciatingly bored at Yalta; or at least became so after being there three weeks and suffering piles, heart palpitations and a cough. He longed for Melikhovo where he could sit on his own bench, lie on his own grass, walk down the village street in his dressing-gown. He preferred the northern spring: so sudden, so much more lyrical and Levitanesque than anything which Yalta could offer. It had been a mistake to come here, reflected Chekhov, who, despite the prevalence of so many assorted complaints in his letters, rarely expressed such regrets over a decision once implemented. Writing off his Crimean trip as the product of idle *Wanderlust*, he packed his bags.[4] On 5 April he was back in Melikhovo, counting his blessings and certainly not foreseeing that he would one day make the Crimea his permanent home.

Chekhov's second trip of 1894 was more unsatisfactory still. In early August he and Potapenko boarded a Volga steamer at Yaroslavl, intending to sail via Tsaritsyn (now Volgograd) and the Don to Taganrog. But the fierce wind, the heat and the prevalence of intellectual conversation conspired with the atrocious racket of Nizhny Novgorod's Permanent Fair to send the two travellers scurrying shamefully to the railway station. They caught the train to Moscow, whence Chekhov proceeded to the Ukraine and recovered his high spirits. During six delightful days at Luka as the guest of his old friends the Lintvaryovs he savoured the pleasures of eating, drinking and idling so often denounced by implication in his fiction.[5]

Soon after returning to Melikhovo Chekhov was off on his travels again. He left for Taganrog on 26 August to see his Uncle Mitrofan, now dying. Then he proceeded via Feodosiya, where he stayed at Suvorin's *dacha*, through Yalta, Odessa and Lvov to the seaside resort of Abbazia (now

Opatija), situated on the Adriatic coast and belonging to the Austrian Empire. His family was beginning to resent his wanderings, and so Chekhov left Russian soil secretly, letting his sister think that he was staying on in Feodosiya.[6]

Abbazia was splendid (21 September); was boring (22 September). The hotels were crowded; there were too many Russians in the place; the Adriatic was inferior to the Black Sea at Yalta. These unfavourable impressions were incorporated in Chekhov's story *Ariadne* (1895). Abbazia here features as "a filthy little Slav town" possessing only one street, stinking and negotiable after rain only in galoshes. Already, in the 1890s, it had been ruined by the tourist trade.[7] Chekhov moved on to Fiume (now Rijeka), Trieste, Venice, Milan, Genoa, Nice, Paris and Berlin, now in a mood to prefer things foreign. The beer was so good that he would become a drunkard if it could be had in Russia. After witnessing an Italian stage version of Dostoyevsky's *Crime and Punishment*, he pronounced all Russian actors insipid; compared with their Italian counterparts those pseudo-Thespians were no more than "swine". We are reminded of the strictures on Russian actresses provoked by Duse's Cleopatra in St. Petersburg three years earlier.[8] Chekhov not only disparaged his fellow-Russians, he also turned against the Slavs as a whole: commenting on the luxuries and attractions of Nice, Monte Carlo and San Remo, he added that these centres of Western civilization far outshone Abbazia, "and all that barbarous, Balkan, all-brother-Slavs-together business".[9]

Chekhov's only other extensive trip of these years was a tour of southern Russia and the Caucasus in August and September 1896. We again find him in Taganrog ("deadly boring") and then Novorossiysk, an "excellent town" with its many factories, its Frenchmen, its good restaurant, its grain elevator, and with all the hectic comings and goings. He moved on to Nakhichevan in southern Armenia, then stayed a week at the North Caucasian spa of Kislovodsk. Returning via Novorossiysk, he took the steamer to Feodosiya and spent ten days as Suvorin's guest before going home by train via Kharkov, where he saw Griboyedov's play *Woe from Wit*.[10]

To turn to Chekhov's Moscow and St. Petersburg excursions is to be brought into closer touch with his literary concerns, for his main contacts were with writers, editors, publishers and journalists. Visits to the more distant St. Petersburg were naturally rarer: only seven during the five-year period. The longest occupied nearly six weeks of December and January 1892–3, and was followed by two years during which Chekhov neglected the capital. He was there twice in 1895 and three times in 1896; the last of these sojourns coinciding with his *Seagull*'s disastrous première, to be described below.

St. Petersburg was less convivial than Moscow: its inhabitants were less inclined to sit around in pubs. Evidently feeling that they needed encouragement, Chekhov launched on St. Tatyana's Day, traditionally celebrated by Moscow University on 12 January, a St. Petersburg version of these jollifications in the form of an annual banquet for the city's writers. The first was held in 1893 at the Maly Yaroslavets Restaurant, the eighteen celebrants including Chekhov himself and such senior associates as Suvorin, Leykin and Grigorovich; there were also D. N. Mamin-Sibiryak, whose fiction Chekhov particularly admired, and K. S. Barantsevich, whose company he evidently preferred to his writings. During visits to St. Petersburg Chekhov met other writers too: Shcheglov, Bilibin, Lydia Avilov and his brother Alexander. He attended concerts, operas and plays. He patronized a masked ball in aid of charity. But according to Potapenko, Chekhov had no close friends in St. Petersburg—or anywhere else for that matter; yet he always received a tumultuous welcome. The less rumbustious social habits suited him better than those of Moscow. Indeed, he would have settled there permanently had it not been for the climate: "raw, damp, and very unsettled; woollen underclothing is the best protection against chills".[11]

Despite the violent revulsion against Moscow which had driven Chekhov to Melikhovo in the first place, the city was soon pulling him in the reverse direction. Only a couple of hours' travel separated it from Melikhovo, which meant that his visits could be frequent and made on the spur of the moment. Of Moscow's vigorous social life we find much evidence. A fortnight spent there in November 1893 produced "a sort of delirium ... one long series of junketings and new acquaintanceships ... never felt so free ... girls, girls, girls". In summer 1896 he loses two nights' sleep and all sense of time on a non-stop "staggering round the Yars and the Hermitages", those well-known Muscovite hostelries.[12]

One of these girls, Tatyana Shchepkin-Kupernik, often met Chekhov in Moscow. They would lunch at the office of the theatrical magazine *Artist* ("The Artiste") or take tea with the newspaper *Russkiye vedomosti* ("The Russian Gazette"). Chekhov would put up at his favourite Moscow Grand Hotel in the centre of town, where he regularly stayed in Room Five, and the news "Anton Pavlovich is here" would flash through the city with the speed of wireless telegraphy. For ever concocting nicknames for his friends, he was "an inexhaustible source of jocular sobriquets". Droves of friends welcomed him: the novelist Potapenko; the playwright A. I. Sumbatov-Yuzhin; the joint editors of *Russkaya mysl* (Goltsev and Lavrov). When asked out for dinner and champagne Chekhov would begin by vaguely protesting. Coughing slightly, looking annoyed, he would accompany his friends submissively, but would soon perk up and become the hagiographically obligatory *inexhaustible source* of "charming and excruciatingly comic absurdities and delightful surprises". But he also had an absent air, that of an "observer, not an actor: an observer distant and as it were senior . . . like an adult playing with children and pretending to be interested when he really wasn't". Behind the lenses of his pince-nez, behind his jokes, could be sensed sadness and alienation. He would survey the scene distantly with the "beautiful, wise eyes" invoked by so many memoirists. But he was not really enjoying himself.[13]

CHAPTER TEN

Melikhovo 1892–7: Ladies' Man

The Elusive Bachelor

The young squire of Melikhovo was an eligible bachelor. He was tall, well-built and considered good-looking; though his health was poor, he was not yet known to be suffering from a fatal disease. He was witty, sociable, kind, considerate, fond of children; a successful man, a rising celebrity. Then there was his tantalizing air of remoteness. He seemed to possess some precious, vital secret which he might perhaps one day divulge to the right person. He was fairly well off, too, his ability to support a family in moderate style being proved by the fact that he was already doing so. He could clearly have taken on a wife and children as well. He was thus an attractive prospect to any young woman who saw her vocation as his wife or mistress, especially as he liked girls: liked teasing them, making them laugh, criticizing their clothes, correcting their attempts at fiction-writing. He also met girls in quantity in Moscow and among his many guests at Melikhovo.

One secret of Chekhov's success with women lay in an unusually well-developed ability, which they could sense, to manage without them. What a formidable challenge he presented to any young person who fancied her credentials as a temptress: this talented, well-favoured young man who seemed to be repelled rather than attracted by the more obvious kind of feminine charms; but who might conceivably turn out less deficient in male sensuality than he appeared.

Under these circumstances Chekhov's thoughts were bound to turn to love and marriage, if only negatively; and even if they had not, his friends and relatives would have made sure that they did. The younger Chekhovs, Ivan and Michael, both made the point by themselves marrying locally during the Melikhovo years. Other relatives and friends harped on

Chekhov's duty to wed, Suvorin among them. But Chekhov's reaction was cool. "All right, I'll marry if you want. But I stipulate that everything must be as hitherto: she must live in Moscow and I in the country, and I'll visit her. As for happiness which goes on day in day out, from one morning to another: that I can't stand. . . . I promise to be a superb husband, but give me a wife like the moon: one that won't appear in my sky every day. I shan't write any better for marrying." Chekhov also told Suvorin that he "feared a wife and domestic routines which will cramp my style and somehow don't seem to suit my waywardness".[1]

These attempts to persuade Chekhov to marry remind us of the disastrous results which ensue in his fiction whenever such officious inter-ference brings together a man and a woman who would have been better off if they had never met. There is *In the Hollow*, where the peasant girl Lipa so tragically weds the preposterous Anisim Tsybukin, police detective and coiner of counterfeit money. There is Belikov's doom-fraught engagement in *A Hard Case*. There is the grotesque but less calamitous union promoted in *The Order of St. Anne* by those female busybodies, friends of the beautiful young heroine, who "bestirred themselves and started looking out a husband for her".[2] These and many discouraging pictures of marriage gave Chekhov's answer to those well-wishers who attempted to equip him with a wife. And if they still wondered why he remained single they could go on to read *His Wife*, *My Wife*, *My Life* and many another cogent study of marital disharmony. Their author was obviously the last man in the world to drift casually into wedlock.

Since Chekhov would not marry during his Melikhovo years, what were his amorous experiences, if any, at the time? His was an easy-going society, and temporary liaisons were common in his circle. It was easy for lovers to put up, say, at his own favourite Moscow Grand Hotel, where the management was no more officious in investigating its guests' intimate activities than was that of the Yalta hotel where Gurov and Anna Sergeyevna were to embark on adultery in *A Lady with a Dog* (1899). As for more permanent experiments in extra-marital cohabitation, these were by no means uncommon, and we remember both Chekhov's elder brothers as living with mistresses or common-law wives. Such irregularities naturally offended respectable, pious older folk such as the Chekhov parents, and were much discussed in societies as gossip-ridden as those of Moscow and St. Petersburg. The principals could easily provoke officious censure—but nothing worse. This was not the world of Tolstoy's *Anna Karenin*, written twenty years earlier and set in a different milieu, where the strains of a profound extra-marital love in a disapproving society prove so over-whelming as to compass the heroine's destruction.

Neither a gossip nor a habitual prude, Chekhov himself took his usual tactful, matter-of-fact line in this area. When his friend Bilibin announced that he had set up house with his mistress and expected to incur moral censure, Chekhov at once congratulated him and sent best wishes to the lady.[3] That he himself never embarked on such a long-term arrangement we may be certain, since it would inevitably have left its trace in a biography so thoroughly documented. What of less stable associations? Here was an attractive man, sought after by attractive women in a society which provided few obstacles to casual love affairs. To what extent did he grasp his opportunities?

The problem is beset with difficulties. There is Chekhov's own admirable modesty: he was the last person to advertise his exploits, amorous or not. Regarding love as the business solely of those intimately concerned, he would have resented the prying into his private life which is incumbent on the biographer. Unfortunately Chekhov's reticence has been shared by his literary executors. His sister suppressed certain material when editing the first substantial collection of his letters—that of 1912-16. Then, when these same letters were republished in the Stalin era with many additional items (as part of the *Complete Works* of 1944-51), editorial policy turned out more prudish still. Various crucial excisions have made it difficult to map Chekhov's intimate life, especially as determined post-Stalinist attempts to consult the original letters have so far failed.[4]

And yet the facts are not entirely hidden. We at least know that Chekhov was neither dedicatedly profligate nor unremittingly celibate. But at what point between these extremes should we place him?

The Abstemious Lover

Inside information on Chekhov's intimate life is supplied by the unpublished letters of the actress Lydia Yavorsky, the only woman whom we can name as having been Chekhov's mistress, except for Olga Knipper during the year preceding their marriage in 1901. Lydia was the daughter of a Kiev police officer. She had been married and divorced early in life, and was about twenty-two years old when she arrived in Moscow to join Korsh's Theatre in 1893. That she was an ambitious actress she soon made evident: not least in a letter to Chekhov of February 1894. Here, before they became lovers, she tried to wheedle him into writing a play, if only a one-acter, for her benefit performance on 18 February. Not surprisingly, Chekhov failed to produce such a work at a fortnight's notice, despite her coy promise of a "big thank you" and her assurance that "your name alone will evoke the interest which I lack as a newcomer to the Moscow public".[1]

The following month finds Miss Yavorsky in Rome. On 23 March she writes Chekhov a rambling, hysterical letter imploring him to intercede with a discarded suitor or lover, unnamed, who has been following her around with a revolver, and who has also written to her father accusing her of having been seduced by the allegedly Lesbian Tatyana Shchepkin-Kupernik. ("Your daughter is hurtling into an appalling abyss.") Now, the person who so volubly protests against imputed homosexuality may thereby intend to advertise availability on a heterosexual level. Whether or not Chekhov troubled to make this deduction, we find Lydia (now returned to Russia) inviting him to come and see her that autumn in terms which suggest that, though they are not yet lovers, she is interested in their becoming such. "Come to me, my good, kind darling; with your coming the sun peeps into my soul."[2]

That the affair was consummated on, or possibly before, some date in January 1895, five letters of that month from Lydia to Chekhov establish fairly conclusively. Besides the mode of address ("my darling") and the use of the intimate second person singular form, there is a reference which, despite being lodged in a whimsical verse parody, yet seems unambiguous, to "that room in the Moscow Grand Hotel where she [Yavorsky] tasted with thee unearthly bliss".[3] Then there is Lydia's reference to a rug which is to warm Chekhov "like my hot kisses", together with a mention of "my mad love for you" and sundry other endearments. Now, he is known to have been in Moscow in January 1895, and to have put up at the Grand Hotel from the 4th of that month, returning to Melikhovo seventeen days later. On 9 January he saw Yavorsky play the leading role at Korsh's Theatre in the translation of a French comedy aptly entitled, under the circumstances, *Madame Sans-Gêne*. That they slept together during this stay seems certain. By March, though, the affair seems already over: by then Lydia is complaining of Chekhov's neglect.[4] Nor does their first intimacy appear to have long preceded the "unearthly bliss" episode in the Grand Hotel.

On neither side do we sense an all-consuming passion. Lydia seems to have been more keen on her career than on Chekhov, while he was amiably prepared to help her professionally, recommending her to Suvorin, who eventually took her on at his St. Petersburg theatre. If we did not know better we should never guess, from the various comments on his mistress made by Chekhov to others, that they had been lovers. Lydia is a "very charming woman"; a "very kind woman and an actress who might have come to something if she hadn't been spoilt by her training. She is a bit of a hussy, but that doesn't matter." Lydia "is educated, dresses decently, is sometimes intelligent. . . . If she was a bit less loud and wasn't quite so affected . . . she'd make a real actress. She's an interesting type anyway."[5]

These comments prompt a pregnant reflection. If Chekhov could be so off-hand in referring to the one woman known from independent evidence to have been his mistress, may he not have had love affairs with one or more of the numerous women with whom the record has him on friendly—but no more than friendly—terms during the Melikhovo years? Indeed he may; but we have precious little evidence either that he did or that he did not. Even his liaison with Yavorsky may have been a mere one-night affair. That Chekhov was no compulsive philanderer we already know from evidence of the 1880s, and we can now confirm it from two of his letters to Suvorin—one written on 19 January 1895 at the end of his Lydia-dominated stay in Moscow, the other on 21 January, the day on which he returned to Melikhovo. Here, in the very wake of his sole documented love affair, Chekhov twice writes of women as "stealing one's youth". He relates the first comment to that notorious lecher Isaac Levitan. "I visited Levitan's studio. He's the best Russian landscape-painter; but he's lost his youth, believe it or not. He's now painting without youth but with bravura. I think he's been worn out by women. Those charming creatures bestow love, but they rob a man of just one little thing only: his youth. A landscape can't be painted without feeling and enthusiasm, and enthusiasm's impossible when a man has over-indulged himself. If I was a landscape-painter I'd lead an almost ascetic life. I'd have a woman once a year and eat once a day."[6] The comment underlines the close link which Chekhov often made between artistic creativity and asceticism.

Two days later Chekhov is still more explicit. "Alas and alack! Women rob men of their youth: but not me. . . . I've had few love affairs, and I am to Catherine [Catherine the Great, a proverbially lascivious sovereign] as a walnut is to a battleship. Silk nighties mean nothing to me except for their comfort and softness to the touch. I'm all for comfort; debauchery doesn't attract me, and I couldn't for instance appreciate Mariya Andreyevna [Potapenko's formidable wife]."[7] Thus Chekhov reflected on love immediately after rising from Miss Yavorsky's bed. As has been splendidly remarked, "whatever form the 'unearthly bliss' of room 5 [in the Grand Hotel] had taken, it had not been a prolonged sensual orgy".[8]

It seems astonishing that someone with Chekhov's rigorous medical training should have subscribed, apparently in all seriousness, to the notion that even moderate sexual intercourse is an automatic passport to premature senility. But we are certainly entitled to deduce that he was somewhat undersexed. He would never have pretended to be anything else, and once explicitly rejected the suggestion that sexual potency could be regarded as "an index of real life and health". He also claimed, most improbably, that all the world's "thinkers" had been impotent by the age of forty: by contrast with "ninety-year-old savages who keep ninety wives each", and with serf-owning Russian landowners famous in the old days for continuing "to impregnate their Agashkas and Grushkas until carried off by a stroke in extreme old age". Chekhov adds that he is not moralizing, "and that probably my own old age won't be free from attempts to 'draw my bow', as Apuleius calls it in his *Golden Ass*".[9]

Not always did Chekhov treat this sensitive topic in so temperate a style; he could also show a harsh, puritanical, censorious streak. In the same letter, for example, he offers certain significant comments on Émile Zola's novel *Le Docteur Pascal*. Here Pascal, a man of fifty-nine, falls in love with Clotilde, a girl less than half his age. This young girl naturally desired youth, Chekhov thundered. "And it takes a Frenchman, if you don't mind my saying so, to turn her for some unknown bloody reason into a hot water bottle for a grey-haired Cupid with sinewy legs like a cockerel . . . a melon caught by the autumn frost." The disgraceful thing was not that Zola's Pascal slept with a young girl, which Chekhov called his private business, but that Zola had the impudence to praise Clotilde for accepting so elderly a lover. "How awful to call this perversion [*sic*] love!"[10] Remarkable here is less the intolerance of youth (showing once again that Chekhov was not invariably the paragon of compassion and understanding evoked in legend) than quite a different consideration: he, whose own age was so close to that of Clotilde, was already thinking of himself as a Pascal—and an impotent Pascal at that. Again and again in letters written in his thirties he complains of being an old man. Should we censure him for doing so? Or feel that he was prematurely and perversely renouncing the joys of youth? Hardly, since this feeling of precocious senility is fully accounted for by poor health: the tubercular condition of which he insisted on remaining unaware, combined with his piles and many other ailments. It is in this context that we must assess such glimpses as he affords into his intimate life. When he writes, in July 1894, of the intoxicating smell of hay and adds that "it's enough to sit on a rick for a couple of hours to think you're in the embraces of a naked woman", he is juxtaposing two experiences which a lustier male would be less inclined to regard as equipollent. In another, franker, passage he speaks of himself as "tossing about on the sea of life and riding out the storm in the flimsy boat of profligacy. The fact is, I don't love my mistresses any more, I'm gradually becoming impotent."[11]

That this last point was probably no joke but a serious comment on his condition is confirmed by a letter from Alexander Chekhov of 15 April 1893 replying to a letter (lost) in which Anton had already complained of sexual apathy. "It's a great pity, but it can't be helped", Alexander consoles his brother. Their aged shopkeeping Uncle Mitrofan had, by contrast, been "far more of a lad than us two"; only recently had the old reprobate "begun to yield to the passage of time". But then (continued Alexander)

Uncle Mitrofan had not written *Ivanov* and *Ward Number Six*. There was more brain work behind a single line of Anton's writings than in any amount of shopkeeping and choral singing—Uncle Mitrofan's two other main activities. "It's also very significant, probably . . . that you live like an archimandrite. Your golden years are passing."[12]

Alexander's letter is important. It confirms Anton's life as celibate or nearly so, and also confirms that his sexual drive was in abeyance in his thirties. Not that it had ever, at any stage, been very great. A natural lack of vigour, combined with the inroads of disease, is enough to explain the "indifference" which came over Chekhov in his fourth decade. There is no need to invoke Alexander's explanation: exhaustion from the pangs of creation. Such exhaustion did not deter Chekhov from active involvement in many enterprises besides literary creation: arduous medical toils, educational exploits, other work for the local council, a busy social life.

If Chekhov did indeed, as we suggest, lead less than a "normal" love life (however defined), it emphatically does not follow that he was less than a man. This is an area in which individual needs differ, and one in which he was content to find his own modest level. Fortunately sexual-fulfilment bores, as they have developed in the late twentieth century, were not there to lecture him on what he was missing. We must also beware of excess of zeal in posthumously robbing the young Chekhov of a sex life simply because it cannot be documented. When he said that he had experienced "few" love affairs, he also implied that he had experienced some. "I don't love my mistresses any more." Then he had presumably loved "them", in the plural, once; and Lydia Yavorsky had not been the only one. We note too that the man who, had he chanced to be a landscape-painter, would have led "an almost ascetic life", was not in actual fact a landscape-painter. On the other hand, every single one of these remarks may have been just a joke.

Chekhov wanted to keep his private life private, and he succeeded; but he did not, as we shall shortly see, keep it quite as private as he may have thought.

Lika Mizinov

Chekhov's attitude to love is further illuminated by his relations with a second Lydia, surnamed Mizinov; we remember her as a friend of Mariya's whom he had first met in the late 1880s. Lika, as the Chekhovs called her, was ten years younger than Anton. As we know from her unpublished letters, she was deeply in love with him during the Melikhovo period and beyond. But so well were her feelings concealed that even his sister, the person closest to both, misunderstood them at the time: not noticing that

Lika was secretly in love with Anton, Mariya believed that Anton was secretly in love with Lika.[1]

Lika was not just one more of Chekhov's lady admirers, but a striking creature with the ash-blond hair and sable brows of the Russian legendary Swan Queen. She was lively and affectionate, a girl of spirit who by no means went in awe of Anton. He might be the famous Chekhov, she once told him, but he was also an idiot.[2] She was constantly reproaching him. Why did he answer her letters late or not at all; break a promise to holiday with her in the Caucasus; say he would visit her in Paris and not turn up? Why did he so often fail to call on her when passing through Moscow to St. Petersburg? A man may sometimes measure the strength of a woman's feeling for him by the stridency of her reproaches; but unfortunately Chekhov was not much interested in Lika's feeling for him, except for liking her and evidently drawing some comfort from her nagging. One is reminded of a passage in *My Wife*. "You will understand what entertainment and pleasure I derived from the sound of a woman's voice in a snug little room as she told me what a bad man I was."[3]

The lively, handsome Lika was at least as eligible as Chekhov; but never, so far as we know, did he consider marrying her. She would certainly have accepted him. Or she would have settled for being his mistress, and there were times when she all but told him so. "I'm burning the candle of my life at both ends. Come and help me burn it quickly. . . . You once said you loved immoral women, so you can't have been bored with me."[4] That Lika declared her love to Chekhov, and perhaps urged him to make love to her, also seems implied in another of her letters, referring to an incident on which we have no other information. "You must have been very surprised and displeased by my conduct. . . . I admit I behaved like an absolute ninny and the thought much distresses me. Don't let anyone read this letter. It's quite enough for me to look silly in your eyes; there's no need for me to look silly to others too. Actually it *was* absurd: to forget oneself by misunderstanding a joke and taking it seriously. Well, you certainly won't blame me much because you've probably realized for some time that that's the way things were."[5] Chekhov replied by evading the issue in his usual jocular fashion. He told his dear little cantaloup that, instead of whining and lecturing the two of them on their bad conduct like a governess, she would have done better to give him her personal news. Were the local dragoons paying court to her? Lika must promise to come back to Melikhovo next month "or be beaten with a stick".[6]

Chekhov kept Lika at arm's length, neither wanting her nor wanting to be rid of her. Seldom has such a stream of jokes and ironical badinage been directed from one human being to another. Chekhov signed his letters with idiotic titles, such as "Emperor of the Midians"; he discussed Lika's imaginary love affairs with absurdly named imaginary rivals ("Trophim", "Bucephalus"). He signed himself "vanquished by you", and asked her to help him tighten the noose which she had thrown round his neck. And Lika indeed would have liked to draw that noose tighter, she replied; "but I'm right out of my depth: I never had such poor success in my life". Chekhov later said that Lika had "so turned my head that I can believe twice two is five". But Lika knew this for the teasing which it was. "As for my turning your head until you think twice two is five, what am I to say, poor thing, if it's you who has so turned *my* head that I can actually believe you, and can even believe that you want to see me?"[7] Thus did Chekhov parry Lika's pathetic attempts to lure him into a more intimate relationship. He liked her more, perhaps, than he liked any other woman until he met his future wife. But he did not love her and he would not make love to her. By late 1893 her hopes of capturing Chekhov had nearly disappeared. She accused him of tormenting her deliberately, adding that he always treated her with condescending pity or ignored her entirely. He should help her by not trying to see her, by not inviting her to his home; such self-denial would mean so little to him, and it might help her to forget.[8]

Lika was soon taking more radical steps to increase the distance between herself and Chekhov: "I have fallen completely in love with Potapenko."[9] And the jolly Ignatius Potapenko was a frequent guest at Melikhovo, where he would arrive with Lika and his violin. While he fiddled the two of them would sing duets and the usual "inexhaustible" stream of jokes, beloved of the memoirists, proceeded from the merry Anton Pavlovich.

It was all great fun.

Tired of pursuing Chekhov, Lika yielded to Potapenko, for whom she had some affection, even if it did come "on the rebound". But their liaison turned out less a splendid orgy of lust than one more minor-key Chekhovian tragedy. In March 1894 the two lovers went off to Paris together. But then Potapenko's wife appeared and began staging hysterical scenes. This was the formidable, unpopular and sexually demanding Mariya Andreyevna. When not threatening suicide she was gadding about and squandering the hen-pecked Potapenko's inadequate earnings on Parisian finery. Now that this monster was living in Paris the wretched Potapenko hardly dared sneak away for an adulterous half hour with Lika.[10] And soon both Potapenkos had steamed off to Italy, leaving poor Lika behind in Paris: abandoned, alone—and, *pour comble de malheur*, pregnant. When Chekhov later learnt of this he called Potapenko "a [. . .] and a swine".[11] But Lika did not blame her Ignatius, knowing him for a hopelessly weak-willed individual. He would plan to leave his wife and live with his mistress. But Lika realized that he could not stick to this or any other decision, and extended to her spineless paramour the special consideration which men who behave childishly are often fortunate enough to receive from their women.

Meanwhile Lika was growing more and more pathetic as her pregnancy advanced. From Paris she encouraged Chekhov to write to her as *Madame* rather than *Mademoiselle*; and she plastered her room with his photographs, presumably to create the impression that her unborn child had a legitimate father. Then she moved to Montreux in Switzerland, bombarding Chekhov with letters which long failed to reach him, for this was the period of his wanderings through Abbazia and elsewhere. He was to come and see her, said Lika, but he was to come alone. And he was to expect a great surprise.[12] Thus delicately did she hint at her situation while calling desperately for Chekhov's support. Small wonder that she felt lonely and unhappy, suffering as she was from serious ill health on top of her pregnancy: like Chekhov, she had taken to spitting blood and appeared to have contracted tuberculosis.

When Lika's pleas at last reached Chekhov he refused to visit Switzerland, though he was now aware of her condition. He was travelling with Suvorin whom, he explained, it would have been awkward to drag along to Montreux even if Lika had not expressly commanded him to come alone.[13] In any case Chekhov was still resolved to prevent her from involving her life with his. By refusing his aid in this crisis he behaved unkindly, perhaps, but not outrageously so. No one had appointed him Lika's keeper, and he was ill equipped for such a role. She might have understood him better if she had pondered the dénouement to *A Dreary Story*, written five years earlier, where the dying Professor cannot or will not respond to an anguished appeal for help from his former ward Katya, the only person of whom he is fond and also the victim of an extra-marital pregnancy. When Katya asks the Professor to help her overcome an acute personal crisis he can only utter meaningless platitudes and suggest that they order lunch. For Lika, Chekhov would not even do that.

Lika probably knew Chekhov better than any other woman friend, and her opinions of him provide valuable insights into his character, being refreshingly free from romantic illusions. To her beloved's appearance she seems indifferent, and so we are spared the cloying references to those beautiful, wise, sad, mournful, lustrous etcetera eyes of which others have provided all too many samples. Beautiful herself, Lika attached little importance to appearance in the other sex. Chekhov was similarly inclined, she told him; all he wanted in a woman was intelligence, not beauty.[14]

Since Lika's love for Chekhov was unrequited we are not surprised that she censured his indifference; his lack of passion; his judicious, balanced calm. Contrasting her own verve, her inability to do anything by halves, with his prudence and caution, she says that she could never react in a uniform manner to everyone and everything as he does. She is irritated by the immense self-sufficiency of one who seems not to need people at all, except in bad weather or in long winter evenings when they are required to alleviate his boredom. He doesn't seem to need a personal life at all, says Lika. All he cares about, she rambles on inconsequentially, is his own comfort and peace of mind. He will never take the initiative in proposing a meeting; why must it always be she who has to get in touch with him? As for his complaints of being an old man, coming from anyone else they would be sheer hypocrisy. To be barely thirty, to have all the requisites for happiness and youth, never to have suffered any great sorrow, never to have failed at anything: if such a man could not live in decent, human fashion then it must be because he didn't want to—certainly not because he was prematurely senile. Oh yes, it was easy to vegetate on a sofa at Melikhovo, sleeping seventeen hours in the twenty-four, moaning about being an old man at thirty, and complaining that if one had been young one might have done this that or the other. To hide behind old age just so that one can sleep, eat and write for one's own pleasure: this had nothing to do with being old, it was just due to Chekhov's bad character.[15] Here Lika was unfair to Chekhov, whose activities at Melikhovo were too energetic to merit such jibes. But on the subject of his emotional reserve she had taken his measure well. For if, as Lika said, Chekhov was "frigid and proper" towards her,[16] it was not because he was profoundly involved with anyone else. Must we add to the lack of sexual drive, to the impotence or near-impotence mentioned above, the additional defect of general emotional atrophy? Was Chekhov's reserve so profound that he found it difficult or impossible to establish intimate terms with anyone, man or woman, outside as well as inside the sexual sphere?

Lika's lover Potapenko, who liked and admired Chekhov enormously, held opinions of him similar to hers. This lively Ukrainian writer found it hard to understand Chekhov: so calm, so even, so outwardly cold that he seemed encased in armour. Even those closest to him were always conscious of a certain distance, says Potapenko—adding that Chekhov had no friends, though many sincerely believed themselves his friends. "He carefully preserved his soul from any casual glance"; he "never opened his soul to anyone".[17]

Here, then, is a man capable of touching the depths of emotion in his works, yet virtually unable to make intimate contact with others, even with those closest to him. That one of his major fictional themes is failure of communication we are once again reminded. Was it this very remoteness, this very lack of vigour and passion which most appealed to that aspect of Lika's personality which we may term sexually accident-prone? A cousin whom she had once loved in secret and who had never even noticed her sufferings; then Chekhov; then Potapenko: surely there was more to this than mere bad luck? For so attractive a girl, surrounded by so many admirers, to despise all others and fix her affections on these three no-hopers: this cannot, surely, have been purely accidental. Not that Lika seems to have relished the miseries which she may to some extent have courted. She was a resilient person whose emotional incontinence, though not inconsiderable, was well below par for her period and country; which helps to explain why Chekhov put up with her. Despite the repeated moanings of her correspondence, there was a certain toughness about Miss Mizinov.

In his play *The Seagull*, written in October–November 1895, Chekhov played a trick on Lika and the Potapenkos like that which he had once played on Levitan and his mistress in *The Butterfly*. He reproduced, that is, in an imaginative work the essentials of their real-life situation: not in faithful detail, but in such a way that the principals themselves—and the numerous gossips of the capital—were bound to be struck by the parallels. As Mariya Chekhov has pointed out, *The Seagull*'s "Nina" is modelled on Lika; her lover "Trigorin" on Potapenko; and "Irina Arkadin" on Potapenko's assertive wife, the much-disliked Mariya Andreyevna. For one of the author's woman-friends these and other echoes of actuality made it impossible to judge the play dispassionately.[18] The main resemblance lay in the fate of the heroine, Nina, a young actress abandoned pregnant by her author-lover. The latter, Trigorin, is described as under the thumb of the masterful Irina. No matter that the portraits might not coincide exactly; the general outline was close enough to embarrass all concerned.

As we have seen, it was only exceptionally that Chekhov drew on his friends' personal affairs in this way. Was it deliberate mischief? Or was he just blundering along in a creative trance? It is hard to know. A month after finishing the play he shows surprise at the affinities with real life which others have pointed out. "My *Seagull* has flopped without being staged; if it really looks as if it describes Potapenko then it clearly can't be performed and printed." We are reminded of Chekhov's surely disingenuous pretence not to have portrayed Levitan and Levitan's mistress in *The Butterfly* (1892).[19] Somehow, though, the Potapenko–Trigorin link was forgotten during the many months which elapsed before *The Seagull*'s first performance. And in any case Potapenko himself cannot have been much offended since he acted as Chekhov's agent in the troublesome business of getting the play passed by the St. Petersburg censor.

Perhaps these negotiations taxed poor Ignatius's energies, for on the eve of *The Seagull*'s first performance Chekhov speaks of his friend as a changed man. Potapenko has given up singing and drinking; he has aged, he is bored, he is more dominated than ever by the insufferable Mariya

Andreyevna, who never lets him out of her sight. The Potapenkos have, Chekhov further reports, taken a box for *The Seagull*'s first night, a performance which Lika also proposes to attend with the Chekhov family. Noting that the Potapenkos' and the Chekhovs' boxes might turn out to be adjacent, Anton said that this would "just serve Lika right".[20] Serve her right! How could so sensitive a man speak in this callous way? His attitude seems especially unkind in view of the poignantly distraught lines given to Nina in Act Four of the play. Here, to those familiar with Lika's unpublished letters, he seems to parody the style of the desperate missives from Montreux in which the abandoned unmarried mother had so vainly appealed for her author-friend's presence and support.

Lydia Avilov

Yet another (a third) Lydia has left traces in the text of *The Seagull*, having played—or, more probably, not having played—a significant role in Chekhov's emotional evolution during the 1890s. This was Mrs. Avilov: authoress, St. Petersburg housewife, multiple mother. Her impact or lack of impact on Chekhov's life contributes, in my view, one of the most pathetically farcical episodes in his biography, though the facts of their relationship remain in dispute. Some are embedded in a long memoir by Mrs. Avilov, "A. P. Chekhov in My Life",[1] most of which cannot be checked from independent sources and which may consist in part of delusionary fantasies.

Let us begin with what lies beyond dispute. Chekhov met Lydia Avilov at least six times in the years 1889–99. Their first encounter occurred in St. Petersburg at the house of her brother-in-law, S. N. Khudekov, editor of *Peterburgskaya gazeta* to which Chekhov had once been a frequent contributor. They met again at the same house on 1 January 1892 at a celebration marking the twenty-fifth anniversary of Khudekov's paper. Then the two met twice, at Leykin's and at Lydia's own house, in February 1895; also at a masked ball in January 1896. She visited Chekhov when he was ill in Moscow in March 1897 and was to meet him briefly in the same city two years after that. She sent her writings to him for criticism, and in 1899 we shall find her helping to prepare his first "Collected Works" by arranging for the copying of certain early material in St. Petersburg. We have thirty-two letters from Chekhov to Mrs. Avilov, supplied in copies by herself; the originals were stolen from her in 1919, she has claimed.[2] As for her letters to Chekhov, only fragments survive after she had extracted them from his sister after his death;[3] she appears to have destroyed or suppressed them. She has thus allowed posterity access only to such parts of her correspondence with Chekhov as she has seen fit to divulge—and those in a form which cannot be checked against the original documents. Chekhov's letters to Mrs. Avilov are relaxed, casual and bantering in his usual style, except where he rebuts certain of her accusations based on his failure to live up to her preconceptions of how he ought to behave. These are not at all the letters of a man to the one great love of his life: the role in which the lady has billed herself for posterity.

She has not, be it noted, claimed that they were lovers, but has merely made the most of the emotional currents which, she most implausibly maintains, surged and swirled whenever male and female author caught sight of each other. "We just looked closely into each other's eyes, but what a lot it meant [she writes of their first meeting in 1889]! It seemed as if my soul had exploded and a rocket had soared aloft; brightly, joyously, triumphantly, ecstatically. I had not the remotest doubt that Anton Pavlovich felt the same as we looked at each other in amazement and delight."⁴ After a series of similar electric shocks experienced at later meetings spread over half a dozen years, Chekhov meets Lydia alone at her house at her invitation in February 1895. It is now, according to the lady novelist's memoirs, that he confesses his love, albeit in the past tense. "Do you know, I was seriously attracted by you?... I loved you. I thought there was no other woman in the world whom I could love so much. You were beautiful and touching, and there was so much freshness and vivid charm in your youth. I loved you and thought only of you.... I knew that you were not like other women... and that it was possible to love you only with a pure and happy love which would last all my life."⁵

Lydia, now obsessed by her own love for Chekhov, responded to his alleged effusion by sending him a fob for his watch in the form of a book, and inscribed "PAGE 267, LINES 6–7". Reference to a volume of stories published by Chekhov in the previous year revealed the message, embodied in his *Neighbours*, as "if you should ever need my life, then come and take it". After this nothing happened for about a year until, Lydia reports, a romantic meeting occurred between herself and Chekhov, both disguised, at a masked ball at Suvorin's theatre in St. Petersburg. He then promised to give her his "answer" to the watch-fob message from the stage in the text of his new play *The Seagull*.⁶ When that play opened on 17 October 1896 Mrs. Avilov was in the audience; she was straining her ears amid the boos and catcalls which attended that disastrous first night, hoping to catch Chekhov's private message to herself. At last, in Act Three, her patience was rewarded as she saw Nina present her lover Trigorin with a medallion— inscribed, like Avilov's gift, but with a different reference: "PAGE 121, LINES 11–12". In the *play* this reference leads to the same passage as that indicated on Avilov's watch-fob: "If you should ever need my life, then come and take it." But that was only for the audience. A different message, one

intended for Avilov's eyes only, was surely to be found under the same
page-and-line reference, if only she could think where to look. Hurrying
home after the performance, Lydia feverishly consulted her library: and
there, sure enough, a recently published volume of her own stories called
The Happy Man enabled her to decode the reply. After so much fuss and
emotion, and some eighteen months after her original declaration of
devotion, Chekhov's riposte had all the impact of one of those grand anticlimaxes in which that inverted romantic specialized. "Young ladies
should not attend masked balls."[7]

That this was a deliberate, well-merited snub Lydia does not appear to
have recognized. Nor was this all. Chekhov had never even acknowledged
the celebrated watch-fob but had casually presented it to another woman,
the actress Vera Komissarzhevsky, who took the part of Nina in The
Seagull, where Lydia's precious gift was used as a stage prop.[8] On another
occasion at about the same period Mrs. Avilov went to Moscow, hoping
to visit Chekhov at Melikhovo; but when she enquired at the offices of
Russkaya mysl she was told (incorrectly) that he had gone to distant
Taganrog. That this was a false trail deliberately laid by Chekhov to
prevent such as Lydia from intruding on his privacy is the view of Nicholas
Leykin, Chekhov's former editor. But Leykin is unfair to Lydia when he
calls her a dilettante writer; she was at least sufficiently professional to have
her works published regularly.[9]

There is no point in further rehearsing the many inconsistencies and
implausibilities in Lydia Avilov's memoirs. They have been thoroughly
analysed by Ernest J. Simmons and Virginia Llewellyn Smith, both of
whom convincingly refute the lady's claims to have aroused an undying
passion in Chekhov. I agree with them, and also with Chekhov's sister,
who has taken a similar view. Others—Chekhov's contemporary Ivan
Bunin and a biographer, David Magarshack—have supported the Avilov
version on grounds which seem inadequate.[10]

To various considerations discrediting Lydia's claims to have been
Chekhov's one great love I would add those of timing and tone. Though
she does not state when her reminiscences were written (the first substantial
fragments appeared in 1910),[11] the bulk of them first surfaced many years
after the events described. Yet the speeches of the main characters are given,
at length, verbatim. Few people could accurately record a conversation in
this way two minutes after it had occurred, let alone several decades or up
to half a century later. Avilov neither claims to have made notes at the
time, nor provides evidence of being endowed with total recall. Was this
a deliberate attempt to mislead posterity? Or did she genuinely see herself
as the only begetter of a pure and sacred passion in her most elusive and
talented contemporary? Had she taken Chekhov's facetious gallantries and

built upon them a vast superstructure of fantasy in which she figures as Isolde to his Tristan? If so, the poor woman deserves pity rather than contempt. Yet the element of emotional incontinence, and of sheer silliness, in her memoirs is not easily forgotten or forgiven. From a woman who attracts him a man may overlook much of what would irritate him in anyone else. But can Chekhov, of all people, conceivably have become emotionally committed to someone capable of signing her name to this mawkish drivel? Did his, of all people's, soul—in heaven's name!—*explode*? It seems downright incredible. But we have no evidence which enables us to assert positively that it was not so.

The Women of Chekhov's Fiction

The three Lydias—Yavorsky, Mizinov, Avilov—were by no means the only interesting young women whom Chekhov met during his Melikhovo years. There was the authoress Helen Shavrov, on whom he continued to lavish literary advice in the playful style reserved for his communications with women. Of her non-literary relations with Chekhov we know nothing, except that Lika Mizinov once referred to his "romance with a lady writer" who, from the context, appears to have been Miss Shavrov.[1] There was also a Miss Pokhlyobin, a pianist who wrote Chekhov hopeless love letters (unpublished),[2] and whom he seems to have taken even less seriously than Lika. There was the mentally unstable, occasionally irritating and intellectually formidable lady mathematician Olga Kundasov, a frequent visitor to Melikhovo, whom Chekhov for a time subsidized financially without her knowledge. There was Tatyana Shchepkin-Kupernik, whom he teased almost as unmercifully as he teased Lika. There was the Ukrainian actress Mariya Zankovetsky with whom he went tobogganing and drank champagne until four in the morning, and who rebuked him for not writing in his "native" language, by which she meant Ukrainian.[3] Such, and many more, were Chekhov's celebrated lady admirers or fans. From them he required that they should be beautiful, elegant, well-dressed, intelligent, witty and amusing; and above all that they should keep their distance.

Considering the three Lydias, none of them exactly sylph-like, together with other women whose company Chekhov cultivated or of whom he expressed approval—Natalya Lintvaryov of the booming laugh, the hearty Sasha Selivanov, the dashing Mariya Zankovetsky[4]—we find a marked preference on his part for robust, outgoing, active girls. It is remarkable then that his fiction appears to idealize a type of woman who possesses none of these qualities: such romantic heroines as Kisochka (*Lights*), Tanya (*The Black Monk*), Zhenya (*The Artist's Story*). In these obviously much admired figures Chekhov stresses the qualities of youth, *naïveté*, purity, defenceless-ness and physical weakness.⁵ There is talk of their thin arms and undeveloped breasts, and they lack the liveliness and humour which Chekhov valued in his real-life lady friends. Here, once again, Chekhov the creator implies standards more ascetic than those which he followed in real life; just as this fictional denigrator of eating and drinking was less abstemious in practice than might be deduced from his works. Certainly Chekhov did not draw on any real-life figure who can be traced when he created these wilting, waif-like heroines.

There is also, in Chekhov's imaginative work, a very different female type: such harpies as Ariadne (*Ariadne*), Olga (*His Wife*), Irina (*The Seagull*), Natasha (*Three Sisters*). Confident, predatory and sensual, these disrupters of male calm were by implication as distasteful to Chekhov as the young and innocent romantic heroines were attractive. Who, if any, were his models? Lydia Yavorsky? The infamous Mrs. Potapenko? We cannot say. The concept of Ariadne may go back to Chekhov's schooldays, for one of his teachers was married to a similar monster who bore the same name, while the atrocious Olga of *His Wife* is known to be based on a certain Mrs. Sablin, whom Chekhov did not know but of whom he learnt from his brother Michael.⁶

As all this emphasizes, we can trace only fragmentary connections between Chekhov's fictional characters and his real-life associates. Real men and women did furnish him with literary "copy", but only in limited degree, as did his travels, his medical practice, his educational work. And yet no theme is more prominent in Chekhov's mature fiction than love. Or should we call it "non-love"? On this, as on all other facts of life, he took his own independent, idiosyncratic view. The harmony, the mutual attraction, the delights, rewards or satisfactions, spiritual and physical, which many other fiction-writers do at least occasionally portray as deriving from the relations between lovers and married people—these are emphatically not Chekhov's main preoccupation. When treating love he is usually concerned, as when handling any other fictional topic, with the collapse of illusions, not with the fulfilment of hopes. But though it is estrangement which chiefly interests him, there are occasions when, in order to show his lovers drifting apart, he must first show them growing together. In such cases the development of their love is described with far less literary skill than is the inevitable estrangement. Rarely indeed do Chekhovian lovers and married couples enjoy any established, long-term contentment. Such instances may be traced, exceptionally, in *Peasants* and *Angel*; but in neither story does the reader contemplate any idyll of marital bliss, for the author kills off or permanently removes the male partners concerned. A single major story, *The Duel*, supplies the happy ending otherwise missing in the mature fiction; but it is the cohabitational misery of the magnificent first ninety-odd pages, not the reconciliation so unconvincingly portrayed in the fictionally disastrous last four, which help to make this one of Chekhov's finest works. As for his drama, contented love plays no part in it.

As a rough indication of the importance of frustrated love, it is fairly prominent in some three-quarters of the post-Sakhalin stories, predominating in quite a few of these over all other themes. At the opposite pole we have *Ward Number Six*, perhaps the finest of all Chekhov's works, but one which he himself professed to find "very boring, as it completely lacks women and any love element".[7] But so too, in great measure, did its author's life.

CHAPTER ELEVEN

Melikhovo 1892–7:
Patterns of Art

The Literary Life

During the Melikhovo years Chekhov maintains his general publishing pattern, as followed since 1888, but varies it in two important particulars.

This pattern, we remember, involved him in first publishing nearly all his works in periodicals, while distributing most of them according to length between two specific favoured vehicles; the longer items had gone to a Thick Journal and the shorter to a daily newspaper. So far the favoured Thick Journal had been *Severny vestnik* and the favoured newspaper had been *Novoye vremya*; but Chekhov had continued all along to publish sporadically elsewhere. At Melikhovo the pattern remained unchanged, except that Chekhov now abandoned his previously favoured periodicals for two new outlets: the Thick Journal *Russkaya mysl* and the newspaper *Russkiye vedomosti*. These switches involved a change of cities as well as a change of vehicles, for the abandoned publications were both based in St. Petersburg, while the newly favoured were in Moscow. Melikhovo thus marks the end of a publishing era for Chekhov. Right through from his début in the comic weekly *Strekoza* back in March 1880 he had published the bulk of his work, including virtually all of any importance, in St. Petersburg. Now Moscow takes over. Thus it came about that, when *Severny vestnik* carried *My Wife* in January 1892, it was publishing Chekhov for the last time; as was *Novoye vremya*, except for odd journalism, when it brought out *Terror* in December of the same year. But neither the author nor his editors had any idea at the time that these were to prove Chekhov's final appearances. Drifting away from the two St. Petersburg publications, not breaking with them in a fit of pique, Chekhov had no lack of other outlets. Nor had his favours to specific vehicles ever been exclusive. So free was he to pick and choose that the year 1892 sees his seven chief new works of fiction appearing in seven different publications; besides which he even re-emerged briefly and unexpectedly with four short, trivial items in an eighth: Leykin's *Oskolki*.

It was through this confused publishing situation that Chekhov, no little confused himself, was groping his way towards the Moscow monthly review *Russkaya mysl*, and the Moscow daily newspaper *Russkiye vedomosti*. The switch to *Russkaya mysl*, of all Thick Journals, reminds us of Chekhov's earlier disastrous contacts with that review. They had been abruptly terminated by the furious letter which he had fired off in April 1890 to the editor, Lavrov. But Chekhov was reconciled with Lavrov by a mutual friend, the actor Svobodin, soon after moving to Melikhovo. A friendly invitation to contribute to *Russkaya mysl* followed.[1] Chekhov at once set about disengaging two of his finest works, already promised elsewhere, and sent them off to Lavrov: *An Anonymous Story* and *Ward Number Six*. Minor disagreements with both the periodicals from which he was now withdrawing made the switch especially welcome, though it meant returning advances of 900 roubles: scrupulousness utterly astounding to the editors, says Potapenko.[2]

Chekhov soon took to calling in at the offices of *Russkaya mysl* during his many Moscow excursions from Melikhovo. Cordial terms were established with Lavrov and his co-editor, V. A. Goltsev; for, as often happens, the composing of a silly quarrel created a close bond between former enemies. From now on *Russkaya mysl* is to be the main outlet for Chekhov's finest work. Beginning with the outstanding *Ward Number Six* in November 1892, and ending with the renowned *Lady with a Dog* in December 1899, Lavrov's review secures the first publication of thirteen stories in all; as also of *Sakhalin Island* and two major plays, *The Seagull* and *Three Sisters*. *Russkaya mysl* is therefore by far the most important Thick Journal of Chekhov's life. We remember its political complexion as liberal, in marked contrast to the reactionary *Novoye vremya*, now abandoned. But to interpret the move as a "swing to the left" by Chekhov is to invoke a mentality alien to one whose primary concerns always remained artistic, intellectual, humanitarian; never political.

The abandonment of *Novoye vremya* comes as no surprise after the criticisms of Suvorin's paper and publishing habits scattered through Chekhov's letters. Neither quarrelling with Suvorin personally nor suspending the publication of his books by Suvorin's firm, Chekhov found *Russkiye vedomosti* more convenient for works too short to require publication in a Thick Journal. The editor, V. M. Sobolevsky, was as congenial as Suvorin, but would surely prove easier to deal with. Moreover, *Russkiye vedomosti* was, like *Russkaya mysl*, conveniently near at hand in Moscow. And it too had a liberal complexion: not a motive for the change, but no great inconvenience either. Eleven of Chekhov's stories were first published in *Russkiye vedomosti*, beginning with *The Two Volodyas* in December 1893 and ending with *New Villa* in January 1899.

How far Chekhov was from deciding in advance to break with *Novoye vremya* is clear from plans which he mentioned as late as August 1893. He then told Suvorin that he would send him a new story of between 600 and 700 lines *every fortnight* in the new year, 1894; he even specified his fee as 200 roubles per item.[3] Far from carrying out this ambitious programme, however, he was never to write another single word of fiction for *Novoye vremya*.

During the Melikhovo years Chekhov continued to write, as he had always written, for money. A few months after his move to the country, which temporarily increased his debts, he reported his innermost being as "tormented by the thought of writing for cash, and of money being the centre of my activity". He knew nothing more tedious and unromantic than this prosaic struggle for existence which robbed him of all enjoyment in life. "I hold that true happiness is impossible without idleness. My ideal is to be idle and love a fat girl. My greatest pleasure is to walk about or sit around doing nothing. . . . But I'm a writer, so write I must."[4] His sources of income were erratic. So too were his business methods and those of his paymasters: one lot of editors would urge on him advances for unwritten work, while others were scandalously slow in paying for copy long delivered and published. The most slovenly of his main sources was Suvorin's publishing house, which was to issue his books for several years after the break with *Novoye vremya*. But so long as Suvorin remained both a major creditor and a major source of income, Chekhov would never know where he stood. It was demoralizing to learn suddenly that he owed his old friend 7,000 roubles—even if it did turn out soon afterwards that he was really 5,000 roubles in credit. On such matters we know more than we otherwise should through the "reticent" Chekhov's habit of confiding detailed information on his finances to fairly distant acquaintances as well as intimates.[5]

During the Melikhovo period Chekhov's writing habits became more secretive—by contrast with the 1880s, when he had often read his stories aloud to friends and relatives, and when he would even compose them in company. Potapenko reports that Chekhov was constantly engaged in subconscious creation at Melikhovo, but adds that he never, now, wrote in the presence of other people. When he had guests he would repeatedly slip away to his study, write two or three lines in private, and then rejoin the company a few minutes later.[6] Chekhov's sister reports that she could always tell from his mood when he was in the throes of creation. "His way of walking and his voice changed, a sort of absent-mindedness appeared, and he often answered questions at random. He usually looked a bit odd at these times. This continued until the moment he began writing, when he became his old self again: obviously the theme and images had now fully matured, and his creative tension was ending."[7]

Chekhov considered himself an unsatisfactory working mechanism. He was lazy, slovenly, slow; he wrote in dribs and drabs; he often did nothing for days on end. He was the least dependable of writers, for never could he predict when he might finish a story. Deploring his inability to meet deadlines, he said that it was no use editors extracting promises from him or trying to hold him to undertakings. He saw the creative process as independent of his volition, and compared it to the voyage of a steamer, governed by such external and unpredictable factors as wind and weather. He could, he said, as little forecast his own future performance as he could an eclipse of the sun. His muse, in a word, was capricious. Hence the money worries which continued even after he had become a popular and recognized writer; for if nothing else about his mature output was predictable, it was at least predictably small.[8]

Somehow, though, Chekhov believed that this unsatisfactory situation must end; that he would some day become as prolific as his friend Potapenko, who had once churned out 1,100 roubles' worth of fiction in five days.[9] And, after all, Chekhov himself had been comparably prolific in his Antosha Chekhonte days. Perhaps that good fortune might return? He once claimed to have 1,036 story subjects in his head; but, alas, at least a thousand of these were to remain unexplored. Nor did anything come of the phantom novel or novels which continued to exercise him; by January 1895 he was planning one "a hundred versts long", but it never materialized. Nor did many another projected work: the play which he was going to write first at Yalta and then by Lake Como; another play to be written in collaboration with Suvorin; a tale about "volcanic women and wizards"; a non-fictional treatise on the sixty council schools of Serpukhov County.[10] These plans went the way of his proposed visits to Tahiti, Chicago, the Arctic and the like, reminding us that, as the bard of visions unattained and illusions frustrated, Chekhov was drawing on a rich vein of personal experience.

Was writing such a terrible burden? It was and it was not. Which was the true Chekhov? The man who found the creative process inseparable from gnashing his teeth? Who repeatedly cursed the obligation to write, finding it incompatible with the urge to live? Who described his longest work of the period, My Life, as "hellishly boring"? Who lamented that it was "depressing to be a man of letters"? Or was it the author who "found pleasure in the very process of writing ... a process meticulous and slow"? Whose hands itched to write? Who was "up to his ears in his inkpot"?

Who had taken root in literature ... who felt like publishing a hundred books? Chekhov owes literature the happiest days of his life; he will throw up medicine, having "paid his debt to it", and devote the rest of his life to fiction; he is so attached to literature that he has begun to despise medicine.[11]

In traditional accounts of Chekhov no article is more firmly established than his modesty. Seldom did he praise his own imaginative work, though he once claimed merit for parts of his treatise *Sakhalin Island*. Of two outstanding contributions, *Ward Number Six* and *An Anonymous Story*, he remarked that he had written "two short tales: the one tolerable, the other vile"; and we do not even know which of the two, in his mind, was which. All his work would be forgotten in seven and a half years, he once told Tatyana Shchepkin-Kupernik; but added that interest in his writings would then revive after an interval.[12] As for personal appearances, promotion, exposure and publicity, he loathed them utterly: hence his unwillingness to recite from his works at Moscow and St. Petersburg "literary evenings". "I don't recite. . . . If I do it for three or five minutes my mouth dries up, my voice grows hoarse and I can't stop coughing." "I recite abominably. The main thing is, I'm terrified. There's a complaint called 'fear of open spaces'. Well, I suffer from fear of the public and publicity." This phobia troubled him when he was asked to supply personal details for publicity purposes. To one editor who asked for a potted autobiography he replied that this was like sticking a knife in his side. "I can't write about myself."[13]

And yet, modest though he undoubtedly was, and prominent though "immodest" was among his terms of disapproval, there was yet something about him which led Suvorin, perhaps his closest friend, to speak of Chekhov as "self-important": something which caused another good friend, Potapenko, to emphasize Chekhov's "pride" and "vanity".[14] May we perhaps discern these qualities, however dimly, in his very reticence? A man may be shy and retiring without wholly lacking pride, vanity and self-importance; and we sense as much, for instance, in Chekhov's protest to the editors of *Vsemirnaya illyustratsiya* ("World Illustrated") for tastelessly publicizing his work. "Please tell the editors ... that I have been disagreeably impressed by their announcement dubbing me 'highly talented' and printing my story's title in poster-size letters. It looks like an advertisement for a dentist or masseuse; and is in any case unworthy of an intellectual. I know the value of publicity and have nothing against it. But modesty and good literary manners towards readers and colleagues are a writer's best and surest recommendation."[15]

As this extract shows, there could be something militant about Chekhov's very modesty, and he was by no means always self-effacing. Certainly he derived immense satisfaction from the status of "literary man" (*literator*), and sometimes spoke as if authorship were an order of knighthood imposing special standards of forbearance and chivalry. The critic, philosopher and novelist Merezhkovsky was one of Chekhov's *bêtes noires*, but an undeniable "literary man"; and for this reason he should not (said Chekhov) have lectured in public, as he had, on the decline of literature. A writer should not make disparaging remarks about "his own sort" to strangers. Where was Merezhkovsky's *esprit de corps*? In his own home, in a newspaper office or at a literary gathering he could have said what he liked. As it was he had let the side down by abusing colleagues to "young ladies, policemen, students, tradesmen and all other sorts of persons who constitute the public. . . . However low literature may have fallen, the public is lower still."[16]

Remembering Chekhov's rigorous standards of etiquette, we can understand his indignation over one unedifying literary episode of the period. Suvorin's son Alexis, himself a minor writer, had been annoyed by an unfavourable notice of his work in *Russkaya mysl*, and had so far forgotten the lofty status of literary man as to seek out editor Lavrov and slap his face. Young Suvorin had then, it seems, written certain "whining letters" to Chekhov giving his version of this fracas. But Chekhov would not listen. All was over between him and that "son of a bitch" Suvorin Junior. "Himself notorious for abusing people daily, he goes and hits someone for abusing him! A fine piece of sportsmanship, that! Nauseating."[17] Perhaps this attitude to Suvorin *fils* helped to convince Suvorin *père* of Chekhov's self-importance. As for the pride and vanity recorded by Potapenko, we note that the same witness goes on to stress Chekhov's ability to control these and other weaknesses. Had he possessed no flaws at all he would have been one-sided, claims Potapenko. Chekhov was not the cold-blooded paragon of common repute, but a man with normal live human passions and weaknesses.[18] Well said, indeed.

To be a literary man was, for Chekhov, to be many things besides an author pure and simple. He was still busy as an informal editorial counsellor to fellow-writers; as an unofficial literary agent; as a casual but penetrating off-the-cuff critic of literature. These activities were exacting and comprehensive, but Chekhov was conscious of his own limitations. His chief concern was with Russian fiction and Russian drama of his own day. He was interested, too, in older contemporaries and predecessors in the field of Russian fiction: in Tolstoy most of all, but also in Turgenev, Pisemsky, Mamin-Sibiryak and others. Yet verse, for example, was "not my line". He had never written it, he couldn't hold it in his mind; he was sensitive to poetry, yes, as he was to music, but without being able to explain why. A story, though: that he could criticize.[19] Similarly, he showed little detailed interest in foreign literature despite some acquaintance with Shakespeare, who is often quoted in his work. If he was interested in playwrights such as Ibsen and Björnson it was in their suitability for the Russian stage. If he was interested in Maupassant he was concerned with the quality of a specific translation into Russian and its suitability for inclusion among his many gifts to Taganrog town library.[20] For literature in general Chekhov's concern was that of a dilettante, but of contemporary Russian prose fiction and drama he spoke with the total assurance of an established professional, one who knew how these things were put together and whose authority was too great to require strident assertion.

In the self-imposed role of unpaid literary agent, Chekhov generously championed other writers less successful than himself. He would intervene with an editor to secure overdue payment for a neglected contributor; or, if an editor friend lost his job with one publication, Chekhov would fix him up with another. He told Helen Shavrov that her fee from *Russkaya mysl* was fair: the stars, of whom Chekhov himself was one, received from 150 to 250 roubles a printer's sheet, but beginners could only expect from 50 to 75 roubles. Chekhov placed a short story from his younger brother Michael; consoled a columnist hired by Suvorin at a disappointingly low salary; intervened on behalf of a playwright (Bilibin) with a theatrical impresario (Korsh). He freely dispensed patronage: a feature of the literary world everywhere, and one which could be particularly helpful in Russia. When his brother Alexander reproached him for indulging in the practice, Chekhov replied that even holiday cottages were let on the old-boy network. "So why shouldn't one confer patronage, if it's useful and won't insult or offend anyone?"[21]

Though Chekhov often rejected offers to do editorial work on a regular, paid basis, he was lavish with informal advice when, as often happened, other writers solicited his opinion. During the Melikhovo years he gave Lydia Avilov and Helen Shavrov much counsel mixed with his usual flirtatious banter. But he also found time for male scribes of the period, including such obscure figures as a Ye. P. Goslavsky, an A. V. Zhirkevich and his own brother Alexander.

Chekhov's advice was always practical. It was crisply and wittily expressed, ranging from minor technicalities to problems of general policy, and it incidentally illuminates his own literary practice. Concentrating on concrete detail, he sternly sifted the titles of his correspondents' stories: a reflection of the extreme care which he took over his own titles. Here, as so often, Chekhov could smell pomposity where others might not notice it. The title *Women* was pretentious, he wrote. So too was "*Against his Convictions . . .*". "It lacks simplicity; there's a contrived pretentiousness about those inverted commas and the three dots at the end." As for peasant speech, a fictional muzhik must of course talk muzhik language, but one should not overdo the yokelese: Goslavsky should avoid such bumpkin-like allocutions as *my-sta* ("the likes of us"). One should eschew provincialisms too. And Chekhov also disliked official jargon, as he told Suvorin. "What a loathsome thing bureaucratic language is! 'Basing ourselves on the supposition that.... On the one hand ... but on the other hand....' It makes me spit when I read it." Chekhov himself occasionally made use of such language but only to characterize a self-important nonentity like his Modeste Alekseyevich, the discomfited husband of *The Order of St. Anne.* As for clichés such as "a face framed in hair", Chekhov withered Zhirkevich with the comment that "only ladies write like that nowadays".[22] He criticized Lydia Avilov for sentimentality, while indicating his own very different method of playing on his readers' emotions. "When you depict the poor and downtrodden ... try to be cooler. It gives a background to another's grief, and sets it in relief. As it is, your heroes weep and you sigh. Oh, do be cool!" "One may weep and groan over one's stories, one may share one's heroes' sufferings; but one should, I infer, do so without letting the reader notice. The more objective you are, the more powerful the impression."[23] We also find Chekhov recommending his own methods, his spare and laconic technique, in criticisms of Helen Shavrov's stories. These were overloaded: too many characters, too many descriptions, too many details. "You're an observant person and you'd have grudged scrapping these particulars. But there's nothing for it, you must sacrifice them for the sake of the whole.... When writing one must remember that details, however interesting, tire the brain."[24] To Zhirkevich Chekhov offered an essay on descriptive technique which well illustrates his own practice. "A nature description must above all be so vivid that the reader can conjure up your landscape immediately after he has read it and closed his eyes. But the piling up of such features as twilight, leaden hues, ponds, dampness, the silveriness of poplars, horizons with storm clouds, sparrows, distant meadows: that's no picture, because I just can't visualize it as a harmonious whole however hard I try. In stories like yours nature descriptions are appropriate and innocuous only when they're *à propos* and help you communicate some mood to the reader."[25]

Always polite in criticizing others' work, Chekhov could combine courtesy with bluntness on occasion. He did so in his comments on a story in which Helen Shavrov self-righteously denounced sufferers from syphilis. Rebuking her for treating medical topics without medical knowledge, while apparently reprimanding her own characters for being ill, Chekhov claimed that syphilis was a disease like any other, and that there was no call for Miss Shavrov to moralize about it. "An author must be humane to his fingertips."[26]

Literature should try to stand above contemporary controversies, in Chekhov's view. Living persons' names should be kept out of stories; leave them to journalists. Nor was there any point in dragging in such topical themes as Tolstoy's theories: like ladies' bustles and crinolines, they were liable to seem dated in ten or fifteen years' time. Chekhov accordingly criticized the novelist Pisemsky, whom in general he admired, for jeering at the critics and liberals of his day—all very petty and naïve. "The serious novelist must stand aloof from everything ephemeral." Nor was it any use spoiling one's reader with happy endings such as that of *The Polaniecki Family* by the Polish novelist Sienkiewicz, whose aim was to comfort the bourgeoisie. "Be faithful to your wife, say your prayers . . . make money, love sport, and all is for the best in this world and the next. The bourgeoisie is very fond of so-called 'positive' types, and of novels with happy endings, because they soothingly suggest that one can make money while preserving one's innocence and remain happy while behaving like a swine."[27]

Patient, helpful and sometimes severe with other creative writers, Chekhov retained in his Melikhovo period and beyond the general detestation of critics, reviewers and journalists which we remember him conceiving in the 1880s. "About reviews I observe the following rule. I never ask anyone, either in writing or orally, to say a word about a book of mine. I have never made such requests, and I advise you not to either: one somehow feels less spiritually polluted. To ask for a notice of one's book is to risk encountering vulgarity insulting to an author's feelings."[28] About M. Protopopov, the journalist whose abusive article had caused Suvorin Junior to slap Lavrov's face, Chekhov wrote to Suvorin Senior as follows. "I'm no journalist. I'm nauseated by abuse, no matter who its object may be. I say that because, after reading Protopopov, Zhitel, Burenin [various reviewers] and other judges of humanity I always have a foul taste in my mouth. It spoils my day, I simply feel ill. . . . This isn't criticism, you see, it's not a point of view, but hatred and insatiable, bestial malice. . . . Why this tone as if they were judging criminals instead of writers and artists? I simply can't stand it."[29] Not content with denouncing contemporary critics, Chekhov also delved into the past to censure the deceased radical author D. I. Pisarev for his attacks on Pushkin's *Eugene Onegin*, and for his attitude to the hero and heroine of that celebrated verse novel. "Terribly naïve. The man debunks Onegin and Tatyana, but Pushkin remains unscathed." Speaking of Pisarev's crude tone, Chekhov complains that his criticism "stinks of a contumaciously niggling prosecuting counsel". Pisarev was the very "father and grandfather of all present-day critics".[30]

Another recurrent nuisance was the censorship, trifling though its impact now appears if compared with the rigour of literary controls in post-Imperial Russia. The censors were largely concerned to remove or tone down material considered indecorous or thought-provoking. To call a famine a famine, and not a "temporary food shortage", was to risk trouble; and Chekhov's editor was therefore surprised when the famine story *My Wife* escaped unscathed. To portray even so feeble a socialist or revolutionary as the hero of *An Anonymous Story* was, again, to enter the danger area. "The Narrator is a former socialist, while Hero Number One is the son of a Deputy Home Secretary. My socialist and my Deputy Minister's son are both quiet lads, and don't go in for politics . . . but I'm still afraid . . . of announcing publication." In this case the fears again proved groundless, for this story too passed the censor without difficulty.[31]

On other occasions Chekhov was less lucky. His *Peasants* was reported as purveying too "gloomy" a picture of Russian village life by a censor who caused the offending page of *Russkaya mysl* to be jettisoned and another, lacking the material found objectionable, to be hastily substituted. When *Peasants* appeared in book form, however, Chekhov was able to do what he had already done when publishing *Sakhalin Island*: to restore in a bound volume the cuts which had been imposed by the censor on periodical-published work.[32] As this reminds us, books were less vulnerable to censorship than periodicals; and periodicals with a small circulation were less under attack than those with a large circulation. There was also the point that individual censors varied widely in severity.

Indecorous pictures of family relationships were liable to suffer mutilation; as witness the objection made to a passage in *My Life* where the hero's sister is described as no longer on speaking terms with her father. This was only one among many censor's interventions which caused Chekhov to regret publishing the story in *Niva* ("The Meadow)", a weekly with a wide "family" readership. As such it came under especially close scrutiny by a censor who also slashed from the same work an eloquent tirade on the horrors of Russian provincial life. Excised too were the hero's denunciations of a society where the strong have enslaved the weak and where a parasitical minority battens on an exploited majority. This profusion of cuts reduced the author to despair. "What the censor has done to my story! Horrible, horrible! He has devastated the ending." Fortunately Chekhov was again able to restore much of the excised material when publishing *My Life* in book form.[33] As this story further reminds us, there is often more to censorship than officially imposed cuts and changes. There is also self-censorship such as a prudent author applies to work in progress so as to avoid trouble later on. "Even when printed *in toto* the story is obviously bound to make a mutilated impression, since when writing it I couldn't forget for a moment that it was . . . subject to censorship."[34] Pre-censorship might also be applied editorially and without the author's permission. When *Russkiye vedomosti* turned out to have treated Chekhov's first contribution, *The Two Volodyas*, in this way, he was furious. "They cropped it so hard that they cut off the head with the hair. What absolutely infantile prudishness and astonishing cowardice! I wouldn't mind if they'd only thrown out a line or two, but they've gutted the middle and docked the tail."[35] But when publishing *The Two Volodyas* in book form Chekhov did not restore the passages so officiously excised, and they have not survived.

The Seagull provoked arguments over references to the liaison between Irina Arkadin and her lover Trigorin. The point here, the censor explained, was not that an actress and a writer were portrayed as cohabiting, but that her son and her brother were described as adopting so casual an attitude to this affair. Perhaps it would be best, Chekhov ironically suggested, to put Irina–Trigorin relations in perspective by giving her brother a new line: "What, at her age! Really! She should be ashamed of herself!" Chekhov wearily agreed to cut the phrase "lives openly with this novelist", and to tone down his already chaste text in other ways. But that was all he would do. Should the censor raise any more footling objections, "then to hell with the play, I don't want to mess around with it any more".[36]

The censorship was growing stricter and crustier, complained Chekhov towards the end of his Melikhovo period, concluding that "in general it's not much fun being a writer". Censorship robbed one of all wish to write freely. "It's like writing with a bone stuck in your throat."[37]

Encounters with Tolstoy

Chekhov's record as a follower of Tolstoy in the late 1880s has been considered above. We now come to the phase in which Chekhov firmly rejects Tolstoy the thinker while becoming a personal friend of Tolstoy the man.

By the mid-1890s it seemed strange that the two most important living Russian authors had never met. Tolstoy was accustomed to hold informal court at his country home at Yasnaya Polyana, south of Melikhovo, and Chekhov had long been urged to visit that place of pilgrimage and pay homage to the *genius loci*. Amongst others P. A. Sergeyenko, an old schoolfellow of Chekhov's and a Tolstoyan disciple, had long been pressing him to go. But Chekhov was never one for doing the expected thing. When he did visit Tolstoy he intended to go without intermediaries or nannies such as Sergeyenko, whom he thought a pompous bore.[1]

On 8 August 1895 Chekhov at last made his way to Yasnaya Polyana, where he spent a day and a half with Tolstoy and his family. Excellent relations were established, and were to last until Chekhov's death, being based on mutual respect which did not preclude mutual criticism. Tolstoy used to say that Chekhov's plays were even worse than Shakespeare's, while Chekhov's criticisms of Tolstoy covered many aspects of the sage's work and teaching. During their first meeting, when some of Tolstoy's novel *Resurrection* was read aloud to the company, Chekhov pointed out a legal error. The heroine was described as being sentenced to two years' Siberian penal servitude; but, as Chekhov well knew from his work among convicts, such short sentences were never imposed. Later, when Chekhov had read *Resurrection* as a whole, he condemned the ending as unconvincing and arbitrarily based on a Gospel text.[2] For Tolstoy's two supreme fictional masterpieces, *War and Peace* and *Anna Karenin*, Chekhov expressed great admiration. Compared with Anna Karenin herself all Turgenev's heroines "with their seductive shoulders" could go to hell. *War and Peace* Chekhov found superb, except for the scenes in which Napoleon figures. Reflecting on the wounded Prince Andrew's death in the same novel, the practical-minded Chekhov typically deplored the state of medicine in the early 1800s; he himself could easily have cured Tolstoy's hero.[3]

Enormously though Chekhov continued to admire Tolstoy the novelist and Tolstoy the man, the sage's teachings had become a different proposition. Chekhov's progressive disillusionment can be traced in comments on a single work of fiction by Tolstoy, *The Kreutzer Sonata*. First considering this famous call for sexual abstinence in early 1890, Chekhov was already criticizing Tolstoy's cavalier treatment of scientific evidence; he condemned Tolstoy for brashly handling topics of which he knew nothing and which he refused to understand out of stubbornness. Tolstoy's views on syphilis, on foundling homes, on women's alleged revulsion against the sexual act: they were not so much disputable as downright ignorant. Never in a long life had Tolstoy bothered to read two or three specialist works on these topics. Still, the story was so good that its defects were like chaff before the wind.[4]

In December of the same year Chekhov, newly returned from Sakhalin, recorded a more severe judgement of the same work. "Before my journey *The Kreutzer Sonata* was a major event to me; but now I find it ludicrous, it seems pointless." And by the following September Chekhov was lashing out against *The Kreutzer Sonata*'s author for pontificating from ignorance, for disparaging medicine, for providing his story with a stupid, stuffy epilogue. "To hell with all Great Men and their philosophy [he writes to Suvorin]. All pundits are despotic as mandarins. They're impolite and coarse ... because they think they can get away with anything. Diogenes spat at peoples' beards because he knew he was immune, and Tolstoy abuses doctors as scoundrels, treating major problems ignorantly because he's another Diogenes who can't be put under arrest or attacked in the newspapers!" All this philosophy was not worth a single mare in Tolstoy's famous horse story *Kholstomer*.[5]

Tolstoy's slights to the doctors' profession derived from his faith in the Simple Life, medical care being only one among the many complex trappings of modern civilization which he sought to renounce wholesale. This entire anti-intellectual, anti-cultural core of Tolstoyism Chekhov categorically rejected. In August 1891 he mentions his yearning for carpets, fireplaces, bronzes and intellectual conversations. "Alas, I shall never be a Tolstoyan. The qualities which I most prize are: women's beauty ... and civilization expressed in carpets, sprung carriages and wit." Reflecting on his own and his fellow-doctors' success in combating cholera in 1892, Chekhov said that they were performing miracles which should compel Tolstoy to respect medicine and civilizing activities in general.[6]

Nowhere does Chekhov more explicitly renounce Tolstoy's teachings than in a letter of March 1894, where he incidentally pulverizes Tolstoy the muzhik-fancier in a passage which anticipates his own no-nonsense picture of village life in *Peasants*.

Tolstoy's morality has ceased to move me. .... I have peasant blood in my veins, and you can't impress me with peasant virtues. ... I have loved intelligent people, sensitivity, courtesy, wit. As for peasants picking at their corns, as for the stifling stink of their footrags: to those things I've been as indifferent as to young ladies going round in the mornings in their curling-papers. But Tolstoy's philosophy greatly moved me. It obsessed me for six or seven years. It wasn't Tolstoy's basic premises, previously familiar to me, which impressed me, but his way of putting things, his judiciousness, and probably some kind of hypnotism. But now something in me protests. Reason and justice tell me there's more love for humanity in electricity and steam than in chastity and vegetarianism. War's evil, litigation's evil. But that doesn't mean I have to wear clogs and sleep on a stove with a workman and his wife and that sort of thing. The pros and cons are neither here nor there, though: the fact is, Tolstoy has somehow sailed away, there's no place for him in my heart. He has left me.[7]

Chekhov's most outspoken fictional attack on Tolstoyism occurs in the novella-length story *My Life*, where he carefully avoids invoking the sage's name in accordance with his policy of not cluttering a work of art with ephemeral topical themes. The hero, Misail Poloznev, is the son of a successful provincial architect. As such he is expected to embark on some respectable professional career like other young men in his position; instead of which he flouts convention by working as a navvy, a farm labourer, a house-painter. Thus does Misail opt for the Simple Life as preached by Tolstoy; thus does he reject such trappings of advanced civilization and culture as his dreary provincial home town can offer. While treating his hero with personal sympathy, such as he also felt for Tolstoy the Man as opposed to Tolstoy the Thinker, Chekhov yet strongly implies that Misail has chosen the wrong course in cutting himself off from the professions and from a more intellectual form of life. While discrediting his sympathetic hero, Chekhov simultaneously implies approval for his associates: anti-Tolstoyan in openly enjoying privileges, soft carpets, cultured surroundings and professional or business careers. These are the talkative Dr. Blagovo; the railway tycoon Dolzhikov; Misail's estranged wife Masha, who grievously sins against Tolstoyan morality by pursuing a career as an opera singer and—worse still—by possessing the attribute of physical beauty.

Anti-Tolstoyan too is the earlier and even finer story *Ward Number Six*. Here Chekhov dissects the Tolstoyan doctrine of non-resistance to evil, again without invoking the sage's name. The ideological villain is a Doctor Ragin who will not lift a finger to improve the filthy, stinking mental ward of his slummy provincial hospital. The ward smells like a zoo, the patients are cruelly beaten by a brutal caretaker; but Ragin has sound philosophical reasons for leaving things as they are. Since lunatic asylums and prisons exist someone or other is bound to occupy them. In any case suffering is only in the mind; given the right philosophical approach one can ignore it. For this excessive addiction to Tolstoyan quietism, for this flat refusal to resist evil, Ragin is denounced by one of his own mental patients, a certain Gromov, who in effect takes Chekhov's part against Tolstoy. In the end, through a chain of unfortunate accidents, Dr. Ragin is forcibly consigned to his own atrocious Ward Number Six. The door slams and the implications of his serene Tolstoyan indifference are brought home, leaving us to reflect on the typical Chekhovian device whereby the author's own mouthpiece in the story (Gromov) is paraded as the inmate of a mental ward. This ploy has enabled Chekhov to present a "message" without seeming to preach it.

What reader, after all, can possibly feel "got at" by an author who chooses to put his own point of view into the mouth of a raving lunatic?

Short Story Writer

Having ranged here and there among Chekhov's Melikhovo stories, while relating their themes to his experiences and thought of the period, we must now briefly review them as a group. These stories form the main achievement of the Melikhovo years. They comprise twenty-seven published items in all, one of which (*An Anonymous Story*) had been written in part before the move to the country. Besides that masterpiece they also include three other long and significant works: *Ward Number Six, Three Years, My Life*. Among them too are over a dozen superb medium-length or shorter studies, of which *Peasants* has been noted above as the most influential. But there are also some inconsiderable trifles, including four published in *Oskolki* which Chekhov was to exclude from his "Collected Works" of 1899-1902.

The Melikhovo stories of 1892-7 form a central block lodged chronologically within the mature 1888-1904 period as a whole, but they do not form a self-contained literary group. Neither by quality, nor by theme, nor by technique, nor by any other overriding factor are they collectively distinguished from the other stories of the mature period: from the sixteen titles which preceded March 1892 or from the seventeen which were to follow March 1897. The switch to two newly favoured periodicals, *Russkaya mysl* and *Russkiye vedomosti*, was accordingly accompanied by no significant change of style or content. We can, if we choose, detect a somewhat greater emphasis on social and philosophical protest. *The Duel*, published in 1891 and implicitly recommending in its unconvincing dénouement a policy of repentance and resignation, offers a marked contrast to *Ward Number Six*, issued in the following year and militant in its rejection of Tolstoyan quietism. This new element of implied protest comes and goes in the stories of the later 1890s, progressively increasing on the whole, as we shall see when we return to the topic. But to make this factor a dividing line in Chekhov's literary evolution, as I unfortunately did in my own previous biography, is to exaggerate a secondary characteristic.[1]

Nor does this central block of Melikhovo stories differ significantly from the splendid group of stories which was to follow between mid-1897 and the end of the century, except in one formal particular: Chekhov abandoned, after quitting Melikhovo as his permanent home, the longer, novella-length works such as *The Duel* and *Three Years*. The ninety-page *My Life* (1896) was to be the last of these.

Can we trace any significant, exclusively Melikhovite, periodicity within the short stories of 1892-7? There was a tendency during these years for Chekhov to be creatively active in late spring and early winter, but this is no less true of the preceding and succeeding phases. There was also a continuing failure to resurrect the high productivity of the mid-1880s. Publishing only a few stories each year and averaging a bare hundred pages of fiction per annum, Chekhov continued the course set in 1888: delighting connoisseurs by the quality of his work, no longer overwhelming them with sheer bulk. Altogether the twenty-seven Melikhovo stories, from the trifling *After the Theatre* (1892) to the momentous *Peasants*

Part of a page from the Notebooks in which Chekhov commonly jotted down
ideas for his stories and plays

(1897), barely exceed six hundred pages in length. That this was less by a few pages than Chekhov had once published in the single year 1886, admittedly the most prolific of his life, is a consideration eloquent to those who wish to keep his over-all productivity pattern under review.

Throughout Chekhov's mature period as a whole his creativity was governed by instinctive timing which he could neither analyse nor consciously regulate. Hence the apparent lack of stability and system in his output. In spring 1892, for instance, he celebrates his move to Melikhovo with what, for his mature period, was a positive spate of new fiction—his response to new financial worries, including his mortgage and other debts. During his first three months in the country he writes eight short stories, though only three of them (Neighbours, In Exile, Ward Number Six) are of major importance. After this burst of creativity he is immobilized for months by his duties as cholera doctor, though he does complete and send off An Anonymous Story. Then, during a visit to St. Petersburg and as if to demonstrate the waywardness of his muse, he dashes off the splendid Terror on Christmas Eve 1892, and has it published on Christmas Day in Novoye vremya—his last fictional contribution to that newspaper.

The year 1893 was comparatively unproductive in short stories, perhaps because Chekhov was heavily engaged with Sakhalin Island. The fiction yield amounted to three items only: the wonderful but nightmarish Black Monk; and two memorable studies of frustration published in January of the following year, A Woman's Kingdom and The Two Volodyas. Comparatively prolific were the years 1894–5, when Chekhov wrote twelve new stories; of these the longest is certainly Three Years and the best probably Ariadne. In 1896 a decline in output followed. Only My Life, but that one of his finest and longest stories, emerged during the year; after which a sole item, Peasants, preceded the breakdown in health which terminates the Melikhovo period proper in early 1897.

Producing irregularly and unpredictably at Melikhovo, as in his mature period as a whole, Chekhov also conformed during these years with his usual limitations. Except for the tiresome legend embodied in The Head Gardener's Story, he wisely confined himself to contemporary themes. And he used the European Russian setting most familiar to himself, straying only exceptionally: with the trips to Western Europe in An Anonymous Story and Ariadne; with the Siberia-based In Exile and the Sakhalin-based dénouement of Murder.

Within his preferred European Russian setting he keeps a fair balance between rural and urban material. Still preferring not to identify his localities, he will speak of the "town of S", "our town", "T . . . Province" or various imaginary villages—named, but not traceable in any gazetteer. Occasionally he will offer a mixed background within a single story, as in

My Life, where country scenes alternate with those set in "the town where I did not know a single honest man": a definition which, given Chekhov's opinion of provincial Russia, provides no basis whatever for identifying this particular locality.

In their social setting the peasant tales discussed above are exceptional, despite their great importance in Chekhov's work and life. So too are other stories based on the lower classes: coffin-makers (*Rothschild's Fiddle*); exiles (*In Exile*); village inn-keepers ultimately destined to be convicts (*Murder*). As these examples demonstrate, Chekhov achieves considerable variety of setting within the world of the lower orders. So does he also when treating his preferred milieu, that of the privileged classes which he himself, as a doctor and writer, had joined during his adult life. Here too we find considerable range among characters who include several fellow-doctors but fellow-writers hardly at all. Among them are also landowners, officials, schoolmasters, students, painters and architects. In *A Woman's Kingdom* and *Three Years* we enter, exceptionally, the world of factory-owners, businessmen and merchants known to Chekhov from his father's experiences as an employee at Gavrilov's in Moscow, and later from his own tours of various factories sited in the Melikhovo area. Chekhov also deals occasionally in mixed social settings and presents clashes between the two. We have already mentioned the son of a local architect who flouts taboo by becoming a manual worker in *My Life*. In *At a Country House* Chekhov portrays a memorable clash within the privileged world, between a snobbish elderly aristocratic landowner and a young, self-made plebeian lawyer.

That there are many points where Chekhov's life may be suspected or proved to intersect with his art we have already noted when relating his love affairs, peasant contacts and other Melikhovo experiences to individual works in which these topics figure. What general impression emerges of the links between life and fiction? That Chekhov often embodied real-life experiences in his works, but did so somewhat sparsely and sporadically, and often after a considerable delay. He was not one of those writers, such as Tolstoy, who make a practice of incorporating in their fiction barely disguised, detailed portraits of friends and close relatives, and who also bring in major historical figures. Still less was he a Dostoyevsky drawing heavily on an introspective imagination to create a gallery of distorted or inverted self-portraits. Themes from real life do crop up repeatedly in Chekhov's work, but generally as odd glimpses of detail—rarely as topics to be exploited in depth. The brilliant but brief *His Wife* is therefore exceptional, being "practically a biography" of a certain Yaroslavl official whose unhappy family life Michael Chekhov had chanced to describe to his brother in detail.[2]

Despite such occasional aberrations it is rarely possible to regard Chekhov's experiences as literary "copy", especially as so long a period often elapsed before a given real-life detail, often much changed, would resurface in an imaginative work. This point is made explicit in a letter of late 1897 from Chekhov to an editor who had unsuccessfully solicited a story based on his experiences in Nice, where he was residing at the time. Chekhov replied that he could only write such a story in retrospect, after returning to Russia. "That's the only way I can write: from memory. I've never done live portraits from nature. I need my memory to sieve the subject, filtering out just what is essential and typical."[3] This statement helps to explain how the stories most saturated with Melikhovo themes (*Peasants, In the Hollow* and others) came to be written only when Chekhov was on the point of leaving, or had already left, his Melikhovo estate. Other themes from childhood in Taganrog spent twenty years filtering through his imagination before taking on fictional flesh: Butcher Prokofy and Schoolmaster Dyakonov, for instance, as resurrected in *My Life* and *A Hard Case* respectively. But that this was not invariably the rule is shown by *The Black Monk*, incorporating a nightmare recently experienced by its author at Melikhovo.[4]

Playwright

The Seagull is the only long play by Chekhov which can be assigned to the Melikhovo period with certainty. He wrote it in October–November 1895 in a small cottage which he had recently built in the grounds of his estate, and to the sound of distant music made by his guests as they sang and played the piano in the main house. The first reference to the new drama in Chekhov's correspondence occurs on 21 October 1895, when he speaks of enjoying the work; of playing fast and loose with stage conventions; of providing a landscape with a view of a lake, a lot of talk about literature, little action and a hundredweight and a half of love. One month later Chekhov reports the play finished, and is still harping on his rejection of theatrical conventions. "I began it *forte* and finished it *pianissimo*, contrary to all the laws of the theatre."[1] As these comments indicate, *The Seagull* represents an experiment in dramatic technique new to Chekhov. He here abandons the traditional concentration on a single star part and on strong, carefully prepared dramatic crises, which had characterized *Ivanov*. *The Seagull* stands, as it were, half way between that earlier four-acter and Chekhov's mature drama: *Uncle Vanya, Three Sisters* and *The Cherry Orchard*.

From all Chekhov's major plays, earlier or later, *The Seagull* differs in the sombre tone of its ending. It differs too in concentrating so heavily on the experiences of creative and performing artists—two actresses and two writers. And it differs yet again by a somewhat self-conscious flaunting of "modernistic" devices. There is the heavily obtruded symbol of the shot seagull, which represents the wanton ruining of Nina's life by Trigorin. No other such ponderous symbol, Ibsenite rather than Chekhovian, occurs anywhere else in the Russian master's work. It appears to derive from an episode which occurred at Melikhovo in April 1892. Isaac Levitan, who was out shooting with Chekhov, chanced to wing a woodcock, and Chekhov had to put the wounded bird out of its misery by a blow on the head; then the two men went home to supper full of regrets at having robbed the world of "one beautiful creature".[2] Another "modernistic" feature of The Seagull is the interrupted play-within-the-play of Act One. This insert, consisting of a rhetorical monologue by a World Spirit, is itself a fragment of non-realistic drama such as Russian contemporaries called "decadent". "We need new forms", proclaims Chekhov's "Treplev", the author of that encapsulated playlet; and we have Potapenko's word for it that this same sentiment was constantly on Chekhov's own lips at the time when he was writing The Seagull.[3]

Though dramatic novelties in plenty were to come from Chekhov's pen in future, such items as dead fowl and tirades—however ironically intended—by a World Spirit were not to be among them. His new, unfamiliar and (as it was later to prove) still transitional dramatic technique contributed to the spectacular failure of The Seagull at its first performance at the Alexandrine Theatre in St. Petersburg: perhaps the most traumatic episode of Chekhov's life. It occurred on 17 October 1896, almost a year after the play had been completed, the interval having been largely devoted to tiresome negotiations with the dramatic censor.

The real cause of the play's failure lay less with Chekhov's unorthodox text than with the circumstances of the performance. For some reason a popular comic actress, Elizabeth Levkeyev, had chosen it for her benefit night, the twenty-fifth anniversary of her début on the stage. She was one of those "fine old character actresses" who has only to emerge from the wings to provoke eruptions of mirth. Her large following consisted of unintellectual fans who liked their bit of fun; and who, if they knew Chekhov's work at all, would be familiar only with Antosha Chekhonte, the comic writer of the 1880s.[4]

Such benefit performances as Elizabeth Levkeyev's played a great role in Russian theatrical life. Inflated—threefold—prices might be charged; theatre-goers would call on the beneficiary to buy their tickets in person and express their devotion to an admired artiste. But though Miss Levkeyev's fans might be glad to buy expensive tickets to The Seagull in her boudoir, they were bound to be disappointed at not seeing her—as they naturally expected on her own benefit night—in the actual play. That was quite out of the question, though, for the mere appearance on stage of so robust, so earthy, so grand a comic old trouper would have slashed the delicate fabric of Chekhov's eccentric drama to ribbons. Thus was the failure of *The Seagull* doubly assured in advance. The body of the theatre was in mutinous mood before the curtain had even gone up on the fateful night. Enraged by the absence of their favourite actress from the cast, these lovers of broad farce were not going to be fobbed off with any decadent highbrow rubbish. Knowing little or nothing of Chekhov, they cared still less about "new forms", whether in the theatre or anywhere else. And if there was to be none of the usual riotous fun on stage they were damn well going to create it in the auditorium.

The Seagull would thus have been foredoomed even if it had not been grossly under-rehearsed, as it was, by a cast which barely knew its lines and had little confidence in the text. The actors and producer took the play seriously, but the decision to stage it at only nine days' notice was absurd. Not until 8 October was the text first read through by the cast, which left hardly any time to learn parts and rehearse.[5] Chekhov himself had arrived in St. Petersburg in time to attend rehearsals in person. Visiting the theatre every day, he discussed interpretation with the actors, stressing the need to avoid theatricality. According to the producer, "everything that could be done in this incredibly short space of time, with only eight rehearsals, for so subtly shaded a play as *The Seagull* . . . was done".[6] But it was not enough, and the author himself was left with no illusions about the prospects for 17 October.

The unhappy first night outdid his most gloomy forebodings, and has inevitably been described as "a spectacle truly unprecedented in the history of the theatre".[7] The trouble began in Act One when Vera Komissarzhevsky, as Nina, had to pronounce the long World Spirit monologue in her secondary role as an actress in the play-within-the-play. This speech, beginning "Men, lions, eagles and partridges, horned deer, geese, spiders and silent fishes", evoked jeers and derisive guffaws, being particularly ill-adapted for the ears of Levkeyev's fans. As the play proceeded, spectators in the front rows demonstratively turned their backs, hissed, whistled, laughed and started rowdy private conversations. The uproar increased until the play was inaudible. But at least certain visual effects could still strike home. Treplev's appearance (in Act Three), his head bandaged after his unsuccessful attempt to shoot himself, evoked raucous laughter and catcalls. Never had Anna Suvorin witnessed so appalling a scene.[8] Chekhov quitted the auditorium in Act Three and sat in a dressing-room. After the performance he left the theatre and wandered the streets on his own, and not until 2 a.m. did he return to Suvorin's house, where he was staying. By that time his sister, who had come to St. Petersburg specially for *The Seagull*, was in great distress and attempts had been made to trace him all over town. That night he told Suvorin that he would never offer another play to be staged even if he lived another seven hundred years.[9]

On the following morning Chekhov left for Melikhovo without taking farewell of the Suvorins. Had he remained in St. Petersburg he would have been able to confirm what his friends tried to explain to him by letter and telegram: that the later performances of *The Seagull* had been well received now that the special conditions of the catastrophic first night were no longer operative. But the management decided, against the protest of the producer, to take *The Seagull* off after eight performances. They were probably influenced by the many vicious reviews which appeared in the press, Chekhov's work being no exception to the tendency for creative originality to attract the malice of mediocrities. There were hostile notices in serious publications such as *Peterburgskaya gazeta* and *Novosti* ("News"); there was abusive doggerel verse in the less edifying comic papers. The magazine *Teatral* ("Playgoer") summed up this campaign. "The press pounced on *The Seagull* and its author with gusto. . . . Chekhov was denied all talent, and written off as an enormous bubble blown up by his sycophantic friends. . . . The gloating of certain critics was downright cynical."[10]

That Chekhov was deeply hurt his letters of the following months witness. Before fleeing St. Petersburg he left a note asking Suvorin to cancel publication, now pending, of his collected plays, *The Seagull* being one of seven items involved: an instruction given in the heat of the moment and tacitly ignored in the event. "I shall *never* write or stage more plays," Chekhov predicted.[11] Suvorin replied upbraiding him for cravenly running away from St. Petersburg. Nothing of the sort, Chekhov retorted. He had taken supper at Romanov's Restaurant after the play; he had slept well in Suvorin's guest room; he had gone home next day "without uttering a single squeak". He had behaved rationally and coolly, like a man whose proposal of marriage has been turned down and who has no recourse but to take his leave. The shock had not been too great since he had foreseen the disaster all along. It was his sister who had really taken the affair to heart, for she had come rushing home from St. Petersburg to Melikhovo in his wake. "She probably thought I was about to hang myself", Anton wrote to Suvorin: a revealing sardonic aside at the expense of one whose kindly ministrations Anton tended to find over-fussy in the intervals between taking them for granted. How profoundly distressed he himself had indeed been by *The Seagull*'s failure, inevitably shattering to so sensitive an artist, is evident from the way in which he kept harping on this "fiasco beyond my wildest imaginings". It wasn't so much *The*

Seagull's failure which grated on him, he said, as the failure of his own personality, and when the proofs of his collected plays came along it was as much as he could do to read them at all.[12]

We must now consider an even greater anomaly than *The Seagull*. *Uncle Vanya* represents, as is noted above, a reworking of the earlier unsuccessful *Wood Demon* (1889). In creating a new play out of an old one, Chekhov reduced the length by about a third and scrapped four major characters entirely: the Zheltukhins, brother and sister; the Orlovskys, father and son. Yet he somehow retained substantial sections of the original dialogue, while yet transforming a play of action into a play of emotional content;[13] and, incidentally, a by no means negligible piece of light entertainment into a work of genius. I know of no parallel for such a process; there is certainly none in Chekhov's other works. Here is the transformation of an immature and fairly conventional comedy into a mature work of startling originality. Everything which had been too clear-cut and brightly-lit in the earlier play becomes enchantingly indefinite, blurred and atmospheric in its successor. For instance, the unfortunate Uncle *George* Voynitsky, who had straightforwardly shot himself in Act Three of *The Wood Demon*, is replaced in the later play by the more puzzling Uncle *Vanya* Voynitsky whose main achievement or non-achievement is to fire a revolver at the hated Professor Serebryakov—and, of course, to miss. Then again, each play has its "Sonya". But how different the two girls are. *The Wood Demon*'s had been an elegant, rather silly, rich young woman who had cloyingly paired off in the finale with Michael Khrushchov, the play's doctor–forester. *Uncle Vanya*'s Sonya is a less handsome, more sensitive girl. She too loves the play's doctor–forester, Astrov, the counterpart to *The Wood Demon*'s Khrushchov, but a more subtly drawn character. And this later Sonya's love remains unrequited, for Astrov barely notices her, having eyes only for the beautiful Helen Serebryakov with whom (in the earlier play) his brash predecessor Khrushchov had provoked a needless quarrel.

The conclusion of *Uncle Vanya* leaves the frustrated Sonya and her frustrated uncle facing a boring future together. This non-solution contrasts vividly with the fates of their counterparts in the earlier play, which had Sonya evidently destined to live her life happily ever after, and which had left her uncle dead by his own hand. Thus had *The Wood Demon* offered a tragic Act Three followed by a happy ending in Act Four, and no nonsense about either of them. With *Uncle Vanya*, though, we shall do better to look neither for tragedy nor comedy, but to realize that we have entered a strange anti-climactic, anti-romantic, anti-dramatic world such as had never existed on the stage before Chekhov: a world with its own laws, its own dimensions, its own brand of humour.

To the mysteries surrounding the relationship of *Uncle Vanya* with its predecessor must be added the mystery of the second play's dating. When, precisely, did Demon become Uncle? We do not know, but we can be fairly certain that the transformation took place either in early 1890 or at least five years later: not at any intermediate point. The evidence for the earlier date is well summarized by N. I. Gitovich. As she points out, Chekhov referred in December 1898 to *Uncle Vanya* as written "long, long ago"; moreover, he expressly gave 1890 as the year of the play's composition in a letter of December 1901. We also know, from a letter of Chekhov's to the actor P. M. Svobodin, that he had intended to submit an unnamed play for production in April 1890.[14] It could have been *Uncle Vanya*. But was it?

I am not convinced by Gitovich's argument. In making the above observations Chekhov may well have meant *The Wood Demon* when he said *Uncle Vanya*, since the two plays so closely resemble each other in sustained sections and in detail. There is also some evidence pointing to a later date. The playwright Shcheglov recounts Chekhov's doings in 1896–7 at first hand, and states that *The Wood Demon* was converted to *Uncle Vanya* at about this time.[15] A more valuable indication is Chekhov's reply to A. I. Urusov's proposal of November 1895 to revive the neglected *Wood Demon* by publishing it in *Severny vestnik*. Chekhov offered to "get hold of *The Wood Demon*, read it and then give a proper answer".[16] He wrote this a day or two after finishing *The Seagull*, and it seems possible that Urusov's suggestion was the stimulus which led to work beginning on the conversion. At all events it is most unlikely that Chekhov would have replied in precisely those terms to Urusov if the conversion had already taken place. It is unlikely, too, that Chekhov would have considered, even temporarily, the republication of a work which such a conversion would naturally (had it already taken place) have rendered obsolete in the mind of its creator.

That *Uncle Vanya* was not concocted at any intermediate point between 1890 and mid-1895 seems clear from Chekhov's statement, made in April 1895, that he had "written nothing for the theatre during the last five or six years".[17] We also find him assuring Suvorin, in the following June, of his firm intention to write a play; and it seems possible that he had *Uncle Vanya* in mind. That the new drama had taken shape by November 1896 we learn from a reference to the intended publication of Chekhov's collected plays: a publication designed to include three long works, of which *Uncle Vanya* must inevitably have been one, as well as four one-acters. Finally, in December of the same year we meet the play's title for the first time, when Chekhov again refers to the scheduled volume of his plays. "Two long plays remain to be set up in type: *The Seagull*, which you know, and *Uncle Vanya*, which no one on this earth knows." This statement strongly suggests that Chekhov had for some reason made it a matter of deliberate policy to shroud the writing of *Uncle Vanya* in mystery; but we still cannot tell whether it was for five or six years, or merely for a few months, that he had kept its existence secret.[18] In any case *Uncle Vanya* first became known through its publication in Chekhov's collected *Plays* of 1897.

Uncle Vanya's quality also seems to argue for a later date. Here is a drama as original and mature as the later *Three Sisters* and *Cherry Orchard*. Could an author capable of creating such a work in 1890 conceivably have reverted in 1895 to so uneasy and transitional a piece of writing as *The Seagull*? That chronology would seem to make nonsense of Chekhov's evolution as a dramatist, and has been commonly rejected.[19] But so elusive a process is artistic creativity that only a rash scholar would rely heavily on such a "hunch" to fix the date of a composition by so unpredictable an artist.

Intimations of Mortality

Chekhov was far from being an invalid during his Melikhovo period, but he was by no means a healthy man either. That he "never complained" about feeling ill is perhaps the most misleading cliché in the litany of the Chekhov Cult, and can easily be disproved. Whatever may have been his practice in conversation, Chekhov the letter-writer did repeatedly complain about his health. He did so in detail, and he did so to persons with whom he was far from intimate; were this not the case we should be more ignorant about his medical history than we are. And yet, as Potapenko rightly says, Chekhov was no hypochondriac. Suffering from so many troublesome ailments besides the tuberculosis, not yet diagnosed, which eventually destroyed him, he would not permit these maladies to halt his many activities.[1]

Piles remained one of the greatest torments, driving him almost frantic at times. In April 1893 he wrote of "an appalling grape-like haemorrhoid which irritates me to the tips of my finger nails. . . . Piles makes me angry, makes me say silly things, ages me." This "generals' disease worse than syphilis" prevented Chekhov from visiting Moscow, for it was torture to ride an ill-sprung trap over the bumpy lanes from his house to Lopasnya station. It was piles which turned Anton into a pessimist, says his brother Michael. Relief might have come in 1895 when doctor colleagues, grateful for Chekhov's efforts to save the medical journal *Khirurgiya* ("Surgery"), suggested operating on him gratis; but he did not make up his mind to face the knife.[2] To piles we must add gastritis, termed by Chekhov "catarrh of the bowels", and bouts of migraine. His eyes also gave him trouble: he suffered from defective vision, one eye being short-sighted and the other long-sighted, and he was still afflicted with scotoma; he had nearly lost the sight of his right eye in 1895, he said. There were also dizzy spells dating from his second year as a student, and heart palpitations which made him fear embarrassing strangers by dropping dead in front of them.³ On another occasion he said that he was not frightened by his heart symptoms, for these thuds, bangs and dizzy spells were not at all what they might seem. The real killer-disease would be something altogether different, something which "steals up unobtrusively, wearing a mask. One may for example have tuberculosis, but one thinks it's something else quite minor. . . . So the real menace is the one you don't fear, while the alarming one is no danger. . . . When nature kills us she craftily deceives us as a nanny deceives a child when she takes him off to bed from the drawing-room. I know I shall die of a disease which I shan't be afraid of. If I fear, therefore, I shan't die. Anyway, this is all nonsense."⁴ And nonsense it indeed was—all too familiar nonsense at that, reminding us of previous attempts by Chekhov to rationalize his tubercular symptoms out of existence.

Now in the mid-1890s, as then in the late 1880s, he was still subject to the consumptive's chronic cough, which he sought to alleviate by giving up smoking. He was still spitting blood regularly each spring. And he was still the physician who, far from seeking to cure himself, insisted on ignoring the danger signals. "I'm alive and healthy [he reports on 11 November 1893]. My cough's worse; but I'm nowhere near tuberculosis, I think. I've cut down smoking to one cigar a day." Two weeks later we again meet this perverse insistence on not suffering from tuberculosis. "I haven't got tuberculosis and haven't discharged blood from the lungs for ages."⁵ But however much he might complain about his health in letters, Chekhov always tried to hide his tubercular symptoms from his mother and sister. This came all the easier to a doctor who was so much his own worst diagnostician that he could still conceal the significance of those symptoms from himself.

It is in the light of health so undermined that we must understand Chekhov's complaints about becoming impotent and such a passage as the following, written only a month after he had taken over the Melikhovo estate. "I'm well over thirty, and feel as if I was nearly forty. I've grown crassly indifferent to everything in the world. . . . I get out of bed and go to bed feeling as if I'd lost all interest in life. It's either . . . excessive fatigue or some kind of unconscious . . . process which novelists call a spiritual upheaval."⁶ Michael Chekhov confirms the decline in his brother's health in the Melikhovo period, tracing the first serious deterioration back to Anton's visit to Tolstoy in August 1895; but without, of course, claiming this a matter of cause and effect. It was then that Anton lost his vitality, says Michael; he became old, yellow and pinched. And Michael ascribes further deterioration to *The Seagull*'s disastrous first night in St. Petersburg in October 1896.[7]

Can Anton really have been unaware, still, that he suffered from tuberculosis? It seems incredible that a practising doctor could continue to ignore symptoms of which the possible purport might have struck any layman. On the other hand, as Chekhov's own works richly illustrate, human beings have an almost infinite capacity for self-deception. Did the man who deluded others about the desperate condition of his health also delude himself? Or did he hover between self-deception and self-knowledge? To ignore, consciously or unconsciously, what cannot be mended can sometimes be the highest form of wisdom. Perhaps it was so in this case.

In March 1897 further self-deception became impossible. Chekhov took the train to Moscow on the morning of the twenty-second and put up at the Grand Hotel. At six o'clock he sat down with Suvorin in the Hermitage Restaurant and at once had a violent haemorrhage from the lungs. Suvorin took him to the suite which he was occupying in another hotel, the Slav Fair, and Chekhov's physician, a Doctor Obolonsky, was called. That Dr. Chekhov did now at last accurately identify his trouble is evident: speaking of the bleeding from his right lung, he compared himself to his unfortunate brother Nicholas, and to another relative who had also died of tuberculosis.[8] Chekhov spent 23 March in Suvorin's suite, but insisted on returning to his hotel next morning, having letters to write and people to see. Then a further severe haemorrhage led to his removal to Professor Ostroumov's clinic in southern Moscow soon afterwards. He remained for sixteen days, being discharged on 10 April. And here tuberculosis was at last firmly diagnosed. Writing of this on 1 April, Chekhov reported that a complete change of life had been prescribed: something easier said than done, he added, for it was as hard to avoid troubles in the countryside as to escape flames in hell.[9]

Occupying Ward Number Sixteen at the clinic, the author of *Ward Number Six* had strict orders to rest, but visitors just could not be kept away. On 6 April the popular Anton Pavlovich had people coming and going all day. "Simply awful! They arrive in pairs, and all beg me not to speak while simultaneously asking me questions." The visitors included Mariya Chekhov, Shcheglov and Suvorin. Lydia Avilov came twice, and took or did not take part in the romantic exchanges coyly assigned to these occasions in her memoirs.[10] One fascinating—far too fascinating— visitor was Tolstoy. Turning up on 28 March, he harangued the sick man on immortality and art, but Chekhov was not convinced. Immortality *à la*

Tolstoy sounded too vague, like a gelatinous mass, and Chekhov wanted no part of it. As for the sage's views on art, which conformed with the general theme of "simplification" underlying his whole philosophy; as for his thesis that art is invalid unless intelligible to peasants: Chekhov wrote that such ideas were not new, but had been repeated again and again in various keys by clever old men throughout the ages.[11]

After talking to Tolstoy Chekhov suffered another serious lung haemorrhage.[12]

CHAPTER TWELVE

Between Melikhovo and Yalta
1897-9

Fifteen superb stories, written in groups of three or four with gaps of several months between each group: such is to be Chekhov's creative harvest in the transitional years between his health crisis of spring 1897 and the end of 1899. He also becomes the major dramatist of a newly founded theatre; edits his "Collected Works"; transfers his home to the Crimea; establishes himself as a prospective lover and husband.

Melikhovo
(April–August 1897)

In a letter of 1 April Chekhov defines his future regimen. His doctors say he must change his way of life and he will comply as well as he can at Melikhovo, with all the "endless fuss over peasants, animals and various other elemental forces". He will give up medical practice and working for the local council; buy a dressing-gown; sit in the sun and eat a lot. There will be no more swimming, no excessive talking. But he is not keen on wintering in the south, as his doctors have ordered. The Crimea, his eventual home, is "grotesquely boring"; the Caucasus is malarial; foreign residence always makes him homesick. His first choice would be Taganrog, but he fears his home town's winter climate.[1]

Meanwhile, with summer in prospect, this problem could be shelved. Returning to Melikhovo from the clinic on 11 April, Chekhov began a four-and-a-half month sojourn punctuated by several trips to Moscow and one to St. Petersburg. He took life easily without being incapacitated or bedridden. He was feeling well; were it not for all the medicines which had been prescribed for him, he would have supposed himself cured.[2] Producing no new literary works during this spring and summer, he continued to advise other writers. He visited his new village school at

Novosyolki, attending its formal opening on 13 July; he also descended on Talezh and Chirkovo to conduct oral examinations.

At Melikhovo guests, welcome and unwelcome, came and went as usual. We can trace and name dozens: neighbours, relatives, fellow-writers and admiring young ladies from Lika Mizinov downwards. The artist I. E. Braz came to paint Chekhov's portrait on commission for the Tretyakov Gallery in Moscow, but disliked what he produced after seventeen days of sittings. Another visitor, the talented caricaturist Alexandra Khotyaintsev, also turned up and sketched her host, combining the two roles of portraitist and lady admirer.[3] One visitor, Ivan Shcheglov, aroused mixed feelings. He has claimed credit for persuading Chekhov to publish the stories *My Life* and *Peasants* together in book form, as was done in a volume brought out by Suvorin later in the year. Shcheglov also persuaded Chekhov to expunge from *Peasants* a few lines written in the manner of Tolstoy. Meanwhile Chekhov privately complained that Shcheglov was talking too much; laughing too loudly; foisting on his host the proofs of his atrocious play about the Russian literary world; getting bits of cabbage soup stuck in his moustache.[4]

France
(September 1897–May 1898)

On 1 September 1897 Chekhov begins the third of his five excursions to western Europe. These happen to have occurred at three-year intervals, from the first in 1891 until the last in 1904: an accidental regularity in the pattern of a somewhat haphazard traveller.

The foreign expedition of 1897–8 was imposed by the need to avoid central Russia during the winter. It was to prove Chekhov's longest by far, lasting eight months in all. He spent a few days in Paris, and then moved on to Biarritz where he relaxed for a fortnight before settling in Nice, his base until the following April. With its palms, eucalyptuses, oleanders, orange-trees and fashionable women, the Riviera resort enchanted him. Nice was warm, cheap, full of life. Polite as ever, the French addressed their servants and cabbies as *Monsieur*. What with the street bands, the carnival, the dancing and the laughter, what with the civilization which seemed to rub off even on the dogs, Chekhov began to regret having never stayed so long in a foreign city before. Here the very street musicians were better than Russian opera singers. Never would Chekhov winter in Moscow again. He would spend all his winters in Nice; he would become mayor of that splendid city, even if its matches, cigarettes, sugar and footwear were inferior to those obtainable in Russia. He was making headway with his French, and could read a newspaper or write a short letter in that tongue, yet could not express his thoughts fluently. Though confessing himself a poor linguist, he showed keen interest in French sounds and grammar, discoursing on these technicalities in letters to Mariya.[1]

During eight months in France Chekhov did not try to go native. Far from cultivating French society in Nice, he settled down none too cosily with his fellow-countrymen in the local *Pension Russe*, inconveniently situated in a narrow, smelly street. Here there was a Russian cook, here Chekhov could talk his native language at table while consuming authentic cabbage soup and salted fungi; but he often chose silence, irked by the lady guests: "reptiles, ninnies, rows of ugly mugs with their malice and gossip". They were boring, idle, complacent; he feared to grow like them.[2]

Fortunately there were other Russians in Nice besides the *pension* ladies, so that Chekhov could enjoy contacts with fellow-countrymen as varied as Moscow itself could provide. He particularly liked Maxim Kovalevsky. That historian, jurist and sociologist possessed the Russian Empire's highest academic distinction: he had been stripped of his professorial chair in Moscow for ideological unreliability. The friends planned to visit Algiers—one of Chekhov's many abortive travel projects, others being trips to Corsica and Egypt. He also met Professor A. A. Korotnyov, head of the biological research establishment at Villefranche; N. I. Yurasov, the Russian Vice-Consul at Menton; the painter V. I. Yakobi; a fellow-playwright, Prince Sumbatov-Yuzhin; Vasily Nemirovich-Danchenko, author and brother of the well-known theatrical producer; his old friend Potapenko, seducer of his other old friend Lika Mizinov. The painter Braz came and did a second portrait of Chekhov as unsatisfactory as the first. Alexandra Khotyaintsev also arrived, put up at the *Pension Russe* and resumed her sketches of Chekhov. He described her as the most intellectual of the *pension* ladies—perhaps because she still wore the same old dress in which he remembered her at Melikhovo, which was no way to impress one who liked his women stylish and elegant. Nor did Alexandra respond to the casino when Chekhov took her to Monte Carlo.[3]

Miss Khotyaintsev's brief, recently published memoirs in no way suggest that she and Chekhov were more than friends.[4] But we do find a few scattered references to his erotic interests. In Biarritz he had "taken on" a nineteen-year-old French girl for exercises in the language. So he unkindly teased Lika Mizinov by letter, inviting her to interpret these "exercises" in the broadest sense. And Margot had followed him from Biarritz to Nice, where he had lost track of her. All the same, he was somehow contriving to "make offerings to the Goddess of love".[5] But despite such oracular hints in his letters, the devoted Lika could not see her Anton Pavlovich as a Don Juan. His Margot was to be pitied, she replied. "Tell

Chekhov, probably at Melikhovo.

Vladimir Nemirovich-Danchenko (1858–1943), stage director and co-founder of the Moscow Art Theatre.

Chekhov's wife, the actress Olga Knipper (1868–1959).

Chekhov reads his *Seagull* to directors and actors of the Moscow Art Theatre, 1898.

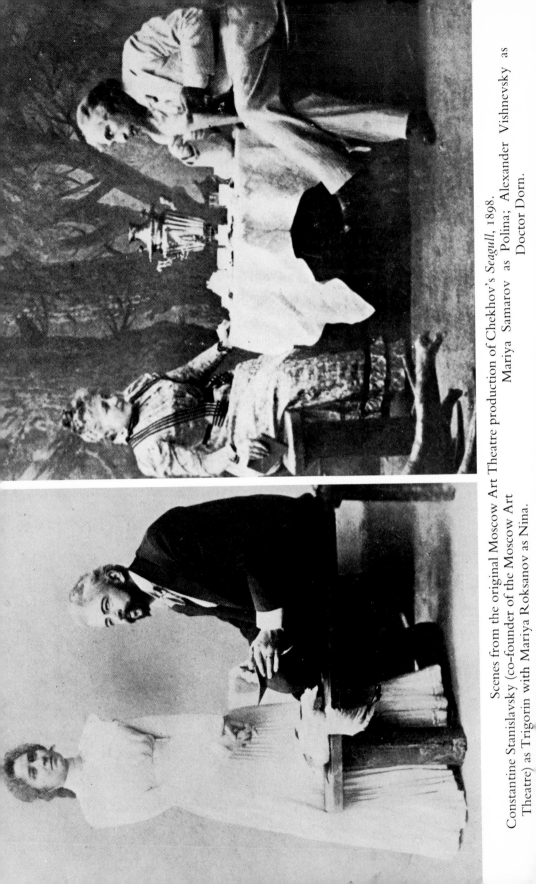

Scenes from the original Moscow Art Theatre production of Chekhov's *Seagull*, 1898. Constantine Stanislavsky (co-founder of the Moscow Art Theatre) as Trigorin with Mariya Roksanov as Nina. Mariya Samarov as Polina; Alexander Vishnevsky as Doctor Dorn.

Above: The sea front at Yalta, where Chekhov lived between 1898 and 1904. *Left*: Chekhov with Maxim Gorky (1868–1936) and Leo Tolstoy (1828–1910).

Chekhov in his study at Yalta.

Chekhov in his garden, 1901.

Chekhov's villa at Yalta.

her a fellow-sufferer sends her regards; I once stupidly acted as the cheese you refused to eat." Of "cheese", a symbol for love-making in this correspondence, Chekhov understood nothing, jeered Lika. "You only like looking at it from afar, even when you're hungry: not eating it. . . . I hope she [Margot] will shake you up and awake qualities long dormant. Perhaps you'll be less of a drip; perhaps you'll be a real human being, a proper man, when you're back in Russia." In that case, said Lika, Mariya Chekhov's girl friends would have to watch out.[6]

At Nice, in October 1897, Chekhov resumes creative writing after a six-month gap since *Peasants*. By December he has produced a little clutch of four stories, each from ten to fifteen pages long, each indicating that declining health had not impaired his skill. The first three were written for *Russkiye vedomosti*, and two (*Home* and *The Savage*) portray the steppe north of Taganrog, an area familiar to Chekhov from childhood. *Home* introduces a lively and attractive young heroine, Vera Kardin, who is gradually demoralized by the relentless triviality of life on a provincial estate. She capitulates in the end by agreeing to marry the lugubrious Dr. Neshchapov, who lacks spiritual resonance and is one of the few unsympathetic doctors in Chekhov's work. *The Savage*, set in the same area, presents a retired Cossack officer and his family. Here is another marital clash with the husband as villain: a monster who terrorizes his pathetic wife, and has brought up his sons to behave as barbarously as himself.

Sympathy for women's misfortunes is also a theme of *In the Cart*, the last story in this trio. It too is set in the countryside, deriving its inspiration from the Melikhovo area, where Chekhov's educational activities had introduced him to just such rural schoolmistresses as *In the Cart*'s harassed, ill-paid, ill-appreciated Mariya. And though the heroines of all three *Russkiye vedomosti* stories are shown as defeated by life, Mariya's defeat is the most complete of all. A tribute to those who persist with unrewarding work under hopeless conditions, *In the Cart* also contains a significant comment on high-minded idealists such as the heroine emphatically is not. "It is a hard, dull life and no one puts up with it for long except silent drudges like Mariya. Vivacious, highly-strung, sensitive souls may talk of their vocation and service to ideals, but they wilt and throw in their hand soon enough."[7]

Chekhov's fourth and last story of the winter, *All Friends Together*, was written for the journal *Kosmopolis*. He later slighted this brain-child by excluding it, perhaps unintentionally, from his "Collected Works".[8] Yet it is a notable study in non-rapprochement, and another work in which Chekhov seems to be explaining why he has never married. The heroine, Nadya, has reached the precise make-or-break age for Chekhovian spinsters, being twenty-three years old, and her relatives have decided to marry her off to her childhood friend Misha Podgorin, a young lawyer. But Podgorin, a vintage Chekhovian hero, cannot accept the role of husband-designate. Far from succumbing to Nadya's feminine charms, he finds them acutely embarrassing. When she appears in a white, open-necked dress the sight of her long, white, bare neck is "not altogether nice". Distasteful too is the spectacle of her legs in flesh-coloured stockings as revealed when her skirt billows up.[9] Podgorin, disconcerted by these sinful glimpses, hurriedly flees by the first train and resumes his comfortable bachelor existence in Moscow.

On Chekhov's writing habits in Nice we are informed by Kovalevsky. Working erratically, by no means one to put in a regular stint at his desk, Chekhov was liable to disappear for days on end when pregnant with a story. He would not even show up for meals; and when he at last re-appeared after parturition his face would be pale and thin; during walks he would be silent and pensive, brooding on his creation.[10]

Superb though the four Nice stories of late 1897 are, their author was not satisfied. A mere fifty pages of print was very little to show for a winter's work. In late 1897 he repeatedly castigated his own idleness, only to lapse into yet greater idleness in the first months of the new year. It was difficult for him to write at a strange desk—like being hung upside down by one foot. Nor did the cuisine of the *pension* aid creativity. What with all the eggs, the steaks, the cheeses, the fruit, the cups of chocolate, one never seemed to stop guzzling, whereas "for writing purposes it's imperative to avoid eating too much". Once again we are reminded of the symbolism of Chekhov's fiction, in which to be detected eating and drinking is so often to seem accused of deepest moral turpitude.[11]

Uprooted from Russia for eight months, Chekhov did not abandon civic responsibilities on home territory. In November he instructed Mariya to give Christmas gifts to the children in his village schools. He became honorary patron of the schools in Taganrog, while continuing to present books to the public library of that city; these included 319 volumes of French literature. He also arranged for the sculptor M. M. Antokolsky to supply Taganrog with a statue of its founder, Peter the Great. When the medical journal *Khirurgiya* again fell on evil days, Chekhov used his influence to enlist financial backing. Kind on the domestic plane, too, he made sure that a maidservant at Melikhovo, who had recently given birth to a daughter, should be permitted to rear her child in his household.[12]

A new civic preoccupation arose when Chekhov took up the great French scandal of the decade: the Dreyfus Case. A Jew and a captain on the French General Staff, Dreyfus had been arrested in 1894 for treason and had been sent to Devil's Island, Cayenne, by a secret court-martial. That he had been condemned through forged documents soon became evident. But Dreyfus's main champion, the novelist Émile Zola, was himself to be convicted of libel after denouncing the French military for "framing" Dreyfus. The scandal, which was to outlive Chekhov, dramatized a rift in world opinion between the conservative, reactionary, anti-Semitic anti-Dreyfusards and their opponents, who proclaimed and eventually vindicated Dreyfus's innocence. Chekhov's interest in the Affair dates from November 1897, when the name Dreyfus first crops up in his correspondence. Reading newspaper reports, studying stenographic records, Chekhov concluded that Dreyfus was innocent and entered the lists on his behalf. He was provoked into doing so by *Novoye vremya*, once a vehicle for his own fiction and owned by Suvorin, who was still one of his closest friends. But that friendship was now strained by the hostility to Dreyfus predictably expressed by Suvorin's notoriously anti-Semitic newspaper; and that after a decade in which Chekhov had somehow kept his personal relations with Suvorin separate from *Novoye vremya*'s politics. These had never been congenial to Chekhov, and he was beginning to find them downright nauseating now that the innocent victims Dreyfus and Zola had fallen foul of the newspaper.

Nowhere in his works or letters does Chekhov so explicitly proclaim the writer's duty to fight injustice as when championing Zola's defence of Dreyfus. The main thing about Zola, he tells Suvorin, "is that he's sincere: that is, he builds his conclusions only on the evidence of his eyes and not on chimeras like other people. . . . Even if Dreyfus is guilty Zola's still right because it's not the writer's job to accuse and persecute, but to champion even the guilty once they've been sentenced and are suffering punishment. 'What about politics?' you ask. 'What about interests of state?' But great writers and artists should take part in politics only as a defence against politics. There are plenty of prosecutors and policemen about already; anyway, Paul's role fits them [writers] better than Saul's." As an instance of what a writer could do for his fellow-citizens, Chekhov cited the intervention of his contemporary, Vladimir Korolenko, in a Dreyfus Affair *à la russe* which had erupted two summers previously. Some peasants (Votyaks, members of a Finnic tribe resident in the Russian Empire) had been falsely accused of performing human sacrifices and put on trial; and only the stand taken by Korolenko, Russia's Zola of the hour, had prevented a miscarriage of justice.[13] And Chekhov's indignation over the Affair is further illustrated in a letter to Alexander. To abuse Zola while publishing one of his novels in translation without paying for it, as *Novoye vremya* was now doing—this was, said Chekhov, reaching for the strongest term of abuse in his vocabulary, "unworthy of a man of letters".[14]

As time rolled by and the Dreyfus scandal showed no signs of dying down, Suvorin's paper persisted in its anti-Semitic line. Knowing that his representations had been in vain, Chekhov periodically mentioned how "odious", "shameful", "loathsome" and "disgusting" was the behaviour of *Novoye vremya* over the Affair.[15] As for Chekhov's relations with Suvorin, these cooled at the time of the Affair and never regained their former cordiality.

Nice seems to have been good for Chekhov's health, though evidence on this is as conflicting as usual. The weather at least was superb; he did not need an overcoat or galoshes all winter, and could wear a straw hat. There was some blood-spitting in the autumn, but that did not stop him "leaping like an unmarried calf" and congratulating himself on his good luck in not having a wife. But frisky though the patient might feel, blood-spitting persisted off and on into the early winter. He was "not preparing to die", but found it hard to walk upstairs and had begun to feel eighty-nine years old. With the new year 1898 his health seemed to improve, despite an infection of the gum following a dental extraction. The blood-spitting had long ago stopped, he reported on 16 March.[16]

When spring arrived Chekhov's thoughts turned more and more to Russia, and he began to send Mariya instructions about the Melikhovo garden. Longing to return, he took the train for Paris on 14 April and awaited the telegram from his sister which would proclaim the Melikhovo weather fine enough to permit his return.[17] He left on 2 May, reaching home three days later.

Melikhovo
(May–September 1898)

Between May and September 1898 Chekhov lived in Melikhovo, making one or two brief trips to Moscow and elsewhere. During this, his seventh and penultimate summer on the estate, his guests still came and went, and he was still occupied with peasant affairs. There were schools to be inspected, pupils to be examined; and his third village school, that in Melikhovo itself, was already under way. He also continued, by corres-pondence, his work as Taganrog's roving ambassador. But the chief event was the revival of creative urges dormant during the previous six months.

Eager to make up for lost time, Chekhov now writes or completes the masterly story *Doctor Startsev*, which he may have begun in Nice.[1] Its theme is the quintessentially Chekhovian tendency for life, especially in the Russian provinces, to sink into a rut. Not that the young, energetic Dr. Dmitry Startsev seems liable to such degeneration when he arrives to take up a medical post near the town of S. and meets the piano-playing Catherine Turkin. Against the stifling background of S. ("What . . . could be said of a town in which the most brilliant people were so dim?") Startsev falls in love with Catherine, who happens—a sinister portent in any of Chekhov's fictional young women—to have particularly well-developed breasts; but she rejects him because she wants to train as a concert pianist in Moscow. Returning to S. a sadder, wiser, more mature woman, who now knows the limits of her musical talents, Catherine is at last ready for Startsev's love. But by now he has been sucked into the provincial mire from which she shows signs of emerging; he has grown fat and grasping, he has become a successful local property speculator— anything but the ardent young lover of former years. Thus, in an exquisitely symmetrical plot, both miss the happiness which each might otherwise have found with the other, had they not been characters in Chekhov and therefore by definition precluded from all prospect of united bliss.

During this penultimate Melikhovo summer Chekhov wrote three more stories, sometimes called "the Trilogy": *A Hard Case*, *Gooseberries* and *Concerning Love*. They are linked structurally and thematically in a fashion unparalleled in his other fiction. Each consists largely of a story-within-a-story told by one of three narrators (Burkin, Ivan Ivanovich, Alyokhin) to one or both of the others. And each is a fictional sermon on freedom. "Why do you get so little out of life?" Again and again Chekhov causes this question to be asked of his characters, often explicitly; and nowhere does he seem to be asking it more pointedly than in the Trilogy. The three heroes of the stories-within-the-stories have each signally failed to seize their opportunities. Belikov, the straitlaced schoolteaching fuddy-duddy of *A Hard Case*, has bullied his fellow-townsfolk into being ashamed of enjoying themselves. The pig-like Nicholas Ivanovich of *Gooseberries* has dedicated his existence to becoming a landed gentleman by acquiring, through years of tedious self-denial, an unprepossessing estate with a gooseberry patch. The hard-working farmer Alyokhin of *Concerning Love* misses the one great romance of his life through lack of initiative. Despite the infinite scope for free and adventurous action which human existence can offer, each has chosen to dig himself a grave and to lie down in it. Each has, in other words, rejected his own freedom.

Chekhov himself was, like his own "Nicholas Ivanovich", the owner of an estate which boasted its gooseberry patch. He too had behaved like his own "Belikov" and "Alyokhin" by spurning young women who would have liked to unite their lives with his. To some extent, then, the Trilogy offers an ironical comment on his own predicament. With these three stories, his last to be written at Melikhovo, we see him taking a fictional farewell of that estate. They are among his most pithy, elegant and profound works. Though these three works form a unity, they could easily have been expanded by adding more stories within the same general framework. This is what Chekhov planned, for he later described the Trilogy as part of "a series still far from complete".[2] But his projected sequel never materialized.

Despite creative achievements so impressive, the summer of 1898 finds Chekhov at an unstable period of his life. He has neither given up his Melikhovo home, though he now suspects that this may soon become necessary, nor has he found a new home anywhere else. Autumn is at hand, and he knows that he must again flee to the south, but has his usual difficulty in making firm travel plans. Should he go abroad again? To Taganrog? To Sochi? Or to Yalta? All he knew for the moment was that all these prospects bored and dismayed him. "This nomad existence . . . has knocked me right off the rails."[3] By 9 September he had settled on Yalta as his provisional destination, and took the train for Moscow, intending to stay in that city for a few days in transit to the south. That this was to prove a key date in his life and career he could not suspect. All he knew was that he was about to meet a newly formed stage company, the Moscow Art Theatre, which was now engaged in preparing his *Seagull* as part of its impending first season's repertoire.

The Art Theatre's choice of *The Seagull* had come about through Vladimir Nemirovich-Danchenko. Co-founder with Constantine Stanislavsky of the new enterprise, and also an old friend of Chekhov's, Nemirovich-Danchenko well knew that the play had flopped disastrously in St. Petersburg in October 1896. But that fiasco had neither changed his high opinion of *The Seagull* nor eroded his conviction that the play could establish itself if sensitively produced and acted. He had therefore written to Chekhov asking permission for the Art Theatre to stage it, and guaranteeing an "artistic triumph"; to which Chekhov, unwilling to face any more theatrical crises, had replied with an outright refusal. But Nemirovich-Danchenko would not take no for an answer. Insisting that *The Seagull* was the only modern play which attracted him as a producer, he offered to go to Melikhovo and explain his production plans in person. His letter caught the hospitable Chekhov in receptive mood. "You can't imagine how keen I am to see you! Just for the pleasure of meeting you and talking to you I'm ready to yield you *all* my plays." Hence the rehearsals which Chekhov was now to attend in Moscow.[4]

It was, then, on 9 September and on the evening of his arrival in Moscow from Melikhovo that Chekhov first met the Moscow Art Theatre Company, including the actress Olga Leonardovna Knipper. At the Hunt Club in Moscow, where *The Seagull* was under rehearsal, the great man's arrival was awaited in a mood of "fluttering nervousness" by Miss Knipper and others who supposed him about to expatiate on certain dimly sensed profundities lurking in the text of his play. But Chekhov turned out no less nervous than they, continually plucking his beard and jerking back his pince-nez.⁵ No profundities emerged, but the author continued to attend rehearsals. On 14 September he witnessed work in progress on Alexis Tolstoy's *Tsar Theodore*, the historical blank-verse play, based on the life of Ivan the Terrible's son, which headed the new theatre's repertoire and with which it intended to introduce itself to the world. Whatever he may have thought of this costume drama, Chekhov was in no doubt about his views on Olga Knipper as its Tsaritsa Irina. "If I'd stayed in Moscow I'd have fallen in love with that Irina", he was soon writing from the south.⁶

Thus did Chekhov first meet the theatre which was to choose him as its favourite pioneering dramatist. By reviving his existing plays, while also inspiring him to create new, specially written plays, the young enterprise was to give a fresh turn and stimulus to his literary activity. And the actress whom he had so admired was to become his wife.

Not suspecting that Chekhov had now met his future bride, his relatives were still urging him to marry. It was in response to such a prompting from his brother Michael, combined perhaps with recent romantic memories of Olga Knipper, that Anton wrote his most considered appraisal of marriage in the abstract. It is typically sensible, untypically free of irony and badinage. It is also, for a man with such original and generally unpredictable views, surprisingly conventional, until we recall his advice given ten years earlier when his brother Alexander had been considering proposing to Helen Lintvaryov. "As for my marrying [he now writes, in 1898, to Michael] . . . what can I say? There's no point in marrying except for love. To marry a girl just because she's congenial is like buying something in the market not because you need it, but because you like the look of it. The most important thing in family life is love, sexual attraction, being 'one flesh'. All else is unreliable and boring, however ingeniously we may rationalize it. So it's a girl one loves, not a girl one just likes, that's needed."⁷

Yalta
(September 1898–April 1899)

Chekhov arrived in Yalta on 18 September 1898, resenting the need to abandon central Russia but without yet planning to take root in this particular locality. He meant to stay "about a month or perhaps even longer" and then seek some other refuge.¹ Having visited Yalta several times before, he was in no mood to succumb uncritically to its charms now, though the town—set in its spectacular bay, surrounded by its crescent of mountains—was appreciated by less blasé Russian visitors as an alien wonderland. Barely a century had passed since the incorporation of the Crimean peninsula in the Empire, and Russians were not yet ready to think of it as wholly Russian. Yalta had been Turkish until 1783, and there was still a large Turkic population of Crimean Tatars.

The town's population had grown rapidly to over 20,000 in the mid-1890s. That figure was regularly doubled by the seasonal influx of tourists, for by now Yalta was the premier Russian seaside resort. It was a haunt of the smart set, including the most august tourist of all, the very Tsar-Emperor, who had a palace at near-by Livadiya. Proximity to that imperial residence kept the Yalta police on their toes; private correspondence was more likely to be intercepted and read by the authorities here than else-where, while other special features included the recently imposed ban on Jewish residents.

Arrived in this sub-tropical sub-paradise, Chekhov wearily weighed its pros and cons. Yalta was more beautiful than Nice and its amenities included that rarity, a sewerage system; but Yalta was also more expensive than Nice—it was dull, dull, dull, while the surrounding countryside was purely oriental. Lodging in a succession of private houses during what was to be a seven-month stay, he was soon considering buying a plot of building land. But then an unexpected blow from the north further emphasized that these were transitional times for the Chekhovs. Anton's father died on 12 October 1898 after a short, painful illness: a constriction of the intestine complicated by an unsuccessful operation. Though con-scious of his father's many limitations, Chekhov had always been a dutiful son. He felt the blow deeply, especially as the old gentleman's life could have been saved had Anton been there at the time; so he himself claimed when he learnt the details. At all events Paul Chekhov's death implied radical changes for the family, as was immediately clear to Anton. "I don't think [he wrote to Mariya] that existence at Melikhovo will be the same again after Father's death; it's as if the course of life there had been cut short at the same time as his Diary." The main cog had now been removed from the mechanism of Melikhovo: surely his mother and sister would not want to live there on their own?²

Soon after the funeral, which Anton was unable to attend, Mariya came to Yalta to discuss plans. These hinged on Anton's recent purchase of a small building plot in Upper Autka. Lying just outside Yalta, and soon to be swallowed by it, this has been described as a noisy, dirty village, with a predominant Asiatic element. Still, Chekhov's new plot offered reasonable prospects of privacy. He had picked it up cheap, for a mere 4,000 roubles, from a vendor who threw in an interest-free mortgage out of respect for the purchaser's literary gifts. There was a well, there was sewerage, there was a fine outlook on mountains and sea. But Mariya was utterly dismayed when her brother proudly displayed his new acquisition. The site was too far from the sea; the steep slope was an utter wilderness of barren, stone-hard earth on which only wild vines flourished. It abutted on a Tatar cemetery where, to complete her distress, a funeral was all too symbolically in progress at the time of her joint inspection with the ailing Anton. Poor Mariya could not help contrasting Melikhovo, where she had worked so hard to create order out of chaos. Now she would have to start again. Still, she made the best of things as usual; and was soon helping to plan the new home under the supervision of a local architect. Meanwhile brother and sister had jointly agreed to retain the Melikhovo estate for the moment. He still intended to spend his summers there, wintering in his new abode.[3]

By mid-November building operations at Upper Autka had converted the barren hillside into a chaos of black sand, holes in the ground, dumps of lime, broken fences, bewildered Tatars, smoke and mud. There was also trouble with the water supply. Still, the view was magical, as was the thought of future amenities: a splendid kitchen, a cellar, a drying-room, a telephone and all other "American" conveniences.[4]

Not content with building his villa at Yalta, Chekhov also snapped up for 2,000 roubles a seaside cottage near the Tatar village of Kuchuk-Koy, on the coast road to Sevastopol about eighteen miles to the south-west. Perched on a precipitous slope, this offered sea bathing, preferably with the aid of a donkey for haulage purposes. It was as weird and wild as Syria or parts of Africa, said Chekhov, boasting that he had acquired one of the most beautiful and unusual properties in the Crimea; with such a country cottage and his Yalta villa as well, he would be perfectly equipped for his old age.[5]

Thus did the casual Crimean visitor of autumn 1898 gradually assume the status of permanent Crimean resident. But for geographical reasons alone Yalta could never become as suitable a home as Melikhovo. There was a vast difference between the former base, a mere two hours' journey from the social and cultural amenities of Moscow, and this new head-quarters from which the once-detested Moscow, soon to be eagerly desired, could be reached only by a complicated route and two full days' travelling. Since Yalta was not yet on the railway system, the first stage of the journey north was a steamer trip of several hours to the west, to the railhead at Sevastopol. There were regular sailings, and it could be a pleasant excursion on a fine summer day. Alternatively, rougher weather and seasickness could be avoided by hiring a carriage and driving the sixty-odd miles to Sevastopol; one could also make one's way overland to other inland railway stations further up the line: Bakhchisaray or Simferopol. These were all spectacular expeditions past Crimean cliffs and mountains, but they were not the ideal prescription for an invalid.

Given these conditions it was inevitable that Chekhov should feel marooned in Yalta as he had never felt marooned in Melikhovo. His periods of uninterrupted residence in the Crimea were bound to be more protracted and were apt to drag on for months. Yet he was to spend no more than three-fifths of his remaining days, an average of some seven months a year, in the Crimea. As we shall see, the rest of his time was to be divided on no fixed pattern between hotels and flats in Moscow; short holidays in the Russian countryside; and two further expeditions to western Europe. But though these absences were often prolonged, Chekhov the creator was yet essentially a Yalta man from autumn 1898 onwards, and it was there that almost all his remaining works were to be written.

Yalta's first literary harvest was gathered in November and December 1898 when Chekhov followed a four-month creative hiatus with a new clutch of four stories. Among these *Angel* is outstanding. It breaks what had become almost an unwritten rule for Chekhov, since it not only portrays marriage as a happy, harmonious state, but presents no less than three happy marriages or marital unions, all entered into by the heroine, Olga. She is a simple, kind-hearted woman who can live only through her love for a husband, lover or child; and having blissfully cohabited with a succession of three very different adult partners, she eventually lavishes her splendidly generous affections on a small foster-son. On Tolstoy, with his dislike of sophistication in art, this superb, seemingly simple tale—in which Chekhov's attitude to his heroine deliciously mingles sympathy with irony—made a strong impression, and he read it out several times to his family.[6]

Although Olga's marital associations had all been happy, while they lasted, we also note that all three unions had ended in death or enforced separation. For a picture, unique in Chekhov's mature work, of a marital union unmarred by such frustration—unmarred too by the disillusionment on which love so often founders elsewhere in Chekhov's work—we must turn to another story of late 1898, *New Villa*. Here the peasant couple Rodion and Stepanida "always sat side by side at home, and always walked down the street side by side. They always ate, drank and slept together, and the more they aged the more they loved each other." All we have in the way of let-down here is the appended information that "it was hot and crowded in their hut, and there were children everywhere".[7] There is also the point that this "Darby and Joan" pair are presented as primitive, illiterate and extremely limited human beings; which is perhaps why

Chekhov permits them the felicity so sternly denied to better-educated and more privileged individuals.

As this reminds us, *New Villa* shares a major theme with two other stories which complete the quartet of Chekhov's late 1898 fiction: *A Case History* and *On Official Business*. This is the rift between the privileged classes—industrialists, engineers, other professional persons—and the benighted mass of peasants and manual workers. The engineer of *New Villa* successfully bridges a river near a village. But his well-meaning wife can build no bridge between herself and the local villagers, for all her attempts to fraternize with Rodion, Stepanida and their kind. A bemused and sorry crew—some kind-hearted men and women, others malicious hooligans— Chekhov's muzhiks are once again presented in a manner contrary to the stereotype of Russian populist and Slavophile literature about the noble peasant: canons which he had so notoriously flouted in *Peasants*. A similar rift is studied in *On Official Business*. A magistrate and a coroner have been summoned to conduct an inquest in a village. Here they make memorable lack of contact with the local constable, or *sotsky*, a downtrodden elderly messenger whose life consists largely of trudging through snowdrifts to deliver official forms. The *sotsky* in this story was modelled on the real-life *sotsky* of Melikhovo, who had long performed similar services for Chekhov.

A comparable contrast between the privileged and unprivileged figures in *A Case History*, but with two differences. Firstly, the background, though rural, is yet industrial: a reflection of the common habit of siting Russian factories, whether of the Melikhovo area or elsewhere, in the heart of the countryside. And, secondly, only the privileged characters (the mill-owner Mrs. Lyalikov, her daughter, the governess) are studied in detail. The unprivileged (the workers) are seen as an undifferentiated mass, probably because Chekhov had little first-hand knowledge of the industrial proletariat: by contrast with peasants like those so skilfully characterized in *New Villa* and *On Official Business*. That Russian workers of the 1890s, a period of intense industrialization, were often miserable and exploited Chekhov well knew. But he did not draw the too obvious conclusion that all factory-owners must inevitably be deliberate and heartless oppressors. In this, as in earlier works describing industrial conditions (*A Woman's Kingdom*, *Three Years*), he suggests that the very capitalists may be as much victims of a hopeless situation as their employees. Mrs. Lyalikov and her heiress-daughter are no happier than the thousand or so dimly-discerned workers who toil so gloomily on their behalf. It is only the family governess—the ludicrous Miss Christine, a vulgar, silly old maid in a pince-nez—who derives any benefits from the Russian industrial revolution, being one of those disapproved Chekhovian characters whose lives centre on eating and drinking. "What are those five mills working for? Just so that Miss Christine can eat her sturgeon and drink her Madeira."[8]

In all these three studies of rural failure to communicate Chekhov follows his policy of stating a problem without offering to solve it. He makes this point explicit in *A Case History* when writing as follows of his Dr. Korolyov, who appears to be that Chekhovian rarity, a mouthpiece of the author. "As a doctor accustomed to forming accurate diagnoses of incurable chronic ailments deriving from some unknown ultimate cause, he [Korolyov] considered factories a mystery of comparably vague and intractable antecedents. As for improvements in the workers' lives, he didn't think them unnecessary, but compared them to the treatment of incurable diseases."[9]

A Case History, *New Villa* and *On Official Business* all convey keen sympathy for the unfortunate, and a concern for social justice which recalls the concern for individual justice revealed by Chekhov's recent interventions in the Dreyfus Affair. Such elements had always been present in his attitude. Now, in the years of his physical decline, they grow more prominent. But Chekhov still did not come near to expounding a social message at the expense of artistic quality. Never was he one of those Champions of the Little Man beloved of cliché-ridden Russian criticism, as all four Yalta stories of 1898 triumphantly confirm. For some reason, though, they do not quite maintain the pre-eminent standard set by the four Melikhovo stories which had preceded them in the summer of the same year.

December 1898 witnesses a further literary triumph—but one staged by others and in Chekhov's enforced absence. On the seventeenth of the month, after twelve weeks' intensive study and rehearsals, the Moscow Art Theatre at last presents its *Seagull*. As described in the memoirs of the Art Theatre's joint founders, Nemirovich-Danchenko and Stanislavsky, this event was a major drama in its own right. On 14 October the Art Theatre had been successfully launched on the world with its production of A. K. Tolstoy's *Tsar Theodore*. But then public interest had flagged, and there were fears for the future of the infant enterprise. Could Chekhov's *Seagull* possibly revive its fortunes? It seemed too much to ask of a play so experimental and unorthodox. Thus the night of 17 December, which opened to a house far from full, had become a make-or-break occasion for the new company. Fears for the author's health, supposedly undermined by the same play's disastrous première in St. Petersburg two years earlier, contributed to the general nervousness; especially when his sister intervened at the last moment with an appeal to take *The Seagull* off in view of the catastrophic effect which a second failure might have on him.

Such is the version of both producers, but Mariya Chekhov herself has robustly denied making this craven appeal.[10]

When the curtain rose on *The Seagull's* Act One the actors were all very worked up. Everyone had taken valerian drops, the tranquillizer of the period; Stanislavsky, as Trigorin, found it hard to control a twitching of his leg. As Act One proceeded audience reactions were hard to gauge, and when the curtain came down the house seemed frozen into immobility. Standing on the curtained stage, Olga Knipper fought to control hysterical sobs amid the silence of the tomb; until, at last, when it seemed that not a single clap would reward so carefully nurtured a production, a delayed action fuse seemed to have been detonated. "Like the bursting of a dam, like an exploding bomb a sudden deafening eruption of applause broke out." Members of the audience rushed the stage amid tears of joy and kissing so general as to recall the Orthodox custom of mass ritual osculation at Easter. People were "rolling round in hysterics", says Stanislavsky, who himself celebrated by dancing a jig. After the remaining three acts had been received with comparable enthusiasm, Nemirovich-Danchenko sent an ecstatic telegram to Chekhov in Yalta. Drafted on the audience's insistence, it recorded a colossal success with endless curtain calls and was signed "mad with joy".[11] Now at last the shameful fiasco of the St. Petersburg première had been wiped out. Chekhov had been restored to the theatre.

Early 1899 witnesses another major event in Chekhov's career: he sells the copyright of his entire works, past and future, to the St. Petersburg publisher A. F. Marks. For many years Chekhov had been dissatisfied with the haphazard issuing and marketing of his works. From the beginning, as already noted, each new item had regularly made its first appearance in the periodical press; after which it might be consigned to seemingly permanent oblivion, except that many of the better and later items had been unsystematically reassembled as books of stories or plays. Some of these collections had run through edition after edition. In 1898 alone, on the eve of the negotiations with Marks, *Motley Tales* achieved its eleventh and twelfth printings. *In the Twilight* had been issued for the eleventh time too, and *Tales* for the twelfth. *Gloomy People* had attained its eighth printing, and even the more recent volume combining *Peasants* with *My Life* had come up for the third time.[12] Issued in varying formats by diverse publishers at unpredictable intervals, these collections had vied with odd single items included with the author's permission in occasional literary symposia published for charity. Such were Chekhov's best-documented products. Of unregarded early items which had never been republished the author possessed neither copies nor records, except for odd scraps which might have survived accidentally.

It was a messy, irritating, untidy situation, unworthy of one now accepted as a major author. How natural, then, that Chekhov should seek to regularize matters. First he flirted with a publisher called Sytin, but turned him down. Then he made a vague arrangement for a multi-volume *Works* with Suvorin. It was while preparing that edition, and even after type-setting had begun at Suvorin's, that Chekhov suddenly switched to Marks.[13] Negotiations occupied January 1899, and the deal was settled with fantastic speed: in a month; in Chekhov's absence; by his appointed St. Petersburg representative, Sergeyenko; and on terms which were later to prove highly disadvantageous.

For 75,000 roubles, to be paid in three instalments, Chekhov assigned his entire existing writings to Marks, undertaking to retrieve and edit the whole corpus for a "Collected Works". As for future writings, first publication could take place as usual, for a fee in the periodical press. But they were then to revert to Marks, who would publish them in book form, paying an additional 250 roubles per printer's sheet of about sixteen pages during the first five years after signature; there was to be an increment of 200 roubles per sheet in each succeeding five-year period. When Chekhov threatened to live to the age of eighty, by which time these supplements would have become formidable, Marks took fright at the joke and nearly withdrew. He need not have worried. Far from living until 1940, Chekhov was to die within six years, and very substantial profits went to the publisher from the start.[14]

On one point Chekhov was adamant: he reserved to himself and his heirs the performance rights of all his drama. He was wise to do so, since his play royalties were now bringing in over a thousand roubles a year, besides which he was keen to preserve his personal links with the theatre.[15]

It all reminds us of the purchase of Melikhovo—also an over-hasty operation, but one which had turned out more luckily. Among those who warned Chekhov against dealing with Marks was that practical woman his sister. Another was Suvorin. Informed of the Marks negotiations, Suvorin had attempted to intervene, particularly warning Chekhov against the supreme folly of signing away his future work. Suvorin also offered 20,000 roubles to tide Chekhov over current financial difficulties. But Suvorin made no firm counter-offer to continue publishing the *Works* which he had begun, seeming highly evasive on this point. In any case, as we have seen, one of Chekhov's main motives in seeking a new publisher was to escape from Suvorin's firm.[16]

For striking this particular bargain Chekhov had many cogent reasons, ill-founded though some were to prove. At last he would see his writings in a model, uniform edition; no longer need he argue with printers and sales managers; his work would not appear on poor paper; he would not be cheated any more, nor be involved in problems of format, price and title. Above all, he would be able to work calmly.[17] In thus miscalculating, Chekhov attributed unproven virtues to the hitherto unknown quantity, Marks. That Marks was a more competent book publisher than Suvorin seems clear, but Chekhov was never to free himself from editorial and production problems. Nor could he avoid such preferably friendly tussles between author and publisher as often precede the appearance of a serious and worthwhile edition.

When making what was to prove his bad bargain of early 1899, Chekhov certainly overestimated Marks's efficiency. But it was not in this particular that the author's most grievous error lay. It was, rather, in failing to negotiate terms guaranteeing a more adequate return from any future rise in the profitability of his work. Such a rise—and a steep rise at that—did in fact occur almost while the ink on Chekhov's signature was still drying, as part of a general increase in the financial rewards of Russian authorship at the turn of the century. But by now it was too late: all Chekhov's work, including anything which he might yet write in the future, was already mortgaged to Marks on terms which were to seem increasingly loaded against the author as the few remaining years of his life passed by. Was this the reason why Chekhov was to concentrate so heavily, once the implications of his 1899 deal had become clear, on dramatic writing, still relatively profitable owing to the author's retention of performance rights? Was this why he was to neglect the short story so markedly in the years 1900–4? If so this was only a logical reaction in one who had rarely pretended to write except for money. How unfortunate that Chekhov, by no means inexperienced or foolish in practical matters, should have shown on this single occasion so catastrophic a lack of prudence in failing to defend the fruits of his labours from exploitation by a shrewder businessman.

Another of Chekhov's miscalculations of early 1899 was to underestimate the immediate and formidable task imposed on him by the Marks contract: to assemble and read his entire published *œuvre*; to supply copies of all items; to select those which he wished to preserve and mark the rest for rejection; to edit, revise and read proofs. These cares immobilized him as a creative writer during most of 1899, and were to continue long afterwards. Soon after the draft contract had been agreed, on 20 January 1899, Chekhov was contemplating with horror the chore of tracing all his early work, and of arranging for it to be copied and submitted by July. This impossible task was made no easier by his exile in Yalta, since his Melikhovo study still housed such relevant documents as he had not mislaid over the years. Of his voluminous early published work he had not bothered to preserve copies; nor in many cases could he even remember the title or contents. Whenever individual items had already been reissued in books, tracing presented no problem, for at least Chekhov had copies of *Motley Tales, In the Twilight* and his other collections. But for long-forgotten, never-republished material he was compelled to enlist allies, chiefly in St. Petersburg: his brother Alexander, Lydia Avilov, sundry bibliographers and editors. They consulted the files of *Budilnik, Razvle-cheniye, Peterburgskaya gazeta* and the like; identified Chekhov's pseudony-mous contributions when they could; and arranged for them to be copied into relays of exercise-books. Fortunately copyists could be hired, and soon this material was being freighted to Yalta and piling up in Chekhov's study.

To the harassed author this was sheer hard labour. He might as well be asked to list all the dates and hours at which he had ever caught a fish. Small wonder that his relief at signing the contract swiftly gave way to disillusionment. He was soon complaining that the sale was a catastrophe, even if he could now afford to eat fresh caviare. As for his juvenilia—now that he re-read them after so long, far from feeling any pride, he was absolutely aghast. The stuff was "revolting"; it was "a load of rubbish" which could only make him throw up his arms in astonishment. "I'm reading the manuscripts which you sent [he told Lydia Avilov]. Horrors, what gibberish! While reading I remember how boring it was to write in days of yore when you and I were younger."[18]

By mid-May, through friends' help and through his own intensive efforts, Chekhov had supplied Marks with copies of about 400 early stories, marking about a half for exclusion. He was also excluding non-fictional work, but was still left with over 3,000 pages of publishable material, enough to fill twelve to thirteen volumes. He wished to publish in chronological order, but "not strictly": a loophole of which he and the publisher availed themselves freely.[19] But though Chekhov had assembled most of the material by mid-1899, his editorial sufferings were only beginning. They spilt into the following years, and he was soon learning that misunderstandings and muddles were no monopoly of Suvorin's firm. Marks's people also had the knack of losing material and misinterpreting explicit instructions. It is therefore not surprising that, when Chekhov's first "Collected Works" appeared in ten volumes in 1899-1902, it was no scholarly and systematic edition. But it was at least a big improvement on the previous haphazard issues of his writings.

To Chekhov's first Yalta winter belong his earliest contacts with Maxim Gorky, now thirty years old but already an established writer. Though Gorky owed his vogue to literary skill and originality, other, non-literary, factors were also involved: his wide-ranging experience of Russia as tramp, down-and-out, wanderer and itinerant odd-job-man; his fame as a revolutionary persecuted by the police. Exploiting these themes, Gorky had tapped a new readership—that of proletariat-fanciers. But he had not allowed early success to go to his head; rather did he lack confidence in his literary technique and sensibly seek advice on improving it. With this in view he had written to Chekhov in November 1898, sending two volumes of stories and requesting comments.

Chekhov was happy to oblige Gorky, the most important, apart from Tolstoy, of the many authors whom he advised. And Chekhov's counsel all tended to concentrate on Gorky's extravagance. Gorky was too expansive, too verbose, too demonstrative, too rhetorical. He was as unrestrained as the naïve kind of theatre-goer who makes so lively a display of emotion and enthusiasm that he ruins the play for himself and others. Gorky should cultivate compactness, especially in nature descriptions and love scenes. He should shun words like "langour", "whisper" and "velvetiness", which create a rhetorical effect chilling to the reader. Gorky should cultivate gracefulness based on economy of effort. He should avoid personifying nature by making his sea "breathe", his sky "look" and his steppe "snuggle". He should cultivate simple statements: "the sun set"; "it grew dark"; "it rained". When reading proofs, Gorky should "where possible expunge the qualifications of nouns and verbs. You have so many qualifications that the reader finds it hard to focus and his attention flags. 'The man sat on the grass': if I write that it's comprehensible . . . because it's clear. . . . Conversely, I'm obscure, I tax the brain if I write 'a tall, narrow-chested, ginger-bearded man of medium height sat down on the grass which was green and already crumpled by passers-by: sat noiselessly, timidly and gazing about him fearfully.' That doesn't go home at once, which is what fiction should do: straight away, in a second."[20]

Chekhov spiced such plain speaking with tributes to Gorky's positive qualities: a "musical element"; an ability to convey the sight and texture of objects. Of certain short works by Gorky he spoke with great enthusiasm: he wished that he himself had written the short story In the Steppes, for instance.[21] But his early enthusiasm soon waned, as is not surprising. When were two writers more opposed to each other: Chekhov so elegant, so elusive, so understated; Gorky—despite all attempts to follow Chekhov's good advice—so loud, so strident, so embarrassingly emphatic? Chekhov was soon remarking that Gorky had started writing "disgraceful rubbish", and that he, Chekhov, would have to give up reading him.[22] But for Gorky the man Chekhov's affection remained constant, though the two never became close friends. They first met on 19 March 1899 during a visit to Yalta by Gorky. Both agreed to grace a literary evening in aid of famine relief, and Gorky saw a lot of Chekhov during the next few weeks. They would spend the whole day together, and once sat talking until six in the morning. Chekhov also took Gorky to his cliff-side cottage at

Kuchuk-Koy. Evidently feeling more a man of the world than his brash younger colleague, Chekhov decided to "introduce Gorky to women"; but we have no evidence that he ever carried out this threat.[23] And Gorky liked Chekhov, valuing his good opinion. To be taken seriously by Chekhov, "that vast and original talent, one of those authors who create an epoch in literary history and social consciousness"—it was deeply moving. Two of Chekhov's qualities in particular, his independence and his loneliness, impressed Gorky. "I think you [Chekhov] are the first free man I've ever seen: the first who never kow-tows to anything." "How lonely Chekhov is, how little he's understood."[24]

What of Chekhov's health during his first Yalta winter? On this we have the evidence of his doctor, I. N. Altshuller, who was struck at their first meeting in autumn 1898 by Chekhov's tired look, by his shortness of breath, by his slow, deliberate gait, and by the cough which betrayed his disease "to our physician's eye"; and, one might suppose, to many a layman's ear. Chekhov was always belittling his disease, attributing its symptoms to influenza, refusing treatment and so on. When Altshuller first seriously examined his patient he found both lungs extensively affected, especially the right; there were several cavities resulting (or so Altshuller impossibly claimed) from pleurisy; the heart muscle was weak; the functioning of the bowels was so impaired that the patient could not take proper nourishment. All in all, the illness was advanced beyond all hope of cure, though there might have been a hope of retarding its course and relieving its symptoms.[25]

However ill Chekhov might be he did not forget those yet more unfortunate, being particularly distressed by the plight of indigent consumptives callously "sent" to Yalta by their doctors or relatives without means of support. "To see their faces as they beg, to see their pathetic blankets when they're dying: it's depressing." Chekhov was soon organizing a subscription to set up a special sanatorium for these sufferers. A *pension* with twenty beds was eventually built on his initiative, and he contributed 5,000 roubles from his own resources.[26] In winter 1898-9 Chekhov also collected funds for the children of Samara Province, then a famine area. Nor were Melikhovo's children forgotten, for Chekhov's third village school was still on his mind, and he sent sums from his Art Theatre royalties to cover expenses. But school affairs in his old home district also evoked flashes of irritation such as the hagiographical biographies conceal. When the peasants of Novosyolki withheld the trifling sum which they had promised towards their own school, Chekhov spoke of taking legal action. He was also annoyed when the Talezh school-mistress kept complaining that she had no blackboards or firewood. "I can't write to her twenty times about one and the same thing", fulminated the author of *In the Cart*, in which just such a downtrodden school-mistress is portrayed with sympathy difficult to maintain in his present irritated mood. He was now trying to resign as Visitor to the Talezh and Chirkovo schools, being particularly fed up with the quarrels, the priest, the peasants breaking the windows.[27]

In Yalta Chekhov became a governor of the local girls' grammar school, which entitled him to wear the uniform of an official of the Sixth Grade and to be greeted by juvenile curtsies. He also helped to sponsor Yalta's centennial celebration of Pushkin's birth, securing from Suvorin the loan of a Chinese gong for a local production of the poet's historical play *Boris Godunov*. Wide-ranging in benefactions cultural, religious and political, he wrote recommendations for actors aspiring to join the Moscow Art Theatre; donated twenty-five roubles to the local mosque; spoke up for a neighbour's son, young Yelpatyevsky, who was in trouble with the police through the student riots of early 1899.[28] Nor was Taganrog forgotten. Chekhov continued to send books to the public library; maintained his interest in the local museum; decided to present the town with drawings by his deceased brother Nicholas. He also took an interest in the activities of his other brother Alexander, now attempting to establish a home for alcoholics on a Finnish island.[29]

Moscow, Melikhovo, Yalta
(April–August 1899)

In spring and summer 1899 Chekhov divided his time between his Melikhovo estate and a newly rented flat in Moscow. He was now briefly a fourfold householder, for he also had his Kuchuk-Koy cottage and his half-built Yalta villa. What he really needed was a wife in each of these homes.[1]

Arriving in Moscow from the south on 12 April, Chekhov was at once embroiled in a contretemps over *Uncle Vanya*. As we remember, this play had suddenly emerged in Chekhov's collected *Plays*, as published by Suvorin in 1897. It had since been staged with fair success in several provincial towns. They included Nizhny Novgorod, whence Gorky had written to Chekhov explaining in his usual rib-crushing prose that the performance had made him "weep as only a peasant woman can"; that he felt "deafened and trampled on" by a play of which "the saw-teeth run directly across one's heart".[2] This was no doubt very gratifying, but it was a far cry from the major metropolitan production which *Uncle Vanya* still awaited two years after its first appearance in print. That the Moscow Art Theatre was keen to snap up the play, after triumphing with *The Seagull*, need hardly be said. By now Nemirovich-Danchenko and his colleagues could almost claim proprietary rights over Chekhov, who returned their regard and affection. Unfortunately, though, *Uncle Vanya* was already pledged to a rival, longer-established, Moscow house: the Maly Theatre. That promise had been made "long ago", as Chekhov had to explain, most regretfully, to Nemirovich-Danchenko in a letter of 8 February 1899. On 1 March the play was, accordingly, given a collective reading by the Maly Company and approved for the repertoire provisionally³—only to provoke one of the most absurd minor episodes in Russian stage history.

Unlike the privately owned Moscow Art Theatre, the property of its shareholders, the Maly was one of the so-called Imperial Theatres directly administered by the Emperor's Court and controlled by an official Theatrical and Literary Committee. On 8 April 1899 this committee's three-man Moscow branch met in solemn conclave to determine whether *Uncle Vanya* was suitable for the boards of a theatre belonging in a sense to His Imperial Majesty the Tsar-Emperor Nicholas II. Coming down neither for nor yet entirely against the project, these worthies had soon produced a verbose report referring *Uncle Vanya* back to the author for certain far-reaching cuts and alterations. One heroine, Helen Serebryakov, was described as "too dreary" to interest an audience. There were said to be many long, boring passages, especially Astrov's harangues about forestry problems. Then there was the question of Vanya Voynitsky's behaviour in attempting to shoot Professor Serebryakov, that preposterous fuddy-duddy, in Act Three. Irritated though Vanya might naturally feel by the old man's high-handed attitude during the preceding family council, that was no excuse (pronounced the committee) for Vanya behaving "in so irresponsible a fashion". As for the exchange between Helen and Astrov, also in Act Three, there was nothing in the preceding text to prepare the audience for *so powerful an explosion of passion*. "On whose part?" Chekhov wearily scribbled in the margin at this point of his copy of the report. To him, as we know from other evidence, the mutual attraction between Astrov and the lovely Helen was a desultory, muted, Chekhovian sort of passion; that there was nothing in the least explosive about it was the chief point which he had hoped to make. Nor was there about the rest of the play, which subtly emphasizes the very untheatricality of life as Chekhov saw it. He was delineating a crisis of a new type, familiar enough in reality but still strange to the theatre: that which consists in the very absence of crisis. No wonder, then, that this tribunal of pedants— this moot of Serebryakovs militant—deemed his deliberately calculated chain of miscued clashes unsuitable for any self-respecting theatre.⁴

A very different view of *Uncle Vanya* was taken by the Administrator of the Imperial Theatres in Moscow, V. A. Telyakovsky. He was wholeheartedly on Chekhov's side, and offered to complain against the committee's decision; or even to go ahead and present *Uncle Vanya* at the Maly in defiance of that decision. But Chekhov was glad of the excuse to withdraw the play and give it to the Moscow Art Theatre. Pacifically inclined as ever, he offered to write another play for the Maly; but never did so. *Uncle Vanya* was already in preparation for the Art Theatre's coming season by 24 May, when Chekhov arrived in Moscow from Melikhovo, went straight from the station to see his play in rehearsal, and found it "coming along splendidly".[5]

So much for *Uncle Vanya*. But there was also *The Seagull*. So far Chekhov had had no chance to see the Art Theatre's outstandingly successful interpretation of that play, and on arriving from the south he "demanded" a special performance. The theatrical season was over, props and sets were in storage. But the company gladly put on a showing for the author on 1 May in the gloom of a barn-like, almost empty theatre. Chekhov's reaction was mixed. The presentation "wasn't bad on the whole"; it was "gripping". But he dismissed Mariya Roksanov's rendering of Nina Zarechny as downright "disgusting". He even tried to have her removed from the cast, according to Stanislavsky: for, "despite his extreme delicacy, sensitivity and kindness . . . he was stern, implacable and absolutely uncompromising over artistic issues". In fact, though, Chekhov had been every bit as disgusted, though too tactful to say so directly, by Stanislavsky's own performance as Trigorin. Stanislavsky had presented this worldly, middle-aged, successful author in a particularly flabby and spiritless manner. It was "a nauseating spectacle", said Chekhov privately; so "impotent" was this Trigorin that he really needed "an injection of sperm". Here Stanislavsky offended by overdoing things as usual: even the underplaying of a part. Trigorin was to be soft-pedalled, so he must be soft-pedalled out of existence. But the only comment which Stanislavsky could extract from Chekhov was that Trigorin should wear dilapidated boots and check trousers; an oracular evasion which the puzzled actor-director eventually infused with deep symbolical meaning.[6]

By contrast with his co-director Nemirovich-Danchenko, Stanislavsky never really spoke the same language as Chekhov. This emerges from the caricatured portrayal of Chekhov in Stanislavsky's memoirs: a dear little old comic, pince-nez-wearing eccentric, a kind of lovable, absent-minded, prissy, ailing dodderer not unlike the ludicrous "Telegin" in *Uncle Vanya*. And yet, despite the ugly notes of condescension in these memoirs, and despite all the memoirist's flamboyancy and impressive façade, Stanislavsky was anything but a megalomaniac seeking to impose himself on others. Decently lacking *au fond* in the sublime self-confidence which he could so skilfully simulate, he would defer in all modesty to the opinion of colleagues. Wherein Chekhov's genius lay, Stanislavsky could not properly decide; who, indeed, could? But Stanislavsky had the honesty to admit this, confessing that he neither understood Chekhov the playwright nor felt at ease with Chekhov the man:[7] not at least until the year 1902, when a dawning comprehension of both seemed to replace his previous uncritical enthusiasm.

April 1899 saw a further deterioration in relations between Chekhov and his old friend and former publisher Suvorin, with whom he had recently clashed over the Dreyfus Affair. Their new disagreement arose from the preceding February's serious student unrest in St. Petersburg. Undergraduate street demonstrations had been viciously repressed by mounted police; and this event, unprecedented in Russian university annals, had provoked widespread public protest, together with student strikes throughout the country. In its handling of the episode Suvorin's *Novoye vremya* had run true to tradition. Suvorin himself had published two articles condemning the students and praising as conciliatory the Emperor's decision to appoint a commission of enquiry into the matter.[8]

To imply that Russian governmental policies fell short in any degree of evil incarnate was to incur odium among students, liberals, intellectuals and "decent" or "honest" men (as they called themselves) generally. *Novoye vremya* was accordingly boycotted by the students, who at one stage proposed to delegate an emissary to slap Suvorin's face. Also descending into farce, the Mutual Aid Association of Russian Writers and Scholars solemnly instituted a Court of Honour before which Suvorin was indicted—in his absence, though he supplied a written defence—for conduct unbecoming a Russian publisher and gentleman. As Chekhov was no doubt reminded, his own election to this same professional association had been vigorously though unsuccessfully opposed by certain members, who had censured him in October 1897 for presuming (in his *Peasants*) to convey a view of bucolic Russia at variance with the yokel-fancying formulae deemed mandatory for a high-minded intellectual.[9] His attitude to the Association, to its Court of Honour, and to the complex issues behind these matters, is expressed in two fascinating letters to Suvorin of April 1899. Seldom, one feels, have politico-literary issues been articulated with such clarity and good sense. As Chekhov explains in the first of these missives, his own sympathies are with the students. "When people lack the right to express their views freely they express them provocatively and irritably; and often, from the state's point of view, in an ugly and disquieting form."[10]

So much for Chekhov's attitude to rioting students, an issue on which he firmly opposed Suvorin. But it by no means follows that Chekhov supported anything so palpably fatuous and pompous as a writers' Court of

Honour instituted in order to put Suvorin on trial. "It's nonsensical, it's absurd [Chekhov fulminated]. In our Asiatic country, lacking freedom of the press and freedom of conscience, where the government and nine-tenths of society regard journalists as their enemies, where life is so cramped and vile, where there's so little hope for better times, such entertainments as pouring slops over each other, Courts of Honour and so forth: they place writers in the ludicrous, pathetic position of caged animals biting each other's tails. . . . To arraign you for openly expressing your views (be they what they may) in print: it's a risky business, that; it's an attack on freedom of speech, it tends to make the journalist's job intolerable."[11]

Thus forcibly did Chekhov vindicate Suvorin's right to express his views. Thus admirably did he denounce attempts to politicize the literary and scholarly community by those who would erect a new and yet more rigid system of obligatory—albeit dissident—opinions in opposition to those prescribed and imposed, however feebly, by the Imperial government. But though Chekhov thought it nonsense for a Court of Honour to try Suvorin, he had no hesitation whatever in doing so himself in his private capacity. By this one-man court Suvorin stood condemned on many counts, and Chekhov spells these out in the same letter. *Novoye vremya* was generally believed to be in the pay of the Russian government, and also of the French, Dreyfus-obsessed, General Staff: for which Suvorin had only himself to blame, Chekhov told him. Why do everything possible to confirm so discreditable an impression? There was Suvorin's support of current government policy in suppressing the considerable autonomy hitherto enjoyed by Finland despite its status as a dependency of the Russian Empire. There was also Suvorin's habit of denouncing unfortunate rival publications which had been banned by officialdom for advocating policies less congenial to the government than those of *Novoye vremya*. Such actions were, said Chekhov, "unworthy of a literary man".[12] As this letter confirms, Chekhov's political attitudes—more accurately, anti-political attitudes—were hardening in the last years of his life. Particularly eloquent and sensitive on the issue of freedom, he showed again and again how committed he was to the liberty of the individual; how implacably opposed to all forms of collective bullying. For those who, whether from the pro-government or the anti-government camp, sought to impose systems of prescriptive ideas in package form Chekhov reserved the withering contempt of which, in his letters and private utterances, he shows himself such a master.

In this, his last Melikhovo summer, Chekhov spent little time on the estate which he had bought seven years earlier. After reaching Moscow from the south he had stayed in that city nearly a month, busy with theatrical and other affairs, before going out to Melikhovo on 7 May.

A month after that he had definitely decided to sell the property. He would not have returned to Melikhovo at all in 1899, perhaps, had it not been for his and Mariya's new village school—now nearing completion. Once again he was involved with carpenters, bricklayers, plasterers, and with the usual haggling, arguments and site inspections, until, by 20 June, the building was at last finished. After that there was nothing to detain him in his old home and he left it for Moscow, never to return, on 6 July. By early August the property had been sold to a timber merchant who failed to pay the balance of the purchase price after assuming possession, and who neglected the place appallingly before it was eventually resold to a Baron Stewart.[13]

Contact between Chekhov and Olga Knipper had been resumed in April 1899 after a seven-month gap following their previous September's brief encounter. He called on her in Easter week, they visited an art exhibition together, and he invited her out to Melikhovo where she spent three days before leaving for a holiday in the south. Then, on 16 June, Chekhov wrote his first letter to Olga, thus starting a correspondence which was eventually to be published in three large volumes and to include nearly a thousand items.[14] The exchange begins with flirtatious badinage, familiar to us from his earlier dealings with women. Chekhov and Olga refer to each other archly, in the third person, as "the Actress, and "the Author". "The Author has been forgotten—oh, how terrible, how cruel, how treacherous", Chekhov writes; and soon receives from Mtskhet in Georgia, where Olga is now holidaying, a suitably whimsical counter-accusation. Complaining that it is Author Chekhov who has forgotten Actress Knipper, she invites him to join her out in Georgia and escort her thence to Yalta. Signifying his acceptance of so charming a proposition, he agrees to meet her in the Caucasus; but only on condition that the Actress promises not to turn the Author's head.[15]

On 8 July Chekhov wired to arrange a rendezvous on a Yalta-bound steamer at Novorossiysk, also writing to explain that he must call at Taganrog "on urgent business". This turned out to be medical in character when, after arriving on 13 July, he investigated his prospects for making a permanent home there, even as his new villa in Yalta was nearing completion. He consulted a Taganrog doctor, I. Ya. Shimkovich, asking whether residence in the town was compatible with his state of health, but was firmly told that Yalta was less harmful to a consumptive.[16] Thus did the quadruple householder of mid-1899 consider acquiring a fifth home. The episode reminds us of the affection which he had increasingly felt for his native town since his departure at the age of nineteen. Whether Taganrog would have satisfied him as a permanent home we may doubt. Absence usually made Chekhov's heart grow fonder, and we suspect that

Taganrog's chief hold on his affections was that he so rarely visited the place.

After settling this question Chekhov kept his rendezvous with Olga Knipper in Novorossiysk. They steamed, as arranged, across the Black Sea to Yalta, where Olga stayed with Anton's friends the Sredins, while he put up at a hotel. They spent two weeks there, visiting Chekhov's nearly-completed villa; watching performing fleas on the Esplanade; making excursions in the picturesque environs.[17] Then, on 2 August, they set off for Moscow by carriage through the spectacular mountains to Bakhchisaray. Traversing the romantic Kokkoz Valley, they experienced some degree of amorous rapprochement to which Miss Knipper would later cryptically allude.[18] But it seems unlikely that the Actress was yet the elusive Author's mistress, for they continued to address each other by the formal second person plural *vy*, not by the intimate *ty* of lovers.

Reaching Moscow with Olga on 4 August, Chekhov spent three weeks in the city before returning to winter in Yalta. He felt too unwell to attend rehearsals of *Uncle Vanya*, now being prepared for its Art Theatre première, but illness did not prevent him from attempting one kind deed. He interceded with Moscow University for a Jewish student who wished to enrol there in this age when Jews were admitted to Russian institutes of higher learning only on sufferance and by quota. The Moscow Vice-Chancellor snubbed Chekhov, keeping him waiting in a stuffy anteroom for an hour and a half, and addressing him discourteously before brusquely rejecting his request. Chekhov left with a headache, sickened by this brush with the Establishment and ruefully comparing his *alma mater* to a criminal investigation office rather than a temple of learning.[19]

Throughout this disturbed summer Chekhov had continued preparing his "Collected Works", being now deeply involved in proof-reading. By 6 August he had corrected all the proofs of Volume One, which was one hurdle crossed in this arduous obstacle course.[20]

Yalta
(August–December 1899)

On 27 August 1899 Chekhov reached Yalta from Moscow and began an eight-month sojourn, his longest, in that resort.

His new house was already a landmark on the hillside. Of eccentric shape, painted white, it would (the owner joked) make an obvious target if the British fleet should ever shell Yalta. When he moved in, the builders had nowhere near finished work: there were no doors, parquet was being laid, painters and decorators were still banging about. Among other distractions, modern and traditional, were a telephone which Chekhov thought a nuisance, and the cry of the local muezzin calling the Tatar faithful to prayer.[1] Less disrupted by these cries, nowadays, owing to Stalin's deportation of the Crimean Tatars and the suppression of their and other religions, Chekhov's Yalta residence is preserved (like the Melikhovo manor and the Moscow house on Sadovy-Kudrinsky Street) as a museum dedicated to his memory. Its director was for many years his sister Mariya, who died in 1957.

In early September 1899 Mariya Chekhov arrived in Yalta with her mother to inspect the new residence. Anton also took them to see his seaside cottage at Kuchuk-Koy, where the old lady was terrified by the precipitous descent to that out-of-the-way property. Soon Mariya was on her way back to her teaching post in Moscow, while Chekhov's mother stayed behind in Yalta with their ancient cook to look after the master of the house. But, as Dr. Altshuller has pointed out, the two old ladies were not competent to maintain in Mariya's absence the strict regimen which the invalid required.[2]

Still a gardening addict, Chekhov delighted in the novelties of sub-tropical horticulture. His Tatar odd-job-man Mustafa and other befezzed labourers laid out paths while their master studied seed catalogues and placed orders, besides wielding a spade in person. He planted oranges, lemons, quinces, almonds, acacias, oleanders, mulberries, camellias, lilies, roses, tulips, hyacinths, keeping accurate records and affixing labels with the correct botanical names.[3] These preoccupations continued when Mustafa was replaced by a pious Russian, Arseny; a tame crane and an assortment of dogs completed the ménage. But despite such satisfactions the invalid was even more bored, bored, bored during his second Yalta winter than he had been during the first. Never had the months dragged on so drearily. Having lost the habit of the north without acquiring a taste for the south, he still felt uprooted on the periphery and needed letters from the hub of events to boost his flagging morale.

From Chekhov's frequent complaints of loneliness we must not deduce that he lacked company. His numerous visitors included "scholars, writers, welfare workers, doctors, officers, painters ... professors, society notabilities ... priests, actors and God knows who else".[4] There was always the odd uninvited intruder who would arrive, plant himself in an armchair and sit talking for hours on end. Too courteous or feeble to send these nuisances packing, the infuriated author would fume internally and think himself lucky if they did not set him coughing with their accursed cigarettes: and that despite the "no smoking" notice in his study. Such pests were also liable, like Mrs. Kharkeyevich (headmistress of the local girls' grammar school), to commiserate with him for hours about the inhumanity of visitors who insisted on commiserating with him for hours when his only wish was to be rid of them.[5] Then there were his various more distant admirers. Many were female, being notorious locally as *antonovki* or "pippins"; the word denotes a juicy and tangy brand of apple. These fans would nudge each other and point him out on the Esplanade. Or, should he step into Sinani's bookshop, they would "happen" to browse on the shelves or buy cigarettes, while casting sidelong glances at their idol.[6] Such nuisances reduced the value of this otherwise admirable shop; an unofficial club, a clearing house for gossip and very much a Yalta institution. Its proprietor, Isaac Sinani, was delighted to become the factotum of the town's most distinguished resident, serving as Chekhov's messenger, agent and confidant.

Though Chekhov's visits to the town centre decreased as his health deteriorated, his bolder admirers were always liable to call at his villa uninvited: yet another penalty for becoming one of Yalta's tourist attractions, on a par with Uchan-Su Falls and Mount Ay-Petri. Depressing too was Yalta's climate, which had turned out less benign than expected. Rain, snow, sleet, high winds and cold weather confined Chekhov to his house for days on end. He even slept in his hat and slippers at times; for his stoves were a constant source of trouble, hardly warming the place at all except when they occasionally turned it into a smoke-filled, overheated inferno.[7]

While Chekhov languished in Yalta, his plays led a life of their own in the north. The big Muscovite theatrical event of that autumn was *Uncle Vanya*'s première at the Art Theatre on 26 October. Chekhov nearly froze in his poorly-heated villa as he kept rising from his bed to answer the telephone over which telegrams on the play's reception were relayed throughout the night. Their phraseology was naturally lush, for to speak in terms less than grandiloquent of any cultural phenomenon would have been a gross breach of etiquette. But Chekhov could read between the high-flown lines that *Uncle Vanya*'s reception had been no unqualified triumph. What did it matter, though? Moderation, even in success, was always best for an actor and writer; it would be healthy for the Art Theatre to prosper more modestly than hitherto.[8]

Of Chekhov's yearning for the Moscow Art Theatre we learn again and again from his correspondence of the winter. Here is the only theatre which holds his affection, though he has never been inside it; he would be glad to serve there himself, if only as caretaker; he envies the very rats who live under the boards. Acclaiming its first anniversary, he telegraphs on 1 October. "SEND INFINITE THANKS CONGRATULATIONS WISHES FROM DEPTHS OF SOUL LET US WORK CONSCIOUSLY EAGERLY INDEFATIGABLY UNANIMOUSLY THAT THIS GLORIOUS BEGINNING MAY BE PLEDGE OF FURTHER TRIUMPHS." To these months also belongs the first mention, albeit negative, of Chekhov's next play. "I am *not* writing a play," he states in November. But he does have a subject: "three sisters".[9]

Between October and December 1899 Chekhov takes farewell of the nineteenth century by writing his last stories to appear in a group: *A Lady with a Dog*; *At Christmas*; *In the Hollow*.

A Lady with a Dog, Chekhov's last story for *Russkaya mysl*, has closer links with his new home than any of his other works, for the action begins in Yalta and its surroundings. In this renowned study of love among the professional classes, the banker and experienced libertine Gurov, husband of an unloved wife, casually seduces Anne von Diederitz as she holidays apart from her flunkey-like husband, a provincial civil servant whom she utterly despises. Their first brief encounter leads to a furtive and sporadic liaison which becomes poignantly frustrating as the two partners fall deeply in love while facing an uncertain future left typically unresolved by their creator. Without reproducing the situation which was now developing in his own life, and most emphatically without portraying himself as Gurov or Olga Knipper as Anne, Chekhov yet infused this masterpiece, which movingly depicts the enforced separation of two imagined lovers, with yearnings of his own. These include the longing for once-detested Moscow which he had come to feel during his winters in the south; for Moscow where—as he writes in the story, deliberately emphasizing the contrast with boring Yalta—"it is always such a joy to see the white ground and white roofs when the snow first falls, on that first day of sleigh-riding. The air is so fresh and good to breathe, and you remember the years of your youth. White with frost, the old limes and birches have a kindly look, they are dearer to your heart than any cypresses or palm-trees, and near them you no longer hanker after mountains and sea."[10]

At Christmas, the second story of late 1899, is a short, lightweight work which Chekhov published in *Peterburgskaya gazeta*, thus reviving a connection broken some years earlier. The action takes place partly in a village, partly in Moscow; and Chekhov again depicts weak, helpless people maltreated by callous, brutal associates. All are drawn from the lower classes.

Such too, on a far larger scale, are the theme and setting of *In the Hollow*, the last and (with *Peasants*) finest of Chekhov's village studies. Its material embraces murder and other crime, and derives from the author's Sakhalin memories, according to his brother Michael, who adds that the setting is near Melikhovo.[11] *In the Hollow* is an intricately tailored work which triumphantly refutes the thesis that an ingenious plot was beyond Chekhov's powers. The climax has the calculating, snake-like Aksinya pouring boiling water over her ill-used sister-in-law's baby to prevent its inheriting land on which the murderess is operating a profitable brick-works. That such atrocities were not uncommon in the Russian countryside Chekhov informed the memoirist Shchukin, adding that *In the Hollow* was set in the Russian midlands, the milieu which he knew best. He also stated that such businessmen as his exploiting Khrymins of *In the Hollow* did exist in real life, being even worse than those of his story; their debauched children were swilling vodka from the age of eight, and had infected the entire district with syphilis.[12]

Only after despatching *In the Hollow* to *Zhizn* ("Life") on 20 December 1899 did Chekhov discover that this magazine had a definite political complexion. It was one of those Marxist organs which, despite the revolutionary nature of Marxist doctrine, were permitted to appear during the declining years of the Russian Empire—partly because the authorities regarded Marx's teachings as no more than harmless, boring exercises in recondite economic theory. Even worse informed on Marxism than the authorities, Chekhov assumed, on learning of the magazine's affiliations at the last moment, that *In the Hollow* would prove ideologically unacceptable to the editors. "I describe factory life, treating it as a melancholy affair. But only yesterday I chanced to discover that *Zhizn* is a Marxist or factory organ. What *am* I to do now."[13] That the peasants and factory hands of *In the Hollow* by no means contravene Marxist assumptions, but rather conform closely with Marxist teaching on the "contradictions of village life"; that the story could therefore not fail to delight the editors of *Zhizn*: of these things Chekhov had no inkling. Why should he? Marxism was still an obscure doctrine in the 1890s. A familiarity with its tenets could certainly not be claimed as part of an educated Russian's intellectual baggage.

Further developing the lesson of *Peasants*, and of other earlier works with rural settings, *In the Hollow* reflects Chekhov's steadfast refusal to idealize Russian village life. The story is thus the last literary item in his continuing implicit polemic against the Narodniks. That the invalid of Yalta was as implacably opposed as the Squire of Melikhovo to trendy yokel-fancying we are further reminded in a letter of January 1899. Here Chekhov discusses the Russian peasantry's most controversial social institution, the *obshchina* or Village Commune. Its main manifestation was the regulation of certain village affairs at informal outdoor assemblies of local heads of households. The Commune was hailed by certain Russian "thinkers" as the very embodiment of collectively functioning innate peasant wisdom. It was also considered to provide a short cut to socialism, an amenity not available to less fortunate societies. But Chekhov was "against the Commune". He called it a rabble, and said that its links were as arbitrary as those uniting a chain-gang. In any case the institution was "coming apart at the seams because Commune and Culture are incompatible". What, then, did the Commune promote in Chekhov's view? "The universal drunkenness and profound ignorance of the Russian peasant."[14]

Though essential to a full understanding of Chekhov and *In the Hollow*, these complex considerations affect the story's quality not at all. It is one of his very best, but marks almost the end of his career as a short-story writer. Only two more examples of the genre, both on an inferior level, were to follow in the years of life remaining to him.

CHAPTER THIRTEEN

Yalta:
The Years of "Three Sisters"
1900–1

In the new century Chekhov's preoccupations become more theatrical. His main personal concern remains the actress Olga Knipper, with whom he contracts one of the most fully-documented short marriages on record. And his main literary involvement is with two four-act plays specially written for the Moscow Art Theatre. It is the first of these, *Three Sisters*, which absorbs most of his creative energies in 1900–1, when he wrote no short stories at all.

Yalta
(January–April 1900)

Resuming our narrative in the middle of Chekhov's second Yalta winter, we find him elected in January 1900 to the dignity of Honorary Academician by the Imperial Academy of Sciences, Russia's most exalted learned institute, founded by Peter the Great in 1724. The new honour brought no tangible benefits except notional immunity from arrest and the right to travel on a special passport. Nor was Chekhov one to savour this or any other rank for its own sake. It probably meant as little to him as the humble and indeed ridiculous Order of St. Stanislaus, Third Class, which he had received for services to education. Still, he at least took the Academy award seriously enough to propose certain fellow-writers for the same dignity. It is typical of his generous spirit or sense of irony that these proposals included N. K. Mikhaylovsky, the celebrated Populist and occasional Chekhov-baiter.[1] In due course we shall find Chekhov paying his honorary academicianship the compliment of resigning from it on an issue of principle.

Thus honoured in distant St. Petersburg, Chekhov continued to put down roots in the Crimea. In mid-January he bought yet another local property, his third, at Gurzuf, on the coast about ten miles north-east of Yalta and thus on the opposite side to his other seaside home at Kuchuk-Koy. The Gurzuf property included a little bay, a mulberry-tree and a four-room cottage with a tiled roof.² But Chekhov was not to make very much use of either of these charming coastal cottages which straddled his Yalta home. Meanwhile his new way of life was paying off in improved health. Not once did illness confine him to bed that winter, and the very tubercle bacillus seemed in full retreat: some consolation for continuing piles, diarrhoea and eye-ache.³

During eight long months of enforced separation Olga Knipper was patiently grooming Chekhov by correspondence for the husband's role so ill-suited, he had once believed, to his aptitudes. As part of this campaign Olga cultivated her friendship with his sister, and a February pancake party at the Ivan Chekhovs' saw the two young women solemnly drinking *Brüderschaft* together. This ceremony conferred on Olga the right, as she quickly informed Chekhov, to allude to Mariya Pavlovna by the intimate form "Masha". Now on "thou" and "Masha" terms with the sister, Olga was in sighting distance of "thou" and "Antosha" terms with the brother, from whom for the moment she was still distanced grammatically by the formal second person plural and geographically by the Moscow–Sevastopol railway. But Olga was already staking her claim on Chekhov. "Do say we can spend the summer together", she begged on 5 February. Her flirtatious banter includes cryptic references to whatever had passed between the two during their previous August's carriage ride through the Crimean mountains. Since then, she teased Anton, rumour had reached her of his betrothal to a Yalta priest's daughter. But Olga intended to come along and upset his domestic bliss. "We did make a pact, didn't we? Remember Kokkoz Valley?"⁴

In early April 1900 this threatened disruption materialized as Olga turned up with Mariya to take a short holiday in Yalta. Only a few days were available, since the main body of the Art Theatre was soon to appear in the south and embark on a two-week Crimean tour. This event, eagerly awaited by Chekhov, was to begin in Sevastopol on 10 April. *The Seagull* and *Uncle Vanya* were in the repertoire. What with all this excitement, theatrical and amatory, Chekhov unfortunately succumbed to severe haemorrhoidal bleeding on 8 April, but recovered sufficiently to sail for Sevastopol two days later, pale, ill, thin, protesting his perfect health. Now at last he could see Art Theatre performances of his plays before audiences. *The Seagull* and *Uncle Vanya*, together with works by Ibsen and Hauptmann, were presented in Sevastopol with élan, to packed houses and thunderous ovations. Then the company sailed for Yalta with its attendant "fans", nannies, maids, children; and with scenery and stage props strewn over the deck. The actors were all in a great pother, all smartly dressed, all bubbling over with exuberance while yet preserving the self-consciously correct deportment befitting a prestigious metropolitan troupe surrounded by gawping provincials.[5]

It was all great fun.

Duly docked in Yalta, the company spent ten days there in all. The Chekhovs kept open house for them and various writers who had congregated for the occasion—Bunin, Gorky, Mamin-Sibiryak and others. Meanwhile Knipper was scurrying about the villa with her sleeves rolled up, helping Chekhov's mother and sister to keep the food and drink flowing; now clearly promoted to rival mistress of the household, she may have superficially resembled the officious jam-making Aunt Dasha of Anton's story *Home*.[6]

For the Art Theatre's Yalta performances tickets had been sold out in advance, and to audiences which included metropolitan visitors besides dazzled locals. On 16 April Chekhov attended *Uncle Vanya*, and suffered the ordeal of making his bow on stage in response to insistent curtain-calls. This was sheer torment, as was the elaborate honorific address presented to him after *The Seagull* on the 23rd. Chekhov loved the theatre. But he loved only its informal aspects, not these public posturings. Rather than be fêted by the playgoing public, he preferred mooching about back-stage dispensing brief and cryptic advice. He was still teasing poor Stanislavsky— now by mysteriously pronouncing that Astrov (in *Uncle Vanya*) should "whistle" in Act Four.[7]

After a farewell banquet with fireworks on the flat roof of a luxurious local villa, the Art Theatre departed for Moscow, leaving *Uncle Vanya's* exhausted author with two mementoes which had been used as props in that play: a garden bench and a swing.[8]

Union and Separation
(May–October 1900)

Released in spring 1900 from medically imposed confinement in tedious Yalta, Chekhov is in no hurry to escape north. Not until 6 May does he leave for Moscow, where he meets Olga, attends a wrestling bout in the Aquarium amusement gardens, and visits Isaac Levitan, another sufferer from tuberculosis and now on the point of death. Nine days later he returns to Yalta, and then goes on to tour the Caucasus with Gorky and the painter V. M. Vasnetsov. They visit the ancient Georgian city of Mtskhet and spend a week in the Georgian capital Tiflis, where a Joseph Dzhugashvili (the future dictator Stalin) is now humbly employed as a clerk at the local observatory. Returning via Batum, Chekhov enjoys six hours on the train with Olga, who happens to be holidaying in these parts with her mother. After this short excursion Chekhov again returns to Yalta, but considers leaving for China, where the Boxer Rising is now in full cry, to serve as a medical officer in the field:[1] one of the most bizarre among the invalid's sudden hankerings for far-away places. In fact he barely strays beyond his Yalta doorstep, where adventure seeks him out; for it is now at last that Olga becomes his mistress.

Olga was not in her first youth, since their original meeting of 9 September 1898 had coincided with her thirtieth birthday. She had thus long outlived all prospect of marriage by the standards of Anton's fiction, in which spinsters of twenty-three tend to be "on the shelf".

Both Olga's parents were German. Her engineer father had left his native Alsace to seek his fortune in Russia, succeeding well enough to provide his family with the usual comforts of the Russian bourgeoisie. Olga herself had been brought up as a typical "young lady" of the period. She had wanted to act or to pursue some other career, but her loving father had firmly banned such frivolities—only to die suddenly, leaving wife and daughter to make their own living after so long protecting them from learning how to do so. The girl and her mother dismissed their servants, gave up their expensive flat, moved in with Olga's maternal uncles, and supported themselves by music lessons. Olga enrolled at a drama school; she was taught by Nemirovich-Danchenko, and graduated straight into leading roles at the newly established Moscow Art Theatre, of which her teacher had become a co-founder.[2]

Simultaneously meeting her future husband, entering her fourth decade and emerging as a fully-fledged actress, Olga had become a person of consequence almost overnight. She was an impressive self-made woman, and her relations with Chekhov were based from the start on the respect of one talented artist for another. Such a relationship had not been possible between him and the charming but ungifted Lika Mizinov. Not that Chekhov's actress was thought as good-looking as Lika. Olga was a well-built, rather strong-featured woman; handsome, but not regarded as a raging beauty. Neither in physique nor character was she one of those wilting, wispy heroines with their weak arms, undeveloped breasts and air of helplessness whom we remember as Chekhov's fictional feminine ideal. She little resembled the Kisochka of *Lights* and the Zhenya of *The Artist's Story*, being more like such real girls as Natalya Lintvaryov, the tomboy of Luka, and Mariya Zankovetsky, the tobogganing Ukrainian actress. She was sociable and outgoing; liked laughter, fun, horseplay. And she shared with Chekhov a lively sense of the ridiculous. As for the subtler elements in his humour, as for the deep-laid strata of his irony—it was all *terra incognita* to the jolly Olga. Of the "Chekhovian humour" attributed to her by one editor, we find little trace in her letters to Chekhov.[3]

Olga was not a multi-level personality like Chekhov; she had little feel for nuances, innuendoes, delicate intimations and the like. When she was happy she laughed; when she was unhappy she cried. And that was that. She was an up-and-down person, her lusty guffaws alternating with bouts of self-pity. She was also insecure by nature, needing constant reassurance, flattery and expressions of devotion: tributes which the self-sufficient Anton scouted as superfluous and irritating when they were paid to himself. The bond between them was, accordingly, less that of communing fellow-spirits than of mutually attracted opposites. Chekhov delighted in Olga as she was. Why should he need to see his own temperament mirrored in hers?

We have watched Olga enter her career at the top, skipping ingénue roles and bursting on to the stage as a reigning monarch: the Tsaritsa Irina in Alexis Tolstoy's play *Tsar Theodore*. Then we saw her as another mature "Irina": *The Seagull*'s Madame Arkadin, a queen of the theatre with a grown-up son. And yet, despite the reservations about her looks ungallantly suggested above, Olga could also carry off *Uncle Vanya*'s Helen, whose physical beauty is repeatedly emphasized in Chekhov's text. Her favourite Chekhov role was to be Masha in *Three Sisters*, a part written especially for her. And Masha, a dashing "daughter of the regiment", was the nearest thing to a Knipper in any of Chekhov's plays. In this unhappy young woman, cruelly separated from her lover Colonel Vershinin, Olga was to invest her frustrations over separation from her Anton. But Olga could also triumph as the slightly absurd Lyuba Ranevsky in Chekhov's *Cherry Orchard*, and as the dying Sarah in a revival of his *Ivanov*. Throughout her long career Olga Knipper also appeared in many plays by other authors and was, all in all, a versatile major artist.

Though we cannot be quite sure that Olga had not become Anton's mistress at some earlier stage, she certainly was so in July 1900. Staying at his Yalta home while his mother and sister were also resident, she would creep into his bedroom at night. "Remember taking me to the stairs, and how treacherously they creaked. I absolutely adored it. God, I'm writing like a schoolgirl."[4] Thus Olga wrote to Anton after her return to Moscow, the change in their relations being signalized at last by the intimate *ty*. But these midnight adventures created a painfully false situation in the villa. Chekhov's pious old mother and highly respectable sister, both menaced as controllers of his household by Olga, could not help noticing the staircase's treacherous creaking—while being expected to pretend that they had not. Shocked, threatened, forced to behave hypocritically, they could not conceal their distress. Anton was blind to all this, of course. But Olga at least could see how deeply such antics upset the other ladies of the house. She could also see how these embarrassments might be applied as a lever in her campaign to marry Chekhov.

Detesting fuss as he did, Chekhov was now to learn at first hand a truth of which he could have reminded himself by reading his own stories: there may be more to taking a mistress than acquiring a delightful bed-mate. The association is apt to involve a load of uncovenanted emotional presuppositions and implied duties. Separated from her lover between 6 August and 23 October, Olga began to spell out these implications.

Olga being Olga (forthright, determined, knowing what she wanted) and Chekhov being Chekhov (evasive, elusive, accustomed to dodging attractive girls), we need not wonder that it was the woman who continued to take the initiative by sending her lover letters almost too obviously designed to manœuvre him into wedlock. Olga "could not move", she wrote to him, for people who were convinced that she already was Mrs. Chekhov. This news, she insisted, was the talk of the Crimean coast from Kastropol to Alupka. But if Chekhov's name was now everywhere linked with hers she had only herself to blame; for she was already telling Nemirovich-Danchenko (who reported it to Stanislavsky) that their marriage was "a settled thing". In fact we have no evidence of any formal agreement to marry at this time—a point on which Chekhov was probably as enigmatic as usual. It was, perhaps, with some hope of jerking him out of this condition that Olga began to dwell, in her letters to her lover, on her association with another man, the actor Alexander Vishnevsky, a friend of Chekhov's with whom he had been at school in Taganrog, and Olga's assiduous escort in Moscow. On 19 August Olga saw an operetta with Vishnevsky, as she informed Chekhov. A week later she reports, whimsically of course, that she is thinking of marrying Vishnevsky. What would Anton advise? Two weeks later she is boasting of having invited another male escort, L. A. Sulerzhitsky, to her flat late one night, where he sang songs and played the fool until 2 a.m.; Olga had never laughed so much in her life. But how little she knew Anton if she thought he could be manipulated by such crude attempts to engage his jealousy.[5]

As autumn drew on Olga became more and more exasperated with Chekhov, for a reason which becomes a leitmotiv in their correspondence. To be forcibly separated for six months of the year by demands which kept her in Moscow while he was confined in the south—that she could reluctantly accept. As Chekhov put it, "if we aren't together it's not my fault or yours, it's the devil's for lodging the bacillus in me and a love of art in you."[6] During the long winter months these separations were clearly unavoidable. However, as Olga was acutely aware in the year 1900, August and September are not winter months. Chekhov was free to visit

Moscow, where the weather was still fine and warm; so why, oh why, did he insist on remaining in Yalta? No wonder Olga wrote that "either you don't want to know me or you can't bear the thought of uniting your fate with mine."[7]

To the crime of unnecessarily remaining in Yalta Chekhov added the further offence of infuriating vagueness about his travel plans. He was ready to come to Moscow "not before 22 September" or "on 12 October"; but as autumn drew on the date of his proposed visit seemed to recede indefinitely. "Why have these lovely autumn months been wasted?" asked Olga. But she knew better than to press the point, continuing "don't be afraid; I don't want a talk with serious faces and consequences, as you feared."[8] And to avoid such a talk may have been sensible, since signs were accumulating that, for Chekhov, a little of Olga went a long way. That he was fond of her we do not doubt; but it does not follow that he could tolerate her uninterrupted presence, day and night, for months on end. He longed for her unbearably when she was away, he cherished her tenderly when she was with him; but after a few weeks he needed to be rid of her. The fact is that he had precious little talent for prolonged intimacy, and had detected this trait in himself long before meeting Olga, when remarking that he could not bear a bliss unrelieved; and that, if he must have a wife, it should be one who (like the moon) would not appear in his sky every day.

To such motives for cultivating solitude in autumn 1900 more cogent considerations must be added. After a gap of seven months since *In the Hollow* Chekhov had again taken up creative work, and was heavily engaged with *Three Sisters*. Part of the play had been written as early as August, but progress was slow, being hampered by influenza and visitors. At one time he anticipated finishing the work in September; at other times he spoke of it unenthusiastically and said that he had no idea when it would be finished. Meanwhile he was exhorted to get on with the job by Nemirovich-Danchenko, by Stanislavsky and not least by his absent mistress, who told him that he should for God's sake write his play and not keep everyone on tenterhooks.[9] It was, then, *Three Sisters* more than ill health or a distaste for Olga's company which detained Chekhov in Yalta until mid-October, when he was at last ready to take the first draft of the play to Moscow.[10]

Moscow, Nice, Italy
(October 1900–February 1901)

On 23 October 1900 Chekhov arrived in Moscow with his manuscript of *Three Sisters*, put up at the Dresden Hotel on Tver Street, was reunited with Olga and embarked on an orgy of theatrical activity. With Gorky he attended his own *Uncle Vanya* and *Seagull* on 27 and 28 October, being presented with a laurel wreath by directors and cast. He saw the same two plays again in November, also attending two Ibsen plays in the Art Theatre's repertoire. And he was still revising *Three Sisters*. But when he at last read the text to the Art Theatre actors and producers it fell flat. It was unplayable, they found; it contained no proper parts, only hints.[1]

Why did *Three Sisters* so disappoint its first interpreters? Like all Chekhov's serious drama it has the air of seeming to make, yet of never quite making, some statement about human life. One main theme is provincial frustration as it affects the three daughters and son of the deceased General Prozorov. Andrew Prozorov would have liked to be a professor in Moscow, but works for the municipal council of which his wife's lover is chairman. The three girls are all disappointed in love: Olga regrets being an old maid; Masha has married the wrong man; Irina's fiancé—unloved at that—is killed in a duel in Act Four. Olga dislikes being a schoolmistress, Masha dislikes being a schoolmaster's wife, Irina dislikes working in a post office. But all their problems would, they fervently believe, magically disappear if they could only fulfil their burning ambition to return to Moscow, their childhood home. With these unhappy, ill-organized creatures is contrasted their vulgar, insensitive, selfish sister-in-law Natasha. She intrudes on the ménage, marries the brother, drools over her children, converts the Prozorov family house into the opposite of a home. What does all this prove? Is the play sad or funny? Does the tragedy reside in the characters' failure to rise to the level of tragedy? Or are they not tragic even in that restricted sense? Since these questions have never been fully resolved we need not wonder that the first cast of *Three Sisters* was so baffled.

Meanwhile the Moscow so ardently desired by Chekhov's three sisters was becoming increasingly irksome to their creator. Thoroughly depressed, he considered snatching a visit to St. Petersburg and the actress Vera Komissarzhevsky, whom he much admired and seems to have used as a counter-irritant to Olga Knipper. His present stay in Moscow was beginning to seem like Siberian hard labour, he disloyally wrote to Vera, who has been described as "possibly the only woman for whom Chekhov's feelings were stronger than hers for him". But there is nothing to support the contention that this relationship constituted a romance manqué.[2] Still irked with Moscow in December, Chekhov informed another correspondent that he had originally come to the city in October with the intention, most certainly never communicated to his mistress, of staying a mere couple of days, instead of which he had hung on for two whole dreary months.[3] No wonder Knipper grew exasperated with her lover. She could forgive his indecisiveness and vagueness, but not the ease with which he could dispense with her company. That he appreciated her in small doses, and in her absence, we cannot doubt; but there were too many times when he was able to do without her. The fact is that she—with all the satisfactions, amusements and distractions of a busy social and professional life—needed him far more than he, for all his much-advertised loneliness, needed her.

In 1900 Chekhov promises contributions to various publications: one to *Russkaya mysl*, another to *Zhizn*, but all in vain, for he was not to complete a single story in that or the following year. For this abandonment of narrative fiction his previous career offers no parallel. But he was still editing his "Collected Works" for A. F. Marks, whose minions were ignoring his instructions and bungling his proof corrections, just as if that notorious muddler Suvorin had taken over. All the same, Volume Two did appear in September 1900.[4]

From editing cares, theatre, mistress and Muscovite winter Chekhov fled in December, crossing the Russian frontier on the 11th of the month and pausing in Vienna to lament his celibate status; he "looked with lust" at the two beds in his hotel room, he told Olga.[5] He reached Nice on the 14th and stayed seven weeks. Putting up again at the *Pension Russe*, as in 1897–8, he repeated many experiences of that previous, longer stay on the French Riviera. Again he ate too much and resolved to eat less; again he brooded on an African trip which never came off, besides also abortively planning an expedition to Spitzbergen and the Solovki islands of far northern Russia; he enjoyed fabulous weather; he "felt ten years younger"; he visited, made small winnings at, grew bored by Monte Carlo; he reflected once more on the superiority of Nice over Yalta, that Crimean Siberia. In Nice, by contrast with the premier Russian seaside resort, people were merry, bustling, laughing; there were no police officers to be seen, nor any "Marxists with their arrogant physiognomies".[6]

Chekhov found that he knew even more people in the French than in the Russian resort. It was delightful to renew friendships with Russian expatriates, among whom Kovalevsky, Yurasov and Yakobi were still available; and it was less than delightful to be pestered by the usual relays of uncongenial visitors. The Vladimir Nemirovich-Danchenkos, who were also staying in Nice at the time, supplied examples of both sorts. With the husband, Chekhov would have liked to discuss his *Three Sisters*, now in rehearsal; but his old friend was unfortunately kept "under close arrest" by an impossible wife with an unspeakable laugh.[7]

Throughout this seven-week period Chekhov's main concern was *Three Sisters*. He was still revising and copying the play when he reached Nice, and he sent improved versions of Acts Three and Four to Russia within a few days of his arrival. From Nice Chekhov also wrote polemical letters on the play, providing insights into his view of the theatre. As usual Stanislavsky as producer simply could not get anything right. "Four responsible female parts, four educated young women: I can't leave them to Stanislavsky with all my respect for his talent and understanding."[8] This lament, penned back in September, foreshadows Chekhov's later apprehensions about the play's progress. He was anxious that the unhappy situation of Masha, played by Olga Knipper, should not be falsified by over-acting *à la* Stanislavsky. Olga might therefore play Masha with feeling, "but not desperately". She must not look sad, because "people who have long been unhappy, and grown used to it, don't get beyond whistling and are often wrapped up in their thoughts". Nor should Masha be seen leading her equally unhappy sister Irina round by the arm in Act Three. That was inconsistent with the play's mood. "Don't you think Irina can get about on her own?"[9] Then again, in Act Three the monstrous Natasha should not, Chekhov told Stanislavsky, wander round the stage putting out lights and looking for burglars under the furniture. She should cross the stage in a straight line without looking at anybody or anything, like Lady Macbeth with a candle. "It's quicker and more frightening that way."[10]

It was, as always, Stanislavsky's exuberance which Chekhov most feared. How on earth could his drama of understatement ever be conveyed by such a dedicated apostle of overstatement as his producer? Why must Stanislavsky make such a cacophonous din with the noises off in Act Three? True, the local town is supposed to be on fire at the time, the alarm is being rung on church bells, and fire-engines are clattering about. But that was no reason to overdo things. "The noise is only in the distance: off stage, a vague, muffled sound." Nor, after Tuzenbakh's death in the off-stage duel of Act Four, need his body be solemnly borne across the stage, as Stanislavsky at one time proposed.[11] So subtle an internal drama would be wrecked by these ham-handed methods, Chekhov felt. But at one point he did require an actor to pull out all the stops: when dilating on the horrors of provincial life in Act Four, Andrew Prozorov should be "very excited", and "just about ready to square up to the audience with his fists".[12] Very excited! Though a quiet tone might often be appropriate with Chekhov, this instruction is a warning against *any* glib generalization about him or his work.

Primed with this advice from Nice, the Moscow Art Theatre presented its first performance of *Three Sisters* on 31 January 1901: the third major première of a Chekhov play to be performed by the same theatre in the author's absence. This time the reception was disappointing, proceeding in diminuendo from about a dozen "shattering" curtain-calls after Act One to a single half-hearted curtain-call after the finale. Such was Stanislavsky's

Title page of Chekhov's *Three Sisters*, published by A. F. Marks, St. Petersburg, 1902

recollection; others (Lavrov, Nemirovich-Danchenko) preserved a more favourable impression.[13] Here, then, was neither disaster nor the success which might have been hoped for. Once again a play of Chekhov's was to need acclimatization before its unfamiliar atmosphere could establish itself.

By the time of the première Chekhov had left Nice. His stay had been a success: living was still cheap, the weather was mild, and there had been no more blood-spitting. Still, he was already complaining of boredom, and had soon had enough of the place.[14] On 26 January he started on a twelve-day tour of Italy, his third and final expedition to that country. After visiting Pisa and Florence he went to Rome for a week, and it was there that he happened to be staying when *Three Sisters* received its first performance. In Italy he seemed once again to be reliving an experience of the past as he reiterated the ecstatic praise which he reserved for this country above all others. Before the usual reaction of boredom could set in he was on his way back to Yalta.

Yalta
(February–May 1901)

Returning to his Yalta home on 15 February, Chekhov learnt of further theatrical developments in the north. The Moscow Art Theatre was now making its annual visit to St. Petersburg with a repertoire which included *Uncle Vanya* and *Three Sisters*; their author was soon receiving telegrams recording the jubilant ovations of metropolitan audiences, but the notoriously crabby St. Petersburg press was hostile to the troupe from the former capital. Disgusted by the press notices relayed to him by Knipper, Chekhov proclaimed for the *n*th time his intention of writing no more for the stage: "I personally am abandoning the theatre, and I shall never write for it again. One may write for the theatre in Germany, in Sweden, even in Spain: but not in Russia where actors aren't respected, where they're brutally savaged, where neither success nor failure is forgiven them."[1] Despite this outburst Chekhov was already discerning the shape of his next drama. He felt impelled, he said, to write a four-act vaudeville or comedy for the Art Theatre. But he intended to take his time. He predicted— correctly, as it happens—that this hitherto unnamed play, identifiable as the future *Cherry Orchard*, would not be ready before late 1903.

Meanwhile he was still selecting, editing and proof-reading his works for Marks's collected edition. Volume Seven (the plays) and another volume of fiction (Volume Four) both appeared in early 1901. He was also vaguely toying with a short story, *The Bishop*.[2]

While he was thus engaged in Yalta his actress friend was bombarding him with sprightly accounts of her doings in each of the "two capitals". In Moscow she had been to a ball given by Savva Morozov, the theatre's financial backer: an orgy lasting until 7 a.m. at which the Art Theatre boys and girls had let down their hair among masses of flowers, semi-naked women and officers. It made Olga's eyes pop out, what with the champagne, the dancing and the excitement of flirting with the stage-struck adjutant of Moscow's Governor-General. By 2 March the Art Theatre's high jinks had moved on to St. Petersburg with a party lasting until 6 a.m. and rendering Olga so helpless with laughter that she nearly made herself ill.[3]

The Art Theatre's St. Petersburg tour witnessed a clash between Chekhov's current actress–mistress and the other no less famous actress who had previously been his mistress. Since we parted from Lydia Yavorsky, whose favours Chekhov had briefly enjoyed in the Moscow Grand Hotel in January 1895, she had become a star of the St. Petersburg stage; had married a titled playwright, Prince Baryatynsky; and was just about to open her own theatre in the capital. No wonder that the new princess patronized the touring players from Moscow, who, though even a St. Petersburger could hardly call them provincial, yet did not rate as fully metropolitan. Descending in full majesty on Knipper's dressing-room during an Art Theatre performance, Yavorsky turned on her rival a stream of "crude and odious flattery"—Olga's words in her report of the incident to Chekhov. Soon wearying of Lydia's endlessly repeated "darling, you were absolutely *marvellous*", Olga decided that she could not stand the sight of "that impudent woman", and gave strict orders for Lydia not to be admitted to her dressing-room again.[4] It was a rash prima donna, this, who dared tangle with a Knipper.

From St. Petersburg Olga made an excursion to the resort of Imatra in near-by Finland, where the amenities included skiing and boating near a waterfall. Olga and the rest of the gang came back sunburnt, feeling like a troupe of Nansens returning from the Arctic. Meanwhile Olga's doomed lover was glumly reporting that he felt more like a grandfather than a spouse.[5]

Yet it was still the dying man who dominated this relationship; not the dashing, healthy, sought-after young actress, the toast of both capitals. This emerges clearly from their duel of wills in early 1901, when the question of Olga's next meeting with Chekhov arose. Both longed to be reunited. But Olga was firmly against meeting in the home which her lover shared with his mother and sister. They should meet anywhere but Yalta, Olga sensibly urged. "More concealment, more sufferings for your mother, more hide-and-seek: I really do find it hard, honestly. *You somehow don't understand this point, or don't want to understand it.*" She and Anton can no longer be "just friends" to each other. "To see your mother's sufferings again, and Masha's flabbergasted face: horrible! I'm between two fires. Do tell me what you think about it. *You never say anything.*[6] We have italicized here the salient complaint which Olga, and not Olga alone among Chekhov's womenfolk, could justly make against the most subtle delineator of emotion in Russian literature: extreme evasiveness in emotional contexts affecting himself. Like the earlier women in Chekhov's life, Olga wanted to know where she stood. How infuriating that when she tried to find out the wretched man pretended not to hear. Perhaps he thought emotional problems would go away if everyone would just pretend that they did not exist? Or perhaps, as his fiction seems to bear out, he was so sensitive to emotional resonances that he could not endure them except in his imagination? One sympathizes with his aversion to fuss, but one must also sympathize with Olga. How maddening a lover this was who, when his mistress wrote that she was dying to meet him anywhere except Yalta, blandly replied that he wouldn't try to force her to come if she was unwilling.[7] He was surely not conscious of having triumphed when Olga finally gave way, meekly arrived at his villa at the end of March and stayed two weeks.

Besides Olga Knipper, Chekhov's Yalta visitors of early 1901 included many other friends old and new. Among associates of long standing were Lavrov, editor of *Russkaya mysl*; the Art Theatre director Nemirovich-Danchenko; the liberal jurist Koni. Valuable contacts were also made with two writers, each ten years younger than Chekhov, and each destined to literary fame in later years: Alexander Kuprin and Ivan Bunin.

Kuprin was still a struggling author, who tried to conceal his destitute condition when visiting Chekhov; but without deceiving his host, who ensured that he was given plenty to eat. Kuprin repaid the debt with a memorable account of Chekhov in his Yalta period. He describes Chekhov's study, sombre in atmosphere with dark gold wallpaper and yellow stained glass set in a square window. There were photographs of Tolstoy, Turgenev and Chekhov's old patron Grigorovich on the walls; and there were masses of other photographs of writers and actors displayed on a separate table. A landscape by Chekhov's now deceased friend Levitan, showing haycocks receding into the distance, was set into the chimney-piece. There was much ornamental bric-à-brac: carved elephants; a model of a sailing schooner; a box of mint pastilles; eccentrically shaped candlesticks and inkwells. Some of these details are added from Dr. Altshuller, who says that each object had its precisely determined position in the room, for Chekhov liked to keep his study so tidy that it had an almost inhuman air.[8] Kuprin also evokes the white dust in the Tatar village near the villa, and reminds us of the wealth of trees—pears, apples, apricots, peaches, almonds—introduced by Chekhov, whom he depicts weeding beds; squatting by his rose bushes as he smears the stems with a sulphur preparation; rejoicing as a rain shower fills his water-butts. All this was his own work, Chekhov proudly pointed out; it had been a wilderness of stones and thistles just a couple of years ago. So far so good. But Kuprin goes on to evoke a Chekhov spectacularly un-Chekhovian. " 'Do you know,' he [Kuprin's Chekhov] suddenly added *with an earnest face and in tones of deep faith.* 'Do you know that, within three or four hundred years the whole earth will be transformed into a blossoming garden? And life will then be remarkably easy and convenient.' "9

Tones of deep faith! How could anyone familiar with Chekhov's work, as Kuprin was, conceivably introduce this of all clichés? Such touches make Kuprin seem determined to set his dead friend squirming in his grave, as he also does by reference to the "profound, lofty sadness" shining in Chekhov's "lovely eyes"; to those same eyes as "aglow with lustrous laughter"; to Chekhov's "intellectual ears", rivalled in their intellectuality only by Tolstoy's. That Chekhov utterly loathed such idiot babble Kuprin should have realized; indeed, he himself elsewhere underlines his friend's distaste for all forms of posing, emotional self-indulgence and theatricality.10 Kuprin was also aware of the instinctive reserve which sharply distinguished Chekhov from his more excitable fellow-countrymen. "I think he never opened or fully gave his heart to anyone." Kuprin, like Stanislavsky before him, at first found Chekhov off-hand or even arrogant; he would keep tilting back his head and surveying one through the bottom of his pince-nez lenses. As Kuprin had noticed, Chekhov was a creature of contrasts. However severe, even forbidding, his manner might seem, he was a great provoker of laughter in which he himself most heartily joined. But then again, his vivacity was always liable to be succeeded by reserve. He was highly secretive, now, about his writing. And this air of reserve was accentuated by his invariably faultless turn-out, for he was never one of your slipper-and-dressing-gown authors.11

With Kuprin, so much more sentimentally inclined than Chekhov, we may contrast Bunin: even more caustic than Chekhov, and a memoirist far more closely attuned to his subject. This is especially true of the short passage where Bunin sums up what he calls the defects of nine-tenths of what has been written, in Russia and elsewhere, about Chekhov during his life and after his death. "For a long time people only called him a 'gloomy' writer, 'the bard of twilight moods', 'an ailing talent', a man who looked at everything hopelessly and indifferently. Now they are going to the other extreme: 'Chekhov's tenderness, sadness, warmth', 'Chekhov's Love of Man'. I can just imagine what his own feelings would have been if he had read about his 'tenderness'. As for the 'warmth' and the 'sadness', they would have disgusted him even more."12

Bunin was closer to Chekhov, and knew him longer, than the compara-tively alien Kuprin. They had first met briefly in Moscow in 1895 and then in Yalta four years later, when Bunin had been horrified by the change in his friend. Chekhov had grown thin, his complexion was darker, his movements were sluggish, his voice rang hollow; and yet it was still the same old Chekhov. Bunin soon became a regular visitor at the Yalta villa. He was a friend of Mariya's too, and describes himself as practically one of the family. Yet Bunin also stresses the distance which Chekhov, with his "enormous sense of his own dignity and independence", always kept between himself and other people. Refusing, with characteristic good sense, to describe his friend as either the gloomy pessimist or the ebullient optimist of legend, Bunin takes a more detached and sensible view. As he reminds us, Chekhov himself tended to insist that he was not a "whiner" or pessimist in his work; and would quote, not very convincingly, his story *The Student* to prove it. In general, Bunin recalls Chekhov as buoyant and smiling rather than gloomy and irritable, even though their friendship coincided with the acutest stage of Chekhov's illness. However sick Chekhov might be, jokes, laughter and even horseplay were always liable to break through.[13] By refusing to depict his friend as a stereotyped Great Man or cult object, by never forcing this complex individual into such simple moulds as "pessimist", "optimist" and the like, and not least by avoiding the usual emotive clichés, Bunin has earned the gratitude of all who prefer to see Chekhov as he was.

Married Bliss
(May–June 1901)

Endless ironies surround the drama or inverted drama of Chekhov's wedding. Here was a bridegroom who had spent years disparaging the institution of marriage and his own eligibility for the role of husband. With greater or lesser artistry and in countless imaginative works he had demonstrated over and over again his unwillingness to contemplate even the theoretical prospect of felicitous cohabitation by man and woman, whether inside or outside wedlock. Taken as a whole, his numerous fictional studies of married love might have been expressly designed to cast doubt not only on the trite concept of "living happily ever after", but even on the possibility of the most fleeting happiness in love beyond the momentary pathetic illusions of the very young. He who now approached this major crisis was a master of the minor key and the miscued effect: a bard of romantic fantasies which collapse in bathos and disappointment. We also know Chekhov for his intense dislike of ceremony, particularly of any centred on his own person. To approach the altar was, for such a man, like laying his head on the chopping block. It is a tribute to his love for Olga that he was prepared even to consider so harrowing an ordeal.

Marriage negotiations between Olga and Anton were intensified after she left him at Yalta in mid-April 1901. A letter of hers, written to him shortly after her arrival in Moscow, shows that her departure from Yalta had been a kind of demonstration. She had, she reminds him, been free to stay on had she wished, but when she had announced her intention of going Chekhov had not said one word to detain her. He had simply said nothing. And so Olga had swept out, piqued to discover yet again, from this test of her lover's devotion, that she was not wanted. The visit had left an unpleasant after-taste, she writes; but adds "come here in early May and we'll get married and live together". On the next day she writes again to stress that no definite decision has yet been taken about the marriage, and on the day after that she repeats her invitation to marry; so that the wedding can take place as quickly as possible, Chekhov must bring his documents with him.[1] To all this Chekhov responds by at last agreeing to marry, while also defining some of his inhibitions as a bridegroom. "If you promise that not a soul in Moscow will know about our wedding till it's over, I'll marry you the day I arrive, if you like. For some reason I'm horribly afraid of the ceremony, the congratulations, and the champagne which one must hold in one's hand while giving a vague smile."[2]

In further letters from Moscow, Olga reports various pieces of intelligence bearing on the marriage theme. "That odious Vishnevsky is crossing his heart and swearing solemn oaths that I'll be his wife in a couple of years. Isn't it awful! He's always making these jokes." More embarrassing still was the Grand Duchess Elizabeth Fyodorovna, the Moscow Governor-General's wife, who waylaid Olga's mother after a charity concert and overwhelmed her with questions. "Is your dear daughter in Moscow? When is she getting married? And how is *his* health?"[3] Undeterred even by this exalted piece of impertinence, Chekhov eventually arrives in Moscow on 11 May and puts up again at the Dresden. Far from keeping his promise to wed Olga at once, he takes the more prudent step of consulting an eminent specialist, Dr. Shchurovsky, in order to determine how much of a permanent invalid he must consider himself. The verdict is discouraging: Chekhov's tubercular condition has deteriorated, both lungs being seriously affected. But the doctor at least has treatment of a sort to prescribe. Chekhov is to go to the prairies of Ufa Province in south-eastern European Russia, and take a "koumiss cure"—drinking the fermented mares' milk brewed by the Bashkir tribesmen of those remote parts.[4] This, assuming that Chekhov is to go through with the marriage, at least solves the problem of where he is to spend the honeymoon.

After what Dr. Shchurovsky had told him Chekhov had second thoughts about marriage. Writing (on 20 May) to his sister, now in Yalta with his mother, to inform her of his intention to take the koumiss cure, he adds the following enigmatic words: "Travelling on one's own is boring, the koumiss cure is boring, while *to take someone with one* would be selfish and therefore unpleasant. I would marry, but *I have no documents*: they're all in my desk in Yalta."⁵ This passage seems to express an intention not to marry, suggesting that Chekhov had deliberately put himself in a position where he could not marry by leaving the necessary papers at home in Yalta. But to Mariya, who was no fool, these evasive remarks sounded an alarm-bell. The man who uses terms such as these to protest his intention of *not* marrying must surely be poised on the very brink of wedlock. Mariya at once replied, urging him not to marry because she feared the effect on his health. Let him keep Olga as his mistress, says Mariya by implication; they can always "get spliced" at some later stage. "Above all we must think about getting you well."⁶ That Mariya feared the emotional stress of the wedding ceremony, as it would affect her brother, shows how well she understood his sensitivity in such contexts. Her letter was posted on 24 May, the very eve of the wedding, and eventually reached Anton on his honeymoon.

Just when the groom decided to take the plunge we do not know. Whatever qualms he may have felt, his bride betrayed no hesitations; nor was she deterred by his poor health prospects. The wedding was celebrated on 25 May in the Church of the Exaltation of the Cross in Moscow eight days after Dr. Shchurovsky had delivered his discouraging diagnosis. Only the four witnesses required by law were present; they were Olga's brother, her uncle A. I. Salz and two students.⁷ Whether Chekhov in fact drank champagne and gave a vague smile we do not know; but we do know that he wore a frock-coat. After the ceremony bride and groom briefly visited Olga's mother before leaving Moscow by train, other friends and relatives having been diverted by what seems an unkind trick. Anton and Olga had invited them all to a dinner well away from the church where the ceremony was taking place; by the time they realized that the host and hostess were not going to turn up, both dinner and wedding were over and it was too late to do anything about it.

So much for the bride's family. What of Chekhov's mother and sister, whom he had so recently left behind in Yalta still ignorant of any specific plans? They had his letter of 20 May for what it was worth, in which he had expressed the intention *not* to marry in terms which created the contrary impression. Then, on the day of the ceremony, a telegram from Chekhov to his mother suddenly and fatefully descended on Yalta, informing her that the marriage had already taken place and asking for her blessing.⁸ The effect was shattering: less on the mother than on poor Mariya, who for some time could not eat and felt physically nauseated. She was bitterly hurt, she told him in a letter dated 28 May, by his failure to give her advance notice—and even more by the bride's callousness. Olga was now Mariya's best friend; *she* might surely have sent word. Mariya can hardly be blamed if she felt lonely and abandoned during this crisis. It was as if Olga had taken everything away from her: her home, her beloved brother. So Olga herself has told us in a diary entry which takes the form of a "letter" written to Chekhov shortly after his death.[9]

Mariya had, we remember, given up her own marriage chances to care for her ailing brother. And though she had retained her Moscow post, living with him only in the holidays, she had worked loyally to make Melikhovo a home. Then, after the disappointment of the move to Yalta, she had devoted herself to establishing his Crimean ménage. Now all this was menaced. What if Olga should dislike the Yalta villa and refuse to live there? Then Anton would not go there either, and how sad that would be.[10] But the main preoccupation of this well-intentioned young woman was less the injury to her own ego and domestic prospects than an agonized concern for the health of the brother in whom she had, perhaps unwisely, invested an excess of sisterly emotion.

While Mariya thus brooded in Yalta, Dr. and Mrs. Anton Chekhov had called on Gorky in Nizhny Novgorod before sailing down the Volga towards Ufa and the koumiss. A misinterpreted timetable had them marooned at the desolate harbour of Drunken Copse for twenty-four hours. But eventually, after a week's travel, they arrived at a sanatorium in the oakwoods of Aksyonovo, a village of Ufa Province, where the amenities were minimal.[11]

On the day after his arrival Chekhov wrote to Mariya assuring her that marriage would not change his life at all; his relations with his sister and mother would be as warm as ever.[12] Only after this letter had been dispatched did Mariya's letter of 24 May, in which she had appealed to him not to marry for health reasons, at last reach him. He hastened to console her with a second, much franker, letter from Aksyonovo: a document long suppressed, presumably as revealing thought processes derogatory to his widow. He might or might not have erred in marrying Olga, said Anton. In either event his reasons were that he was over forty; that Olga's relatives held old-fashioned views; that "if we have to separate I can leave her without a moment's hesitation, as easily as if we weren't married, because she's financially independent and lives on her own resources".[13] Chekhov further reassured his sister by saying how boring life was out in the wilds. But try though he might to soothe her, Mariya well knew that things could not be the same again. Relations between herself and her best friend, now disturbingly promoted to sister-in-law, were bound to be strained for a time. In the event, however, their friendship was to survive two world wars and three Russian revolutions until both

Chekhov's ladies eventually died in the late 1950s, each in her tenth decade.

At the time Mariya had expressed her distress most keenly in one particular letter to Anton, that of 28 May, to which we have already alluded. This was, she later told him, the only occasion on which she had ever addressed him with complete frankness. Her letter was written in deep sorrow, but without a trace of anger. Far, indeed, from bristling with indignant home truths, it contains only the mildest reproaches. Even they are oblique in the sense that they emphasize her own suffering rather than the tactlessness of those who had caused it. Moreover, it was (as we saw) the bride, not the groom, whom the slighted sister blamed for so cruelly failing to send advance notice of the wedding.[14] And this sad, mild missive represents the nearest that poor Mariya Pavlovna, now in her late thirties, had ever come to mutiny against the casual despotism of her famous brother.

Yet Mariya was surely wise in her reluctance to condemn, for the mere foible of male inconsiderateness, a bridegroom who was also a dying man. The submissive Mariya had always acted as if she expected to be trampled on, and we cannot blame the harassed invalid for taking her so much for granted. It would be pleasant to report him behaving more considerately, but we may at least note that his treatment of his sister once again lacked the insipid superhuman saintliness so often and erroneously attributed to him. It should also be remembered that he had dithered on the brink of wedlock right up to the last moment. How on earth could he and Olga have told his mother and sister of their plans if they had not really had any plans?

It was not only Mariya who received from Chekhov an unromantic account of his Aksyonovo honeymoon. "Well, I've gone and got married [he told one of his editors]. To my new state—that is, to the removal of certain rights and privileges—I'm already accustomed, or nearly so, and feel well. My wife's a very decent, intelligent woman and a good soul." To his brother Alexander he phrased his situation in a manner more befitting his status as invalid bridegroom: "I have, in a manner of speaking, got married." After a fortnight's koumiss Chekhov told another correspondent that he had gained ten pounds and could not decide whether his marriage was good or bad. Two days later he again complained to Mariya about the boredom of Aksyonovo: the koumiss had begun to upset his stomach; the scenery was wonderful, but the local Bashkir tribesmen were dim, apathetic and ugly.[15] On 1 July Dr. and Mrs. Chekhov quitted this backwater, sailed down the Volga to Tsaritsyn and proceeded to Yalta via Novorossiysk.

Thus began the three years of the Chekhovs' married life. The time during which husband and wife lived together worked out almost exactly equal to the time during which they were apart. The basic reason for their frequent separations has already been indicated: the wife's career, the husband's illness. However, there was more to the situation than the anguish of two loving hearts cruelly parted by circumstance. In each summer–autumn season of 1901-3 which they could have spent living uninterruptedly together there were not a few occasions when Chekhov resumed his maddening bachelor habit of contriving avoidable separations. No wonder his wife felt hurt and rejected, bombarding him with reproaches while he remained infuriatingly evasive. To point this out is not to denigrate the marriage, but only to suggest that it fell short of the romantic illusions with which Olga, and Chekhov too at times, tended to invest it: as the union of two people content to live only for each other, whose happiness is to be measured solely by the length of the hours, days and years which they can spend together. If all marriages which fall short of this specification are failures we may doubt whether there have ever been any successes. Perhaps the Chekhovs' marriage can best be understood and interpreted, like many another, in the light of a passage from his story *Concerning Love*. "So far we've only heard one incontrovertible truth about love: the biblical 'this is a great mystery'. Everything else written and spoken about love has offered no solution, but has just posed questions which have simply remained unanswered. What seems to explain one instance doesn't fit a dozen others."16

To the 1,300 pages of the Chekhov–Knipper correspondence the wife— more demonstrative, busier and therefore having more to impart—has contributed the longer but less interesting letters. While Anton's contributions are terse, elegant, ironical and rarely dull, his wife's are ill fitted to amuse the general reader. But to the investigator this is absorbing material: partly, on Knipper's side, for insights into the Moscow Art Theatre's intimate history. In her six years' association with the living Chekhov she appeared in five of his plays, as also in plays by Gorky, Turgenev, Hauptmann, Ibsen and many others. Her comments take us behind the scenes of these and other productions: a topic important to our theme, but not central to it. Much of the other, highly repetitive, material consists of endearments tedious to any third party; hopes of having children; discussions of when and where husband and wife should next meet; recriminations suggesting that he is deliberately avoiding her; arguments about whether she should abandon the stage to look after him; accounts of the high jinks—champagne-drinking, dancing, skiing, opera-going and so on— enjoyed by Olga while her husband languished alone in the south; complaints about how unhappy Olga feels, how she senses life passing her by, how she knows herself to be a bad wife who ought to kneel and implore her husband's forgiveness; requests for special information on the purpose of life such as Olga, and not Olga alone, was convinced that Chekhov must possess despite his sincere protestations that this was not so.

The mutual endearments were intended for two pairs of eyes only; but though they quickly pall there are significant points in them. That Chekhov called his wife his little dog, his little horse, his little cockroach, his little German and so on, while she called him her handsome husband or her lustrous-eyed poet: none of this need detain us. But we do deduce that this was a true marriage, and no mere "platonic" union, from the many references to the tedium of sleeping alone, to Olga's coyly confessed "sinful thoughts" and the like. Though the most intimate material has been understandably cut by her, much residue remains. As for the endearments, Olga's were often physically orientated: she would refer to Anton's eyes, his hair, his habit of plucking on his beard or sitting with his back to her, waistcoatless, of a morning. But Anton's endearments might, by contrast, have been addressed to a disembodied spirit rather than a real woman; the physical consciousness of his wife does not seem to have been present in his mind during her absence. They had been so long parted, he once observed, that he had forgotten whether she was a blonde or a brunette; this was a joke, of course, but one might well wonder briefly whether the remark was not seriously intended.[17]

Was this or was this not a "good" marriage? Were Chekhov and Olga wise to unite their fates? If husband and wife had consented to answer these large and impertinent questions both would probably have replied that they loved each other, and would not have wished to unscramble their union. But it must also be recorded that two level-headed, well-informed observers took a contrary view.

I. N. Altshuller, Chekhov's Yalta doctor, roundly condemns the marriage in his memoirs. He claims that Chekhov's sister would have been glad to move to Yalta as full-time nurse-housekeeper, thus solving his domestic problems, had such a move not been made psychologically impossible by his marriage. Medically speaking, this marriage was sheer disaster, Altshuller adds. And so too was Chekhov's whole association with the Moscow Art Theatre, for that too provoked emotions detrimental to his health. Altshuller memorably depicts the future Dr. and Mrs. Chekhov as they once appeared to him in spring 1900. In a white dress, at the top of the stairs, stood radiant Olga; beaming, glowing with health and happiness, conscious of her prestige as leading actress of a leading metropolitan company. What a contrast with the stooping, thin, yellow, ageing, hope-lessly ill figure of poor Chekhov, who stood gazing at her from ground level.[18] And how well the doctor has pictured the barrier which must always, love or no love, separate the healthy from the incurably ill.

Bunin gives an even more scathing view of the marriage. There was no great love at all in Chekhov's life, he suggests in his memoirs. He later modified this view by accepting Lydia Avilov's romantic version of *her* relationship with Chekhov, but that only makes Bunin's comment the more damning to any over-sentimental version of the relations between Chekhov and his wife. Like Dr. Altshuller, the layman Bunin also condemns the marriage as harmful to Chekhov's health, exactly echoing Mariya's arguments in her letters to her brother. Bunin knew Olga well, he regarded her as a friend, but he also knew that her milieu and way of life were alien to her husband. Bunin had foreseen at an early stage the inevitable clash between Olga and Mariya. Regarding Chekhov as torn (an exaggeration, surely) by suffering for both women, Bunin even considered Chekhov's marriage a form of suicide; it was "worse than Sakhalin".[19]

Though we can accept all these strictures as reasonable and inspired by concern for the invalid, it yet remains likely that Chekhov himself, given the choice, would have preferred three hectic years as Olga's husband and Art Theatre dramatist to a longer period of inglorious coddling by his devoted sister in the doldrums of Yalta.

Yalta and Moscow
(July–October 1901)

Reaching Yalta with his bride in early July, Chekhov settled down with her in the villa for six weeks. He felt unwell, he was coughing, he was spitting blood, and he decided to make his will. Olga was to receive the Gurzuf property and 5,000 roubles; Mariya was bequeathed the income from his plays and a life interest in the Yalta villa; and his three brothers were all to receive sums of money. Chekhov further willed that, after Mariya's and his mother's deaths, his residual estate should go to Taganrog Town Council for elementary education.[1]

In late July Chekhov received a letter from Gorky pointing out what he already knew: that the Marks contract had turned out disproportionately profitable to the publisher and outrageously unfair to the author. Gorky claimed that Chekhov could break the contract, returning the 75,000 roubles received from Marks. Gorky's own publishing firm, Znaniye, could then take over all Chekhov's works, guaranteeing an income of at least 25,000 roubles a year. But Chekhov replied that he could neither lay his hands on 75,000 roubles nor face a prolonged struggle with his publisher, especially now that Marks had already brought out half the "Collected Works".[2]

On 20 August Olga went to Moscow on her own and began looking for a flat to share with Mariya during the winter. Chekhov was to join her almost at once, but instead of rushing to her side he preferred to send her letters explaining how bored he was with sleeping alone. By mid-September Olga was tired of his procrastinations. "Yet another week to wait. Why? Why? What's delaying you?" Separated from her husband for the first time, the bride wrote him dithyrambs about his gentle, loving, soft eyes. "My soul aches when I remember the quiet anguish which seems so deeply seated in your soul." To these ill-chosen words Chekhov pithily riposted: "What nonsense, darling." Olga also wrote that relations with her sister-in-law and future flat-mate would never be harmonious. "I'll always come between the two of you, and I feel she'll never accept me as your wife." Fearing a quarrel between the two women closest to him, Chekhov sent Olga his well-tried cure for emotional complications: pretend that they don't exist. "Put up with things and keep quiet for just one year, that's all, and then all will be clear to you."[3]

Having previously disposed of Anton's presumptuous ex-mistress Lydia Yavorsky, Olga now confronted another of his old flames, Lika Mizinov. But this was no clash of prima donnas. Still unable to find her niche in life, and possessing no particular vocation or talent, Lika had recently decided to try the stage, and came up for audition by members of the Art Theatre. She offered them a rendering from Helen Serebryakov's lines in *Uncle Vanya*: not the happiest choice, for it was one of Knipper's own parts and Knipper turned out to be a member of the panel. Though poor Lika was offered walking-on parts she was unanimously rejected as a serious actress, and one of the examiners unkindly suggested that she should open a fashion shop.[4] How humiliating for her: to be turned down as an aspiring actress by the highly successful actress recently married to the man who had spurned her, Lika, as a woman over a period of ten years. But Lika had an irrepressible streak, and proposed at some later Art Theatre orgy to drink *Brüderschaft* with Olga. The offer was declined, and the snub shows us an uncharitable Olga who could, surely, have been more generous to so pathetic a rival? Soon after this Lika married—happily, it appears—one of the Art Theatre producers, A. A. Sanin, and we last meet her in Knipper's letters on 1 March 1903: "terribly stout, colossal, imposingly dressed, rustling".[5] Evidently Olga felt outshone, in spite of everything, by one generally reputed far and away the finer figure of a woman.

Arrived at last in Moscow by mid-September 1901, Chekhov spent six weeks united with wife and theatre: a period of stage contacts as intensive as any in his life. He was soon plunged into rehearsals of the new season's *Three Sisters*, concentrating on Act Three. The third acts of Chekhov's dramas are always those in which he comes nearest to creating the mirage of a climax, and Act Three of this play is no exception. Here the ministrations of an untutored Stanislavsky might be particularly disastrous, and

Chekhov personally produced Act Three. He also took V. V. Luzhsky, as "Andrew", through his lines three times individually.[6]

In Stanislavsky's account Chekhov is still the same old comic, lovable, eccentric little genius. He is still fussing about Act Three's noises off and the need to reproduce the cracked, soul-searing tone of Russian provincial church bells. He therefore turns up for one rehearsal with a cab full of saucepans, basins and tins, disposes them here and there, and gives an elaborate, embarrassed briefing to the sound-effects men. The result is cacophony which drowns the actors' lines. Here Stanislavsky gets his own back on Chekhov, who several times complained that Stanislavsky's noises off tended to be too frequent and too loud. Chekhov also intervened by telling the play's "Colonel Vershinin" that he was saluting like a mere lieutenant and should acquire the nonchalant assurance appropriate to an officer of field rank. Much concerned with the many military aspects of *Three Sisters*, Chekhov had imported a Colonel Petrov to advise on uniform and deportment; on no account were his officers to be the heel-clicking popinjays of Russian theatrical cliché.[7]

Chekhov saw *Three Sisters* on 21 September and took two tumultuous curtain calls. For once he was thoroughly satisfied with an interpretation of his work. "*Three Sisters* is going splendidly, brilliantly, much better than the play is written. I've done a little producing, exercising my author's influence on one or two of them, and it's now said to be going better than last season."[8]

CHAPTER FOURTEEN

Yalta: The Years of "The Cherry Orchard" 1901-4

The Cherry Orchard, the second of Chekhov's two plays written specially for the Moscow Art Theatre, is the main creative preoccupation of his final years. To these years also belong his last two short stories: *The Bishop* and *A Marriageable Girl*.

Yalta
(October 1901–May 1902)

In late October 1901 Chekhov returned from Moscow to Yalta and stayed for seven months until late May 1902. That winter's diarrhoea, piles and blood-spitting mark a further deterioration in his health; never had he been so ill before. He also felt lonely and more bored than ever. Tired of the view from his study window, he felt homesick for the north. Wretched Yalta seemed as cold as Kamchatka, while longed-for Moscow was as remote as Australia. So demoralized was Chekhov that he retired to bed at 9 o'clock on New Year's Eve expressly to avoid witnessing the advent of 1902. Meanwhile he yearned, as usual, to travel: to Novaya Zemlya, to Spitzbergen, to Lake Baikal, to Switzerland, to the Nile; he planned an entire world tour. But he was neither to realize any of these ambitions nor to act out another recurrent dream: that of moving from accursed Yalta to congenial Taganrog.[1] Yalta was still more intolerable now that Chekhov's medical advisers were no longer unanimous in recommending its climate. "Some doctors say I can go to Moscow, others say it's out of the question; but I can't, can't, can't stay here!" In Yalta he did stay, though, trapping an occasional mouse, fondling his dogs, observing his tame crane, complaining of his temperamental stoves, ordering trees and attending to his garden, though so fatigued that he must rest after pruning a single rose. Still, he would rather garden than write: to be a full-time gardener would give him an extra ten years' life.[2]

He was still in close contact with other writers, one of whom, the aged Tolstoy, was now residing at Gaspra on the coast only six miles from Yalta. Chekhov visited the ailing sage, for whom as a man his admiration had only increased over the years; he spoke to Tolstoy on the telephone, he worried about Tolstoy's health. Chekhov also valued his continuing contacts with Gorky, who was under police supervision as a revolutionary sympathizer. Chekhov put Gorky up in his villa for a week in November 1901, and remained in touch after his turbulent guest had moved on to Oleiz, a near-by coastal village.[3]

Chekhov was now urging his author-friends to write plays for the Moscow Art Theatre. Gorky was doing so already, and Chekhov approached Andreyev, Balmont and Teleshov. But his own playwriting was still in abeyance. He planned a comedy with a part for Knipper: a "funny" play for the Art Theatre in which we again discern the phantom of *The Cherry Orchard*. But it glimmers only to recede. "I shan't write any play because there are so many playwrights already." Meanwhile he was still editing and proof-reading the works which were now swiftly rolling off Marks's presses: Volumes Eight and Nine in December 1901, Volume Ten in the following April.[4]

As for new fiction, in February 1902 Chekhov at last sent *The Bishop* to the magazine *Zhurnal dlya vsekh* ("Everybody's Journal"). It appeared in April; and marks, together with the later *Marriageable Girl*, his last, sparse phase as a short-story writer. Written by a dying author, it chronicles a dying hero. Here, for the first time in a long career, we at last sense a flagging of creative energy. Not all readers would agree, and we are not impugning the high repute in which *The Bishop* and *A Marriageable Girl* are both rightly held. But they are not on the master's highest level. Both betray stylistic weariness and slackness of texture arguably appropriate to the theme of death, common to both works. This same theme had been handled more effectively and without comparable fatigue symptoms in a work of Chekhov's early prime, *A Dreary Story* (1889). The plight of *A Dreary Story*'s Professor, depicted by an author in his late twenties, is far more moving than that of his Bishop, depicted when Chekhov must have known that his own life had only a short while to run. But how, he asked, could he possibly write anything worthwhile in his present mood, and "in a lousy dump like Yalta"?[5]

The Bishop's hero was modelled on a whole trio of real-life clerics and its theme had been with Chekhov for fifteen years, though the title is first recorded in a letter of December 1899. This was, on available evidence, a uniquely lengthy gestation period for a Chekhov story.[6] Knowing that the ecclesiastical theme was particularly vulnerable to censorship, Chekhov ordered that the story should be withdrawn entirely if a single word were to be cut. Thus vigorously, so late in his life, does he speak on this sensitive topic. His tone reflects the pride of an accepted major writer impatient of petty bureaucracy and official oppressiveness in general; it also reflects a measure of financial security which made him relatively indifferent to his fee. But despite his insistence it does appear that censor's changes, of which no trace survives, were imposed on *The Bishop*: interference particularly galling to an author who had already pre-censored the story himself by tailoring it to officialdom's presumed requirements as he wrote.[7]

While Chekhov worked and brooded his wife was enjoying herself with the Moscow Art Theatre set as usual, these orgies being lovingly reported in her letters to Yalta. The première of Nemirovich-Danchenko's new play *In Dreams* ended in an all-night party and the reading of press notices at breakfast time. A special performance of *Uncle Vanya*, on 11 January for a doctors' conference, was received with tumultuous ovations, torrents of weeping and outbursts of hysterics followed by kvass, champagne and ("do you mind?") flirting with Stanislavsky. There was also dalliance ("please don't be jealous") over champagne with the genial Morozov. There was a Christmas party attended by the sullen Chaliapin in his jerkin and high boots: sullen until the great bass suddenly found his voice at 7 a.m., bellowed for beer and sang gipsy songs. There was a party for *Three Sisters*'s fiftieth performance, a medley of roast beef, salami, ham, wine, horseplay and guitar-playing. Rarely outdone when laughter and jokes were in demand, Olga mimicked a crying baby, and was congratulated amid drunken guffaws on having spawned a tiny Chekhov.[8]

Once again, as the dying man was continually being reminded, life was all great fun.

Herself singing, playing piano duets, visiting art exhibitions and artists' studios, Olga seemed determined to reproduce the relationship between serious doctor-husband and flighty, artistically versatile wife (also an "Olga") as portrayed in one of Chekhov's finest stories, *The Butterfly*, written long before he had heard of Miss Knipper. Not least did Chekhov's Olga resemble her fictional counterpart by deferring to persons unlikely to impress her husband. After meeting the wife of A. A. Stakhovich, the stage-struck upper-crust adjutant of Moscow's Governor-General, Mrs. Chekhov reported with awe that "one could sense her breeding".[9] Such preoccupations were alien to the healthily plebeian Anton, as little of a snob as he was of an inverted snob.

From Yalta Chekhov protests that these late nights are bad for Olga, who is paying for her high jinks with constant headaches. More prone than ever to depression and self-pity, she blames herself bitterly and tediously for not abandoning the stage, which she both loves and hates, to care for her sick husband. Well aware how much he dislikes her "brooding on life and whining", she just cannot stop herself. She is a bad actress. She is a bad wife. She is a total nonentity. Life is passing her by. All she ever sees is the theatre and actors. Nagging herself in this way, she also nags her husband. Why are his letters so short? Why does he never open his soul to her? Why is he receding from her? Either he doesn't like her any more, or else he never has been genuinely fond of her. She is "just a woman" to him, not a "person". And why, unkindest cut of all, has he been discussing his projected new play with his sister and not with his wife? "All right, then, you don't trust me, and I'll never ask you about anything again, don't worry! I shan't interfere, I'll just learn about things from others."[10] Chekhov soothes her as best he can, pointing out that her reason for not quitting the stage is simply because that is neither her wish nor his. But such quiet comments fail to calm the tempestuous actress. There were better ways of soothing her than this. On the eve of a flying visit to Yalta in February, she writes asking her husband to talk of his love for her when she arrives. "I know you do it very little, but if you do say something it will flash through all my veins."[11] Such touches help to relieve the self-pity, the whining and the nagging. We sense how strong her need of Chekhov was; as, in its own way, was his need for her.

Husband and wife both longed for a child, seeing parenthood as a solution to their problems. They had whimsically christened the infant "Pamfil" in anticipation; and now at last, after her brief February visit to Yalta, Olga becomes pregnant. But Chekhov's ability to provoke the miscued effect is, alas, fully maintained even in this most intimate matter. That Olga was with child she suddenly discovered in the worst possible way: by suffering a miscarriage in St. Petersburg at the end of March, during an Art Theatre tour of the capital. Thus did Yalta's exile simultaneously learn that he had been about to become, and that he was not going to be, a father. In his life, as so often in his works, anticlimax had triumphed again.

After an operation in a St. Petersburg clinic on 31 March, Olga was confined to bed seriously ill for a fortnight until she felt well enough to travel. Arriving at Yalta by the Sevastopol steamer, she was removed on a stretcher and taken home, still ill and feverish, to her ailing husband.[12]

Wifemanship
(May–November 1902)

Not until late May were husband and wife both well enough to face the journey to Moscow, where Olga unfortunately suffered a sudden relapse so severe that her life was feared for. On 1–2 June she had abdominal pains, and spent the night groaning, shouting and weeping. Ten days later a further acute crisis occurred; peritonitis was diagnosed, an operation recommended. But then she took a sudden turn for the better, though many weeks were to pass before she recovered completely.[1] Chekhov now had to care for his sick wife during the precious season when they had looked forward to a happier life together. Helped by the serviceable Vishnevsky, whose good offices proved invaluable, Anton looked after her effectively, but not with the saintly patience often incorrectly attributed to him. He complained of feeling imprisoned; and when, in mid-June, Olga seemed able to manage without him, he quickly grasped his opportunity. She was now sitting up in an armchair and was permitted chicken soup, he reported. "But *the main thing is* [emphasis added] I have permission to leave. I go with Morozov to Perm tomorrow."[2]

The Art Theatre backer had invited Chekhov to the family estate by his factory at Vsevolodo-Vilva, near the Urals some eight hundred miles east of Moscow. They went by train to Nizhny Novgorod; by steamer down the Volga and up the Kama, to Perm; further by steamer to Usolye, and then by rail and carriage. Chekhov enjoyed river cruising and eating sturgeon bouillabaisse, as he had on his way through to Sakhalin in 1890; but he found Perm dull and the weather too hot. He spent only four days on Morozov's property—a far from perfect guest, according to a lugubrious eye-witness account by the student mining engineer A. N. Tikhonov. A stooping, black-coated figure with a rumpled bow-tie, Chekhov burst into a great coughing fit on arrival, stepped awkwardly to one side and spat "a reddish, viscous phlegm" into a portable spittoon before silently giving Tikhonov his "damp hand". At a dinner attended by all the local intelligentsia the celebrity from Moscow resisted attempts to draw him out; and went to bed early without saying good night, complaining that he was tired. He later recovered sufficiently to offer some scathing criticisms of Gorky's prose style. Through this unsympathetic description we discern a Chekhov too ill to maintain his normal convivial manner. Tikhonov also has him denouncing his host as an ugly combination of parlour revolutionary and exploiting factory-owner, while another source shows him browbeating Morozov on the need to introduce an eight-hour day in his distillery and wood-vinegar processing plant at Vsevolodo-Vilva.[3]

When Anton arrived back in Moscow, Olga was ready to convalesce at Lyubimovka, Stanislavsky's family estate north-east of Moscow. Here husband and wife spent six weeks in idyllic surroundings and in "peace, health, warmth and satisfaction". This was paradise compared with Yalta, Chekhov wrote. He was too busy fishing to work on the play which he still had in mind, for excellent angling was available in a river which flowed only a few yards away from his guest cottage on the estate. That Olga enjoyed this respite we learn from her reference to the "blissful month" at Lyubimovka. But bliss had not been unalloyed, as we also learn from the same source: apologizing later for each "unpleasant minute" which she had caused her husband to suffer at Lyubimovka, she adds that "there were plenty of them and I'm furious with my lack of self-control".[4] While thus blaming herself, Olga was also nursing a grievance against Chekhov for going off to Yalta, as he did on 14 August, neither indicating when they were to meet again nor deigning to explain his departure. He later wrote that blood-spitting and business had taken him from his wife's side.[5] But we have no evidence of business requiring him in the Crimea; nor, in mid-summer, would a consumptive have been worse off in the balmy north than in stuffy, dusty, torrid Yalta. Once again Anton had gratuitously sacrificed Olga's company after a few weeks' close proximity. But instead of taxing him with this real offence, she first fired off unreasonable accusations inconsistent with the good sense which was often hers when she was in better health. She sent Mariya an offensive letter, which has not survived, accusing her of monopolizing Anton and deliberately luring him back to Yalta without his wife. Chekhov read the letter himself and wrote back reprimanding Olga for being unfair to Mariya. During the next few weeks wild accusations and counter-accusations flew between husband and wife. Olga protested to Anton about Mariya's tactlessness in showing him her letter when she, Mariya, must have known that it was bound to upset him; when Olga had received letters from Mariya likely to distress him, *she* had kept quiet. But Chekhov replied that Mariya had not shown him the offending missive; he had just chanced to pick it up and read it.[6] Sensing that his real offence had been to abandon his convalescent wife, Chekhov pointed out that he had lived with her since Easter without moving one step from her side. (But what about his trip to Perm, a full 800 miles from her side?) Olga responded with sarcasms. She was so glad that he was happy in Yalta, and he certainly need not trouble to hurry back on her account. Chekhov noted her hostility, saying that he feared for their marriage; and seemed, yet more infuriatingly, to contemplate a breach with equanimity. "Don't leave me . . . until we have a little boy or girl, and then you can do what you like."[7]

This epistolary quarrel sputtered on for a month until, on 14 September, the wife at last expressed her real grievance. "We're so much apart anyway, and you have to engineer an unnecessary separation." To find her partner thus self-sufficient was galling to a woman who so needed to be needed. On 29 August, in one of her non-nagging spells, she well analysed their relationship. "You're lucky. You're always so calm and untroubled that I sometimes think no separations, feelings or changes affect you. This isn't due to frigidity or apathy, but to something that won't let you bother about everyday things. Are you smiling? I can just see your face as you read this letter: all your wrinkles which I love so much, and the soft lines of your mouth. My darling!"8 Nor was even Chekhov so reserved as to scorn such displays of affection. He told Olga that the longer they lived together the deeper his love for her would be. "So note that, little actress. And if I wasn't ill you'd hardly find a greater stay-at-home than I."9 We may doubt the second of these propositions, but not the first. Chekhov may have been temperamentally unfitted for settled married life, but it by no means followed that he did not love his wife.

One of Chekhov's first acts on reaching Yalta in August 1902 was to resign the Honorary Academicianship conferred in January 1900. Such was his response to a recent ugly episode: the abrupt expulsion from the Academy of his friend Maxim Gorky, elected in December 1901. The annulment had been ordered by Nicholas II, who so resented this politically undesirable academician that, scrawling "how very original" on the paper informing him of Gorky's election, he had then personally ordained the miscreant's summary ejection. And the incident had been handled in a particularly shabby way because Gorky's expulsion had been announced as if it had been the Academy's independent decision and not an autocratic ukase.10 The disgusted Chekhov conferred with his fellow-academician Korolenko, who shared his indignation, also consulting Tolstoy, who had received the same honour; but Tolstoy said that he had never considered himself an academician, and thrust his nose in a book. Chekhov and Korolenko then went ahead and resigned without him.11 In his resignation letter of 25 August 1902 Chekhov wrote that he had originally congratulated Gorky in all sincerity on his Academy election, only to find that election annulled in the Academy's name, and therefore in his own name. Unable to reconcile such a contradiction with his conscience, he most respectfully begged to be relieved of his academicianship.12 This was not quite an act of bold political defiance, for there was no danger of reprisals in the context. But the episode does reflect the declining Chekhov's growing exasperation with official repressiveness.

Of the two months' "unnecessary separation" from Olga engineered between mid-August and mid-October 1902 Chekhov made little literary use. He was still sure that he had a "splendid subject" for a play; as he indeed had, for that play was the embryonic Cherry Orchard. But he just could not get down to work. All he did was to revise yet again his sixteen-year-old comic monologue Smoking is Bad for You; calling this final recension "an entirely new play", he sent it to Marks for publication in the "Collected Works".13 Then, in mid-October, Chekhov returned to Moscow and rejoined his wife. He was also reunited with her theatre, now housed in a new building. Here *Uncle Vanya* was being superbly performed, its author reported. Partly housebound by ill health, he was besieged by hordes of visitors, as usual. They included such literary friends, old and new, as Suvorin, Gorky and Bunin.

Bunin scathingly depicts relations between the ailing husband and the now blooming wife. Far from abandoning social engagements out of sympathy for the invalid, she was still gadding about as ever. We meet Nemirovich-Danchenko resplendent in tails, redolent of cigars and eau-de-Cologne, as he carries off the dynamic "scented, beautiful, young" Mrs. Chekhov to a play or charity concert. "Don't be bored while I'm away, pet", coos the departing wife. Bunin would sit up all night with his friend until Madame sailed back on a gust of wine and scent. "Oh, why aren't you asleep, duckie? It *is* so bad for you."[14] The scene absurdly recalls, once again, the flighty "Olga" of poor Anton's *The Butterfly* (1892); and even the yet more flighty "Olga" of *His Wife* (1895)—two works in which he had by anticipation created caricatures of the wife whom he had not then met.

Yalta
(November 1902–April 1903)

Chekhov went back to Yalta in late November 1902, and stayed until late April of 1903. His tubercular symptoms seemed to be receding, for he spat little blood that winter, but suffered from toothache, disorders of the bowels, influenza and pleurisy. His beard was turning grey, he felt old. He cultivated his garden, visited Gorky, approved of a newly built church with bells reminiscent of central Russia. But neither these distractions nor his usual vague and never-realized travel plans, to visit Vienna, Dresden and Switzerland, could relieve Yalta's boredom. He abstained from alcohol all winter because, he said, he had no one to drink with; but took a keener interest in food, especially when the town acquired a new delicatessen shop where he could buy caviare, olives, salami, ham and mushrooms.[1]

During this five-month exile Chekhov experienced his longest separation from his wife, whose letters were more than ever charged with self-pity this winter. She was a bad wife, she should leave the theatre, she wanted a child, she had a loathsome feeling in her soul. She wanted someone to teach her how to live, but was at last sensing that Chekhov genuinely did not feel himself to possess any exclusive clue to this or any other ultimate mystery. His elusiveness still tantalized her. Why did he conceal his state of health? Why did he never tell her about his literary activities? "I was practically the last person to read *The Bishop*."² Chekhov did his best to calm her. There was nothing wrong with their marriage except that it had come too late, he said. Another handicap was her quick temper, he told her, for it was risky to come near her when she was in a bad mood. And the volatile, spirited Olga still envied her husband's tranquillity. But when she told him so, by no means for the first time, in February 1903, she provoked an astonishing reply. "You say you envy my character. Well, I must tell you that I have a harsh character. I'm quick-tempered and so on and so forth." An irascible Chekhov! However firmly we may reject the angelically patient Anton Pavlovich of popular misconception, this hardly seems to fit until we read his own qualification. "I'm used to controlling myself, since it ill becomes a decent man to lose his temper. In the old days I was a holy terror."³

Meanwhile Olga was still enjoying herself party-going, laughing, skiing, planning a trip along the Finnish coast by that new-fangled device the motor-car. And still the great friend of the family, her colleague and long-standing escort Vishnevsky, danced attendance on her. Much as he valued Vishnevsky—who sometimes irritated him by declaiming long passages from his roles in Chekhov plays—Anton drew the line this winter, flatly refusing to share the coming summer's marital *dacha* with their faithful old friend. Meanwhile Art Theatre gossips were describing the Chekhovs as on the point of divorce, saying that Vishnevsky was going to marry Olga. So Olga was unkind enough to inform Chekhov. It was a topic better passed over in silence, and the drama-loving Olga probably brought it up only to provoke *some* reaction from her maddeningly equable husband. A more jealous invalid would have suffered—as perhaps he did, and as perhaps Olga intended him to—from her harping on the close association between herself and her all-too-healthy actor-escort.⁴

As Chekhov himself had once illustrated in *The Butterfly*, the morals of Moscow artistic circles were not a model of rigour. And though we have no hard evidence to suggest a liaison between Olga and the devoted Vishnevsky, a shadow must surely have crossed Chekhov's mind. Vishnevsky was no monk, at least to the extent that Chekhov had once suspected him of making one of the Melikhovo servants pregnant.⁵ Might not the maid's seducer have moved on to the mistress? The thought must have occurred to Chekhov, as it is bound to occur to his biographers. We certainly cannot dismiss such a possibility outright, inconsistent though it may seem with the authentic love for Chekhov which one senses behind all Olga's naggings, accusations and protestations.

As a good literary wife Olga took a keen interest in the business side of her husband's profession. By no means mercenary, she was less unworldly than he. She often urged him, for example, to seek fees for the translations of his works which, to his intense exasperation, were now appearing in several languages.[6] She also supported efforts made by Gorky and others to persuade Chekhov to break the grossly disadvantageous contract with A. F. Marks. Could a legal loophole be found? What of the contract's penalty clause invoking certain sanctions for the author's failure to meet certain undertakings? Had Chekhov actually signed that document? Then again, had Chekhov actually signed an instrument conferring on Sergeyenko, his agent in the Marks negotiations, the formal power of attorney? If not, Marks might find the contract impossible to enforce. In a letter of 23 January 1903 Olga raised these points, but Chekhov believed that he should stick to his bargain. To exploit such legal technicalities would be "unworthy of a literary man".[7]

We now take farewell of Chekhov the short-story writer. He began *A Marriageable Girl*, his last completed essay in the genre, in late 1902 after a gap of nearly a year since finishing its predecessor, *The Bishop*. And, like *The Bishop*, this last story was an unconscionable time in the writing. The title is first mentioned on 20 October 1902, and a version was sent to *Zhurnal dlya vsekh* on 27 February 1903, only to undergo extensive revisions, carried out on the wide margins of succeeding sets of proofs, before it was at last published in December of the same year. More evidence survives on the different stages of composition than is furnished by the textual history of any other Chekhov story.[8]

A Marriageable Girl depicts a young woman called Nadya who lives an unfulfilled life in a dreary Russian provincial town where she has become engaged to a worthy, lazy, complacent, dim young man. Depressed by an inspection of her future marital home, where the mere sight of the new bath-taps particularly upsets her, she suddenly decides to run away from her town, from her fiancé and from her no less dreary mother and grandmother. And Nadya, more determined than any of the Three Sisters, actually does effect a getaway: not to Moscow, but to St. Petersburg, where she pursues an unspecified course of studies. In this she is abetted by an old friend of the family, one Sasha. He dispenses Chekhovian advice while dying of consumption, and we seem to recognize him as that rarity: a fictional portrait, admittedly distorted, of the author himself.

Since *A Marriageable Girl* has an ardent young woman erupting from the stuffy provinces to pursue a course of studies in the capital, it has been interpreted by Kremlin-instructed Russian literary processers as a work of revolutionary significance.[9] And we must agree to this extent: that Nadya, under the censorship conditions of the time, was clearly recognizable as an embryonic revolutionary by those who could read between the lines; as what Russian reader could not? To leave home, to reject a conventional marriage, to embark on university studies on one's own: there was, in

Russia of the early 1900s, the merest hair's breadth between these activities and conspiracy against the state. Unfortunately, though, Chekhov tells us nothing of Nadya's new activities beyond indicating that they are vaguely exciting and satisfying, whereas the stifling atmosphere of the provinces— that vintage Chekhov theme—is skilfully evoked. Neither a call to revolution nor a sermon on the virtues of facile optimism, the story shows its author's genius sputtering, not scintillating. "I've written such stories umpteen times before, so you won't find anything new there": such was his own verdict on *A Marriageable Girl*.[10] He is too harsh, but his words fit better than the hackneyed Kremlin-sponsored interpretation: dying genius with trembling hand points ardent youth way to glorious future.

While writing his *Marriageable Girl* Chekhov did not think of it as his last story. There were still masses of subjects in his head, he claimed; he was still vaguely agreeing to contribute to his old favourite *Russkaya mysl* and other periodicals. On 1 March 1903, just after sending in the completed first draft of *A Marriageable Girl*, he spoke of having started a second story, and even a third. It is to these plans that we must relate three uncompleted, posthumously-published fictional fragments: *The Cripple, Poor Compensation* and *A Letter*. The last-mentioned features two brothers, one a convict and the other insane. It may therefore be the projected story of which Chekhov spoke on 12 December 1902 as so frightening that it would even "put Leonid Andreyev's nose out of joint", for Andreyev's plots often hinge on crimes and mental illness. But neither the few surviving pages of *A Letter* nor those of *The Cripple* and *Poor Compensation* look like potential masterpieces. Rather do they seem to show the ebbing of the master's strength.[11]

That these scraps were the work of a dying man the emphasis, in all three, on physical and mental disablement pathetically confirms.

"*The Cherry Orchard*"
(*March 1903–January 1904*)

Chekhov might be dying, and finished as a short-story writer. Yet his most famous play was still to come. He had been brooding on the theme off and on for about two years before we meet the first recorded mention of its title, *The Cherry Orchard*, in a letter of 24 December 1902. It had been conceived as "funny, very funny", and was to be a four-act farce. By February 1903 it was "already completed", but only in Chekhov's head. On 1 March he laid out paper, inscribed the title and worked on it for a period, only to put it aside on leaving Yalta for Moscow on 22 April.[1]

In Moscow Chekhov consulted yet another doctor, the eminent and eccentric Professor Ostroumov, whose diagnosis was as depressing as his bluff manner was disconcerting. Chekhov's right lung was in poor condition, he suffered from emphysema; "you're a cripple, chum", Ostroumov crudely put it. That news came as no surprise. But Chekhov was downright astonished when so weighty an authority expressly ordered him to spend his winters in a *dacha* near Moscow, not in Yalta or abroad.[2]

During a brief trip to St. Petersburg Chekhov met his publisher Marks, but apparently without raising the ticklish question of circumventing his contract. He then spent six weeks with his wife in a cottage near the town of Naro-Fominskoye about fifty miles south-west of Moscow. The cripple's health seemed fair despite Ostroumov's diagnosis; the weather was lovely; there was a river full of fish; there were excellent walks. Part of the time was spent travelling in the near-by countryside with stops at the small towns of Voskresensk and Zvenigorod, those old haunts of the 1880s, in desultory search of a small country property to substitute for the discredited Yalta.[3]

Content to relax in his cottage, Chekhov toyed with *The Cherry Orchard* and the proofs of *A Marriageable Girl*; he also worked as fiction editor of *Russkaya mysl*, once the vehicle for some of his own finest stories. Refusing payment, he read stories submitted to this journal, and returned them with brief, crisp and matter-of-fact recommendations—to accept, to reject or to revise—delivered in the calm tones of one who knew his worth as a judge of modern Russian fiction. He also received an invitation from the well-known impresario Diaghilev to join the editorial staff of the famous St. Petersburg journal *Mir iskusstva* ("World of Art"), pioneer of a new and in many ways un-Chekhovian approach to the arts. Chekhov refused, telling Diaghilev that he could neither live in the capital nor function as an absentee editor.[4]

On 7 July the Chekhovs left for Yalta, where Olga took a daily swim, while Anton tackled his *Cherry Orchard* so effectively that the end seemed in sight by 2 September. But then he started coughing again. When Olga left for Moscow on 19 September the manuscript remained unfinished, and she could not take it with her, as had been hoped. Within a month of her departure, however, Chekhov had completed the play and made a revised fair copy. On 14 October he sent it to Moscow, where it had long been eagerly awaited by the Art Theatre.[5]

While work had been in progress Chekhov's morale had been high, but it slumped once the pangs of creation were over. Everything seemed to irritate him. Now, if ever in his life, we find traces of the quick temper which he had implausibly claimed as his; perhaps prolonged ill health had at last sapped his exemplary self-control. He shouted at his cook for not maintaining his medically-prescribed diet. He resented repeated requests, channelled through his wife, for permission to translate his work into foreign languages. That foreigners could neither understand nor appreciate Russian literature was an axiom with Chekhov, who regarded all translation of his writings as an aberration, whether English, French or German was the vehicle. "Tell them you know nothing [he instructed Olga], tell them I don't answer your questions and all that. I can't stop them, can I? So let them translate away; no sense will come of it anyway." Another offence was the celebration by his native Taganrog, in autumn 1903, of the "twenty-fifth anniversary" of his literary début: a proceeding which he would have resented in any case, even if he had not regarded it as two or three years premature. Always hostile to such rituals, he had hitherto kept his irritation within bounds, but now it seemed to overflow in all directions.[6]

The main nuisance was his recently completed play, which everyone seemed determined to misunderstand, from Stanislavsky and Nemirovich-Danchenko downwards. Stanislavsky had reacted to the advent of *The Cherry Orchard* in his usual over-demonstrative idiom and with characteristic glandular secretions. When reading Act Three, the exuberant actor-producer had sweated; he had sobbed through the whole of Act Four. All in all, the play had "driven him out of his mind". That this might be no mere figure of speech was suggested by Stanislavsky's wire to Chekhov giving his first reaction to the play: JUST READ PLAY SHAKEN CANNOT COME TO SENSES IN UNPRECEDENTED ECSTASY . . . SINCERELY CONGRATULATE AUTHOR GENIUS. Chekhov was disgusted by this telegram. To call his play a work of genius was, he told Olga, to over-praise it and rob it of half the success which it might otherwise have had. Even Nemirovich-Danchenko was not spared after obtusely comparing the childlike Anya of *The Cherry Orchard* to Irina of *Three Sisters*. And how had the absurd idea arisen that all the play's characters were permanently in tears, when the opposite was the case?[7]

Worse was to follow when the drama critic N. Ye. Efros published a garbled digest of Chekhov's plot with Act Three taking place in a "hotel"; Efros also described the play's self-made businessman Lopakhin as a vulgar "son of a bitch", when Chekhov had tried to portray him as subtle and sensitive. Calling the critic a "noxious animal", feeling as if he had been made to drink slops as well as having them poured all over him, Chekhov compared himself to the father of a small daughter debauched by the unspeakable Efros. He dashed off a telegram to Nemirovich-Danchenko, accusing or appearing to accuse him of having supplied Efros with these false details. Never would he have sent the play to the Art Theatre in the first place if he had known that Efros would annoy him so much. The problem of the "hotel" alleged by Efros to be the scene for Act Three, in fact set in a drawing-room, naturally troubled Chekhov, who feared a consequential error in the production; especially as no one in the Art Theatre seemed capable of understanding the simplest instructions.[8]

Chekhov's distraught condition may be judged from his carelessness or folly in burning all the drafts of The Cherry Orchard at Yalta at a time when only a single copy existed. Entrusted to the keeping of his wife, not the ideal custodian of an irreplaceable manuscript, that precious text was being passed from hand to hand in the Art Theatre. "Mind you don't lose it, or the upshot will be highly amusing", Chekhov admonished Olga— one of his many masterly understatements. Meanwhile this author so careless about the security of his masterpiece was nagging poor Olga: for not sealing her letters properly; for putting on the wrong stamps; for not posting her letters herself, but giving them to other people who carried them round in their pockets.[9] To such lengths was the patient, courteous Chekhov reduced in the autumn and early winter of 1903. He himself referred to his "very bad mood", and said that he feared to write letters because he could not avoid being rude; he had, he added, "an intolerable character". Not all his letters of the period are so crabby, though. Many contain recommendations, couched in moderate language, on the casting of The Cherry Orchard and on the interpretation of individual roles. These still form an indispensable guide to the staging of the play.[10]

Meanwhile Chekhov longed for Moscow. He needed the slush and bad weather of the north; he could not manage without literature and the theatre. " 'To Moscow, to Moscow': it's not Three Sisters, but One Husband speaking." So he told his wife. Then why did he not just go to Sevastopol and get on the Moscow train? After all, the great Professor Ostroumov had now commanded winter residence in the north, though Dr. Altshuller, Chekhov's Yalta physician, believed that his eminent colleague's recommendation had been given when he was drunk. But it was not the good Altshuller, it was Mrs. Chekhov who now stood in his way. For some perverse reason it had been agreed between them that Anton was not to travel north until Olga gave him her "permission". That summons he now eagerly awaited. But Olga, who had suffered so much in the past from the ease with which Chekhov could dispense with her, seems to have been getting her own back now. After chiding her for detaining him in the south he eventually left, arriving in Moscow on 4 December.[11]

The move to Moscow seemed to improve Chekhov's health, though it was a trial to mount the many stairs to the flat which Olga had found for them and which unfortunately had no lift. Here he continued literary activities while pestered, as ever, by visitors. He was still editing new fiction for Russkaya mysl; still planning and vaguely promising short stories which were never to be written. But his main energies, in so far as he still had any, were given to *The Cherry Orchard*, now under intensive preparation at the Art Theatre. He altered two short passages after the censor had banned references to contemporary workers' living conditions and to the demoralization bequeathed by serfdom, abolished forty years earlier. He was also preparing the play for the press, reading proofs of it and conducting running revisions in the light of rehearsals.

Chekhov attended rehearsals almost daily, yet without reaching any accord with his producer Stanislavsky. The new play was not flourishing, Stanislavsky complained. "The blossoms were just going to come out when the author appeared and threw us all into confusion. The blooms fell off and only now are new buds appearing." The main difficulty had already arisen with earlier plays and stemmed from a fundamental difference of view between creator and interpreters. Were these plays, as Chekhov maintained, comedies? Did they even contain, as he said of *The Cherry Orchard*, elements of farce? Or were they "ponderous dramas of Russian life"? It was this last interpretation which Stanislavsky, and not he alone, insisted on imposing.[12]

In firmly describing his plays, above all *The Cherry Orchard*, as comedies, Chekhov was perhaps confusing matters by dragging in a traditional theatrical term inapplicable to his new form of drama. What he was really appealing for, we suggest, was a lightness of touch, a throw-away casual style, an abandonment of the traditional over-theatricality of the Russian (and not only the Russian) theatre. But here was Stanislavsky serving up a suet pudding instead of a soufflé, seeming hopelessly addicted to that heavy traditionalism of which he and his theatre believed themselves to have sounded the death-knell. Meanwhile Chekhov was too resigned, too ill, too modest to thrash things out on first principles with his producer. Did he ever, indeed, really probe into his concept of comedy in his own mind to find out exactly what he meant by it? Whatever the reasons, *The Cherry Orchard*'s first night prospects seemed increasingly dim as rehearsal succeeded rehearsal. This was perhaps inevitable with a work so finely balanced between pathos and humour. Here is a plot hinging on the tragic loss, to an upstart businessman, of a family estate which its feckless genteel owners dearly love; in so far, that is, as they are capable of dearly loving anything. Yet the upstart is no vulgar *nouveau riche*, but a sensitive and compassionate man. And the tragic loss of the estate turns out neither a tragedy nor even much of a loss once the blow has fallen. Even so grave a personal crisis as this can provoke no profound reaction in the charmingly superficial evicted proprietors, whom Chekhov gently ridicules, yet from whom he by no means withholds his sympathies. Nothing is quite what it seems, nor yet quite the opposite of what it seems, in a play which calls for rare delicacy of interpretation.

Even Chekhov's own works, in which the mirages of climaxes so deliciously melt into artistically contrived anticlimaxes, contain few examples of irony as poignant as that furnished in real life by *The Cherry Orchard*'s première. Here was a Great Writer's finest hour, the topmost pinnacle of his career, the moment when he was to receive full and ecstatic recognition for a lifetime's achievement. And, of course, the great occasion so developed as to cause him acute suffering.

The ill-starred 17 January 1904 happened to be both Chekhov's name-day and his birthday: his forty-fourth and—as his thin, bowed, shrunken figure suggested—destined to be his last. What better occasion could there be for one of those jubilee celebrations so popular in the Russian literary world? Though his literary début had occurred in 1880, making such an orgy at least twelve months premature, the decision was never-theless taken to mark his twenty-fifth anniversary—in the theatre, at the first night of his new play. Accounts of a premature Chekhov anniversary in Taganrog had already irritated him, we remember. And no wonder. Besides working for nearly a quarter of a century as a writer, Chekhov also had behind him nearly a quarter-of-a-century's experience of literary jubilees. As many references in the letters and memoir material show, there was hardly anything which more disgusted him than these junketings with their pompous speeches about a "dearly-beloved author", his "tender soul", his "love of Man", his "deep compassion for the poor and down-trodden" and the like. To the least cliché-ridden of all Russian authors these excruciating platitudes were sheer torture. Nothing so grated on his tender, suffering soul as references to his own or anyone else's tender, suffering soul: especially when he contrasted such eulogies with the malice expended by these same panegyricists on occasions other than jubilees. "For twenty years they curse a man up hill and down dale [he once told Bunin]. Then they present him with an aluminium goose-quill pen and spend the whole day pestering him with solemn claptrap, tears and kisses."[13]

On 17 January 1904 the collective urge to dramatize the triumph of this dying genius took precedence over all real concern for the poor man's needs and feelings, the interval between Acts Three and Four of *The Cherry Orchard* having been earmarked for elaborate speeches and presentations from the stage. Chekhov was not warned, of course, for that would have been to hazard the whole enterprise. Nor was he even present in the theatre during the first two acts, and he was therefore deliberately missing the fourth première of one of his plays at the Art Theatre on the first occasion when his presence in Moscow would have made it possible for him to attend.[14]

When the second act was over and tumultuous ovations seemed to assure the play's success, Nemirovich-Danchenko sent Chekhov a note begging him to come to the theatre. And Chekhov complied, still not realizing what was afoot when he appeared on stage in the interval after Act Three and was greeted by fervent applause. Coughing, weak, obviously ill, he also aroused the sympathy of those who called out that the sick Anton Pavlovich should at least face his ordeal seated.[15]

The speeches and presentations seemed endless. There was an address from the Society of Lovers of Russian Literature; from *Russkaya mysl*; from the Literary-Artistic Circle; from four daily newspapers. The Art Theatre company supplied an address by Nemirovich-Danchenko, an antique casket containing all their portraits, and a further address from the actor V. V. Luzhsky. Homage came from the rival Maly Theatre too, not to mention innumerable telegrams from other publications and bodies ranging from Diaghilev's *Mir iskusstva* to the Kharkov student body. From these and other sources the helpless author was bombarded with the usual shattering platitudes: the "sincere, ardent love of the public"; "deep love of Man"; "sincerity"; "truth breathed upon by the mysterious exhalation of genius"; "rays of undimmed glory"; "sincerity"; "beloved, darling author"; "our boundless devotion"; "tender heart"; "pure soul"; "great joy"; "sincerity". Even at the supper held after the performance they were still at it, with Russia's most celebrated bass singer Chaliapin dilating on Chekhov's "compassion for Man", as allegedly revealed in his denunciations of *poshlost*. This last term, denoting complacent vulgarity, was hackneyed in literary criticism and had once been described by Chekhov himself as completely outmoded; how wrong he had been these very celebrations were now making depressingly clear.[16]

Chekhov stood it as best he could. When addressed as "dear and most honoured author" he derived wry satisfaction from the coincidence with Gayev's line "dear and most honoured book-case" in Act One of his play. But he had not enjoyed himself. "Yesterday my play was on, so I'm in a bad mood." And he felt like escaping to France or the Crimea. Even after a week he had not recovered from his jubilee, and was testily deploring various expensive folksy *objets d'art* which had been bestowed on him and which he detested. But he had endured his supreme triumph with characteristic stoicism and courtesy. He even sent a cordial message to the drama critic Efros, whose premature, inaccurate disclosures about the play had so irritated him a few months earlier that he had declared himself not on speaking terms with that offensive busybody.[17]

Farewell to Yalta
(February–April 1904)

Chekhov left Moscow for Yalta on 15 February 1904 and stayed ten weeks—his last sojourn in his Crimean home. He was still living in the backwash of *The Cherry Orchard*, still displaying the irritation characteristic of his obsession with this play. Though pleased to learn of a triumphant Art Theatre première of *The Cherry Orchard* in St. Petersburg on 2 April, and though also delighted to hear of several successful provincial performances, he was annoyed when certain "touring riff-raff" had the nerve to stage the play in Yalta itself, practically on his doorstep.[1]

Chekhov's communications with the Art Theatre still reflected acute exasperation, provoked not least by the famous "sound of a breaking string" in Acts Two and Four. His wife was instructed to tell Nemirovich-Danchenko that this sound should be much, much shorter and should seem to come from very far off. "How petty! They can't even cope with a measly noise when my stage directions are so clear."[2] Chekhov also bitterly complained of Stanislavsky on the basis of visitors' reports on his performance as Gayev: for playing Act Four "odiously", for "dragging it out excruciatingly"; for taking forty minutes over a sequence which should have been over in twelve. "All I can say is, Stanislavsky has wrecked my play." And still the Art Theatre as a whole perversely failed to grasp *The Cherry Orchard*'s very essence. "Why is the play so persistently called a drama [as opposed to a *comedy*] in posters and newspaper advertisements? Nemirovich and Stanislavsky definitely see . . . something quite different from what I wrote, and I bet you anything neither of them has read it through carefully even once."[3]

Not realizing that his creative life had ended with *The Cherry Orchard*, Chekhov still planned and promised future works: a story for *Russkaya mysl*, a three-act play for his actor friend P. N. Orlenev. He was still doing editorial work for *Russkaya mysl*, still corresponding about the "Collected Works" with Marks. That there was no point in translating *The Cherry Orchard* for Berlin and Vienna, because the Germans and Austrians had "no billiards, no Lopakhins, no students like Trofimov", Chekhov also lamented. His *Seagull* and *Three Sisters* had been translated into German already, long ago, but not one pfennig had he had out of either.[4]

That Chekhov's irritability also extended to his reviewers and critics need hardly be said, since he always had regarded them as a nuisance, even in his pre-Yalta days. His opinion of them remained unchanged until the end of his life. "Critics are like the gadflies which stop a horse ploughing [he told Gorky]. The horse strains, muscles tensed like double-bass strings.

Meanwhile there's a wretched gadfly tickling and buzzing on his crupper, so he has to twitch his skin and flick his tail. But what's all the buzzing about? The gadfly hardly knows. It just feels restless and wants to proclaim its existence while asserting its ability to buzz away on any subject in the world. For twenty-five years I've been reading criticisms of my stories. But I don't remember one helpful hint; nor have I heard one word of good advice. The only critic to impress me was Skabichevsky who once wrote that I'd die in a ditch, drunk."[5]

Chekhov's sister Mariya spent part of his last weeks in Yalta with him; as also did his brother Alexander, that rare but welcome guest. By other visitors Chekhov tended, as usual, to be bored. Boredom and loneliness remain the themes of his decline, as do stomach troubles, toothache, shortness of breath and the inevitable cough. So, too, do hopes and plans for the future: for the *dacha* which he wants to rent or buy in Moscow Province; for a boat to be purchased in St. Petersburg. Such preoccupations show him far from thoughts of imminent death. So too does his urge, grotesque in one so ill, to enlist as a medical officer in the far eastern war theatre, where the Russian and Japanese Empires were now at war.[6]

Everyone now seemed to be talking of the Russo-Japanese War, which was to end in the following year with a humiliating Russian defeat. Chekhov stoutly maintained that "our lads will beat the Japs".[7] But one witness has him hovering between forecasts of a Russian victory and hopes, arguably more patriotic still, for a Russian defeat—potentially worthwhile should it stimulate radical reform at home.[8] This was, incidentally, a line on the war similar to that taken by the infant Bolshevik movement and by other revolutionaries. Some memoirists have the declining Chekhov directly predicting a Russian revolution: and correctly so, since such an upheaval was indeed to break out in 1905, shortly after his death; and, though suppressed by authority, it was indeed to provoke certain political concessions. To such possibilities Chekhov showed himself more attuned than his Yalta neighbour Dr. Yelpatyevsky, a revolutionary sympathizer. Whenever Yelpatyevsky chanced to show scepticism about Russia's revolutionary prospects Chekhov would *pounce* on him with "harsh, dogmatic, un-Chekhovian objections". "'How can you say such things?' he would *seethe*. 'Can't you see that everything's been turned upside down: both society and the workers?'"[9]

Yelpatyevsky is one among several memoirists who have presented a similar picture of the dying Chekhov. N. D. Teleshov says that Chekhov often spoke of revolution as inevitable. "In a few years we'll have no autocracy, you'll see." And V. V. Veresayev says that "revolutionary electricity ... *rocked Chekhov's soul. His eyes blazed with stern indignation* when he spoke of the outrages of Plehve [the Russian Home Secretary] and the stupidity of Nicholas II." To this may be added the predictions which, according to Kuprin, Chekhov was always making, à propos of nothing and *in his confident tone*, that Russia would soon enjoy constitutional government.[10]

These reports unite in presenting a Chekhov very different from the figure who appears in these pages: a New Man, suddenly lurching, in the evening of his life, into previously eschewed political commitment. There is, surely, some element of romancing in these accounts. And surely such memoirists are reading into Chekhov attitudes of their own which were never his; especially as their accounts are limp and glazed with the stupefying clichés, as italicized above, of "revolutionary" prose. Those *blazing eyes*, this *confident tone*, that *seething*: could anything be further from the temperate, judicious Anton Pavlovich as we know him? We do not necessarily suspect these witnesses of deliberate misrepresentation, but suggest that the "blazing eyes" and associated phenomena, if correctly reported, may have been the clinical symptoms of a patient in the terminal stage of tuberculosis rather than the manifestations of a new-found political ardour. Such scepticism is reinforced by Chekhov's lifelong acute distaste for the many blazing-eyed and firmly confident contemporaries who littered his path—a type widespread indeed in his age and country. But our main reason for impugning this picture of Chekhov the dying revolutionary agitator is the non-prophetic, matter-of-fact tone of his own words where these are more firmly authenticated than they can be in the accounts of memoirists who purport to convey his conversation verbatim. We refer to his letters, where he does indeed often express contempt for existing Russian institutions, together with an underlying hope for the future, but where he never utters a single syllable in the false, jarring, exalted, pseudo-dynamic tone of the Teleshovs, Veresayevs, Yelpatyevskys and Kuprins. Though we cannot positively prove that revolutionary electricity had *not* rocked the dying Chekhov's soul, we most certainly cannot be convinced that it had.

The memoirists may exaggerate Chekhov's belief in the imminent overthrow of the imperial system, but are accurate when they show him increasingly disgusted by the present: by the repressive practices of the Imperial Russian Government and by the general condition of Russian society as it functioned under the grim, paternalistic eye of a cumbrous, inefficient, mindlessly restrictive autocracy. His opposition to current limitations, mild by post-Tsarist standards, on freedom of speech goes back to long before the year 1904, as has been seen above; and it is also true that such opposition had been steadily increasing as the years went by. Chekhov's disagreements with the political traditionalist Suvorin, his stand over the Dreyfus Affair, his resignation from the Academy of

Sciences over the Gorky scandal, his impatience with the blundering interference of the literary censorship, his dislike of the interception of his mail by the Okhrana (political police) in Yalta: all these attitudes reveal a negative view of Imperial society. Did he draw from this negative conclusion the positive rider that revolution offered an acceptable solution? This thesis is difficult to believe, resting as it does on the unsupported evidence of the "blazing eyes" brigade among the memoirists.

Chekhov's alleged new-found air of conviction is still harder to credit when we remember his habitual caution in discussing political issues and his aversion to all over-simplified interpretations. Disgusted though he was by many of the manifestations of contemporary Russian society under the autocracy, he could also temper this disgust by setting it in its historical context. "I'm far from an enthusiast for modernity. But one must be as objective and fair as possible. Bad as things may now be, uncongenial as the present is, the past was quite simply nauseating."[11]

Once again, to descend to a more specific issue, we have seen Chekhov siding with the disaffected students of St. Petersburg during their clashes with authority; and we saw him helping an individual student-rebel, the son of his neighbour Yelpatyevsky. Yet Chekhov could not regard this or any other complex problem as a black-and-white affair, being anything but an unthinking student-fancier. While taking a line generally favourable to these young protesters, he did not fail to point out that, in a few years' time, many of them would join the forces of oppression as grasping officials and the like, and would themselves be found oppressing the next generation of protesting students. Why, the most extreme reactionaries of all—such notorious figures as M. N. Katkov and K. P. Pobedonostsev—were typical products of Russian universities. And so "I don't trust our intelligentsia, hypocritical, bogus, hysterical, uneducated and lazy as it is. I don't even trust these people when they suffer and complain, for they themselves spawn their own persecutors. I believe in individuals, I see salvation in isolated personalities scattered here and there throughout Russia; whether they're intellectuals or peasants they are our strength, few of them though there are."[12]

If we consider another scandal of the period—the persecution of the Jews in the late Russian Empire—we find Chekhov helping individuals to beat the residence restrictions at Yalta or the quota for admissions to Moscow University. That he was horrified by the notorious Kishinyov pogrom of 1903 is not difficult to believe.[13] We also remember his intervention against the anti-Semitic camp involved in the Dreyfus Affair. But Chekhov was not one to speak of Jews or anyone else with the facile, insulting condescension of the inverted racial discriminator as that type has evolved since his death. If he chanced to dislike a Jewish individual he no more hesitated to say so than he hesitated to disparage any of the many Gentiles who annoyed him.

So much for Chekhov's hostility to the Imperial system and attitudes to a hypothetical revolution. What of his belief in progress generally? Here again some memoirists have his eyes blazing, his voice ringing with conviction. As already noted, Kuprin reported him predicting, *with a note of deep faith*, that within three or four hundred years the whole world would become a blossoming garden. Chekhov liked looking at examples of experimental architecture and at ocean liners, adds Kuprin; he was always interested in the latest inventions, he liked talking to specialists. *With firm conviction* he would claim that such crimes or misdemeanours as murder, robbery and adultery would one day disappear. "He believed that the true culture of the future would *ennoble Man*." Another memoirist has Chekhov intuitively predicting and indeed overestimating the activities of Aeroflot, when he speaks of the "air trains" of the future which will enable anyone to leave his bed in Yalta, breakfast in Moscow, lunch in St. Petersburg and be back in Yalta for supper.[14]

Rarely if ever does Chekhov adopt this vein in his letters. The nearest he comes to it is, perhaps, when he makes the not necessarily optimistic prediction that "our great-grandchildren will live to the age of two hundred". That Chekhov did indeed sincerely believe in progress is, however, confirmed; not least by his own persistent efforts to promote elementary education and public health. He also discussed this belief (typically Victorian, it may be thought) in terms no less explicit, but far less extravagant, than those put into his mouth by memoirists of the blazing-eyes school. "Life is passing me by. . . . All I see and understand, luckily, is that life and people are becoming better and better, more intelligent and more honest." Here, in these restrained phrases, is the voice of the real Chekhov: one who indeed did believe in progress, but not at all in Progress.[15]

Such was the tone and style of his "faith in the future", such the context of the many passages in his plays and stories where this or that character forecasts that "life will be wonderful in X years"; the figure varies from fifty upwards. "Mankind marches on, going from strength to strength": when Trofimov, Chekhov's eternal student in *The Cherry Orchard*, utters this and similar sentiments hailing the advent of a "new life", we are not to suppose ourselves undergoing indoctrination in facile optimism by Chekhov the coiner of propagandist slogans. Far from it, for the faith in the future of such as Trofimov often seems to be used by Chekhov to emphasize the futility of the present: and, in this instance, of a character whom we remember as much for his habit of losing his galoshes as for any philosophical profundities. Predictions of a glorious future, lodged in the text of Chekhov's imaginative work, were never intended to be lifted out of context and paraded as sermons on the desirability of mindless euphoria. In any case, there are other, quite different, quotations which enable us to see such interpretations in perspective. When speaking of the grinding poverty and starvation of the Russian countryside, of the dilapidated thatched roofs, of the ignorance, misery, gloom and general depression which he sees around him, the hero of Chekhov's story *The Student* comments: "All these horrors have been, are and will continue to be, and the passage of another thousand years won't make life any better."[16]

On the critical practice of parading out-of-context quotations from fiction as evidence of the author's views the author himself should have the last word. When, in late 1902, a certain O. G. Ettinger proposed to publish a collection of extracts from Chekhov's writings, Chekhov reacted sharply. "These thoughts and musings are not mine, but my heroes'. If, say, a character in one of my plays or stories claims that one should murder or steal, that doesn't entitle Mr. Ettinger to parade me as an advocate of murder and theft."[17]

Whatever Chekhov's views on progress, there can be no doubt that he firmly rejected religious belief. He had long ago lost his faith, he once told Diaghilev, adding that he was utterly bewildered when he saw any intelligent man claiming himself a believer. Educated Russians had abandoned their religion, they were retreating further and further from it; and this despite all contemporary "philosophico-religious societies". Deriding those who based their faith on guesswork or Dostoyevsky, Chekhov yet retained sufficient toe-hold on the eschatological to concede that, in thousands of years' time, humanity might collectively establish the existence of God on the same basis as the proposition twice two equals four. Meanwhile he scorned such fashionable Russian religious philosophers as V. V. Rozanov and D. S. Merezhkovsky.[18] And he especially disliked Russian religious ladies: "that element which causes religion to silt up like the sand-choked Volga". How lucky Muslims were to be spared the activities of any female faithful! He was scathing too whenever some young woman sought to detain him with speculations about "life". "Don't take so tortuous a view of life [he told Lydia Avilov a few months before his death].... Does it—life, that unknown quantity—really merit all the painful ratiocinations which rack our Russian brains?"[19]

Himself no believer, Chekhov continued to respect religious faith in others, provided that they did not egregiously proselytize. Such tolerance runs through his whole life and work, and no uninstructed reader of his penultimate story *The Bishop* would have identified it as the work of so convinced though unmilitant an unbeliever.

As all these considerations show, it is easier to prove what Chekhov did not believe than to deduce any positive faith from the material. He comes nearest to expressing such a credo in a letter of 28 January 1900. Discussing Tolstoy, whose thought he had so sharply criticized in the recent past, he writes that he had never loved any other human being as much as Tolstoy; and while emphasizing that he is "not a believer", he claims Tolstoy's creed as "closest to me, and better adapted to my needs than any other".[20] Had Chekhov, then, suddenly become converted or reconverted to Tolstoyan views such as we remember him tentatively advocating back in the late 1880s? Far from it. Never, for example, did he accept Tolstoy's idealization of the peasant. Nor did Chekhov now dream, if he ever had, of rejecting the trappings of advanced culture and civilization in favour of existence reduced to its crude essentials à la Tolstoy.

He still rejected Tolstoy's view that art must be condemned as invalid unless capable of appealing to the most common of common men. Keenly and practically interested in elementary education, as we have seen, Chekhov was repelled by condescending attempts to "bring culture to the masses". He made this point forcibly in January 1903 when discussing a People's Theatre patronized by Gorky in Nizhny Novgorod. "People's Theatres, People's Literature: that's all rubbish, it's so much People's fudge. We shouldn't degrade Gogol to the People, we should raise the People to Gogol."[21] But despite such points of disagreement, there was still an important residue of belief which Chekhov and Tolstoy held in common. Both accepted the "Christian ethic"—if by this it is legitimate to understand an attempt to behave honestly, decently, unselfishly and with due regard to the claims of others. It was a stark Christianity, this: purged not only of its supernatural beliefs and eschatological trappings, but also— in Chekhov's, not Tolstoy's, case—of its God.

To this belief of Chekhov's, if belief it can be called, must be added his continuing firm but low-key commitment to science and the scientific method. No leaper to conclusions on the basis of instinctive "feel", he remained a hard-headed pragmatist who, when presented with a problem, did not burst into speech before he had carefully reviewed available evidence. He believed, in the last resort, in little more than this: that there is no point in claiming to know the unknowable. This simple faith had the merit of startling originality in the hectic days of *fin-de-siècle* Russia, a period of clamant religiosity and fevered politico-metaphysical panacea-mongering.

Farewell to Moscow
(May 1904)

May 1904 witnesses the penultimate stage in Chekhov's decline. Reaching Moscow on the third of the month, he moves into the new flat which his wife has found, and which at least has a lift: a convenience of little value, though, for he spends most of the month confined to bed or shuffling round in dressing-gown and slippers. Upset stomach, pleurisy, high temperature, sleeplessness, rheumatism: these are among his sufferings. His latest physician, the German Doctor Taube, is in constant attendance, and soon decides to send his patient to Germany for a cure. But Chekhov is, alas, beyond all curing. Teleshov remembers him on a sofa surrounded by cushions: "a little man with narrow shoulders, with a narrow, bloodless face ... thin, emaciated, unrecognizable". It was hard to believe that anyone could have changed so much. As Chekhov held out his thin, wax-like hand to say good-bye, he remarked that he was going abroad on the following day "to die".[1]

Yet still the dying man maintained some of his usual activities. He was still generous with his help and advice: to a bereaved husband who wished to marry his deceased wife's sister, thus contravening Russian ecclesiastical law; to a deacon's son who sought a transfer from one university to another. And he was still reading manuscripts for *Russkaya mysl*, though only the shortest and most clearly legible items were submitted to him now. He also conceived a new dramatic plot markedly un-Chekhovian in its exotic setting. "The hero, a scholar, loves a woman who either fails to return his love or is unfaithful to him, whereupon he goes away to the far north." Act Three was to take place on the deck of an ice-bound ship whence the lonely scholar-hero spied the ghost of his beloved flitting past against the background of the aurora borealis.[2]

Chekhov's last weeks were troubled by a quarrel between A. F. Marks and another of his publishers, Znaniye, the co-operative enterprise headed by Gorky. As we saw, Gorky had already unsuccessfully urged Chekhov to break his contract with Marks. But it was *The Cherry Orchard* which had the two firms at loggerheads now. To Znaniye Chekhov had granted the right, as retained under the contract, of first publishing his play, after which it would revert to Marks in perpetuity. The author's intention had been for Znaniye to publish *The Cherry Orchard* as part of a symposium planned for early 1904, and then for Marks to bring it out later in the year. But two difficulties developed. Firstly, Znaniye's symposium was unexpectedly delayed, incidentally depriving Chekhov of royalties from the play. And, secondly, Marks had infringed the spirit of his contract with

Chekhov by unexpectedly hustling through *his Cherry Orchard*, thereby threatening the sales of Znaniye's delayed publication, since Chekhov's play was the symposium item most attractive to purchasers. When protests against Marks's action reached Chekhov from Znaniye, he admitted himself partly to blame, but was also furious with Marks for deliberately advancing publication in order to cause Znaniye embarrassment. Still, as usual, the soul of correctness in his business transactions, Chekhov offered to reimburse Znaniye the large sum of 4,500 roubles paid to him for his play. Alternatively, he encouraged Znaniye to bring against him a court action which both sides would regard as friendly so that he would then be able to sue Marks in turn. Thus both the author and the symposium's publishers might recover their losses from the unscrupulous Marks, with whom Chekhov now proposed severing personal relations. From this tedious feud the harassed playwright was soon to be released by death.[3]

After a month confined to his quarters in Moscow in May 1904, the sick man felt just well enough to don boots and frock-coat on the 31st of the month and take a cab trip round Moscow. Three days later he left Russia on doctor's orders, never to return.

Badenweiler
(*June–July 1904*)

Chekhov and his wife stopped in Berlin and spent four or five days at a hotel. Anton's appetite had improved and he liked German bread, while disapproving of German women for dressing tastelessly. Though short of breath, he felt that he was recovering his health and visited the zoo. Not planning, evidently, to die in the immediate future, he bought a suit and some jerseys. But this euphoria did not impress the celebrated Berlin medical specialist Professor Ewald, who called on the distinguished Russian visitor for a consultation, only to throw up his hands in despair and leave the room without a single word. A similar impression was received by a layman, G. B. Iollos, Berlin correspondent of Chekhov's old vehicle *Russkiye vedomosti*. Iollos made himself useful to the Chekhovs during their brief stay in Berlin, but had no illusions about the sick man's prospects. "I could see Anton Pavlovich's days were numbered, so ill did he seem; he was terribly thin, he coughed and panted after the least movement, and he always had a high temperature."[1]

Reaching the German spa of Badenweiler, near the Black Forest and the French border, on 9 or 10 June, Chekhov again felt much better. He had a keen appetite; he was sleeping well; he planned a trip to Italy, after which he would return to Yalta *via* Constantinople. But he was also restive, moving from a *pension* to a private guest-house, the Villa Friederike, a nd thence to the more comfortable Hotel Sommer. Convinced that his health was returning "not by the dram but by the hundredweight", he complained that his doctor had forbidden him coffee, which he liked, and ordered him to drink wine, which he disliked. It was warm and sunny, there was a lovely garden at the Villa Friederike, and a balcony with an interesting view of the post office in the Hotel Sommer. But even now he was not so near death as to escape the boredom which had ambushed him throughout life whenever he settled down anywhere, however briefly. He was still harping on the hideous clothes worn by the natives, and on German tastelessness in general; compared with the Germans even the Russians—let alone the Italians and French—led a far more "talented" life.[2]

At Badenweiler Chekhov was treated by a Dr. Schwörer, mentor of his latest Moscow doctor, Taube. The patient's diet accordingly remained unchanged; it was "the same stupid cocoa and porridge", but Chekhov seemed to thrive on it. He also enjoyed fresh air and sunshine, but complained of the heat. He was still sleeping well, and by 26 June his health seemed "really on the mend". He planned to visit Lake Como, he enquired about sailings to Russia from Marseilles and Trieste. In his last letter (of 28 June and to his sister) he is still concerned with timetables and mentions his lack of summer clothes; Olga has just gone to Freiburg to order him a light flannel suit.[3]

Suddenly, on Tuesday 29 June, Chekhov suffers a heart attack, but seems to recover after an injection of morphia and gulps of oxygen. On the next night he again has a heart attack; and again seems to recover, for on Thursday, 1 July, his heart is beating vigorously again, and he still feels lively enough to entertain his wife with the plot of a projected story. At a fashionable resort full of fat, gluttonous bankers, red-cheeked Englishmen and Americans, who have all returned hungry to their hotel after a day's healthy exertion, it suddenly turns out that no evening meal will be served because the chef has run away. The story was to describe the effects of this blow below the belt "on all these spoilt people":[4] a twist reminiscent of Antosha Chekhonte rather than the mature Anton Chekhov.

A few hours later, between midnight and 1 a.m., Chekhov suddenly woke up. He felt as if he was choking, spoke deliriously of some "sailor" and muttered a question about the Japanese. He also asked his wife to send for a doctor. It was the first time in his life that he had ever made such a request, and she found a Russian student, another guest at the hotel, to undertake the errand. In the silence of the sultry night the crunch of the young stranger's footsteps on the gravel drive made poor Olga feel unutterably lonely and desperate while she watched her husband die in a foreign hotel room. As a last resort she prepared an ice pack to press against his heart. Still conscious but now clearly approaching his end,

Chekhov remarked that "you don't put ice on an empty heart".

At 2 a.m. the doctor arrived. He administered camphor injections and whiffs of oxygen, also prescribing champagne: all futile attempts to stimulate the sinking organism into life. Now Anton Pavlovich said his last words. He first explained in German that he was dying (*"ich sterbe"*). Then he took the champagne, smiled at his wife, remarked that he "hadn't drunk champagne for ages", drained the glass and calmly turned on to his left side.

By 3 a.m. he was dead.⁵

Even in death Chekhov was not spared ironies such as had so long haunted both his life and his plots. The coffined corpse was delivered to St. Petersburg in a railway wagon labelled as if to inspire some newly arisen Antosha Chekhonte: FRESH OYSTERS. From there, in greater dignity, Chekhov was conveyed to Moscow's Novodevichy Convent and decently interred by his father's side.

Conclusion

Chekhov's death was immediately greeted in his own country by a volley of tributes couched in precisely the kind of phraseology which the honorand himself had most abominated: tributes to the Sad-Eyed Poet of Twilight Russia; the Blazing-Eyed Prophet of Humanity's Glorious Future; the Wise Observer with a Wistful Smile and an Aching Heart; the Champion of the Little Man; the Gentle, Suffering Soul; the one who Loved People. Fortunately he was not yet sufficiently popular abroad to provoke a comparable avalanche of gush from the world at large; but the world at large has been making up for the deficiency ever since.

Chekhov was powerless in life to stem outpourings of admiration for himself which might have been expressly designed to embarrass him. Nor can a mere biographer hope to save the Tender, Ailing Lyricist from his admirers. But the biographer can at least try to avoid the over-dramatized, over-emotional, pompous language which Chekhov himself so detested. His true worth transcended such absurdities, and an attempt has been made to demonstrate this.

This is not, of course, the first study of Chekhov to reject the traditional tone of feverish exaltation. We have already seen Bunin denouncing conventional panegyrics of the Bard of Twilight Moods with his "warmth", "tenderness" and "Love of Man". Another contemporary and friend, Potapenko, protested against portrayals of Chekhov as a bloodless paragon lacking all human passions and weaknesses. Even a Russian critic from the Stalin period, A. B. Derman, has spoken out boldly to refute the most indefensible hagiographical pretence of all: that which has Chekhov "never uttering a single complaint" during the entire course of his life. And what an insult it is, this charge of "never complaining" which Derman so rightly rejects; for Chekhov was in fact a carper of genius who, in his letters, elevated the parading of minor grievances to a fine art practised with wit and virtuosity throughout his adult life.[1]

The sober, scholarly, empirical, unemotional, decently Chekhovian approach to Chekhov is superbly defined by his earliest major biographer, A. Izmaylov, publishing in 1916. "Chekhov was no saint. . . . His biographer should realize that literary history is not written for the edification of the young, even though it often does fulfil that function. . . . Chekhov the brilliant, Chekhov the witty, Chekhov whose every word glitters, eternally memorable, like a diamond; Chekhov handsome as a demigod, always surrounded by dazzling girls, irresistibly attractive to men and women; Chekhov the philanthropist doing his good deeds left right and centre: that stuff may be all right in a mood-piece or prose poem. . . . It has nothing to do with biographical research."[2]

The present biography is written from an angle close to that expressed by Izmaylov. It has also been stimulated, negatively, by the decades of evocative eulogies which have continued to spurt forth since Izmaylov, Bunin, Potapenko and Derman first issued their warnings. So strongly do I agree with these four, and with many another unavailing voice of sanity, in deploring the traditional idealization that I have gone out of my way to seek evidence of inconsiderate, shabby, inconsistent or downright shameful behaviour. I was looking for anything which pointed to human fallibility rather than the virtues of a saintly ninny. The body of my text contains these findings. Chekhov has, for instance, been seen writing to individuals in an affable manner which seems insincere when collated with the harsh words which he wrote about these same persons behind their backs. Izmaylov makes this point too. "Chekhov's comments *on* Shcheglov, Pleshcheyev and Leykin [he might have added Grigorovich] . . . are not always on the same amicable level as the letters written *to* those people."[3] This kind of hypocrisy is part of ordinary everyday behaviour, and it certainly constitutes no crime. Equally certainly, though, it is inconsistent with the angelic character attributed to Chekhov by the imperceptive.

To the peccadillo of social hypocrisy we must add Chekhov's failure to respond to emotional demands made, not always unreasonably, by wife, sister and women friends. As has been shown, he could be evasive to the point of causing unnecessary suffering. Once again he was committing no crime. But he was also, once again, falling well short of Chekhov the nineteenth-century Messiah as popularly misconceived. That he tended to be unreliable in supplying literary copy, meeting deadlines and predicting his own movements we have also shown. And we have found him censuring himself for servility and bad temper: of which, however, we were able to find little independent evidence. But we did find the occasional hint of vanity and self-importance to set against the impressive structure of his innate modesty.

The purpose of ransacking Chekhov's record for character faults was of course neither to "debunk" nor to defend him, but to discover his true nature. And the result, not altogether unexpected, of assembling his defects in their totality has been to provide a character reference more impressive than can come from those who degrade him with their mindless adulation.

We remember in particular the occasion on which Anton Pavlovich so

effectively used nerve-warfare tactics to prevent his sister marrying
Alexander Smagin. That this episode is fairly discreditable to Chekhov must
be conceded. But the staggering fact is that this, and nothing more heinous
than this, constitutes the most blameworthy single act to have come to
light in the length and breadth of the abundant source material. Let him
cast the first stone who has never behaved worse than Anton behaved to
Mariya over the Smagin affair.

If we can make no more serious accusations than these we are forced
back, on balance, to a view not so far removed in content from the
traditional admiration, however different the tone in which we may choose
to express ourselves. The Chekhov who emerges from our crucible, purged
of evocative claptrap, is enhanced, not impaired, by the discovery that
he was no pious paragon but a human being with a few, so remarkably
few, human faults. That Chekhov was gentle, sensitive, kind, helpful, truly
charitable and philanthropic, free of affectation and remarkably tough-
minded behind his courteous manner—these and many other virtues
completely outweigh the few occasions on which we have, as it were,
been able to catch him out.

In any case none of this matters except for its bearing on Chekhov's art.
Who cares whether he furnished a model of good conduct for humanity
at the beginning of the twentieth century? It is the stories of his maturity
from 1888 onwards which form his main contribution to humanity;
followed at a respectable distance by the three mature plays *Uncle Vanya*,
Three Sisters and *The Cherry Orchard*. These are his major works; but they
are far indeed, as we have seen, from exhausting his literary achievements,
among which the early stories, the other long plays, the farces, the letters
and *Sakhalin Island* also have their importance.

On the comparative merits of the mature stories and the mature plays,
my own view is that the former constitute by far the more significant
body of work. This view remains unchanged since I first expressed it in
the Preface to my 1950 *Chekhov*.[4] Here was not a great dramatist who also
happened to write short stories, but a supreme master of the short story
who also happened to be a great dramatist. In this I again agree with
Bunin, who once stated outright that Chekhov's plays were "far from his
best work". Chekhov himself regarded his drama as of secondary importance, according to Bunin, who suspects that Chekhov must have been
insulted to find his reputation depending, not on the stories which constitute his main achievement, but on the accident of having his far less
remarkable plays taken up by the fashionable Moscow Art Theatre.[5]
Perhaps Bunin goes too far. No degree of admiration, however extravagant,
for Chekhov's narrative fiction need lead us to disparage his drama. The
stories and the plays are not rivals. Rather do they complement each other

in purveying an individual vision of the world which has been delighting and tantalizing readers and theatregoers for nearly a hundred years.

Since Chekhov's essence has never yielded to analysis, and since his very mysteries are so potent an element in his magic, I shall not court disaster by ending this book with an attempted definitive summing up—more appropriate to a critical than a biographical study—of his literary achievement. But I can at least emphasize one prominent ingredient in the special Chekhov formula: the significant contrast, which runs through so much of his best work, between his characters as they really are and as they see themselves. In countless variations, both fictional and dramatic, he studies illusions destined sooner or later to be shattered against the trivialities of everyday life.

That the trivial and the tragic often go hand in hand is perhaps Chekhov's most potent creative discovery. Nowhere is it more effectively expressed than at the funeral feast of *In the Hollow*, after the burial of Lipa's baby, murdered by scalding. We have in mind the point where the local priest thinks to bring the comforts of religion to the pathetic bereaved mother, and where the inattentive reader might easily miss Chekhov's deadly but typically unobtrusive irony.

" 'Grieve not for the babe, for of such,' said the priest, picking up a fork with a pickled mushroom on it, 'is the Kingdom of Heaven.' "[6]

Infanticide and pickled mushrooms: it reminds us of the slaughtered Matthew Terekhov's body slumping in the bloodstained boiled potatoes of *Murder*, and of Chekhov's own body arriving in St. Petersburg in the wagon labelled FRESH OYSTERS. It also reminds us of the high hopes for fulfilment in love or work which, in Chekhov's writings as in his life, are so often seen collapsing among jam-jars, fried onions, copper saucepans and dirty washing. And it calls to mind many another incongruity in this careful, pragmatical, down-to-earth, scientifically trained yet elusive observer whose straightforward prose could hauntingly flick at the unknowable; and who, while capturing on paper the inspired fantasies of his creative genius, was so often simultaneously cursing his lost galoshes, his piles, his diarrhoea, his reviewers.

᠁᠁᠁᠁᠁᠁᠁᠁᠁᠁᠁᠁᠁᠁᠁᠁᠁᠁᠁᠁᠁᠁

The Shape of Chekhov's Work

This appendix offers a general description of Chekhov's *œuvre*, drawing together and expanding material which has already been considered in the body of the text.

We deal first with items which Chekhov intended, at the time of writing, for publication or performance; and then with material not designed for publication. The figures are based on *Works, 1944–51*, but might have to be modified slightly in due course when *Works and Letters, 1974–82* is available in full; for this 30-volume edition, of which the first volumes were promised for 1974 (but became available only in April 1975), see above, pp. xiii ff. and below, pp. 345–6.

I. MATERIAL INTENDED FOR PUBLICATION

A. IMAGINATIVE WORKS

1. Narrative Fiction and Associated Material

Chekhov's main contribution to literature falls under the two headings of short stories and plays. We can be far more precise in describing the latter: Chekhov wrote 17 surviving plays (one uncompleted), as will be noted below. But how many stories did he write? It is impossible to answer this question, even approximately, owing to the large number of works which hover in the limbo between the two genres of narrative fiction and the plotless sketch, while partaking of both genres in every possible degree of admixture. Where Chekhov's earliest and most prolific years, up to 1887, are concerned, the confusion of genres is particularly marked: especially as we find—in addition to stories, sketches, story-sketches and sketch-stories—various miscellaneous absurdities not quite covered by any of these descriptions: e.g. comic calendars and captions, some only one line long, to cartoons and facetious picture jokes. There is also a lengthy semi-absurdity: the detective novel *The Shooting Party*, which runs to 180 pages and is the longest of all Chekhov's imaginative works.

It is the presence of so much miscellaneous and borderline material, especially in Chekhov's earlier work, which has compelled us to give this section of his product the cumbrous title "Narrative Fiction and Associated Material", for which "narrative-type material" will be loosely used as a shorter equivalent.

This is the most important area of Chekhov's achievement. It includes all his short stories, good, bad and indifferent. It is also the most prolific area, accounting in all for 9 volumes of *Works, 1944–51,* and there totalling over 4,000 pages.

(a) The Early and Mature Periods: a Comparison

In the present study the narrative-type material is considered to fall into two main sections: an early period (preceding March 1888); a mature period (from March 1888 onwards).

The over-all total of surviving narrative-type items is formidable, comprising 588 published contributions in all. Of these, 528 belong to the early period, and only 60 to the mature period.

The average length of the mature works (about 24 pages) is roughly four times that of the early works (under 6 pages). Even so, the early period still accounts for two thirds, in bulk, of Chekhov's narrative and associated writings: 6 volumes of *Works, 1944–51,* as opposed to the mere 3 volumes covering the fiction of the mature period.

Since the early period lasted only 8 years (1880–8), as opposed to the 16 years (1888–1904) of the mature period, the quantitative output of narrative-type material in the early period was roughly four times that of the mature period. The difference is yet more marked if expressed in terms of the number of items published: we find an average of $5\frac{1}{2}$ new titles per month during the early period: but only 1 per three months during the mature period.

Fiction is not a commodity to be assessed in bulk, and the relatively sparse mature narrative works constitute Chekhov's most important achievement. In quality they eclipse the voluminous early works. Yet the early works do include numerous individual items (both comic and serious) of high quality; besides which their literary standard may be observed improving, impressively but erratically, over Chekhov's first eight years of authorship.

(b) Chekhov's "Collected Works" as an Index of his Assessment of his Own Writings

Valuable evidence on Chekhov's attitude to his own work is provided by his editorial policy as applied when he selected and revised his first (ten-volume) "Collected Works" (1899–1902) for the St. Petersburg publisher A. F. Marks. Reconsidering his entire *œuvre* as part of this process, Chekhov rejected much material outright, not thinking it worth preserving. As we would expect, his earliest writings were the most ruthlessly axed; and the later a work was the more likely was he to admit it (if necessary with extensive alterations) to his "Collected Works". To this sloppily compiled edition, not formally entitled a *Collected Works*, a further, eleventh, posthumous volume was added by Marks in 1906 to include certain later stories—also revised by Chekhov for the Marks edition, but not featured in the ten volumes of 1899–1902. Meanwhile these same stories had already been published in an intervening, "second", 16-volume, edition issued (in 1903) by the bibliographer's nightmare Marks as a supplement to his magazine *Niva* and over-optimistically entitled a *Complete Works.*

The following table shows the distribution of titles between the early and mature periods, differentiated according to whether Chekhov did or did not include them in his "Collected Works" (including the posthumous eleventh volume of 1906).

PERIOD	INCLUDED IN THE "COLLECTED WORKS" EDITED BY CHEKHOV	EXCLUDED FROM THE "COLLECTED WORKS" EDITED BY CHEKHOV	TOTAL
Early	186	342	528
Mature	54	6	60
TOTAL	240	348	588

(c) *Further Breakdown of the Early Period* (*March 1880–March 1888*)

The early period is here divided into four phases according to Chekhov's publishing policy at the time.

(i) *Pre-"Oskolki" Phase* (March 1880–November 1882)

This begins on 9 March 1880 with the appearance of Chekhov's first traced published work, *A Letter from the Landowner* . . . in the St. Petersburg comic weekly *Strekoza*; see Chapter 2.

(ii) *"Oskolki" Phase* (November 1882–May 1885)

This begins on 20 November 1882, when the story *Running into Trouble* appears in the leading St. Petersburg comic weekly *Oskolki*; see Chapter 3.

(iii) *"Peterburgskaya gazeta" Phase* (May 1885–February 1886)

This begins on 6 May 1885, when the story *The Last Mohican Woman* appears in the St. Petersburg daily newspaper *Peterburgskaya gazeta*; see Chapter 4.

(iv) *"Novoye vremya" Phase* (February 1886–March 1888)

This begins on 15 February 1886 when the story *Requiem* appears in the leading St. Petersburg daily newspaper *Novoye vremya*; see Chapter 5.

This last phase (and the early period as a whole) ends in March 1888 with the publication of *The Steppe* in the St. Petersburg monthly *Severny vestnik*: Chekhov's début in a Thick Journal and the beginning of the mature period covered in Chapters 6 to 14.

Expressed in the number of titles published, the breakdown of narrative-type items of the early period is as follows.

PHASE	NUMBER OF TITLES
Pre-*Oskolki*	42
Oskolki	224
Peterburgskaya gazeta	106
Novoye vremya	156
TOTAL	528

It should be noted that these figures do not relate to the number of items published in the periodical which gives its name to a particular phase, but to the total of new items published in *any* periodical (or other outlet) during a given phase.

In the following table the totals of early-period publications are broken down to show how Chekhov's policy of selection affected individual phases.

PHASE	INCLUDED IN THE "COLLECTED WORKS" EDITED BY CHEKHOV	EXCLUDED FROM THE "COLLECTED WORKS" EDITED BY CHEKHOV	TOTAL
Pre-*Oskolki*	none	42	42
Oskolki	47	177	224
Peterburgskaya gazeta	39	67	106
Novoye vremya	100	56	156
TOTAL	186	342	528

The totals of Chekhov's narrative-type contributions to the three main periodicals of the early period are as follows.

PERIODICAL	INCLUDED IN THE "COLLECTED WORKS" EDITED BY CHEKHOV	EXCLUDED FROM THE "COLLECTED WORKS" EDITED BY CHEKHOV	TOTAL
Oskolki	81	181	262
Peterburgskaya gazeta	63	45	108
Novoye vremya	27	2	29
TOTAL	171	228	399

These three publications thus account for 399 of the 528 early-period narrative-type items. The remaining 129 early-period items went to over a dozen other, largely comic, publications. Of these the Moscow-published *Budilnik* (with 48 titles spread over the years 1881–7) was the most favoured, followed by the Moscow-published *Zritel* (with 27 titles in 1881–3).

(d) Further Breakdown of the Mature Period

Nearly all Chekhov's "narrative-type works" of the mature period are short stories; even here, though, one or two items (notably *The Beauties* and *The Student*) have virtually no narrative element.

(i) Pre-Melikhovo Phase (March 1888–March 1892)

Beginning with *The Steppe*, this straddles Chekhov's expedition to Sakhalin, and ends with his move to Melikhovo; see Chapters 6 to 8.

(ii) *Melikhovo Phase* (March 1892–March 1897)

This begins with Chekhov's move to Melikhovo and ends with his hospitalization in Moscow; see Chapters 9 to 11.

(iii) *Between-Homes Phase* (March 1897–January 1900)

This covers the unsettled interval between March 1897 and January 1900, by which month Chekhov was fully established as a resident of Yalta; see Chapter 12.

(iv) *Declining Phase* (January 1900–July 1904)

This covers Chekhov's last years, during which he completed only two new stories; see Chapters 13 and 14.

In the following table the 60 stories of the mature period are broken down to show how Chekhov's policy of selection for his "Collected Works" operated within individual phases.

PHASE	INCLUDED IN THE "COLLECTED WORKS" EDITED BY CHEKHOV	EXCLUDED FROM THE "COLLECTED WORKS" EDITED BY CHEKHOV	TOTAL
Pre-Melikhovo	15	1	16
Melikhovo	23	4	27
Between-Homes	14	1	15
Declining	2	none	2
TOTAL	54	6	60

For the sake of the record it must be added that Chekhov's last story, *A Marriageable Girl*, has been given the benefit of the doubt and counted among those favoured by inclusion in the "Collected Works"; in fact the question of its inclusion or exclusion does not appear to have arisen.

In the mature period Chekhov no longer cultivates a single most-favoured publication as the main outlet for his work, but goes over to a tandem system: that is, he now favours at any given time a pair of periodicals, consisting of a single Thick Journal for his longer stories and a single newspaper for his shorter stories. Between 1888 and 1892 this brace of most-favoured publications consists of the Thick Journal *Severny vestnik* and the newspaper *Novoye vremya*, both based in St. Petersburg. In 1892–3 Chekhov abandons both as an outlet for fiction and transfers to a new pair of most-favoured publications, both based in Moscow: the Thick Journal *Russkaya mysl* for longer and the newspaper *Russkiye vedomosti* for shorter stories. Neither before nor after this transfer did he abandon the practice of sending work to a wide variety of other periodicals with which he did not cultivate or retain a most-favoured relationship.

The following is a complete list of the 60 narrative-type works published by Chekhov in his mature period, grouped by phase and year according to the publications in which they appeared. An asterisk marks the six items excluded by Chekhov from his "Collected Works".

PRE-MELIKHOVO PHASE
(March 1888–March 1892)

YEAR	*Severny vestnik*	*Novoye vremya*	OTHER VEHICLES
1888	The Steppe *Lights	An Awkward Business The Beauties	The Seizure The Cobbler and the Devil
	The Party	The Bet	
1889	A Dreary Story	The Princess	
1890		Thieves	
		Gusev	
1891		Peasant Women	
		The Duel	
1892	My Wife		The Butterfly

MELIKHOVO PHASE
(March 1892–March 1897)

YEAR	*Russkaya mysl*	*Russkiye vedomosti*	OTHER VEHICLES

1892	Ward Number Six		After the Theatre
			In Exile
			*Fragment
			*The Story of a Com-
			  mercial Venture
			*From a Retired
			  Teacher's Note-
			  book
			*A Fishy Affair
			Neighbours
			Terror

1893	An Anonymous Story	The Two Volodyas	
1894	A Woman's Kingdom	Rothschild's Fiddle The Student The Russian Master At a Country House The Head Gardener's Story	The Black Monk
1895	Three Years	The Order of St. Anne	His Wife
	Murder		Patch
	Ariadne		
1896	The Artist's Story		My Life
1897	Peasants		

	BETWEEN-HOMES PHASE (March 1897–January 1900) and DECLINING PHASE (January 1900–July 1904)		
YEAR	*Russkaya mysl*	*Russkiye vedomosti*	OTHER VEHICLES
1897		The Savage Home In the Cart	
1898	A Hard Case Gooseberries Concerning Love A Case History		*All Friends Together Doctor Startsev Angel
1899	A Lady with a Dog	New Villa	On Official Business
1900			At Christmas In the Hollow
1902			The Bishop
1903			A Marriageable Girl

The following was the distribution of the 23 mature stories listed above as apppearing "in other vehicles".

Terror was Chekhov's last story, and the only one of his Melikhovo phase, to appear in *Novoye vremya*. Three stories appeared in *Peterburgskaya gazeta*: *The Cobbler and the Devil*; *After the Theatre*; *At Christmas*. Four stories appeared in *Oskolki*: *Fragment*; *The Story of a Commercial Venture*; *From a Retired Teacher's Notebook*; *A Fishy Affair*.

Two stories appeared in symposia which also included contributions from other writers: *The Seizure* in *Pamyati V. M. Garshina* ("To the Memory of V. M. Garshin"; St. Petersburg, 1889); *His Wife* in *Pochin* ("New Enterprise"; Moscow, 1895).

Two stories each were published by three St. Petersburg monthlies: *Neighbours* and *On Official Business* by *Knizhki nedeli* ("Books of the Week"), monthly supplement to the weekly *Nedelya* ("The Week"); *My Life* and *Doctor Startsev* by *Niva* ("The Meadow"); *The Bishop* and *A Marriageable Girl* by *Zhurnal dlya vsekh* ("Everybody's Journal").

The remaining seven stories appeared in periodicals to which Chekhov contributed once only, as follows.

St Petersburg publications: *The Butterfly* in the weekly *Sever* ("The North"); *In Exile* in the weekly *Vsemirnaya illyustratsiya* ("World Illustrated"); *All Friends Together* in the monthly *Kosmopolis* ("Cosmopolis"); *In the Hollow* in the monthly *Zhizn* ("Life").

Moscow publications: *The Black Monk* in the monthly *Artist* ("The Artiste"); *Patch* in the monthly *Detskoye chteniye* ("Children's Reading"); *Angel* in the weekly *Semya* ("The Family").

One story, *Mediocrities* (*Obyvateli*), has been excluded from the above account as an anomaly. It was originally published in *Novoye vremya* in 1889 as an independent item. But in 1894, when Chekhov published *The Russian Master*

(*Uchitel slovesnosti*) in *Russkiye vedomosti*, he incorporated *Mediocrities* as the first of the new story's two chapters. *Mediocrities* was thereby superseded as an independent work.

2. Drama

Chekhov's Works include 17 plays, of which 7 are of full length (four-acters) and 10 are short (one-acters).

(a) Four-Act Plays

The first of the four-act plays was not given a title by Chekhov, but is generally known as *Platonov*; it was probably written in the early 1880s, and was neither published nor performed in his lifetime.

The first draft of the second four-acter, *Ivanov*, was written in September–October 1887; the play was extensively revised between October 1888 and January 1889.

Chekhov's third long play, *The Wood Demon*, was written between May and October 1889 and converted into the fourth four-acter, *Uncle Vanya*, at some unknown time: probably either in 1890 or in 1896.

The three remaining long plays have a less complex history, and are as follows: *The Seagull*, written in October–November 1895; *Three Sisters*, written in August–October 1900; *The Cherry Orchard*, written in March–October 1903.

Notable first nights or early performances of the long plays were as follows.

PLAY	THEATRE	CITY	DATE
Ivanov	Korsh's	Moscow	19 Nov. 1887
	Alexandrine	St. Petersburg	31 Jan. 1889
The Wood Demon	Abramov's	Moscow	27 Dec. 1889
The Seagull	Alexandrine	St. Petersburg	17 Oct. 1896
	Moscow Art	Moscow	17 Dec. 1898
Uncle Vanya	Moscow Art	Moscow	26 Oct. 1899
Three Sisters	Moscow Art	Moscow	31 Jan. 1901
The Cherry Orchard	Moscow Art	Moscow	17 Jan. 1904

(b) One-Act Plays

Among Chekhov's short plays *Tatyana Repin* (1889) is a curio not intended for production on the stage; it was written as a private joke between Chekhov and A. S. Suvorin, who published it in two copies.

Two of the remaining one-acters are "tear-jerkers": *On the High Road* (written in 1885, banned by the censor, neither published nor performed during Chekhov's lifetime); *Swan Song*, written in 1887.

The six farces are: *The Bear*, *The Proposal* (1888); *A Tragic Role*, *The Wedding* (1889); *The Anniversary* (1891); the uncompleted, posthumously published *Night before the Trial*, written at some time in the 1890s.

The one-acter *Smoking is Bad for You*, a combined farce and tear-jerker, survives in six recensions spread over the years 1886–1903.

Six of the ten short plays represent adaptations of a previously published story or stories by Chekhov.

TITLE OF PLAY	BASED ON STORY OR STORIES
On the High Road	*In Autumn* (1883)
Swan Song	*Kalchas* (1886)
A Tragic Role	*One among Many* (1887)
The Wedding	*The Wedding Season* (1881); *Marrying for Money* and *A Wedding with a General* (1884)
The Anniversary	*A Defenceless Creature* (1887)
The Night before the Trial	*The Night before the Trial* (1886)

B. WORKS DEALING WITH FACTUAL MATERIAL

1. Learned Studies

Chekhov's single academic work, *Sakhalin Island*, which is in part a travelogue, was first published in serial form in *Russkaya mysl* between October 1893 and July 1894. In its revised, canonical form it occupies vol. 10 of *Works, 1944–51*, which also gives a full history of the text and an account of the numerous variants. *Sakhalin Island* amounts to over 360 pages in *Works, 1944–51*, being more than twice as long as any of Chekhov's other works.

In the years 1884–5 Chekhov also planned a work of historical scholarship, *A History of Russian Medicine*, conducting a considerable amount of preliminary research, but did not reach the stage of writing up his findings.

2. Journalism

(a) Splinters of Moscow Life

Between 2 July 1883 and 12 October 1885 Chekhov published a column on Muscovite affairs entitled *Splinters of Moscow Life* in the St. Petersburg weekly *Oskolki* ("Splinters"). The column appeared 50 times in all.

(b) The Case of Rykov and Company

This series of reports, on the trial (in Moscow) of a certain Rykov and his associates for embezzlement from a provincial bank, appeared in 16 issues of the St. Petersburg daily *Peterburgskaya gazeta* between 24 November and 10 December 1884.

(c) From Siberia

This series of travel articles, comprising 9 items in all, was published in *Novoye vremya* between 24 June and 23 August 1890.

(d) *Miscellaneous*

Between 1881 and 1893 Chekhov published 40 miscellaneous journalistic articles in various periodicals. They include obituaries, theatre notices and an attack on the administration of the Moscow Zoo.

II. MATERIAL NOT INTENDED FOR PUBLICATION

A. LETTERS

Chekhov's correspondence is the principal source of the present biography. At the moment of writing the fullest collection of the letters is that published in the last eight volumes (numbers 13 to 20) of *Works, 1944–51* It contains 4,200 letters printed in chronological order and running from the summer of 1875 to 28 June 1904. It may be supplemented by reference to further sporadic publications of letters, most notably to the 145 items published in *Chekhov: literaturnoye nasledstvo* (1960), pp. 153–258; for a fuller account, see "O sudbe epistolyarnogo naslediya Chekhova" in *Works and Letters, 1974–82, Works* 1:295–318. By now the total of Chekhov's extant letters is "about 4,400" (ibid., p. 305). Of the 487 letters in vols. 1 and 2 of the letters in *Works and Letters, 1974–82*, only four (those to M. M. Dyukovsky) are published for the first time.

B. NOTEBOOKS

To the student of Chekhov's life and art his Notebooks are of particular importance. There are four of these, containing extensive manuscript entries which he began to make in mid-March 1891 and which he continued making until a few days before his death. The notebooks include a wealth of literary material—ideas for plots and characters. Some of these remained unexploited, but many can be related to the stories or plays in which they were used, often after a considerable delay. The Notebooks also contain much miscellaneous material in the form of diary entries; addresses of friends and colleagues; medical prescriptions; jottings relating to the upkeep of houses and gardens; lists of books to be read or acquired for Taganrog Public Library.

C. DIARY

A diary of Chekhov's, covering the years 1896–1903, has survived and is published in W., 12:332–9. Though it does contain some useful material it is too short to serve as a major source.

D. MISCELLANEOUS

Other material, not covered above, includes Chekhov's reports on his service as medical administrator in the Melikhovo area in the years of the cholera epidemics (1892–3); an appeal for needy sufferers from tuberculosis in Yalta; entries in albums; and even two poems, each a comic quatrain.

Chekhov in English

This appendix indicates the availability of Chekhov's work in English translation; also of critical, biographical and other works on Chekhov in the English language.

A. IMAGINATIVE WORKS

Chekhov's major imaginative writings have been translated very frequently. For instance, the present biographer's version of *The Cherry Orchard* (1964) was the seventeenth English translation of that play to appear in print.[1] But the greater part of the voluminous early material remains untranslated, having only limited documentary interest.

Renderings of Chekhov into English are, in general, highly unsystematic and unscholarly. Rarely do translators indicate what principle of selection they have adopted. Nor do they, with rare exceptions, give the date and title of the Russian originals. This omission is especially exasperating in the case of an author whose published contributions total well over 600 items, including several pairs of works identically entitled in Russian. Moreover, not a few stories bear titles of the type *Anguish, Grief, Sorrow, Misery, A Misfortune* and the like. Translations of these can sometimes be related to their originals only at the expense of considerable bibliographical sorrow, grief, anguish etcetera.

The only systematic multi-volume edition of Chekhov's works in English is *The Oxford Chekhov*, edited and translated by the author of the present biography (O.U.P., London, from 1964 onwards).

The Oxford Chekhov contains all the drama: the ten short plays in vol. 1, and the seven long plays in vols. 2–3. It will also contain, when completed, all the fiction of the mature period 1888–1904, in vols. 4–9; at the time of writing vols. 5, 6, 8 and 9 have been published, while vols. 4 and 7 still await publication. Within this framework, and with certain other reservations set out in the prefaces to individual volumes, the works are published in chronological order. To avoid the kind of confusion which makes the bibliography of English translations from Chekhov a nightmare, the Russian title of each work is cited on its title page together with the date of first publication. The edition includes appendixes giving the textual history of each work together with an account of its composition and translations of the main variants. Each volume contains explanatory notes and a bibliography listing earlier English translations. The principles and conventions of the edition are defined in the prefaces, and the work has been accompanied by a close study of earlier versions.

It is hoped to extend this edition, from a tenth volume onwards, with selections from the stories of the early period.

Two selections of stories from *The Oxford Chekhov* have been issued in paperback, as *Chekhov: Seven Stories* (O.U.P., London 1974), and *Eleven Stories* (1975). Also available in paperback editions are the *Oxford Chekhov* translations of all the short plays; and of *Ivanov, The Wood Demon, The Seagull, Uncle Vanya, Three Sisters, The Cherry Orchard*.

The most prolific translator of Chekhov into English has been Constance Garnett. She published 17 volumes of Chekhov translations in all, between 1916 and 1926: 13 volumes of stories, 2 of plays and 2 of selected letters. The stories translated by Garnett total 201, of which 54 are from the mature period (covered by vols. 4–9 of *The Oxford Chekhov*), while 147 are from the early period. Of the 240 stories which Chekhov included in the "Collected Works" edited by himself, Garnett translated 188; of the 348 items which he rejected she translated 13. The order in which her translations of the stories are printed follows no chronological or other discernible pattern.

Though Garnett is far from the least competent of Chekhov translators, her English is marred by an element of quaintness. This has sometimes been romantically misconstrued by readers unfamiliar with Russian as echoing some equivalent element in an original which, whatever qualities it may or may not possess, is most emphatically not quaint. Investigation suggests that the exotic patina of Garnett's and some other renderings may derive from hastiness of execution; and that it is "translationese", not any considered stylistic policy, which has imparted to her Chekhov that curious remoteness sometimes welcomed by the imperceptive as quintessentially "Russian". Garnett's is not, as is sometimes mistakenly believed, deliberately cultivated "period" English; nor, if it were, would that be an appropriate medium in which to render an author who was the last man in the world to write deliberately cultivated "period" Russian. Of English as used shortly after Chekhov's day George Calderon's *The Seagull* and *The Cherry Orchard* (London, 1912) supply a variety more natural than Garnett's, and therefore better attuned to a writer whose Russian is so authentically Russian.[2]

Of the 335 narrative-type works of the early period which eluded Garnett, the great majority remains mercifully untranslated. However, nine translators in all, operating between 1915 and 1960, have mopped up some of this material— unsystematically, for the most part, and often duplicating each other's work. Some 60 to 80 titles from the 335 will be found among the miscellaneous items (many duplicating or anticipating material included in the Garnett corpus) covered by the following 11 volumes.

Stories of Russian Life, tr. Marian Fell (New York, 1915)
Russian Silhouettes: More Stories of Russian Life, tr. Marian Fell (London, 1915)
The Bet and Other Stories, tr. S. Koteliansky and J. M. Murry (Dublin, 1915)

The Grasshopper and Other Stories, tr. A. E. Chamot (London, 1926)

The Shooting Party, tr. A. E. Chamot (London, 1926)

Plays and Stories, tr. S. S. Koteliansky (London, 1937)

Short Stories, tr. A. E. Chamot (London, ?1946)

The Woman in the Case, and Other Stories, tr. April FitzLyon and Kyril Zinovieff (London, 1953)

St. Peter's Day, and Other Tales, tr. Frances H. Jones (New York, 1959)

The Unknown Chekhov, tr. Avrahm Yarmolinsky (London, 1959)

Early Stories, tr. Nora Gottlieb (London, 1960)

For further information on these works, most of which are out of print, see the publications by Heifetz and Yachnin in the Bibliography; see also the Bibliographical Index in Magarshack, *Chekhov: a Life*.

To the above must be added a new publication, issued as the present volume goes to press.

Chuckle with Chekhov: a Selection of Comic Stories by Anton Chekhov, chosen and translated by Harvey Pitcher in collaboration with James Forsyth (Swallow House Books, Cromer, Norfolk, 1975)

This welcome publication of early material is systematic, scholarly, stylistically appropriate and creatively ingenious.

B. WORKS NOT INTENDED FOR PUBLICATION

Letters of Anton Tchehov to his Family and Friends, tr. Constance Garnett (London, 1920)

The Note-books of Anton Tchekhov together with Reminiscences of Tchekhov by Maxim Gorky, tr. S. S. Koteliansky and Leonard Woolf (Richmond, Surrey, 1921)

Letters on the Short Story, the Drama and other Literary Topics. By Anton Chekhov. Selected and ed. Louis S. Friedland (New York, 1924)

The Life and Letters of Anton Tchekhov, tr. and ed. S. S. Koteliansky and Philip Tomlinson (London, 1925)

The Letters of Anton Pavlovitch Tchehov to Olga Leonardovna Knipper, tr. Constance Garnett (London, 1926)

The Personal Papers of Anton Chekhov. Introduction by Matthew Josephson (New York, 1948)

The Selected Letters of Anton Chekhov, ed. Lillian Hellman, tr. Sidonie Lederer (New York, 1955)

Letters of Anton Chekhov, tr. Michael Henry Heim in collaboration with Simon Karlinsky. Selection, Commentary and Introduction by Simon Karlinsky (New York, 1973)

Letters of Anton Chekhov. Selected and ed. Avrahm Yarmolinsky (New York, 1973)

C. BIOGRAPHICAL AND CRITICAL STUDIES

Leon Shestov, *Anton Tchekhov and Other Essays* (Dublin and London, 1916)

William Gerhardi, *Anton Chekhov: a Critical Study* (London, 1923)

Oliver Elton, *Chekhov* (The Taylorian Lecture, 1929; Oxford, 1929)

Nina Andronikova Toumanova, *Anton Chekhov: the Voice of Twilight Russia* (London, 1937)

W. H. Bruford, *Chekhov and his Russia: a Sociological Study* (London, 1948)

Ronald Hingley, *Chekhov: a Biographical and Critical Study* (London, 1950)

Irene Nemirovsky, *A Life of Chekhov*. Tr. from the French by Erik de Mauny (London, 1950)

Lydia Avilov, *Chekhov in my Life: a Love Story*. Tr. with an Introduction by David Magarshack (London, 1950)

David Magarshack, *Chekhov: a Life* (London, 1952)

David Magarshack, *Chekhov the Dramatist* (London, 1952)

Vladimir Yermilov [Ermilov], *Anton Pavlovich Chekhov, 1860–1904*. Tr. Ivy Litvinov (Moscow, 1956; London, 1957)

W. H. Bruford, *Anton Chekhov* (London, 1957)

T. Eekman, ed., *Anton Čechov, 1860–1960* (Leiden, 1960)

Beatrice Saunders, *Tchehov the Man* (London, 1960)

Ernest J. Simmons, *Chekhov: a Biography* (Boston, 1962)

Maurice Valency, *The Breaking String: the Plays of Anton Chekhov* (New York, 1966)

Thomas Winner, *Chekhov and his Prose* (New York, 1966)

Robert Louis Jackson, ed., *Chekhov: a Collection of Critical Essays* (Englewood Cliffs, N. J., 1967)

Nils Åke Nilsson, *Studies in Čechov's Narrative Technique:* The Steppe *and* The Bishop (Stockholm, 1968)

Karl D. Kramer, *The Chameleon and the Dream: the Image of Reality in Čexov's Stories* (The Hague, 1970)

J. L. Styan, *Chekhov in Performance: a Commentary on the Major Plays* (Cambridge, 1971)

David Magarshack, *The Real Chekhov: an Introduction to Chekhov's Last Plays* (London, 1972)

Virginia Llewellyn Smith, *Anton Chekhov and the Lady with the Dog*. Foreword by Ronald Hingley (London, 1973)

Harvey Pitcher, *The Chekhov Play: a New Interpretation* (London, 1973)

Sophie Laffitte, *Chekhov, 1860–1904*. Tr. from the French by Moura Budberg and Gordon Latta (London, 1974)

Donald Rayfield, *Chekhov: the Evolution of his Art* (London, 1975)

Kornei Chukovsky, *Chekhov the Man*. Tr. Pauline Rose (London, n.d.)

REFERENCE NOTES

There are so many references in this book that it has often been necessary to consolidate them in groups at or near the end of the paragraph to which they apply in order to avoid disfiguring the body of the text with an excess of figures.

Except where otherwise indicated, references beginning with the word "to" relate to letters written by Chekhov, as published in *Works, 1944–51*. The references "to Alexander", "to Michael" and "to Mariya" indicate letters from Chekhov to his brothers and sister. The references "from L. S. Mizinova" and "from L. B. Yavorskaya", followed by a date, refer to unpublished letters from these ladies to Chekhov, as preserved in the *Otdel rukopisey* (Manuscript Department) of the Lenin Library, Moscow. Mizinova's letters are there catalogued under 331. 52. 2a; Yavorskaya's under 331. 64. 34.

Other references are by authors' or editors' names, or by book titles, as listed in alphabetical order in the Bibliography of Source Material, pp. 345–8.

The following abbreviations are used.

AChiys	CHEKHOV, M. P., *Anton Chekhov i yego syuzhety* (Moscow, 1923)
Alexander, *Pisma*	CHEKHOV, AL. P., *Pisma A. P. Chekhovu yego brata Aleksandra Chekhova*, ed. I. S. Yezhov (Moscow, 1939)
Chit	SURKOV, YE. D., ed., *Chekhov i teatr: pisma, felyetony, sovremenniki o Chekhove-dramaturge* (Moscow, 1961)
Knip.	DERMAN, A. B., ed., *Perepiska A. P. Chekhova i O. L. Knipper*, 2 vols. (Moscow, 1934, 1936)
Ln	VINOGRADOV, V. V., and others, ed., *Literaturnoye nasledstvo: Chekhov* (Moscow, 1960)
Mariya, *Idp*	CHEKHOVA, M. P., *Iz dalyokogo proshlogo* (Moscow, 1960)
Mariya, *Pisma*	CHEKHOVA, M. P., *Pisma k bratu A. P. Chekhovu* (Moscow, 1954)
Otd. ruk.	*Otdel rukopisey*: the Manuscript Department of the Lenin Library, Moscow
Pisma, 1912–16	CHEKHOV, ANTON, *Pisma*, ed. M. P. Chekhova, 6 vols. (Moscow, 1912–16)
tr.	translated by
Vokrug	CHEKHOV, M. P., *Vokrug Chekhova: vstrechi i vpechatleniya* (Moscow, 1959)
W. and *Works, 1944–51*	CHEKHOV, ANTON, *Polnoye sobraniye sochineniy i pisem*, ed. S. D. Balukhaty and others, 20 vols. (Moscow, 1944–51)
Works, 1960–4	CHEKHOV, ANTON, *Sobraniye sochineniy*, ed. V. V. Yermilov and others, 12 vols. (Moscow, 1960–4)
Works and Letters, 1974–82	CHEKHOV, ANTON, *Polnoye sobraniye sochineniy i pisem A. P. Chekhova*, as announced (in 1974) for publication in 1974–82 (see above, pp. xiii ff. and below, pp. 345–6)

CHAPTER 1 TAGANROG

The Grocer's Son (pp. 1–11)

1 Gitovich, 10–11. **2** To Mariya, 29 Apr. 1890. **3** *Vokrug*, 47–50. **4** Sobolev (1934), 14; Linin, 33. **5** To M. M. Chokhov, 4 Nov. 1877. **6** W., 13:303, 307–9. **7** *AChiys*, 15–17; Izmaylov, 30. **8** Izmaylov, 10; *Vokrug*, 34–6. **9** Sobolev (1934), 6. **10** *Ln*, 916–24. **11** Alexander, in Brodsky, 55–8. **12** M. I. Morozova, in Linin, 26–8. **13** Alexander, in Brodsky, 29–35. **14** Ibid., 30, 42–6; Alexander, in Golubov, 33. **15** Mariya, *Idp*, 16; *Vokrug*, 43. **16** *Vokrug*, 33–4. **17** Mariya, *Idp*, 15–18; *AChiys*, 11. **18** W., 15:339, 344. **19** W., 14:278; 15:403; 16:132. **20** Hingley, 5; Izmaylov, 25–6; Sobolev (1934), 14. **21** W., 8:420. **22** To A. S. Suvorin, 29 Aug. 1888. **23** W., 14:326; Linin, 28, 34. **24** To A. S. Suvorin, 7 Jan. 1889. **25** Alexander, in Brodsky, 36–7; to Alexander, 2 Jan. 1889. **26** To A. S. Suvorin, 21 Jan. 1895. **27** *AChiys*, 12. **28** Mariya, *Idp*, 17. **29** *Vokrug*, 53. **30** Linin, 38.

Early Schooldays (pp. 11–18)

1 Linin, 33. **2** Gitovich, 12–13; Izmaylov, 19–20; Roskin, 11; Sobolev (1934), 13. **3** Izmaylov, 55–6. **4** Florinsky, 2:1038–9. **5** Roskin, 64. **6** W., 5:435. **7** Izmaylov, 42; Sobolev (1934), 37. **8** Izmaylov, 41; Sobolev (1934), 27. **9** Linin, 42; Sobolev (1934), 28–9. **10** *Vokrug*, 32. **11** Ibid. **12** Sobolev (1934), 17; Linin, 36. **13** *Vokrug*, 55–9. **14** To A. S. Suvorin, 29 Aug. 1888. **15** *Vokrug*, 60–2, 65. **16** Gitovich, 14.

Alone in Taganrog (pp. 18–27)

1 Alexander, in Brodsky, 52–4; Gitovich, 20. **2** Gitovich, 15. **3** *Vokrug*, 50. **4** Roskin, 49. **5** *Vokrug*, 64; Roskin, 52. **6** Alexander, *Pisma*, 44; Mariya, *Idp*, 22–3. **7** Alexander, *Pisma*, 45–7. **8** Ibid., 37, 49. **9** Sobolev (1934), 32–3; W., 13:23. **10** W., 13:22, 28; Mariya, *Idp*, 25–6; *Vokrug*, 74; Alexander, *Pisma*, 132–3. **11** W., 13:546. **12** To M. M. Chokhov, 1 Dec. 1876. **13** To the same, 10 May, 29 July 1877. **14** To Michael, 6–8 Apr. 1879. **15** M. A. Rabinovich, in Linin, 44. **16** Linin, 36; W., 13:26. **17** *Vokrug*, 67; W., 13:26; 15:321. **18** Linin, 30–2, 40; *AChiys*, 13; Feyder, 5; Sobolev (1934), 19; Izmaylov, 33, 45. **19** Izmaylov, 45, 47. **20** Feyder, 6–7; Linin, 40; Mariya, *Idp*, 18. **21** I. P. Chekhov, in Feyder, 6. **22** Sobolev (1934), 42; *Vokrug*, 53; Linin, 42. **23** Gitovich, 35; Izmaylov, 39. **24** To Michael, 6–8 Apr. 1879. **25** Alexander, *Pisma*, 47–8, 51; *AChiys*, 23. **26** Alexander, *Pisma*, 50, 427; *AChiys*, 23. **27** *Works and Letters*, 1974–82, *Works* 1:555–7. **28** Izmaylov, 38; W., 13:24; Linin, 44–5. **29** Gitovich, 38–9. **30** Feyder, 11.

CHAPTER 2 EARLY "CHEKHONTE"

Domestic and Student Life (pp. 28–33)

1 *Vokrug*, 80. **2** To S. Kramarev, 8 May 1881. **3** *Vokrug*, 72–3, 78. **4** Ibid., 82. **5** Ibid., 81. **6** Gitovich, 55, 66. **7** W., 13:63, 83, 90, 96. **8** N. I. Korobov, in Gitovich, 46. **9** *Vokrug*, 125–6. **10** W., 1:473–7; *Vokrug*, 88. **11** Z. Ye. Pichugin in *Ln*, 543–4. **12** K. A. Korovin in *Ln*, 550–1. **13** Ibid., 551–4. **14** Alexander, *Pisma*, 69; Gitovich, 42.

Apprentice Author (pp. 33–8)

1 W., 20:210; see also W., 14:422, 583. **2** W., 1:539–40. **3** Gitovich, 41, 44–5. **4** *Vokrug*, 89–92. **5** W., 1:559. **6** *AChiys*, 23. **7** *Oxford Chekhov*, 2:282–3; Gitovich, 45. **8** *Oxford Chekhov*, 2:1–5.

CHAPTER 3 "SPLINTERS"

The Ascendancy of "Oskolki" (pp. 39–50)

1 N. A. Leykin, in Feyder, 22–3. 2 W., 13:45, 76, 115. 3 W., 13:151–2, 462. 4 Myshkovskaya, 104. 5 W., 13:59–60, 63, 71; Myshkovskaya, 30. 6 W., 2:507, 531. 7 W., 1:39. 8 To N. A. Leykin, 7 Oct. 1884. 9 Izmaylov, 179–93. 10 *Works and Letters, 1974–82, Works*, 1:550–2. 11 To N. A. Leykin, 1 Apr. 1885; Gitovich, 97. 12 N. A. Leykin, in Gitovich, 83. 13 To N. A. Leykin, 25–6 June, 26–30 June 1883. 14 W., 13:77, 129. 15 To Alexander, 13 May 1883. 16 To N. A. Leykin, 20–1 Aug. 1883. 17 W., 13:62–3, 112; *Vokrug*, 112. 18 To M. Ye. Chekhov, 31 Jan. 1885.

The Young Doctor (pp. 50–6)

1 To N. A. Leykin, 25 June 1884. 2 *Vokrug*, 132; W., 13:102. 3 *AChiys*, 29–30; *Vokrug*, 129. 4 W., 13:140; Gitovich, 92. 5 *Vokrug*, 134–5. 6 Belchikov, 107 ff. 7 To G. I. Rossolimo, 11 Oct. 1899. 8 Ye. K. Markova, in Gitovich, 98; W., 13:119. 9 To N. A. Leykin, 14 Sept. 1885. 10 W., 2:405. 11 P. Zelenin, in Gitovich, 99. 12 W., 7:174. 13 To Alexander, 17–18 Apr., 13 May 1883. 14 To N. A. Leykin, 27 June 1884. 15 To Alexander, 15–20 Oct. 1883.

CHAPTER 4 "THE ST. PETERSBURG GAZETTE"

The Ascendancy of "Peterburgskaya gazeta" (pp. 57–60)

1 To N. A. Leykin, 26 Nov. 1884. 2 W., 3:573; 13:131. 3 To N. A. Leykin, 12 Oct. 1885. 4 W., 4:376.

Babkino (pp. 60–4)

1 Mariya, *Idp*, 36. 2 To N. A. Leykin, 9 May 1885. 3 W., 13:136, 536–7. 4 N. V. Golubeva, in *Ln*, 562. 5 Mariya, *Idp*, 40. 6 N. V. Golubeva, in *Ln*, 563. 7 *Vokrug*, 139–40; Mariya, *Idp*, 47. 8 Mariya, *Idp*, 34–5, 43–4; *Vokrug*, 124.

CHAPTER 5 "NEW TIME"

The Hub of Empire (pp. 65–71)

1 To M. G. Chekhov, 11 Apr. 1886. 2 W., 13:157, 164. 3 Izmaylov, 6; W., 13:154–6, 171. 4 W., 13:176, 188, 206; *Vokrug*, 168–71. 5 Ambler, 174–5. 6 To V. V. Bilibin, 28 Feb. 1886. 7 To the same, 14 Feb. 1886, in *Ln*, 165; Gitovich, 124. 8 Gitovich, 128–9. 9 To D. V. Grigorovich, 28 Mar. 1886. 10 To V. V. Bilibin, 4 Apr. 1886. 11 To Alexander, 6 Apr. 1886. 12 To Michael, 25 Apr. 1886. 13 W., 13:213–16. 14 Gitovich, 138–9; W., 13:226. 15 Gitovich, 297, 538; W., 13:194.

At Home and on Holiday (pp. 71–8)

1 Mariya, *Idp*, 48. 2 W., 13:369; Mariya, *Idp*, 49–51. 3 W., 13:161, 208. 4 *Vokrug*, 144–5. 5 W., 13:612. 6 *Ln*, 164, 168. 7 W., 13:309, 334, 336, 357, 359. 8 To V. V. Bilibin, 4 Apr. 1886, in *Ln*, 172. 9 To Alexander, 6 Apr. 1886. 10 To N. P. Chekhov, Mar. 1886, in *Works and Letters, 1974–82, Letters*, 1:223–4. 11 To Michael, 3 Dec. 1887. 12 W., 13:165, 201. 13 W., 13:219, 266. 14 To F. O. Shekhtel, 11–14 Mar. 1887; *Works and Letters, 1974–82, Letters* 1:248. 15 To Mariya, 7–19 Apr. 1887. 16 W., 13:303, 309. 17 W., 13:320, 323. 18 W., 6:519; 13:328. 19 To Mariya, 17–19 Apr. 1887.

Metropolitan Triumphs (pp. 78–80)

1 W., 13:293, 365, 383–4, 517. **2** W., 13:372, 401. **3** W., 13:232, 248, 264, 267–8.
4 W., 13:265–6, 268. **5** W., 13:285, 290, 498. **6** To M. V. Kiseleva, 17 Mar. 1887.
7 See Gleb Struve, "Chekhov i Grigorovich", in Eekman, especially pp. 244–5.
8 W., 13:172, 351.

The Ascendancy of "Novoye vremya" (pp. 80–7)

1 W., 4:492, 646; 6:430–1. **2** To G. M. Chekhov, 17 Oct. 1887. **3** To A. S. Suvorin,
27 Mar. 1894. **4** A. S. Lazarev-Gruzinsky, in Gitovich, 148. **5** W., 5:121. **6** To M. V.
Kiseleva, 14 Jan. 1887. **7** To Ya. P. Polonsky, 25 Mar. 1888. **8** To Alexander, 10 May
1886. **9** W., 13:248, 261, 278.

Stage Début (pp. 87–93)

1 Oxford Chekhov, 1:171–3; W., 13:265. **2** To A. F. Marks, 1 Oct. 1902; Oxford Chekhov,
1:189–90. **3** Gitovich, 165; Vokrug, 176. **4** W., 13:392–6. **5** W., 11:540–1; 13:393.
6 Oxford Chekhov, 2:290 ff. **7** W., 14:268, 290; Oxford Chekhov, 2:292. **8** Oxford
Chekhov, 2:208. **9** To Alexander, 10–12 Oct. 1887.

CHAPTER 6 GROWING PAINS
"The Steppe" (pp. 94–8)

1 W., 14:8, 23. **2** W., 14:11, 37. **3** W., 14:14, 28–9, 33. **4** A. N. Pleshcheyev, in
Feyder, 96. **5** Ibid., 94. **6** N. K. Mikhaylovsky, in Feyder, 97–9. **7** Feyder, 99–101.
8 W., 7:524. **9** W., 14:54, 59. **10** To Ya. P. Polonsky, 18 Jan. 1888. **11** W., 14:62,
71, 76–7. **12** A. S. Lazarev-Gruzinsky, in Gitovich, 192. **13** W., 13:387; 14:88. **14** W.,
14:66, 70, 89, 95, 513. **15** W., 14:78, 100.

Southern Travels (pp. 98–102)

1 W., 14:43, 61, 65, 86. **2** Pisma, 1912–16, 2:90. **3** Alexander, Pisma, 210. **4** Vokrug,
163–6, 172–4. **5** Mariya, Idp, 79–80; to A. S. Suvorin, 30 May 1888. **6** W., 14:124,
127–9, 153. **7** W., 14:134–7, 254. **8** To A. S. Suvorin, 25 July 1888. **9** W., 14:146–9.
10 AChiys, 58, 63–4. **11** W., 14:341, 379. **12** To O. L. Knipper, 9 Feb. 1903. **13** Pisma,
1912–16, 2:384. **14** W., 14:133, 386.

Domestic Trials (pp. 102–7)

1 W., 14:259, 429; Vokrug, 191. **2** W., 14:60, 175. **3** Vokrug, 190. **4** To A. S. Suvorin,
14 Oct. 1888; emphasis added. **5** To Alexander, 26 Apr. 1888. **6** To the same, 2 Jan.
1889. **7** W., 14:50, 133–4, 137, 450. **8** To A. S. Suvorin, 17 Mar. 1890. **9** To A. S.
Kiselev, 15 May 1888. **10** W., 14:43, 60, 125; Vokrug, 185. **11** To Alexander, 28 Aug. 1888.
12 W., 14:34, 117; Mariya, Idp, 71. **13** Vokrug, 192; Grossman, passim; Mariya, Idp, 143.

The Theatre (pp. 107–13)

1 To Ya. P. Polonsky, 22 Feb. 1888. **2** To I. L. Leontyev (Shcheglov), 2 Nov. 1888.
3 W., 14:222, 259, 295–6, 358; Ln, 174. **4** Oxford Chekhov, 1:178–9; W., 14:246–9.
5 Oxford Chekhov, 2:284–333; W., 11:465–89, 509–44. **6** Gitovich, 220. **7** W., 14:299,
301, 323; Gitovich, 221. **8** W., 14:223, 296, 357, 427, 431, 441. **9** To Alexander,
11 Apr. 1889. **10** To the same, 8 May 1889. **11** W., 14:293, 316. **12** Oxford Chekhov,
3:3; W., 14:407, 412. **13** P. M. Svobodin, in Chit, 211–12. **14** To A. N. Pleshcheyev,

21 Oct. 1889. **15** A. P. Lensky to Chekhov, in *Chit*, 214. **16** To A. P. Lensky, 2 Nov. 1889. **17** *Vokrug*, 189; Gitovich, 250. **18** Izmaylov, 303. **19** Gitovich, 258–9. **20** To A. I. Urusov, 16 Oct. 1899.

Stories (pp. 113–19)

1 W., 14:187–8, 518. **2** W., 14:325, 405. **3** W., 14:416; *Ln*, 484. **4** To A. S. Suvorin, 1 Apr. 1890. **5** To the same, 12 Nov. 1889. **6** Elton, 20; Hingley, 99 ff. **7** W., 7:188. **8** Gitovich, 259. **9** W., 14:229–30. **10** To A. S. Suvorin, 15 Nov. 1888. **11** W., 14:396, 400–3; 15:37. **12** W., 14:417, 422. **13** To A. N. Pleshcheyev, 30 Sept. 1889.

Unsolved Problems (pp. 119–26)

1 W., 14:183, 208. **2** To A. S. Suvorin, 30 May 1888. **3** *Vokrug*, 129; W., 14:121. **4** W., 14:78, 172, 257–8; 15:36. **5** To A. S. Suvorin, 18–23 Dec. 1889. **6** To the same, 4 May 1889. **7** To the same, 8 Apr. 1889. **8** W., 13:373; 14:36, 150, 209. **9** W., 14:328, 330. **10** W., 14:365, 373. **11** To A. N. Pleshcheyev, 4 Oct. 1888. **12** I. L. Leontyev (Shcheglov), in Feyder, 121. **13** W., 14:154, 177, 508–9. **14** To V. M. Lavrov, 10 Apr. 1890. **15** W., 14:226, 340, 380. **16** W., 14:184, 217. **17** W., 15:45–6; Gitovich, 222, 231, 237. **18** W., 14:421, 437. **19** W., 14:323, 353–4. **20** To I. L. Leontyev (Shcheglov), 22 Mar. 1890.

CHAPTER 7   SAKHALIN

Prelude to a Mission (pp. 127–31)

1 W., 10:493–4; *Vokrug*, 211. **2** W., 15:28, 43. **3** W., 10:535–6; Tupper, 136–7. **4** W., 10:519 ff. **5** W., 15:16–17, 19, 24, 36. **6** To A. S. Suvorin, 9 Mar. 1890. **7** W., 15:13, 30. **8** W., 14:151, 154, 169, 183, 294. **9** W., 15:13, 29, 43. **10** W., 15:56–8. **11** W., 15:483.

Outward Bound (pp. 131–6)

1 W., 15:63–9. **2** To Mariya, 14–17 May 1890. **3** Ibid. **4** To M. V. Kiseleva, 7 May 1890. **5** To Mariya, 14–17 May 1890. **6** W., 10:518; 15:86. **7** W., 15:85–91. **8** W., 10:361–6. **9** *Pisma, 1912–16*, 3:112; to Mariya, 14–17 May 1890. **10** To A. N. Pleshcheyev, 5 June 1890. **11** To N. A. Leykin, 5 June 1890. **12** *Pisma, 1912–16*, 3:106–7. **13** W., 15:111. **14** *Pisma, 1912–16*, 3:129. **15** W., 10:9. **16** W., 15:119–21. **17** W., 10:23.

Devil's Island (pp. 136–41)

1 W., 10:487, 500; 15:9, 464; Gitovich, 252–4. **2** W., 10:26, 31, 384. **3** Gitovich, 271–2. **4** W., 10:64–5, 357–8. **5** W., 10:403–4. **6** Knyazeva, 181–2. **7** To A. S. Suvorin, 11 Sept. 1890. **8** W., 10:22, 63. **9** W., 10:91–107. **10** W., 10:312; 15:126. **11** W., 10:96, 313, 320. **12** W., 10:295, 299 ff.; 15:126. **13** W., 10:232. **14** W., 10:212–13. **15** W., 10:214. **16** W., 10:216. **17** W., 10:235. **18** To A. F. Koni, 26 Jan. 1891. **19** To his mother, 6 Oct. 1890.

Mission Completed (pp. 141–5)

1 W., 15:32, 130. **2** *Pisma, 1912–16*, 3:145. **3** Ibid., 3:146. **4** W., 15:131–41. **5** *Vokrug*, 215–17. **6** W., 15:129–32. **7** W., 15:133, 172. **8** W., 15:201, 205, 208, 238. **9** W., 10:375. **10** W., 16:111–13. **11** W., 10:511–13. **12** To A. S. Suvorin, 20 May 1891. **13** I. A. Bunin, in Golubov, 534.

CHAPTER 8 BETWEEN SAKHALIN AND MELIKHOVO

Reluctant Metropolitan (pp. 146–8)

1 W., 15:134, 144. **2** W., 15:135–41. **3** W., 15:145–56. **4** W., 15:149, 156. **5** W., 15:159–61.

Chekhov goes West (pp. 148–51)

1 *Pisma, 1912–16,* 3:194. **2** To Mariya, 20 Mar. 1891. **3** *Oxford Chekhov,* 6:237–8. **4** W., 15:177, 179. **5** W., 15:181–7, 191. **6** *Oxford Chekhov,* 8:85–6. **7** W., 15:185–7. **8** W., 15:190–2. **9** *Oxford Chekhov,* 6:241–3. **10** W., 15:194–5. **11** W., 15:209; 16:229; D. S. Merezhkovsky, in Feyder, 184.

"Dacha" Life (pp. 151–4)

1 W., 15:197–201. **2** *AChiys,* 84; *Oxford Chekhov,* 8:97; *Vokrug,* 224. **3** *AChiys,* 82–3; *Oxford Chekhov,* 8:104. **4** *Vokrug,* 224–5. **5** W., 7:487–97. **6** *Vokrug,* 225; Mariya, *Idp,* 105; to M. V. Kiseleva, 20 July 1891. **7** To Alexander, 24 Oct. 1891. **8** To A. S. Suvorin, 16 June 1891.

Moscow and Famine (pp. 154–7)

1 To M. N. Albov, 30 Sept. 1891. **2** To A. S. Suvorin, 27 Nov. 1891. **3** To Ye. P. Yegorov, 11 Dec. 1891. **4** W., 15:307–8, 316–18. **5** *Oxford Chekhov,* 6:51–2. **6** To L. A. Avilova, 29 Apr. 1892. **7** T. L. Shchepkina-Kupernik, in Kotov, 222–3; *Oxford Chekhov,* 6:271; Sobolev (1930), 143. **8** W., 15:261–89. **9** To A. S. Suvorin, 30 Nov. 1891; W., 7:499 ff. **10** W., 15:255. **11** W., 15:298–307.

CHAPTER 9 MELIKHOVO, 1892–7: PATTERNS OF LIFE

Landowner, Family Man and Host (pp. 158–67)

1 Gitovich, 310; Mariya, *Idp,* 111–12; *Vokrug,* 227–8. **2** Mariya, *Idp,* 115; *Vokrug,* 229–30. **3** W., 15:338, 340. **4** *Vokrug,* 229. **5** T. L. Shchepkina-Kupernik, in Kotov, 207. **6** *Vokrug,* 232. **7** W., 15:355–6; 16:93, 232; Kotov, 208. **8** To N. A. Leykin, 16 Apr. 1893. **9** W., 16:208, 221; 17:41. **10** Alexander, *Pisma,* 282–3. **11** Ibid., 283. **12** Mariya, *Idp,* 76–7. **13** T. L. Shchepkina-Kupernik, in Kotov, 230. **14** W., 15:427, 452. **15** *Vokrug,* 246. **16** W., 16:94, 298. **17** W., 15:383; 16:80, 361, 417. **18** To V. V. Bilibin, 18 Jan. 1895.

Peasant Benefactor and Chronicler (pp. 167–79)

1 To A. S. Suvorin, 17 Jan. 1897. **2** To the same, 6 Apr. 1892. **3** To the same, 15 May 1892. **4** W., 15:330, 414; Mariya, *Idp,* 119–20. **5** *Vokrug,* 234; W., 16:28, 54; *Pisma, 1912–16,* 4:233. **6** W., 16:73, 314. **7** I. N. Potapenko, in Golubov, 320–3. **8** W., 12:351; 15:415. **9** W., 15:410, 414, 418. **10** To A. S. Suvorin, 16 Aug. 1892. **11** W., 16:81, 118. **12** *Oxford Chekhov,* 9:74. **13** Gitovich, 371; W., 16:350; W., 17:28; Mariya, *Idp,* 123–4. **14** Mariya, *Idp,* 125. **15** Ibid., 124; to A. S. Suvorin, 26 June 1896. **16** W., 12:334; 17:19. **17** To A. S. Suvorin, 18 Aug. 1893. **18** *Oxford Chekhov,* 8:195. **19** Ibid., 8:221. **20** Ibid. **21** Ibid. **22** To A. S. Suvorin, 13 Apr. 1895. **23** W., 9:583–4; Hingley, 160. **24** W., 9:583–4. **25** To A. S. Suvorin, 1 Aug. 1892. **26** To the same, 26 June 1899. **27** W., 9:581–2. **28** *Oxford Chekhov,* 8:163–4. **29** W., 12:335. **30** To A. S. Suvorin, 1 Aug. 1892. **31** Hingley, 135.

Traveller (pp. 179-83)

1 To G. M. Chekhov, 6 Mar. 1894. **2** V. Fausek, in Golubov, 190-4. **3** I. A. Bunin and I. P. Chekhov, in W., 8:564. **4** W., 16:132-7. **5** To A. S. Suvorin, 15 Aug. 1894. **6** To L. S. Mizinova, 18 Sept. 1894. **7** W., 16:167-8; *Oxford Chekhov*, 8:83. **8** *Works, 1960-4*, 12:55. **9** *Pisma 1912-16*, 4:327. **10** W., 12:333; 16:355. **11** Baedeker, 102; I. N. Potapenko, in Kotov, 262. **12** W., 16:97, 336. **13** T. L. Shchepkina-Kupernik, in Kotov, 198-200; I. N. Potapenko, in Kotov, 237-8.

CHAPTER 10   MELIKHOVO 1892-7: LADIES' MAN

The Elusive Bachelor (pp. 184-6)

1 W., 16:228, 279. **2** *Oxford Chekhov*, 8:33. **3** To V. V. Bilibin, 22 Feb. 1892, in *Ln*, 191. **4** Llewellyn Smith, xv-xvi.

The Abstemious Lover (pp. 186-90)

1 From L. B. Yavorskaya, 2 Feb. 1894. **2** From the same, 17 Oct. 1894. **3** From the same, undated. **4** From the same, March (undated) 1895. **5** W., 16:201, 207, 231; *Works, 1960-4*, 12:65. **6** To A. S. Suvorin, 19 Jan. 1895. **7** To the same, 21 Jan. 1895. **8** Llewellyn Smith, 59. **9** To A. S. Suvorin, 11 Nov. 1893. **10** Ibid. **11** *Pisma, 1912-16*, 4:417; W., 16:154. **12** Alexander, *Pisma*, 275.

Lika Mizinov (pp. 190-6)

1 Mariya, *Idp*, 143. **2** From L. S. Mizinova, 17 June 1891. **3** *Oxford Chekhov*, 6:45. **4** From L. S. Mizinova, 8 Oct. 1892. **5** From the same, 18 June 1892. **6** To L. S. Mizinova, 23 June 1892. **7** From L. S. Mizinova, 13 July and 26 Nov. 1892; W., 15:402, 445. **8** From L. S. Mizinova, 2 Nov. 1893. **9** From the same, Dec. (undated) 1893. **10** From the same, 3 Apr. 1894. **11** To Mariya, 2 Oct. 1894. **12** From L. S. Mizinova, 3 Oct. 1894. **13** To L. S. Mizinova, 2 Oct. 1894. **14** From L. S. Mizinova, 20 Feb. 1898. **15** From the same, 22 Aug. 1893. **16** From the same, 24 June 1897. **17** I. N. Potapenko, in Kotov, 235-6. **18** T. L. Shchepkina-Kupernik, in Kotov, 221; Mariya, *Idp*, 151. **19** To A. S. Suvorin, 16 Dec. 1895. **20** To Mariya, 12 Oct. 1896.

Lydia Avilov (pp. 196-9)

1 Golubov, 200 ff. **2** *Ln*, 260; W., 15:596. **3** Mariya, *Idp*, 169. **4** L. A. Avilova, in Golubov, 204. **5** Ibid., 229. **6** W., 16:537. **7** L. A. Avilova, in Golubov, 249-50. **8** Unpublished letter (date illegible) from V. F. Komissarzhevskaya to Chekhov, *Otd. ruk.* 331.48.7. **9** N. A. Leykin, *Diary*, 7 and 9 Mar. 1895, in *Ln*, 502. **10** Bunin, 135; Llewellyn Smith, 97-108; Mariya, *Idp*, 167; see also "Avilova", as indexed in Magarshack (1952) and Simmons. **11** Kotov, 499.

The Women of Chekhov's Fiction (pp. 199-201)

1 From L. S. Mizinova, 12 Sept. 1897. **2** *Otd. ruk.* 331.56.38. **3** M. K. Zankovetskaya, in *Ln*, 593. **4** Llewellyn Smith, 124. **5** Ibid., 74 ff. **6** *AChiys*, 124; Sobolev (1930), 166. **7** To L. A. Avilova, 29 Apr. 1892.

CHAPTER 11   MELIKHOVO 1892-7: PATTERNS OF ART

The Literary Life (pp. 202-12)

1 Gitovich, 320. **2** I. N. Potapenko, in Kotov, 255-6; W., 16:102-3. **3** To A. S. Suvorin, 18 Aug. 1893. **4** W., 15:394; 16:134-5, 155. **5** W., 16:12, 159, 163. **6** I. N. Potapenko, in Kotov, 235, 244. **7** Mariya, *Idp*, 137. **8** W., 16:22, 67. **9** W., 16:104, 206. **10** W., 16:155, 190, 203, 233, 414. **11** W., 15:388; 16:58, 114, 142, 209, 346, 393. **12** T. L. Shchepkina-Kupernik, in Kotov, 232; W., 15:426. **13** W., 16:36, 114, 307. **14** A. S. Suvorin, in Feyder, 261; I. N. Potapenko, in Kotov, 236. **15** To P. V. Bykov, 4 May 1892. **16** To A. S. Suvorin, 17 Dec. 1892. **17** To Mariya, 11 Mar. 1893. **18** I. N. Potapenko, in Kotov, 236. **19** To A. V. Zhirkevich, 10 Mar. 1895. **20** To P. F. Iordanov, 19 Oct. 1896. **21** W., 16:203, 205, 324. **22** W., 15:352; 16:85, 234–5, 336. **23** W., 15:345, 375. **24** W., 16:184, 326. **25** To A. V. Zhirkevich, 2 Apr. 1895. **26** To Ye. M. Shavrova, 28 Feb. 1895. **27** W., 15:406; 16:60, 240. **28** To N. M. Yezhov, 22 Mar. 1893. **29** To A. S. Suvorin, 24 Feb. 1893. **30** To the same, 11 Mar. 1892. **31** W., 8:517; 15:245. **32** W., 9:578–9. **33** W., 16:385; *Oxford Chekhov*, 8:139, 189, 297–8. **34** To M. G. Vecheslov, 7 Nov. 1897, in *Ln*, 213. **35** To V. A. Goltsev, 28 Dec. 1893. **36** W., 16:347; Gitovich, 419. **37** W., 16:206, 393.

Encounters with Tolstoy (pp. 212–15)

1 To A. S. Suvorin, 7 Aug. 1893. **2** W., 18:313; Gitovich, 393. **3** W., 15:259; 16:32. **4** To A. N. Pleshcheyev, 15 Feb. 1890. **5** W., 15:136, 240–1. **6** W., 15:238–9, 415. **7** To A. S. Suvorin, 27 Mar. 1894.

Short Story Writer (pp. 215–20)

1 Hingley, 150. **2** *AChiys*, 124. **3** To F. D. Batyushkov, 15 Dec. 1897. **4** *AChiys*, 15–18, 110.

Playwright (pp. 220–6)

1 W., 16:271, 285. **2** To A. S. Suvorin, 8 Apr. 1892; *Oxford Chekhov*, 2:337. **3** I. N. Potapenko, in *Chit*, 224. **4** Ibid., 228; Ye. Karpov, ibid., 240. **5** Ye. Karpov, in *Chit*, 236. **6** Ibid., 238–9. **7** I. N. Potapenko, in *Chit*, 227. **8** A. I. Suvorina, in *Chit*, 232; Ye. Karpov, ibid., 240–1. **9** A. S. Suvorin, in Feyder, 261. **10** W., 11:575; *Chit*, 230, 233, 242, 475. **11** To A. S. Suvorin, 18 Oct. 1896. **12** W., 16:370–1, 387, 413. **13** Pitcher, 78. **14** Gitovich, 260, 282–3; W., 17:375; 19:199. **15** I. L. Leontyev (Shcheglov), in Kotov, 432. **16** To A. I. Urusov, 21 Nov. 1895. **17** To Yelizaveta Bila, 22 Apr. 1895, in *Ln*, 195. **18** W., 16:338, 386, 409. **19** Simmons, 200.

Intimations of Mortality (pp. 226–9)

1 I. N. Potapenko, in Kotov, 246; *Vokrug*, 260. **2** W., 16:58–60, 274; *AChiys*, 113. **3** W., 15:439; 16:145, 338. **4** To A. S. Suvorin, 24 Aug. 1893. **5** W., 16:97, 103, 328. **6** To A. S. Suvorin, 8 Apr. 1892. **7** *Vokrug*, 259; *AChiys*, 126. **8** Gitovich, 459; Suvorin, 150–1. **9** To A. S. Suvorin, 1 Apr. 1897. **10** L. A. Avilova, in Golubov, 256 ff.; W., 17:59. **11** W., 17:64–5. **12** To A. S. Suvorin, 1 Apr. 1897.

CHAPTER 12　BETWEEN MELIKHOVO AND YALTA
Melikhovo (pp. 230–1)

1 W., 17:54, 62. **2** To N. A. Leykin, 24 Apr. 1897, in *Ln*, 209. **3** W., 17:529; Gitovich, 475, 479. **4** W., 12:336; 17:77.

France (pp. 231–6)

1 W., 17:136–80. **2** W., 17:189–90. **3** To Mariya, 1 Jan. 1898. **4** *Ln*, 605 ff. **5** W., 17:133, 166, 222. **6** From L. S. Mizinova, 4 Oct. 1897. **7** *Oxford Chekhov*, 8:255. **8** Ibid., 9:ix–x. **9** Ibid., 9:229, 237. **10** M. M. Kovalevsky, in Golubov, 448. **11** W., 17:176, 178. **12** W., 17;161–2, 165, 178, 193, 258. **13** To A. S. Suvorin, 6 Feb. 1898;

W., 17:473. **14** To Alexander, 23 Feb. 1898; W., 17:476. **15** E.g. to Alexander, 30 July 1898. **16** W., 17:161, 171–2, 182, 215, 220, 232, 246. **17** To Mariya, 20 Apr. 1898.

Melikhovo (pp. 236–9)

1 To V. M. Lavrov, 25 Feb. 1898. **2** To A. F. Marks, 28 Sept. 1899. **3** To L. A. Avilova, 30 Aug. 1898. **4** W., 17:266, 485; Gitovich, 504, 506. **5** O. L. Knipper, in Kotov, 473. **6** To A. S. Suvorin, 8 Oct. 1898. **7** To Michael, 26 Oct. 1898.

Yalta (pp. 239–51)

1 To A. B. Tarakhovsky, 13 Sept. 1898. **2** W., 17:329–30. **3** Mariya, *Idp*, 190–1; W., 17:341; Golubov, 606. **4** To Mariya, 15 and 22 Nov. 1898. **5** W., 17:326, 335, 381, 386. **6** Gitovich, 540, 544–5. **7** *Oxford Chekhov*, 9:99. **8** Ibid., 9:74. **9** Ibid. **10** Mariya, *Idp*, 187; Vl. I. Nemirovich-Danchenko, in *Chit*, 303–4; K. S. Stanislavsky, in Kotov, 37. **11** *Oxford Chekhov*, 2:353; Vl. I. Nemirovich-Danchenko, in *Chit*, 305–6; K. S. Stanislavsky in Golubov, 375, 744. **12** Gitovich, 538. **13** W., 17:297, 344, 360–1; 18:442. **14** W., 18:27–8, 450. **15** To P. A. Sergeyenko, 1 Feb. 1899. **16** Mariya, *Idp*, 195; Gitovich, 542. **17** W., 18:29, 57–8. **18** W., 18:57, 59, 132. **19** W., 18:91, 156, 169. **20** W., 17:376; 18:221. **21** W., 17:375; 18:11. **22** To L. A. Avilova, 9 Mar. 1899. **23** W., 18:117; Gitovich, 557–9. **24** Maxim Gorky, in Gitovich, 557, 559, 563. **25** I. N. Altshuller, in Golubov, 585–6, 598–600. **26** Gitovich, 645; W., 18:267. **27** W., 17:322–3, 359, 364, 514; 18:76. **28** W., 17:335, 341; 18:22, 50, 98, 229, 238. **29** W., 17:369; 18:121.

Moscow, Melikhovo, Yalta (pp. 251–7)

1 To V. K. Kharkeyevich, 20 May 1899. **2** Maxim Gorky, in *Chit*, 359. **3** V. A. Telyakovsky, in Gitovich, 552. **4** *Chit*, 433–4; W., 18:235. **5** W., 18:167; Gitovich, 561. **6** K. S. Stanislavsky, in *Chit*, 255–6; W., 18:145, 276. **7** K. S. Stanislavsky, in Kotov, 41. **8** Alexander, *Pisma*, 527–8; W., 18:485. **9** A. S. Suvorin, in Gitovich, 485; W., 18:485. **10** To A. S. Suvorin, 2 Apr. 1899. **11** To the same, 24 Apr. 1899. **12** Ibid. **13** Gitovich, 575, 778; W., 18:174. **14** See Bibliography under "Derman" and "Vilenkin". **15** W., 18:172, 186; Knip., 1:53. **16** Knip., 1:61. **17** Gitovich, 574–5; Knip., 1:71. **18** Knip., 1:72, 122. **19** W., 18:199, 207, 212, 503–4. **20** Gitovich, 576.

Yalta (pp. 257–62)

1 W., 18:227–8, 360. **2** I. N. Altshuller, in Golubov, 600; W., 18:245. **3** Mariya, *Idp*, 202. **4** A. I. Kuprin, in Kotov, 140. **5** To Mariya, 21 Jan. 1900. **6** I. N. Altshuller, in Golubov, 587. **7** To Mariya, 19 Nov. 1899. **8** To O. L. Knipper, 30 Oct. 1899. **9** W., 18:235–7, 266. **10** *Oxford Chekhov*, 9:134. **11** W., 9:612. **12** Ibid. **13** To M. O. Menshikov, 26 Dec. 1899. **14** To A. S. Suvorin, 17 Jan. 1899.

CHAPTER 13 YALTA: THE YEARS OF "THREE SISTERS"

Yalta (pp. 263–5)

1 W., 18:294, 315. **2** W., 18:299. **3** W., 18:301–2, 311. **4** Knip., 1:122, 125, 133. **5** K. S. Stanislavsky, in Kotov, 46–51; W., 18:363. **6** *Oxford Chekhov*, 8:245; K. S. Stanislavsky, in Kotov, 52–3. **7** Kotov, 50; Gitovich, 621–2. **8** Kotov, 56; Gitovich, 622.

Union and Separation (pp. 265–9)

1 To Maxim Gorky, 12 July 1900. **2** Knip., 1:21 ff. **3** Vilenkin, 1:38. **4** Knip., 1:161. **5** Ibid., 1:156, 165, 171, 187; Gitovich, 630. **6** To O. L. Knipper, 27 Sept. 1900.

7 Knip, 1:197. **8** W., 18:387, 402; Knip., 1:207. **9** Knip., 1:151–2; W., 18:390–1. **10** To Maxim Gorky, 16 Oct. 1900.

Moscow, Nice, Italy (pp. 269–74)

1 O. L. Knipper, in Gitovich, 637. **2** Brisson, 50; Llewellyn Smith, 122–3; W., 18:411. **3** W., 18:418. **4** Gitovich, 632; W., 18:377, 397. **5** W., 18:421. **6** W., 18:425, 427, 432–3; 19:14, 29. **7** W., 18:425, 431–2; 19:10, 21. **8** To O. L. Knipper, 15 Sept. 1900. **9** To the same, 2, 21, 24 Jan. 1901. **10** To K. S. Stanislavsky, 2 Jan. 1901. **11** To O. L. Knipper, 20 Jan. 1901. **12** V. V. Luzhsky, in *Chit*, 353. **13** K. S. Stanislavsky, in Kotov, 61; Gitovich, 652. **14** W., 19:10, 15, 22.

Yalta (pp. 274–8)

1 To O. L. Knipper, 1 Mar. 1901. **2** W., 19:62, 76. **3** Knip., 1:310–11, 341. **4** Ibid., 1:324–40. **5** W., 19:62; Knip., 1:355. **6** Knip., 1:353, 370. **7** To O. L. Knipper, 11 Mar. 1901. **8** A. I. Kuprin, in Kotov, 137; I. N. Altshuller, in Golubov, 591. **9** A. I. Kuprin, in Kotov, 133; emphasis added. **10** Ibid., 139, 141, 146, 152. **11** Ibid., 139, 147, 150–2. **12** I. A. Bunin, in Golubov, 520. **13** Ibid., 512–14, 521, 534.

Married Bliss (pp. 278–85)

1 Knip., 1:379–86. **2** To O. L. Knipper, 26 Apr. 1901. **3** Knip., 1:398–9. **4** To Mariya, 20 May 1901. **5** Ibid.; emphasis added. **6** Mariya, *Pisma*, 182. **7** Gitovich, 664. **8** W., 19:92. **9** Vilenkin, 1:380; Mariya, *Idp*, 222; Mariya, *Pisma*, 184. **10** Mariya, *Pisma*, 184. **11** Gitovich, 666; to Maxim Gorky, 28 May 1901. **12** To Mariya, 2 June 1901. **13** To the same, 4 June 1901, in *Ln*, 236. **14** Mariya, *Pisma*, 184–6. **15** W., 19:99, 102–7. **16** *Oxford Chekhov*, 9:41. **17** To O. L. Knipper, 10 Mar. 1903. **18** I. N. Altshuller, in Golubov, 601–2. **19** I. A. Bunin, in Golubov, 534; Bunin, 134–5.

Yalta and Moscow (pp. 285–7)

1 W., 19:110, 114–15. **2** W., 19:110–11, 452. **3** W., 19:122, 129; Knip., 1:432, 439. **4** Knip., 1:425. **5** Vilenkin, 1:232. **6** V. V. Luzhsky, in Gitovich, 675–6. **7** Kotov, 64; Golubov, 394, 747; Gitovich, 677. **8** W., 19:139–40; Gitovich, 676.

CHAPTER 14   YALTA: THE YEARS OF "THE CHERRY ORCHARD"

Yalta (pp. 288–91)

1 W., 19:187–279. **2** W., 19:183, 185, 240. **3** W., 19:160, 186, 208, 239; Gitovich, 680–2. **4** W., 19:163, 197, 265. **5** To O. L. Knipper, 27 Nov. 1901. **6** *Oxford Chekhov*, 9:289–90. **7** W., 19:257–8. **8** Knip., 2:169, 199, 230–1, 247, 268–9. **9** Ibid., 2:393. **10** Ibid., 2:240, 242, 245. **11** Ibid., 2:313. **12** W., 19:278; Knip., 2:421; Gitovich, 705.

Wifemanship (pp. 291–5)

1 Gitovich, 709; W., 19:287. **2** W., 19:291, 301. **3** Gitovich, 711; Kotov, 293, 297, 302. **4** W., 19:312–13; Knip., 2:441, 513. **5** To O. L. Knipper, 24 Aug. 1902. **6** Knip., 2:445–6, 454, 464. **7** Ibid., 2:458, 460, 465–6. **8** Ibid., 2:475–6, 504. **9** W., 19:345. **10** Knip., 2:349, 362–3. **11** W., 19:278, 529. **12** To A. N. Veselovsky, 25 Aug. 1902. **13** W., 19:329, 357. **14** I. A. Bunin, in Golubov, 536–8.

Yalta (pp. 295–8)

1 W., 20:9–73. **2** Vilenkin, 1:152–3. **3** W., 19:393; 20:44–5. **4** W., 20:9; Vilenkin, 1:190, 218, 263. **5** To A. L. Vishnevsky, 3 Nov. 1899. **6** *Oxford Chekhov*, 9:xv–xvi.

7 Vilenkin, 1:192, 240–1, 410; W., 19:379; 20:14.   **8** *Oxford Chekhov*, 9:293 ff.   **9** Yermilov (1946), 416 ff.   **10** To O. L. Knipper, 23 Mar. 1903.   **11** W., 19:389; 20:60–1.

"The Cherry Orchard" (pp. 298–304)

1 W., 19:54, 76, 401; 20:37, 61.   **2** W., 20:101, 113.   **3** W., 20:104–12.   **4** W., 20:106–13, 119; Gitovich, 752.   **5** W., 20:121, 129, 131, 153.   **6** W., 20:155, 171; *Oxford Chekhov*, 9:xv–xvi.   **7** W., 20:159–63, 398–9; Gitovich, 769.   **8** W., 20:161–4, 174–7, 399.   **9** W., 20:164, 167, 174.   **10** *Oxford Chekhov*, 3:325–9; W., 20:186.   **11** W., 20:143, 189–90, 193–4.   **12** W., 20:195, 201; Gitovich, 784–5.   **13** Golubov, 514.   **14** Gitovich, 786.   **15** Ibid., 787; Feyder, 443.   **16** To A. S. Suvorin, 23 Jan. 1900; Gitovich, 788–9.   **17** W., 20:209–10, 215–16; K. S. Stanislavsky, in Feyder, 444.

Farewell to Yalta (pp. 305–11)

1 W., 20:236, 265.   **2** To O. L. Knipper, 18 Mar. 1904.   **3** W., 20:258, 265.   **4** To O. L. Knipper, 4 Mar. 1904.   **5** Maxim Gorky, in Kotov, 15.   **6** W., 20:248, 270, 273–4.   **7** W., 20:241.   **8** A. Ya. Beschinsky, in Gitovich, 800.   **9** S. Ya. Yelpatyevsky, in Gitovich, 796.   **10** Kotov, 142, 167, 183.   **11** To I. L. Leontyev (Shcheglov), 20 Jan. 1899.   **12** To I. I. Orlov, 22 Feb. 1899.   **13** M. A. Chlenov, in Golubov, 642.   **14** M. K. Pervukhin, in Golubov, 616; A. I. Kuprin, in Kotov, 133–4.   **15** W., 19:128; 20:181.   **16** W., 8:346; *Oxford Chekhov*, 3:170.   **17** To A. F. Marks, 23 Oct. 1902.   **18** W., 19:195, 406–7; 20:119.   **19** W., 18:295; 20:225.   **20** To M. O. Menshikov, 28 Jan. 1900.   **21** To Vl. I. Nemirovich-Danchenko, 2 Nov. 1903.

Farewell to Moscow (pp. 312–13)

1 N. D. Teleshov, in Gitovich, 809; W., 20:280–4.   **2** O. L. Knipper, V. Gilyarovsky, in Gitovich, 808–9; W., 20:291.   **3** W., 20:291–2, 301–2, 435.

Badenweiler (pp. 313–15)

1 Gitovich, 811; W., 20:293–5; Golubov, 605.   **2** W., 20:295–303; Gitovich, 811.   **3** W., 20:303–6.   **4** Gitovich, 815–16.   **5** G. B. Iollos and O. L. Knipper, in Feyder, 455–6 and Gitovich, 817.

CONCLUSION (pp. 316–19)

1 Derman (1948), 4; Golubov, 520; Kotov, 236.   **2** Izmaylov, 5–6.   **3** Ibid., 6.   **4** Hingley, vi–vii.   **5** I. A. Bunin, in Golubov, 519.   **6** *Oxford Chekhov*, 9:183; emphasis added.

APPENDIX II (pp. 330–3)

1 *Oxford Chekhov*, 3:339–41.   **2** See further, Ronald Hingley, "Chekhov and the Art of Translation", *The Cambridge Review*, 1 May 1965; *Oxford Chekhov*, 9:xiii–xv.

BIBLIOGRAPHY OF SOURCE MATERIAL

The purpose of this highly selective Bibliography is twofold: to provide a key to the Reference Notes; and to indicate the most important sources from which the present biography is drawn.

AChiys—see under CHEKHOV, M. P. (1923)

ALEKSANDROV, B. I., *Seminary po Chekhovu* (Moscow, 1957)

ALEXANDER, *Pisma*—see under CHEKHOV, AL. P.

AMBLER, EFFIE, *The Career of Aleksei S. Suvorin: Russian Journalism and Politics, 1861–1881* (Detroit, 1972)

AMFITEATROV, A. V., *Sochineniya* (St. Petersburg, 1910–14), vol. 14

AVDEYEV, YU. K., *Po chekhovskim mestam Podmoskovya* (Moscow, 1959)

AYKHENVALD, YU., and others, *Pamyati A. P. Chekhova* (Moscow, 1906)

BAEDEKER, KARL, *Russia with Teheran, Port Arthur and Peking* (Leipzig, 1914)

BALABANOVICH, YE., *Dom A. P. Chekhova v Moskve* (Moscow, 1958)

BATYUSHKOV, F. D., *Na pamyatnik A. P. Chekhovu* (St. Petersburg, 1906)

BELCHIKOV, N. F., ed., *Chekhov i yego sreda: sbornik* (Leningrad, 1930)

BELYAYEV, M. D., and A. S. DOLININ, ed., *A. P. Chekhov: zateryannyye proizvedeniya, neizdannyye pisma, vospominaniya, bibliografiya*, (Leningrad, 1925)

BERDNIKOV, G., *Chekhov* (Moscow, 1974)

BRAGIN, S. G., ed., *Khozyayka chekhovskogo doma: vospominaniya, pisma* (Simferopol, 1969)

BRENDER, VLADIMIR, ed., *O Chekhove: vospominaniya i statyi* (Moscow, 1910)

BRISSON, P., *Tchékov et sa vie* (Paris, 1955)

BRODSKY, N. L., and others, ed., *Chekhov v vospominaniyakh sovremennikov* (Moscow, 1954)

BUNIN, I. A., *O Chekhove: nezakonchennaya rukopis* (New York, 1955)

CHEKHOV, AL. P. (Alexander), *Pisma A. P. Chekhovu yego brata Aleksandra Chekhova*, ed. I. S. Yezhov (Moscow, 1939) [abbreviated as "Alexander, *Pisma*"]

CHEKHOV, ANTON

(*a*) *Major editions of his writings in Russian*

(1) The first collected works, as selected and edited by the author and published by A. F. Marks:

Sobraniye sochineniy, vols. 1–10 (St. Petersburg, 1899–1902)

(2) The first attempt at a complete, systematic, critical edition of all the works:

Polnoye sobraniye sochineniy, ed. A. V. Lunacharsky, S. D. Balukhaty and others, 12 vols. (Moscow–Leningrad, 1929)

(3) The first attempt at a complete, systematic, critical edition of all the works, letters and other writings, and the main source of the present biography (for 145 additional letters, newly discovered or printed in full for the first time, see *Ln*, 149–258):

Polnoye sobraniye sochineniy i pisem, ed. S. D. Balukhaty, V. P. Potyomkin, N. S. Tikhonov, A. M. Yegolin, 20 vols. (Moscow, 1944–51) [abbreviated as "*Works, 1944–51*" or "W."]

(4) A new edition, designed to supersede *Works, 1944–51*, and announced for publication in 1974–82 by the Gorky Institute of World Literature of the USSR Academy of Sciences; to consist of 30 volumes, of which 18 will contain the works and 12 the letters:

Polnoye sobraniye sochineniy i pisem [abbreviated as "*Works and Letters, 1974–82*"]
Reference is also made to N. F. Belchikov's edition of *Platonov: neizdannaya pyesa A. P. Chekhova* (Moscow, 1923)
   (b) *Editions of the letters which occasionally preserve intact material censored out of "Works, 1944–51", vols. 13–20:*
   Pisma A. P. Chekhova, ed. M. P. Chekhova, 6 vols. (Moscow, 1912–16) [abbreviated as "*Pisma, 1912–16*"]
   Pisma A. P. Chekhova k O. L. Knipper-Chekhovoy, ed. Ye. Konshina (Berlin, 1924)
   Sobraniye sochineniy, ed. V. V. Yermilov, K. D. Muratova, Z. S. Paperny, A. I. Revyakin, 12 vols., of which vols. 11–12 contain a selection of the letters (Moscow, 1960–4) [abbreviated as "*Works, 1960–4*"]
CHEKHOV, M. P. (Michael), *Anton Chekhov i yego syuzhety* (Moscow, 1923) [abbreviated as "*AChiys*"]
   Anton Chekhov, teatr, aktyory i "Tatyana Repina" (Petrograd, 1924)
   Vokrug Chekhova: vstrechi i vpechatleniya (Moscow, 1959) [abbreviated as "*Vokrug*"]
CHEKHOV, S. M., *O semye Chekhovykh: M. P. Chekhov v Yaroslavle* (Yaroslavl, 1970)
CHEKHOVA, M. P. (Mariya), *Dom-muzey A. P. Chekhova v Yalte* (Moscow, 1951)
   Pisma k bratu A. P. Chekhovu (Moscow, 1954) [abbreviated as "*Mariya, Pisma*"]
   Iz dalyokogo proshlogo (Moscow, 1960) [abbreviated as "*Mariya, Idp*"]
CHEREPAKHOV, M. S., and YE. M. FINGERIT, *Russkaya periodicheskaya pechat: 1895–oktyabr 1917* (Moscow, 1957)
Chit—see under SURKOV, VE. D.
DERMAN, A. B., *Tvorchesky portret Chekhova* (Moscow, 1929)
   Anton Pavlovich Chekhov: kritiko-biografichesky ocherk (Moscow, 1939)
   Moskva v zhizni i tvorchestve A. P. Chekhova (Moscow, 1948)
DERMAN, A. B., ed., *Perepiska A. P. Chekhova i O. L. Knipper*, 2 vols. (Moscow, 1934, 1936) [abbreviated as "Knip."; for remaining Chekhov–Knipper correspondence, see under VILENKIN, V. YA.]
   A. P. Chekhov: sbornik dokumentov i materialov (Moscow, 1947)
DROZDOVA, M. T., "Iz vospominaniy ob A. P. Chekhove", *Novy mir* (Moscow, 1954), no. 7, pp. 211–22
EEKMAN, T., ed., *Anton Čechov, 1860–1960: some Essays* (Leiden, 1960)
ELTON, O., *Chekhov: the Taylorian Lecture* (Oxford, 1929)
FEYDER, VAL., ed., *A. P. Chekhov: literaturny byt i tvorchestvo po memuarnym materialam* (Leningrad, 1928)
FLORINSKY, MICHAEL T., *Russia: a History and an Interpretation*, 2 vols. (New York, 1963)
FRIDKES, L. M., *Opisaniye memuarov o Chekhove* (Moscow, 1930)
GEYZER, I. M., *Chekhov i meditsina* (Moscow, 1954)
GILYAROVSKY, VL., *Moskva i moskvichi: ocherki staromoskovskogo byta* (Moscow, 1959)
GITOVICH, N. I., *Letopis zhizni i tvorchestva A. P. Chekhova* (Moscow, 1955)
GOLUBOV, S. N., and others, ed., *A. P. Chekhov v vospominaniyakh sovremennikov* (Moscow, 1960)
GROSSMAN, LEONID, "Roman Niny Zarechnoy", *Prometey*, vol. 2 (Moscow, 1967), pp. 219–89
HEIFETZ, ANNA, *Chekhov in English: a List of Works by and about Him* (New York, 1949)
HINGLEY, RONALD, *Chekhov: a Biographical and Critical Study* (London, 1950); see also under *Oxford Chekhov, The*
Iz arkhiva A. P. Chekhova: publikatsii (Moscow, 1960)
IZMAYLOV, A., *Chekhov, 1860–1904: biografichesky nabrosok* (Moscow, 1916)
KALLASH, VL., and others, ed., *A. P. Chekhov: sbornik statey* (Moscow, 1910)

KARLINSKY, SIMON, ed., *Letters of Anton Chekhov* (New York, 1973)

KENNAN, GEORGE, *Siberia and the Exile System*, 2 vols. (London, 1891)

KHIZHNYAKOV, V. V., *Anton Pavlovich Chekhov kak vrach* (Moscow, 1947)

KIREYEV, D., *Chekhov: zhizn i tvorchestvo* (Moscow, 1929)

Knip.—see under DERMAN, A. B., ed. (1934, 1936)

KNYAZEVA, K. I., and others, ed., *Anton Pavlovich Chekhov: sbornik statey* (Yuzhno-Sakhalinsk, 1959)

KOGAN, P. S., *A. P. Chekhov: biografichesky ocherk* (Moscow, 1929)

KOTOV, A. K., ed., *A. P. Chekhov v vospominaniyakh sovremennikov* (Moscow, 1947)

KOZMIN, B. P., and others, ed., *Istoriya Moskvy*, vol. 4: *period promyshlennogo kapitalizma* (Moscow, 1954)

KROLENKO, YA. A., ed., *Chekhovsky sbornik: naydyonnyye statyi i pisma, vospominaniya, kritika, bibliografiya* (Moscow, 1929)

LAKSHIN, V. A., *Iskusstvo psikhologicheskoy dramy Chekhova i Tolstogo* (Moscow, 1958)

LEVITAN, I. I., *Vospominaniya i pisma* (Moscow, 1950)

LININ, A. M., ed., *A. P. Chekhov i nash kray: sbornik* (Rostov-on-Don, 1935)

LISOVSKY, N. M., *Bibliografiya russkoy periodicheskoy pechati: materialy dlya istorii russkoy zhurnalistiki* (Petrograd, 1915)

LLEWELLYN SMITH, VIRGINIA, *Anton Chekhov and the Lady with the Dog* (London, 1973)

Ln—see under VINOGRADOV, V. V.

MANUYLOV, V., *A. P. Chekhov* (Leningrad, 1945)

MAGARSHACK, DAVID, *Chekhov: a Life* (London, 1952)

MALOVA, M. M., *Rukopisi Chekhova v sobranii Instituta literatury (Pushkinskogo doma)* (Moscow, 1947)

MARIYA, *Idp*—see under CHEKHOVA, M. P. (1960)

MARIYA, *Pisma*—see under CHEKHOVA, M. P. (1954)

MASANOVA, I. F., *Chekhoviana*, vol. 1 (Moscow, 1929)

MOROZOV, M., "Chekhov v otsenke angliyskoy i amerikanskoy pechati", *Oktyabr* (Moscow, 1944), vols. 7–8, pp. 162–8

MYSHKOVSKAYA, L., *Chekhov i yumoristicheskiye zhurnaly 80-kh godov* (Moscow, 1929)

NECHAYEV, V. P., and YU. M. MURKINA, ed., *A. P. Chekhov: rukopisi, pisma, biograficheskiye dokumenty: opisaniye materialov Tsentralnogo gosudarstvennogo arkhiva literatury i iskusstva* (Moscow, 1960)

NEMIROVICH-DANCHENKO, VL. IV., *Iz proshlogo* (Academia, 1936)

Oxford Chekhov, The, ed. and tr. Ronald Hingley, vols. 1–3, the plays; vols. 4–9, the stories of 1888–1904 (London, 1964–   )

Pisma, 1912–16—see under CHEKHOV, ANTON (1912–16)

PITCHER, HARVEY, *The Chekhov Play: a New Interpretation* (London, 1973)

POKROVSKY, V., ed., *A. P. Chekhov, yego zhizn i sochineniya: sbornik istoriko-kriticheskikh statey* (Moscow, 1907)

POLOTSKAYA, YE. A., *Anton Pavlovich Chekhov: rekomendatelny ukazatel literatury* (Moscow, 1955)

ROSKIN, A., *Antosha Chekhonte* (Moscow, 1940)

RYSKIN, YE. I., *Osnovnyye izdaniya sochineniy russkikh pisateley: xix vek* (Moscow, 1948)

SAKHAROVA, YE. M., ed., *Anton Pavlovich Chekhov, 1860–1904: pamyatka chitatelyu i materialy v pomoshch bibliotekaryu* (Moscow, 1954)

A. P. Chekhov o literature (Moscow, 1955)

SIMMONS, ERNEST J., *Chekhov: a Biography* (Boston, 1962)

SOBOLEV, YURY, *Chekhov: statyi, materialy, bibliografiya* (Moscow, 1930)

Chekhov (Moscow, 1934)

STANISLAVSKY, K. S., *Moya zhizn v iskusstve*, 7th edn. (Moscow–Leningrad, 1941)

A. P. Chekhov v Moskovskom khudozhestvennom teatre (Moscow, 1947)

STROYEVA, M., *Chekhov i Khudozhestvenny teatr: rabota K. S. Stanislavskogo i Vl. I. Nemirovicha-Danchenko nad pyesami A. P. Chekhova* (Moscow, 1955)

STRUVE, GLEB, "Chekhov in Communist Censorship", *Slavonic and East European Review* (London, June 1955), pp. 327–41

SURKOV, YE. D., ed., *Chekhov i teatr: pisma, felyetony, sovremenniki o Chekhove-dramaturge* (Moscow, 1961) [abbreviated as "*Chit*"]

SUVORIN, A. S., *Dnevnik A. S. Suvorina*, ed. M. Krichevsky (Moscow, 1923)

SYSOYEV, N., *Chekhov v Krymu* (Simferopol, 1954)

TUPPER, HARMON, *To the Great Ocean: Siberia and the Trans-Siberian Railway* (London, 1965)

VILENKIN, V. YA., ed., *Olga Leonardovna Knipper-Chekhova*, 2 vols. (Moscow, 1972); vol. I contains the correspondence between Chekhov and his wife from 27 Nov. 1902 onwards; for the first two vols. of Chekhov-Knipper correspondence, see under DERMAN, A. B., ed. (1934, 1936)

VINOGRADOV, V. V., and others, ed., *Literaturnoye nasledstvo: Chekhov* (Moscow, 1960) [abbreviated as "*Ln*"]

Vokrug—see under CHEKHOV, M. P. (1959)

W.—see under CHEKHOV, ANTON (1944–51)

WESTWOOD, J. N., *A History of Russian Railways* (London, 1964)

Works, 1944–51, *Works, 1960–4* and *Works, 1974–82*—see under CHEKHOV, ANTON

YACHNIN, RISSA, *The Chekhov Centennial Chekhov in English: a Selective List of Works by and about Him* (New York, 1960)

YERMILOV, V., *Chekhov* (Moscow, 1946)

Dramaturgiya Chekhova (Moscow, 1948)

ZAYTSEV, BORIS, *Chekhov: literaturnaya biografiya* (New York, 1954)

INDEX OF CHEKHOV'S WORKS

The following works by Chekhov are mentioned in the text and Appendixes. The titles of certain uncompleted, lost or merely projected writings are included.

GENERAL INDEX

Compiled by Patricia Utechin

A NOTE ON THE TYPE

The text of this book was set in Bembo, the well-known monotype
face. The original cutting of Bembo was made by Francesco Griffo
of Bologna only a few years after Columbus discovered America,
and was named for Pietro Bembo, the celebrated Renaissance writer
and humanist scholar who was made a cardinal and
served as secretary to Pope Leo X.
Sturdy, well balanced, and finely proportioned,
Bembo is a face of rare beauty. It is, at the same time,
extremely legible in all of its sizes.

Composed by The Camelot Press Ltd,
Southampton, Great Britain.
Printed and bound by The Haddon Craftsmen, Inc.,
Scranton, Pennsylvania.
Binding design by Susan Mitchell